UKRAINIAN EPIC AND HISTORICAL SONG

Ukrainian Epic
and Historical Song:
Folklore in Context

NATALIE KONONENKO

UNIVERSITY OF TORONTO PRESS
Toronto Buffalo London

© University of Toronto Press 2019
Toronto Buffalo London
utorontopress.com
Printed in the U.S.A.

ISBN 978-1-4875-0263-8 (cloth)

∞ Printed on acid-free paper with vegetable-based inks.

Library and Archives Canada Cataloguing in Publication

Kononenko, Natalie O., author
Ukrainian epic and historical song : folklore in context /
Natalie Kononenko.

Includes bibliographical references and index.
ISBN 978-1-4875-0263-8 (hardcover)

1. Dumy, Ukrainian – History and criticism.   2. Dumy, Ukrainian –
Translations into English.   I. Title.

ML3690.K825 2019   782.42162'91791   C2017-907525-X

 Publication of this book was made possible, in part, by the financial
support of the Shevchenko Scientific Society of
Canada.

 Канадська
фундація
українських
студій
 Canadian Foundation
for Ukrainian Studies
Fondation canadienne
des études ukrainiennes

This publication was made possible in part by the financial support of the Canadian
Foundation for Ukrainian Studies.

University of Toronto Press acknowledges the financial assistance to its publishing
program of the Canada Council for the Arts and the Ontario Arts Council, an agency
of the Government of Ontario.

 Canada Council   Conseil des Arts
for the Arts   du Canada

ONTARIO ARTS COUNCIL
CONSEIL DES ARTS DE L'ONTARIO
an Ontario government agency
un organisme du gouvernement de l'Ontario

Funded by the   Financé par le
Government   gouvernement
of Canada   du Canada

Canadä

To Len,
Staunch defender of all things Ukrainian

Contents

Acknowledgments

Books do not come into being without the help and support of many and this work is no exception. I feel that, if I am to describe something well, I must experience it first-hand. Many people helped me do just that. I am most indebted to the many kobzari and the several lirnyky whose performances I have heard over the years. Special thanks go to Pavlo Suprun and Mykhailo Koval. They not only moved me with their singing, they let me into their homes and into their lives. I would not understand the life of a minstrel without them.

Equally important are the many people in Ukraine who drove me around to see various Kozak sites that figure so prominently in dumy such as Berestechko, Chyhyryn, Subotiv, Bila Tserkva, Pereiaslav, and Baturyn. Seeing these helped me understand strategic positioning and the actions described in the songs translated here. Thanks go to Leonid and Olena Prokopenko, Halyna Kapas, Oleksandr and Maryna Romaniuk, Oleksandr Panchenko, Oleksii and Tetiana Vyhovskyi, Halyna Korniienko, and Oleksandra Britsyna. In addition to accompanying me to important sites, all these people shared their wisdom and offered their guidance. I am also most indebted to the many people who took my travelling companions and me into their homes, allowing me to experience all aspects of Ukrainian life. I would not know the emotional impact of either laments or ballads if I had not had the opportunity to experience life in villages.

I have also had the opportunity to travel to and live in Turkey. I have seen the palaces in Istanbul and other major cities and I have lived in the eastern part of Turkey, the borderlands dotted with fortresses which gave me a sense of the raids and life of conflict that characterize the period described in dumy. My Turkish hosts taught me about their culture and their faith. For this and travel opportunities to Ukraine I thank the American Council of Learned Societies, IREX (the International Research an Exchanges Board), SSHRC (The Social Sciences and Humanities Research Council), and the Kule Chair Endowment. If I have neglected to mention one of my many sponsors, I apologize because I am most grateful for my many opportunities to explore the world of Ukrainian epic.

Dumy are no longer a productive genre and the translations here are based on texts in books and archives. The background information that I give also comes from archival and print sources. Thus, I am most grateful to the many libraries and archives that aided me in my research, including my library at the University of Alberta and the library of my former institution, the University of Virginia. The library at the University of Illinois was especially helpful because it contained newspapers and rare local journals that provided more detailed information on performance traditions than available in large-scale, major publications. The archive of the Rylskyi Institute of Art Studies, Folklore, and Ethnography also deserves special mention because it allowed me to see the field notes of important duma collectors. Seeing these manuscripts was most helpful for getting a sense of the tempo and sound of the songs I would go on to translate. Much of my travel to libraries and archives was also sponsored by the institutions and funding agencies mentioned above.

In addition to the libraries, archives, and their staffs, I was helped by numerous individuals, especially my former graduate student Huseyin Oylupinar, who guided me through Turkish sources. My historian colleagues Frank Sysyn, John-Paul Himka, Zenon Kohut, and Victor Ostapchuk were always available to answer questions about appropriate sources. Leonard Krawchuk, a passionate lover of all things Ukrainian, was my unpaid and most diligent research assistant, searching online and helping me find everything from newspaper articles related to my research to images that would prove useful to my understanding of my material.

As always, I thank my patient and supportive husband Peter Holloway, who has allowed me to wander, not only to archives and other data repositories, but also to various obscure locations in Ukraine, Turkey, Kazakhstan, and elsewhere. Ukrainian dumy and historical songs speak about the support and dedication of one's true love and I thank mine for all that he has done for me.

I thank my outside readers for their work on my manuscript, their attention to detail, and their valuable corrections and suggestions. Any errors that remain are mine.

Geographical Names

Azov (also referred to as Ozov and Oziv). Named Azak by the Polovt-
sians who captured it in 1067, this settlement was part of the Golden
Horde from the 13th century. It was captured by the Ottoman Empire
in 1475 and held by the Don Cossacks in 1637–42. The city became a
part of the Russian Empire in 1774.

Bazavluh (Bazavluk) is a river in the southern part of today's Dnipropetrovsk region. It is a tributary of the Dnipro River. The Zaporozhian Sich was located on this river from 1593 to 1638.

Berestechko – a town in the Volyn region. It was the location of a battle
that went disastrously badly for Bohdan Khmelnytskyi and the
Kozaks, many of whom perished in the swamp.

Bila Tserkva – city south of Kyiv. Its current name is the same. It was
founded in the eleventh century by Yaroslav the Wise. Bohdan
Khmelnytskyi signed a treaty with the Polish-Lithuanian Commonwealth in Bila Tserkva in 1651.

Bohuslav – formerly an important centre and now a smaller city south
of Kyiv.

Bratslav – a city in the Vinnytsia region, mentioned in Khmelnytskyi
dumy. It is a city important to Jews because it was the home Rabbi
Nachman, the founder of one of the major branches of Hasidism.

Cherken-dolyna – Cherken Valley, located in southern Ukraine in the
region of Tavan, a tributary of the Dnipro. It was an important crossing
for traders and Crimean Tatar raiders.

Chyhyryn – a city that currently bears the same name. It has been continuously inhabited since the Iron Age and the remnants of an Iron

Age fortress are still visible. At the time of Khmelnytskyi it became the Hetman's residence and remained so until 1676.

Kefe, Kafa, Keffe, present-day Feodosiia, a city founded in the fourth century and the location of a major slave market in the period from the fifteenth to the seventeenth centuries. The name Feodosiia was restored to the city when Crimea was annexed by the Russian empire in 1783.

Khortytsia – two islands on the Dnipro River, near the city of Zapor-izhzhia. The name is most often associated with the Kozak head-quarters, which, according to legend, provided the Kozaks with great defensive advantages from large vessels such as Ottoman gal-leys. Other Kozak headquarters were Tomakivka (ca.1564–93), Baza-vluk (1593–1638), Mykytyn Rih (1639–52), Chortomlyk (1652–1709), Kamianets (1709–11), Oleshky (1711–34). There was also the New of Pidpilna Sich (1734–75), as well as the Zadunaiska (1775–1828) – but the latter was outside Ukraine. The location of the Sich on Greater Khortytsia Island is now the site of a Kozak museum.

Khotyn – a fortress on the right bank of the Dniester River. Once part of Moldova and now a part of Ukraine, Khotyn was long contested by the Ottomans and the Polish-Lithuanian Commonwealth. It was captured and held by the Kozaks, lead by Tymysh Khmelnytskyi, in 1650 and 1652-3.

Kili, Kiliia – a city in the province of Odesa, located on the Kiliia tributary of the Danube River. It is 45 kilometres downstream from Izmail and 40 kilometres from the Black Sea. It was the location of a major Ottoman fortress.

Kodak – a fortress built by the Polish-Lithuanian Commonwealth in 1635 on the right bank of the Dnipro River. Its purpose was to stop peasants who felt oppressed and exploited from fleeing the Com-monwealth and joining the Zaporozhian Sich.

Kodyma – a tributary of the Southern Bug that flows through the Mykolaiv and Odessa provinces. It forms an especially wide valley where conflicts with Tatars frequently occurred.

Korsun – still has the same name. This city was the site of a major battle during the Khmelnytskyi Uprising.

Kozlov – Gozleve in Ottoman Turkish and Kezlev in Crimean Tatar. The city is currently called Evpatoria. This was the location of a large market where slaves were sold.

Muravskyi Shliakh – the Muravian Way, a trail heading northward from Crimea, through Eastern Ukraine, and into Russia. It was used by the Tatars of the Crimean Khanate for attacks on the Ukrainian lands and beyond.

Pereiaslav – a city southwest of Kyiv. It was the location where Bohdan Khmelnytskyi signed the treaty that recognized the Hetmanate, but also subjugated it.to Russia.

Podillia – a historical region between the Southern Bug and the Dniester. It is mentioned frequently in dumy.

Polonne – a city located on the Vistula. In the Khmelnytskyi dumy the name Polonne refers not only to this city, but to Polish territory in general.

Saltanka/Soltanka (krynytsia) – krynytsia means "well" and the well called either Saltanka or Soltanka appears in the duma about three brothers dying near the Samara River.

Samara – a tributary of the Dnipro River. It originates on the western side of the Donetsk ridge and flows through the regions of present-day Donetsk, Kharkiv, and Dnipropetrovsk.

Savur-mohyla – mohyla refers to a kurgan or burial mound such as one of those left by the Sarmatians on the Ukrainian steppe. Savur-mohyla appears frequently in folklore, both dumy and other folklore forms. It was believed to be a particularly large burial mound and became emblematic of all kurgans. It is located on the Donetsk ridge near the city of Snizhne, not far from the current Russian border. Its height made it strategically important in times of conflict.

Sorochyntsi – a town in the Poltava region, famous for its fairs.

Subotiv – currently a small village near Chyhyryn. At the time of Khmelnytskyi, it was his homestead and the location of his church which, during the uprising that he led, also served as a fortress. The church is reputed to have underground tunnels that allowed the inhabitants of Subotiv to hide when under attack.

Suchava/Suceava – a city in northwest Romania, located on the banks of the Suceava River in the Danube basin.

Tavriia – a region in the southern part of Ukraine that include parts of the current Kherson and Zaporizhzhia regions.

Tiahynia or Tighina in Romanian, Bender in Turkish – the old name for the fortress in the city of Bendery, Moldova. It is located on the Dniester River.

Zhovti Vody – currently a town in the Dnipro Region, located on the river Zhovta. It was the location of one of the important battles of the Khmelnytskyi Uprising.

UKRAINIAN EPIC AND HISTORICAL SONG

Introduction

In the late 1960s, Omeljan Pritsak, a Turkologist at Harvard who would go on to found the Harvard Ukrainian Research Institute, called in a group of graduate students and had us examine a suitcase. Our job was to find a secret compartment. When we could not, Pritsak said something to the effect that, if Harvard graduate students could not find the compartment, then border control agents would not be able to find it either. Not long after, he travelled to the Soviet Union and returned with a microfilm. The microfilm contained a copy of volume 2 of a collection of Ukrainian dumy assembled by Kateryna Hrushevska. Harvard already owned a copy of volume 1 of this work, but volume 2 had been confiscated and destroyed shortly after its publication and was very rare.[1] Pritsak hoped to publish a complete set of Ukrainian dumy and Hrushevska's was the most inclusive collection. Obviously getting a copy of volume 2 was a must. But what were these texts? Why was it so important to publish them and to publish them in full? What made a senior academic willing to commit an act that had the potential of landing him in a Soviet prison? Why had Soviet authorities tried to destroy this material? What could possibly be so dangerous about a collection of folk songs? The answer lies in what dumy are. These are songs important to Ukrainian identity – they are the songs of nation building. They are emblematic of Ukrainian nationhood, proof that Ukraine is its own nation, a separate cultural entity and not part of Russia, not "Little Russia" by any means.

Dumy are songs of Ukrainian identity. The genre came into being along with Ukraine. As songs about the Ukrainian Kozaks, dumy chronicle the birth of national consciousness, the time when the peoples living on the territory of what is now Ukraine began to think of themselves as a polity, when they began to see themselves, not as families or individual clans subject to a foreign overlord, but as a cohesive unit capable of making its own impact on the world stage. As the consolidation of the Kozaks into a formal institution led to the creation of a sense of identity, so dumy, as songs celebrating the lives and deaths of Kozaks, their struggles and their triumphs, became the voice of this new sense of self.

Dumy are folk songs. They were orally composed and their sole means of transmission until the nineteenth century was by word-of-mouth and from one mendicant minstrel to the next. The time when scholars first took notice of them and began to record and publish them was the early nineteenth century. This too is a period of heightened awareness of Ukrainian identity. It saw the growth of national consciousness across Europe and Ukraine was no exception. Nationalism motivated many of the scholars who collected dumy and presented them to the public.[2] The scholars could not exhibit the full extent of their nationalist feelings because Ukraine at that time was part of the Russian Empire and anyone writing about dumy needed to do so in Russian. Nonetheless, the texts themselves could be in Ukrainian. More important, the existence of a specifically Ukrainian epos, a tradition distinct from Russian epic poetry, confirmed that Ukrainians were a separate people, a group with a distinct culture, a nation that could hope to achieve statehood in the future.

Interest in dumy came to the fore again with the independence of Ukraine and new concern with Ukrainian identity. When the Soviet Union collapsed and Ukraine finally became an independent country, dumy were seen as the means of discovering Ukraine's true identity, one that had been hidden, but not destroyed, by the Soviet state. There was a rush to republish Hrushevska and to find and print as many of the suppressed manuscripts as possible. Pritsak's efforts to smuggle volume 2 of Hrushevska into the United States was a precursor to this push. Today dumy are important because of Russian efforts to re-subjugate the Ukrainian nation. Crimea was annexed by Russia in 2014 and the struggle over the eastern portions of Ukraine, the Donbas area, continues. Ukrainian dumy come to the fore whenever the question of Ukrainian identity arises and the present book of dumy in translation is a response to the current situation.

Today dumy are prominent in the popular imagination. Media present these songs as a weapon against oppression and the performers of dumy, minstrels called kobzari or lirnyky, depending on the instrument they play, as defenders of freedom. In films, minstrels are portrayed as dangerous to the political regime that oppresses the Ukrainian people. They are so much of a threat, in fact, that they must be killed. In the 2007 film *Bohdan-Zynovii Khmelnytskyi*, the Polish Prince Jeremi Wiśniowiecki, Bohdan Khmelnytskyi's enemy and the enemy of the Ukrainian people, accidentally comes upon a workshop where a group of craftsmen are making bandury while a kobzar sits in the corner singing a duma.[3] Wiśniowiecki calls over the master craftsman and a dialogue follows. We learn that the two know each other. Wiśniowiecki had punished the master craftsman earlier, cutting off one of his fingers and stabbing him in one eye so that he would no longer make bandury and thus undermine Polish rule. Having discovered the master back at his craft, the prince is furious. He orders the man to lay his hand on a newly made bandura so that he can now cut off the entire hand. The master says that he is willing to lay, not just his hand, but also his head, on the bandura for the sake of his craft. This the Polish prince orders him to do. He brutally executes the master and then calls in his men and orders them to shoot the rest of the workmen and the minstrel and to burn the shop to the ground. This scene graphically displays the belief that dumy and all things associated with this art form cannot be tolerated by the enemies of Ukraine. In the popular imagination, dumy instil fear in the hearts of anyone suppressing Ukrainians because this art form is such a powerful force for resistance.

While the filmic incident described above is almost certainly fictional, another, and far more massive, destruction of minstrels may have basis in fact. Josef Stalin, the ultimate Soviet dictator and the orchestrator of the famine that devastated Ukraine in 1932 and 1933 is believed to have been especially fearful of minstrels and their art. He is rumoured to have seen dumy as songs that encouraged, not simply the maintenance of identity, but active striving to nationhood and thus the overthrow of Soviet power in Ukraine. Stalin is said to have ordered the liquidation of kobzari and lirnyky. The usual description of the massacre goes as follows: a minstrel conference was called in Kharkiv in 1939 and minstrels from all over Ukraine were invited. A similar conference had been held in the same location in 1902 and it had been a great success in terms of promoting minstrelsy and improving the social and economic standing of the performers.[4] Whether attracted by the possibility of another successful event that would help their position or simply obedient to government orders, many kobzari and lirnyky came. At one point, on Stalin's orders, they were all rounded up and trucked out to the forest, where they were shot and buried.

Did this massacre of minstrels really happen? Did Stalin feel so threatened by their artistry and their dumy that, even after the massive destruction of the famine called the Holodomor, he had to destroy the few symbols of resistance that were left? We do not know and so far no documentation that would confirm the massacre has been found. There is a memoir attributed to Shostakovich, but it was not published by him and its authenticity is in doubt.[5] Hiroaki Kuromiya got access to the former Communist Party Archive in Kyiv (the Tsentralnyi derzhavnyi arkhiv hromadskykh obiednan) and published his findings in the book *The Voices of the Dead: Stalin's Great Terror in the 1930s*. He was able to find two cases of the persecution of bandurists, men who played the traditional instrument associated with minstrels and dumy. While the treatment of these men was indeed horrendous, what happened to them does not support the belief that a mass execution of minstrels occurred. In fact, Kuromiya states that bandurists were not wiped out under Stalin, popular belief notwithstanding. As for the two men whose records he examined, they were not traditional folk minstrels, but sighted city musicians.[6] While proof of a massacre of folk minstrels remains elusive, the event is prominent in the popular imagination. Andriy Hladyshewsky, an Edmonton, Alberta, lawyer and a member of the Dnipro Male Chorus, told me that, when he travelled with the chorus to Ukraine, he felt the chill of standing in the same place as the many performers who had died for their art; he felt the awesome responsibility of carrying forth their legacy. He firmly believes that minstrels were indeed executed because they posed a threat to the Soviet regime and this determined his reaction on the trip.

The massacre of minstrels has also become the subject of a recent film. Oles Sanin, the director who produced *Mamai*, a gorgeous and painterly film based on the duma about the escape of three brothers from Azov, also released *Povodyr* (The Guide).[7] It is the story of an American boy who accompanies his industrialist father to the Soviet Union. The father believes that the Soviet Union truly is a workers' paradise and goes there to help. In the short time that he is there, his view is not changed because all that he and his son see is the prosperous life of the nomenclatura, the powerful officials. Then, on a train ride to Moscow, the father is suddenly killed and his orphaned son gets to experience the other side of the Soviet Union. The boy is attacked by homeless youths, but saved by a blind minstrel. The minstrel disguises him as a guide, or povodyr, to protect him, and the two travel through 1930s Ukraine, where the boy witnesses the horrors of collectivization and the impending famine. The boy can speak and read Ukrainian and he sees the edicts which declare the kobzari to be a threat to Communism. He hears comments about the depravity of a regime that would persecute blind people and children. At the end of the film the boy witnesses the massacre of minstrels. In this telling, they are blown up and their massacre is disguised because the explosion which kills them is part of a dam-building project. The story is told by the now-adult eyewitness and the film ends with him saying that he searched for documents which would prove that what he says is true, but could not find them. The documents may never have existed and the kobzari may not have been executed by the Soviet regime, but belief matters more than fact and the belief that dumy and their singers are powerful enough to warrant fear so extreme that kobzari and lirnyky would be killed en masse persists. This belief is used to create a powerful and award-winning film.

The importance assigned to dumy and their performers motivated my undertaking the creation of the book which follows. I could not help but notice that my fellow Diaspora Ukrainians were looking to epic poetry as the source from which a true Ukrainian identity could be derived. But how well did they know these texts and how well did they understand their content? Most people I knew looked at dumy as talismans, but did not really understand this genre that they held in such high esteem. I decided to remedy this situation by providing a new translation of traditional duma texts. A new translation was called for because earlier works, including *Ukrainian Dumy* in which I had played a role as the author of the introduction, were out of print.[8] Further-more, lack of availability was not the only issue. All earlier collections, including the one in which I had participated, printed song texts only. I wondered: given texts and texts alone, could members of the Ukrainian Diaspora understand the content of the songs that they were reading? Did references to slavery and the possibility of ransom from captivity make sense? Did modern readers of duma texts understand why horses featured so prominently in them or why Kozak vessels were so suscep-tible to storms at sea? I thus decided to provide, not only a contempo-rary translation of at least one example of every known duma text, but also discussion of background material, information about Ottoman slavery and the nature of Kozak warfare, both on land and on sea.

It is fortuitous that my own interest in the daily life of the past coin-cided with a turn in historical scholarship away from the lives and deeds of prominent historical figures and to the experience of regular people living in the times described. Thus, I was able to find detailed descriptions of slavery. I could read about the raids that would take people captive and I could find accounts of the transport of captives to market. New studies detailed the lives of the people who became slaves and an entire book described women captives.[9] Information on Kozak life and Kozak warfare was harder to come by as I was unaware of some of the newer Ukrainian publications, yet I was still able to read descriptions of daily life on the territories that would become Ukraine. Here I found information on the importance of horses, both for forays into the steppe to gather game, fish, and honey and for protection from Tatar raiding parties. I also found descriptions of other aspects of life on the steppe and the changes to this life that occurred over time. My plan was to use this information to help dumy make sense to the reader who knew only that dumy were important, but did not know about the times and events which these songs describe. I had originally intended to follow a format close to that used in earlier collections of dumy, namely, I was going to publish the texts I had selected in groups, each group preceded by a historical introduction and followed by a discussion of the artistic devices used in the texts. As I worked on the material, however, it made much more sense to integrate the texts into the historical discussion, to imbed the songs into the descriptive narrative. My attempts to capture and convey the events that inspired dumy also liberated me from notions of genre purity. Earlier scholarship, including the work of Kateryna Hrushevska with whom this introduction began, published dumy and dumy alone. Hrushevska worked hard to determine which texts could be considered part of this genre and which could not and published only those which met her rigorously delineated specifications. If one looked at real life, however, it was clear that genre purity was a non-issue. Performance situations were not restricted to dumy and minstrels sang what the audience wanted, including historical songs, religious songs, and songs requesting alms. Awareness of this led me to include translated samples of other genres from the minstrel repertory when these helped elucidate the context in which dumy functioned. Thus, this is a book of dumy in context. The contexts provided are those which help us understand these texts and their power. The inclusion of genres related to dumy may have an impact beyond our understanding of dumy. Ukrainian epic is related to other epic traditions, as will be described in the following chapter. These traditions, too, may well have been performed in the context of other types of songs. Yet almost none of these "other songs" are available in English. I know of no translations of Ukrainian religious songs and historical songs other than the ones done by me. The "minor" genres of other traditions may be equally sparsely represented. Providing access to genres related to epic seems like a worthwhile contribution to scholarship.

The book of dumy translations in context which follows begins by discussing how scholars and the educated public looked at a folk genre that spoke to them and articulated their feelings and aspirations. It compares dumy to the epic poetries of other national traditions. I strive to show what motifs and themes dumy share with other epic songs. This is followed by a brief history of duma collecting and scholarship. A great many important Ukrainian scholars worked on this genre. The nineteenth century was the time of Romantic nationalism and the beginning of folklore work in many countries, Ukraine included. Because dumy presented historical events, thus demonstrating that Ukraine had its own history and the making of a separate nation, scholars were particularly interested in this genre, collecting and publishing and republishing duma texts, sometimes by themselves and sometimes together with other historical poetries. The work of nineteenth-century collectors, men often inspired by nationalist feelings, influenced not only the sorts of texts that we now have available, but also the ways in which we view these texts. Because nineteenth-century scholars prized duma above other forms of folk expression, they sought to isolate this genre from other types of song. This approach to dumy has impacted our perception of this genre. Early scholars' speculations about the way duma came into existence and developed over time, plus their view of history, carry tremendous weight. This book contests some of those traditional understandings. I argue that the history reflected in the dumy is not the history of famous leaders and well-known battles. I contend that it is the history of the common folk who experienced the results of the policies of famous leaders and the aftermath of well-known battles: the dumy speak about the experience of the common man and are not history-book history. Yet understanding the views of earlier scholars is crucial to appreciating the texts that we have, and so this book begins with a discussion of collecting and scholarship from the nineteenth century to the present.

The duma texts that we have today and that are translated in this book were recorded by nineteenth- and early-twentieth-century scholars from minstrels called kobzari and lirnyky. These were blind mendicants who belonged to minstrel guilds. The guilds admitted only the blind and put them through a rigorous process of apprenticeship and training during which students learned not only the texts of dumy and the other songs which minstrels were expected to perform, but also the ways of managing blindness and the customs of their profession. Performance studies is an important part of folklore scholarship today and draws attention to the performance situation, explaining how the demands of singing in front of an audience influences the text that is produced. If we are to understand dumy texts as they have come down to the present day, then we must understand the situations in which they were performed and the people who performed them. Performance studies inform chapter 2, which deals with minstrels and minstrelsy. It draws heavily on my book *Ukrainian Minstrels: And the Blind Shall Sing*, a monograph I wrote using archival sources as well as articles in little-known journals and studies published in major academic venues. The chapter describes the sorts of people who became minstrels, how they were trained, when and where they performed, and who their audiences were likely to be. It looks at the professional guilds to which minstrels belonged and discusses the impact these might have had on the minstrel tradition. Before delving into the part about which we have a reasonable amount of information, this chapter also explores several conundrums: the two types of minstrels, the kobzari and the lirnyky, played very different types of instruments and yet they belonged to the same guilds. How did musicians who differed so greatly come together and become part of a single tradition? The other conundrum is the issue of blindness. All professional performers from whom dumy were collected were blind – but was blindness always a necessary attribute of the minstrel? Were the original composers of epic songs sighted military bards who witnessed the events which they then described? This is possible and chapter 2 goes through the evidence that supports this hypothesis.

Dumy are traditionally divided into three groups or cycles. The first of these is tied to the events of the fourteenth through sixteenth centuries. The second cycle chronicles the times of Bohdan Khmelnytskyi and the Kozak Uprising. The third cannot be tied to any specific historical period and is usually labelled the cycle of songs about everyday life. Most collections of dumy, this one included, seek to present dumy in chronological order. In fact, the sequence followed here is the one established by Kateryna Hrushevska. However, the approach to history used in this collection differs from the approaches of the past. Early scholars knew that dumy were connected to major historical periods and movements; only what was expressed in folk texts did not quite correspond to what was written in history books. Thus, early researchers sought to match up what appeared in folk texts with what was written about in books and chronicles, an effort that yielded only limited correspondences. But folk performers are precisely that – they are folk and their interests are not the same as the interests of scholars. Their songs reflect the life of the ordinary person and the folk experience of history. With the recent turn away from the chronicling of major actors and events and the interest in describing the ordinary person and his or her life in tumultuous times, we can now compare these new descriptions to what we find in dumy. The correspondence between the two is remarkable. Dumy did capture and preserve the experience of the common man with a remarkable degree of accuracy. Chapter 3, therefore, uses the many new studies of Ottoman slavery to understand dumy about captivity. When we look at the ordinary person's experience of capture and enslavement, dumy make complete sense. The capture of slaves on Slavic territory, Ukraine included, was a regular business, conducted mostly by the Nogais and the Tatars of the Crimean Khanate, who sold what and whom they took to the Ottoman Empire. The process of capture and enslavement was complex and ransom was a desired solution from the point of view both of those taken captive and of their captors. This fact helps us understand the many dumy about captivity and why they discuss the possibility of ransom and return. From recent historical studies we learn that slavery in the Ottoman Empire was not like slavery in the West. There were different categories of slaves and, while becoming a galley slave was close to receiving a death sentence, other forms of slavery were not so onerous and could even be profitable. Slaves were routinely freed after a certain length of time and many former slaves chose to stay in the Ottoman Empire; they did not return to their homeland. Understanding the nature of Ottoman slavery helps make sense of the events and emotions described in dumy. Chapter 3 is devoted to slavery and the dumy about this topic.

Chapter 4 looks at Kozak warfare. The beginnings of Kozak military operations left a limited historical record and what we do know about this period comes as much from duma texts as from traditional sources such as official correspondence or court records. In fact, now that we can appreciate the accuracy of dumy when it comes to depicting the lives of ordinary people, we may find that these songs are our best source of information about this period. Before the Kozaks became an organized unit and a political force, the people on the territory of what would become Ukraine practised self-defence. They were farmers, but they worked in the fields with arms at the ready.

Furthermore, they organized small bands for defensive purposes and for forays into the steppe to gather nature's bounty. These small bands laid the foundation for later Kozak regiments. This chapter looks at the dumy about small-scale steppe warfare and the consequences of such forays.

One of the special features of Kozak military might was their prowess at sea. The Kozaks used a special boat called a *chaika* that allowed great manoeuvrability. Small Kozak boats, because they were low in the water and hard to see from the distance, could sneak up on both enemy ships and cities and towns, which made the Kozaks a formidable maritime force. At the same time, the small size of the chaika made it highly susceptible to storms. Chapter 4 looks at this aspect of Kozak warfare as well, giving translations of dumy about sea operations in the context of what we know about the vessels used by both Kozaks and their Ottoman foes.

As the Kozaks became an organized military force with regular units and commanders, the nature of Kozak warfare changed. Chapter 4 ends with dumy about this more advanced form of combat. Here we see calls for men to enlist in Kozak regiments and take part in organized campaigns. Again, the dumy are given in context, not of famous leaders and events, but of the mundane aspects of recruitment, travel to the battle site, and war. The songs here depict the moral struggles of the ordinary man torn between going into battle and seeking glory and staying home to protect his kin and his land. The horse appears as an important part of being a successful Kozak; wise men keep their mounts close to them as they sleep.

The epitome of Kozak organization occurred under the leadership of the famous and controversial leader Bohdan Zynovii Khmelnytskyi. He led a successful revolt against the Polish-Lithuanian Commonwealth, which was, at that time, in control of Ukrainian territories. The Commonwealth exploited the rich resources of Ukraine in a rapacious manner, often using Jews as intermediaries. Jews were allowed to hold leases over land that belonged to Polish nobles and to collect tolls, taxes, and fees for everything from bridges to fishing and hunting rights. The extreme oppression suffered by the Ukrainian population led to a fierce and bloody revolt. An entire cycle of dumy is devoted to the Khmelnytskyi period and discussed in chapter 5. These songs may not have been of folk origin and they may have been texts put together by literate seminarians living in close proximity to folk minstrels. While likely not folk compositions, Khmelnytskyi songs were indeed a part of the minstrel repertory as it was recorded in the nineteenth and early twentieth centuries. Because folk performers had adopted Khmelnytskyi dumy and sang them alongside other dumy, they are included here.

While initially enormously successful, Khmelnytskyi's uprising against the Polish-Lithuanian Commonwealth did not lead to the establishment of an independent Ukraine. Khmelnytskyi signed a treaty with Muscovy at Pereiaslav recognizing the Hetmanate. But this polity was aligned with Russia and, when Khmelnytskyi's death brought a period of squabbling among Kozak factions, progressive erosion of Ukrainian independence ensued. The turmoil that followed the death of Khmelnytskyi is called The Ruin, and a cycle of dumy called the songs of everyday life is traditionally tied to this period. These are narratives which mention no identifiable battles or political leaders. They are songs about family strife: they sing of sons neglecting the mother who sacrificed her health to raise them properly; they tell of husbands who neglect their wives as they go off to be with their Kozak buddies; they describe sisters who are separated from brothers, and stepfathers who resent their adult stepsons. While not connected to any specific historical period, these songs were popular with the audiences of nineteenth- and early-twentieth-century minstrels precisely because they dealt with the sorts of family conflicts that were a part of their lives. As will be discussed in detail in subsequent chapters, concerns about famous historical figures and well-known battles were the concerns of the elite. Among the folk who consumed dumy, songs about the issues that they themselves dealt with were the ones in greatest demand. Dumy about everyday life are the subject matter of the final chapter.

The epilogue offers a personal reflection on my own obsession with dumy and other epic songs. In addition to being songs about Ukrainian identity, dumy are songs of war. They speak about the struggle to survive in desperate times. They sing about maintaining human dignity under the most adverse of circumstances. I was attracted to dumy because I was a child of war. Dumy, along with other epic songs, helped me deal with the destruction that surrounded me. With the current level of strife and conflict in the world, looking at dumy and the contexts in which they were composed and performed is, unfortunately, most timely. Dumy offer us insight into war and its effect on the lives of ordinary people. It is my hope that such insight can lead to peace.

Text Selection and Translation

The dumy texts translated in this book were all taken from the two-volume duma collection compiled by Kateryna Hrushevska and mentioned at the beginning of this introduction. Almost all duma exist in variants. This means that different performers sang the same basic narrative differently; one performer's version would differ from the version of another singer. Also, since these are longer texts, composed at the moment of performance, a phenomenon which will be discussed below, even the same minstrel was likely to sing a duma at least slightly differently from one occasion to the next. If the same performer were recorded several times, his renditions of a duma would likely differ. Hrushevska assembled and published not only every single available duma, but every variant of that duma that she could find, creating a massive, two-volume work. Translating all of her texts here was out of the question and any scholar who would need access to all variants would surely be someone who knew Ukrainian and could work directly with Hrushevska's texts. What I chose to do was to select at least one variant of every each duma published by Hrushevska and to translate that. All the translations are my own. The selection is my own as well and, while I tried to be as objective as possible and to select the fullest and most representative of all available texts, it is doubtlessly true that my tastes and preferences have influenced my selection. I did choose to translate more than one text in several instances. In the case of certain songs, usually the very popular ones recorded multiple times, different plot lines developed over time. Thus, the song called "The Escape of Three Brothers from Azov" usually ends with the murder of the older brothers by Tatars. In some versions, however, they reach home successfully and are reunited with their parents, only to be banished when the parents learn that they abandoned their youngest sibling to die in the steppe. Both types of texts are translated here. The same has been done for the "Duma about a Widow and Her Three Sons." In some versions the widow returns to live with her sons after they realize the error of their ways; in other versions she does not. I have translated examples of both versions. I also present a rather unusual text where the widow is taken in by a female rather than a male neighbour and where the reason for expelling the mother is motivated less by concern with social standing and more by tensions within the family.

All texts translated below are fully annotated using the information provided by Hrushevska. I give the pages in Hrushevska's work where the text in question can be found and I also reproduce her information about the original collector of the text and the date and place of its first publication. In many cases the performer from whom the text was collected is not known, but when that information is available, I include it also. Historical song texts used in this book come from the highly respected collection of dumy and historical songs compiled by Antonovych and Drahomanov.[10] Here too, in addition to providing page references to the source which I used, I give all available background data, such as collector, performer, and date of original publication. Other sources for the song texts translated here are not used as extensively and some are archival. All are fully annotated.

When writing my translations, my goal was to produce a text that read smoothly and was faithful to the original. This made word-for-word translation impossible. Yet, because most duma lines are end-stopped, line-by-line translation was a realistic approach that produced a rendition that was both readable and accurate. In my attempt to be accurate, I have placed in brackets any words that do not appear in the original Ukrainian but that I inserted to improve readability. Thus, what is not in brackets is what appears in the original line. Certain "filler" words, if they made the English translation awkward, were removed. Rhyme is a common feature of Ukrainian song, dumy included. However, I chose not to try and reproduce rhyme because this would necessitate too much distortion in the structure and meaning of any given line.

In my efforts to provide an accurate rendition of the meaning of dumy I have retained those turns of phrase which may seem odd in English, but do capture the Ukrainian world view. Thus, I have followed the Ukrainian choice of colours for things such as body parts and fluids. When wounded combatants are described, their flesh is said to be white, their bones yellow, and their blood black. I have kept these colours even though these designations differ from standard English practice. Elsewhere I have deviated from previous translations precisely to capture Ukrainian meaning more accurately. The word *syvyi*, usually translated as "grey," is frequently used to describe both men and horses. I have chosen to translate this word as "pale" because my knowledge of Ukrainian folklore tells me that this adjective is used to emphasize lightness of colour. "Pale" is also a better choice because it does not carry the undesirable connotations of old age or deathly pallor that "grey" does in English. Ukrainian epic, like other songs, will often use compounds such as "saying with words," "crying with tears." Because this is a feature of folk poetry, it has been maintained here. Other frequently used word combinations or formulas are rendered in more colloquial English to capture meaning more accurately. For example, texts state that a protagonist "sheds tiny (*dribni*) tears." I have translated this as "copious tears" because the emphasis here is on quantity and not on teardrop size. The adjective in question, whether applied to tears or to rain, implies volume: soaking rain, flowing tears.

Verb tense can also be unusual in dumy. Because these were oral texts, the singer performing them would sometimes shift tense, using the past tense and suddenly switching to the present, especially in those cases where the situation was particularly dramatic. For example, when two individuals confront one another or when the hero finds himself in a life-threatening situation, the performer may chose to switch from the narrative past to the present. I have kept the tense(s) used in the original to capture oral flavor and to maintain the dynamism of the original verse.

Proper nouns, the names of people and places, present a special problem. The easy part was selecting a transliteration system for rendering Cyrillic names using Latin letters. The system chosen was the one adopted by the Ukrainian Cabinet of Ministers in 2010 and posted on a Ukrainian government website.[11] It is similar to the widely used Library of Congress system, but slightly simpler. The spellings this system uses, especially of initial glide-vowel combinations, are more easily recognized by speakers of English. But selecting a way to render proper nouns with Latin letters does not begin to solve the issues that dumy present. For one thing, these songs are oral compositions transmitted by blind and illiterate performers. Both personal names and names of places are rendered in many ways; performers were not cognizant of a standard spelling and its corresponding pronunciation, and so they used what they knew: variants which could differ substantially from the spelling found in written documents. Furthermore, the documents themselves are not consistent. The same name, whether of a person or a place, could be written in different ways. Place names changed over time. The city which is called Kafa, Kefe, or Keffe in dumy texts is present-day Feodosia, and Kozlov, a city which started out with the Turkish name of Gezleve and later became Tatar Kezlev, is now Evpatoriia. The solution used here is to give the place name as it appears in the duma text and to provide a list of the other names attributed to the geographic location. This list appears before this introduction.

Rendering the names of people in English is even more complex. There are variant spellings produced by oral transmission. Family names and patronymics were not used consistently and many names that appear in dumy texts are adjectival, if not actual adjectives. Names appear in the order of given name and then patronymic or descriptor and they also appear in the opposite order. My solution to these problems is as follows: names are given in the order in which they appear in a duma text. Thus, if the hero is called Samiilo Kishka, that is what appears in the translation, and if he is later called Kishka Samiilo, even in the same duma, then that is the sequence used. Adjectival names are given as they appear, except in those cases where the name is clearly meant to be descriptive. I judged appellations to be descriptive when the adjectival part of the name is expanded upon with additional modifiers and entire lines of descriptive text. Thus, I have translated Fedir Bezridnyi as "Fedir the man without kin" because his lack of relatives is underscored by additional lines of text which emphasize his solitude and also because his having no kin is central to the plot. Some historical figures are referred to in dumy, not by their given names, but by their nicknames. For example, Khmelnytskyi's son Yurii is typically called Yevras or Yuras in dumy. When a duma text gives a nickname rather than a given name, that is what appears in the translation here. The last problem with names is that Ukrainians dealt with people from other lands. Polish names appear in the dumy about Khmelnytskyi, and Turkish and Tatar names appear in dumy about captivity and in the songs about fourteenth- through sixteenth-century Kozak warfare. Because this is a book about Ukrainian poetry, I have chosen to give the Ukrainian spelling of all non-Ukrainian names. Essentially, as with place names, what appears in the text being translated is what is given in this book. Many authors of English-language scholarly publications concerning Ukrainian topics, dumy included, are themselves Ukrainian. When referring to those authors, I have used the name that they use in the West. I have not reconstructed the Ukrainian spelling of names like Subtelny and Magosci. The name of the famous historian Mykhailo Hrushevskyi presented a special problem. His name transcribed from the Ukrainian would be rendered the way that I have done in the preceding sentence. However, many translations of this author's work spell his last name as Hrushevsky. When referring to books that use this spelling, I have kept the form that the publication uses. This affects the bibliography and the notes. This seemed to be the best way to help readers find publications, should they wish to do so. Another issue that affects primarily the notes and the bibliography is the transliteration of Ukrainian authors who, because they published at a time when Ukraine was part of the Russian Empire, wrote in Russian. The books they produced were in a mixture of Russian and Ukrainian with the texts that they collected printed in the original and all other materials, including the names of the authors, given in Russian. Again, because mine is a book about Ukrainian epic, when referring to these authors in my discussion, I have given a transliteration of the Ukrainian version of their names. In the notes and in the bibliography I give the Ukrainian version of the name first, followed by the transliteration of the Russian version, the name as it appeared in the publication. This should allow the reader to both identify the authors cited and find their works.

While I have translated most Ukrainian words into English, some terms are so specific to the Ukrainian tradition that I have chosen to use the Ukrainian original. This applies to the name of the genre that is translated here. I call the songs I am translating dumy even as I use this term interchangeably with "epic" and "epic song." Some genres are quite specific to the Ukrainian tradition. This is the case with a special religious song called a psalma and that is the term used here. Similarly minstrels, because they are distinctly Ukrainian, are called kobzari if they played the bandura and lirnyky if they played the lira. All these foreign words are given in italics the first time that they are used. Subsequent usage of the term is not italicized. Plural formation in Ukrainian is different from plural formation in English. With all the terms used above, I have given the Ukrainian plural, typically an "i" or a "y," rather than adding an English "s."

One very easy decision, although one that might startle readers, is my use of the word Kozak instead of the widely used English word "Cossack." This again is motivated by the desire to be accurate. "Cossack" does not sound like the Ukrainian pronunciation of the term used for this special and literally iconic warrior class. Cossack also carries connotations that are undesirable when one is trying to have the reader see this period and its people anew. There are too many associations with elite tsarist troops who massacred protestors at the time of the Soviet Socialist Revolution and with rampaging hordes who devastated civilian populations across the steppe. If we are to look at these men from a different perspective, using a new name, the one that they used when referring to themselves is mandatory. Because Kozaks are known in English, albeit under a different rendition of the name, the plural formation I use here is the English one, namely, the addition of an "s."

Plurals of other terms of Ukrainian derivation that have entered English usage, such as hetman, are also formed by the addition of an "s."

In sum, this book strives to make dumy as comprehensible as possible to the modern reader. It strives for accuracy and fidelity to the original while also considering today's world and the linguistic, cultural, and historical knowledge that a modern consumer of these texts might bring. It is intended as a bridge between the present and the past, between the English-speaking world and Ukraine.

1 The Recording and
Publication of Dumy

Epics are a genre of folklore. European interest in epic began in the early nineteenth century. This was the time of Romantic nationalism, a time when interest in determining what constituted the identity of a particular national group came to the fore. The famous folktale collections of Jacob and Wilhelm Grimm, writings that likely inspired the first recordings of Ukrainian epic poetry, were spurred on by a desire to uncover that which was truly German. For peoples who were not independent, Finland being a prime example, folklore, especially folklore with historical content, was doubly valuable. As Pertti Anttonen writes, having a heroic age, one expressed in epic, indicated "the presence of a national spirit which would guide peoples in their state formation."[1] Thus, even if a particular group did not yet have an independent nation state, the presence of epic song indicated that this group was indeed a separate people, one which could and should develop its own polity.

Ukraine was in a position similar to Finland's. It was part of the Russian Empire and yet sought a separate and distinct identity. Ukrainian nationalists worked to establish the distinctiveness of Ukrainian culture while their Russian masters tried hard to subsume Ukraine into the Russian whole, proclaiming it to be a region, not a nation, and its language to be a dialect of Russian. Panteleimon Kulish, who would go on to be a major collector of Ukrainian epic as well as the first writer to produce a novel in Ukrainian, developed a distinctly Ukrainian alphabet based on phonetics, the sounds of spoken Ukrainian. Yet as much as scholars like Kulish tried to separate the language from Russian, the nineteenth century was also the time of some of the most forceful efforts to subordinate Ukrainian and to label it as a regional version of Russian. The Ems Ukaz, issued in 1876, forbade the use of Ukrainian in public lectures, plays, and publications. The strictures of this declaration were later loosened and folk texts could be published in Ukrainian, even as any scholarly discussion of these texts had to be in Russian. The permission to publish folk texts in Ukrainian was not a concession to Ukrainian nationalism. Rather, it was meant to underscore the definition of Ukrainian as a dialect because folk texts collected in Russia proper were also published as pronounced by the folk. Publishing Ukrainian texts in the same manner as Russian dialect was meant to equate the two; both were texts that deviated from the literary language, but both were dialects of Russian and not distinct languages. The Russian Imperial Geographical Society, located in St Petersburg, Russia, mounted a series of folklore expeditions. One was to the so-called southwestern region, meaning Ukraine. Again, calling this area a region to which an official Russian organ sent its workers was a way to claim Ukraine as a part of the Russian whole.

The Ukrainian scholars who undertook the work of collecting folklore, many of whom were nationalists, were conflicted about the role that they played in the Russian imperial enterprise. On the one hand, because their work as folklorists was encouraged and they were allowed to amass a truly impressive body of data, they felt that they were proving that Ukraine was distinct from Russia. Folklore was considered to be distinctive and to display those aspects of culture that are unique to an ethnos; thus, having rich folk traditions implied a strong culture, one uncontaminated by other national groups. On the other hand, displaying Ukraine's folklore wealth played into the Russian idea that this was a backward land, one in need of Russian stewardship. In the nineteenth century, folklore was associated with the past; it was considered a survival of older ways. Villages were the places where the more pure past was believed to live on even as urban centres were changed by industrialization and interaction with people from other nations. If Ukraine was rich in folklore, then it was precisely what Russia claimed: another underdeveloped region, just like the rural areas where Russian folklore was being recorded. In Western Europe, the fact that the essence of a nation was believed to be preserved in its villages was not a problem and neither was the fact that rural areas were considered retrograde. Nations were seen to have both cosmopolitan urban areas and ethnically pure rural ones. In Germany, for example, scholars could research their village traditions without threatening their nationality's status as a developed people. In Ukraine, folklore riches both implied national distinctiveness and played into the bucolic image of Ukraine promoted by Russia.

The solution to this problem was to concentrate on folklore that reflected history and it was this that Ukrainian scholars found in dumy. These were not "once upon a time" stories; they were not narratives about some fantastic fairytale kingdom. They were not stories aimed at children, as folktales were often thought to be. Dumy were songs of combat. Valiant heroes fought and died. Their bravery was inspiring. The names of real places appeared in dumy, as did the names of historical figures. Dumy reflected Ukraine's past – and this past was heroic. This past was real and fed the hope that Ukraine, too, would be real one day. As a result of Ukrainian nationalism, we have more duma texts than recordings of any other genre. In terms of quantity, the next closest folklore form would be the historical song, followed by the ballad. It was the emphasis that these genres placed on real life that made them attractive. It was the desire to locate dumy in history that led scholars to try and find in them those references to people and places that were attested to in historical documents.

Duma in the Context of Other Epic Poetries

Dumy have a publication history that dates back to the beginning of the nineteenth century. The songs themselves probably existed long before they were ever recorded. They most likely came into being at the time of the events that they describe, meaning as early as the fourteenth century. If we use contemporary phenomena which we can observe to understand past phenomena which we cannot, then dumy may well have been composed to honour Kozaks who died in battle. John McDowell's work in Costa Chica, Mexico, shows that corridos are typically composed shortly after the death of the man to whom the song is dedicated and whose heroism it celebrates.[2] With so many dumy describing the deaths of their heroes, with verses assuring us that a hero's fame will not die and will not perish, it is tempting to see dumy, too, as songs honouring brave fallen Kozaks whom the original singers, the composers of the songs, actually knew. The heroes fell but their songs lived on, just as the singers promised that they would in the concluding lines of the texts they composed – and they have indeed lived on for centuries. These songs went unnoticed for many years. They were a fact of life and no one saw them as special or worthy of attention until the nineteenth century. It was then that the elite, people distant from the folk, finally noticed dumy and were drawn to them.

Folklore becomes accessible to scholarship and enters the debate about nationalism and identity when it makes the transition from oral to written form.[3] The textualization of oral tradition required a number of leaps of the imagination. The development of the concept of national literature was necessary and with it the concomitant notion of "the nation" as its collective author.[4] These shifts in the understanding of culture began in the eighteenth century with the publication of an epic poem that became an international sensation – and was probably a fake. In 1760 James Macpherson published *Fragments of Ancient Poetry Collected in the Highlands of Scotland*, his translations of Gaelic songs that he claimed to have found and noted down in his travels. Encouraged by the attention that this received, Macpherson produced *The Works of Ossian*, an epic poem about the hero Fingal which he presented as his English translation of an ancient manuscript that he had discovered. While the originals that Macpherson supposedly used were never made public and *Ossian* was called a fake on the basis of errors in chronology and in the formation of names, it still became enormously popular and was translated into a number of languages. In many senses, it was *Ossian* which led to the birth of Romanticism and nationalism. As Sabra Webber notes, "The Ossian epics inspired Europeans to collect their homeland's native oral literatures."[5] This work "served as inspiration for the formation of national identities." *Ossian* laid the groundwork for the belief that a native epic provided the proof of a culture's distinctiveness and thus supported its claim to nationhood. As *Ossian* was seen to assert the distinctiveness of the Scots and to work against their assimilation into England, so it established a pattern for using the epic poetries of other minority cultures as a way to fight assimilation and to maintain a separate identity.

The epic poetry celebrated by nationalists and heroism enthusiasts is complicated and multifaceted. It presents a number of themes that resonated with scholars in the nineteenth century and are most appropriate now. Epics are associated with national consciousness because they are creation stories which tell of the establishment of cultures, if not nation states. The sort of creation we see in epic is not the birth of the cosmos; rather, epics tell of the founding of social order as it is at the time when an epic text is performed. Great armies clash in epics. Heroes fight and often die. When the conflict is over, the result is the world as it was known by the singers and audiences of a particular tradition. In the *Iliad* and the *Odyssey*, the epic poems often considered the foundation of Western literature, gods meddle in the lives of men,

but the relationship between the human and the divine is neither created nor altered during the course of the narratives; it pre-exists the
songs and continues after the close of the story. What comes into being
is the social order that characterizes Greek society. In Homeric epic,
the Greeks and the Trojans battle and both sides lose some of their best
men. Noble emotions such as loyalty and honour force leaders to make
choices that lead to tragedy. The overweening pride of Achilles makes
him a wonderful warrior and also leads to the death of his friend Patro-
clus and his valiant antagonist Hector. Epics explore tragic situations
and force their protagonists to make impossible choices. When all the
destruction is over, the result is a situation of stasis that is the known
world. That social order is displayed to and articulated for the audience. After the destruction at Troy, Odysseus makes a tour of the ancient
Greek cosmos as he returns home. He does not intentionally wander for
ten long years, but his journeys display to the listener all the wonders
of the world of the living and even give the audience a glimpse into the
ultimate fate of every human being: the world of the dead. The *Odyssey*
describes the cosmos as it exists at the conclusion of the Trojan War in
all its horror and all its glory.

As stories of conflict and struggles to impose order on chaos, epics
are stories of re-creation rather than creation. The *Enuma Elish*, a more
ancient narrative than the *Iliad* and the *Odyssey*, can show the relationship between epics and accounts of creation or myths. Sometimes called
the Babylonian Genesis and often listed as an epic, the text tells of one
creation followed by a violent reordering or re-creation of things. The
first narrative, one that is akin to myth, tells of the peaceful appearance of heaven and earth, the fresh waters and the salt waters. With
time, conflict among the gods arises. Younger deities are born and their
behaviour troubles the old gods and prevents them from living as they
wish. Eventually a battle ensues and the leader of the younger gods,
Marduk, defeats Tiamat, the vast, primal female entity who heads the
older deities. Upon defeating Tiamat, Marduk rips her body apart to
(re)create the heavens and the earth. While the recording of this text
and perhaps its composition had a political purpose, what matters here
is that it attests to the violent reformation or re-creation of the world.
It is this re-establishment of world order, through violent struggle, that
is the "epic" portion of the *Enuma Elish* and it is re-creation through
conflict that characterizes epic poetry.

Epics are stories of loss. Heroes who are mighty enough to challenge
the gods invariably lose what is dearest to them: a parent, a brother, a

friend. The Gilgamesh epic, an ancient Sumerian text, talks of conflict among men, between men and gods, and between men and nature. Because Gilgamesh, the king of Uruk, is arrogant and mistreats his subjects, a wild man called Enkidu is created to battle him and keep him in line. Enkidu is Gilgamesh's equal in strength and the two do fight but, instead of killing each other, they become friends. This does not solve the problems of the world because the two men team up and decide to gain fame by defeating Humbaba, an ogre-type being and the guardian of the Cedar Forest. The death of Humbaba angers the gods. Gilgamesh then enrages the gods further by rejecting the advances of Ishtar, who unleashes Gugulanna, the Bull of Heaven, and sends him to punish Gilgamesh for his arrogance. Gugulanna causes enormous devastation in Uruk and, when Gilgamesh kills him, he performs a great service for his people. At the same time, he angers the gods even more and this leads them to decree the death of Enkidu. Enkidu does die and Gilgamesh, greatly distressed, sets out on a quest to find the means of reviving his friend. His adventures lead Gilgamesh to a magic plant that confers eternal life. Unfortunately, as he returns to the human realm, Gilgamesh falls asleep and a snake eats his prize. The snake gains the ability to shed its skin and renew itself while mankind is doomed to remain mortal. Gilgamesh, for all his might and for all his struggles, must himself die – and yet his struggles are glorious and he gains the immortality of fame throughout the ages.

In epic traditions we see not only the acceptance of mortality, but also the realization that weakness is the natural state of man. Superhuman warriors are precisely that – they are super or non-human and cannot exist in the human world, at least not in the world of today. Sviatogor in the Russian *bylina* (epic) tradition is enormous in both size and strength. He is so huge and mighty that he towers above the treetops, and he is limited to walking or riding exclusively in the mountains because the earth cannot bear his weight. Sviatogor encounters the human hero Ilia Muromets, a man who, in other songs, is depicted as a cripple, someone who could not walk until he was cured by three wandering holy men. Sviatogor becomes friends with Ilia and the two ride across the mountains together. At one point they come across a coffin cut into the rocks. Ilia tests the coffin and it is far too big. Sviatogor lies down into the stone sepulchre and it proves to be just his size. In fact, it fits him so tightly that he cannot get back out. When he sees that his struggles are in vain, Sviatogor instructs Ilia to strike the stone with his sword, hoping that this will shatter the rock. Ilia does as instructed. Every strike of this sword, however, creates an iron band over Sviatogor's body. It does nothing to chip or crack the stone. When Sviatogor realizes that his struggles are useless and that he is fated to die in the coffin cut into mountain stone, he summons Ilia and tells him to bend down and inhale his dying breaths. Ilia accepts one breath and feels a tremendous surge of strength. He then accepts a second breath and feels stronger still. When Sviatogor offers a third breath, Ilia refuses. Sviatogor praises this decision and commends Ilia for his wisdom, explaining that a third breath would have passed on excessive strength and killed Ilia. Men of the stature of Sviatogor, the song tells us, can no longer exist. Today's heroes, men like Ilia, must be somehow less than the heroes of old; they may even be cripples who overcame their disability.

Epic heroes encounter cosmic forces and cannot overcome them. They are not the heroes of myth. Some heroes discover the nature of the world and, by doing so, teach humanity about the natural order and man's frailty in the face of nature. Heroes in both Russian byliny and in Finnish epic, the *Kalevala*, try to battle the cosmic, not realizing what they are dealing with, and fail. Both Vainemoinen of Finnish epic and Mikula Selianinovich from Russian epic or byliny tackle what seem to be ordinary, even inconsequential, things only to discover that a sack of soil carries the weight of the world that no man, however much of a hero he may be, can lift. Heroes learn that an old woman or a frail nag is actually time and that what seems to be a drinking horn is actually a vessel magically connected to the sea. No man, however mighty, can drink it dry just as no man can outrace time. Heroes cannot conquer time in the sense that they cannot escape death and they are not capable of adjusting to changing circumstances. Koroghlu, the great Turkish hero dies, not in combat, but after being shot by one of his own men. He is a man who fought with dagger and sword, a man who believes that only a man who realizes the enormity of killing a fellow human being can take another man's life. The introduction of firearms means that the age of men like Koroghlu is over. When Koroghlu sees a pistol, he cannot believe that such a weapon could kill a man. To prove himself right, he exposes his own magnificent chest and is shot and killed. The defiance of epic heroes is doomed to fail and yet it is precisely their willingness to face failure and to resist the inevitable that makes them so attractive, so admirable.

The problems that heroes face come from the social order as well as the natural order and historical change. The great power of epic lies in the fact that so many heroes face impossible choices and yet do not shy away from action. The English hero Beowulf battles the huge and powerful Grendel – then Grendel's even more fearsome mother. His most epic battle, however, comes at the end of the song which bears his name. It is a battle with a dragon and Beowulf knows that he is now old and feeble and that this fight will be his last. Yet he confronts the monster because that is his duty. When the narrative concludes, the monster is dead and the threat to the kingdom is gone, but so is Beowulf himself. In the Nibelungenlied, Kriemhild sets things right by avenging the death of her husband, Siegfried. In the process, however, she causes the death of all the Burgundians, including her own brother. Things are as they should be from the point of view of marital relations, but very wrong when one looks at the heroine's relationship to her biological kin. Kriemhild's loyalty to Siegfried might be called into question also because she marries the Hun Etzel (a character likely based on Attila the Hun) to put herself in a position that would make revenge possible. Roland of the chanson which bears his name exhibits exemplary bravery. He refuses to summon help even when the Saracens stage an ambush. His heroism is worthy of praise and the Saracens are eventually defeated, but only at the price of Roland's own death and that of his men. Roland's actions did help defeat the enemy, but his needless sacrifice of his own life and the lives of his retinue is questionable behaviour.

The choices of men like Koroghlu, Roland, Beowulf, Kriemhild, and other epic heroes constitute the epic dilemma. Is it better to insist on honour, as Roland does, or is it preferable to take the more practical approach? Would Roland have accomplished more for his country had he summoned help and saved the lives of his men? Is it more important for Koroghlu to uphold his approach to battle and validate the worth of a human life, or would it be more prudent for him to adapt to modern weapons? Does Kriemhild's revenge justify the death of so many people? What does Beowulf accomplish by allowing the dragon to take his life? Does his ability to overcome fear justify his willingness to die? Epic heroes are both grander than life and flawed and it is precisely their flaws that give the songs in which they appear enormous power. These are heroes who are human, and it is their humanity which allows the reader or the listener to identify with them and dream of fame and grandeur.

Dumy share the traits of other epics poetries. Like them, dumy are songs about a conflict-ridden world. As in the *Enuma Elish*, the world of the Kozaks already exists, but needs to be re-created and set aright. Tatar raids devastate the Ukrainian population. People are constantly under threat; they are attacked in the fields; they are taken as captives; they are treated as chattel. The struggle is one that is on the cosmic as well as human level because it is not merely a struggle between men, but between two faiths, two mighty religions. It is not just the Ukrainians against their Turkish and Tatar foe: it is a struggle between Christianity and Islam and many dumy end with praise for the Christian lands. Like Sviatogor and Vainemoinen and Gilgamesh and Beowulf, dumy heroes are mighty. Many, like Ivan Konovchenko, battle enemy hordes that number in the hundreds – and triumph over their adversaries. Yet, like Gilgamesh and Vainemoinen and Mykula Selianinovich, dumy heroes, as mighty as they may be, cannot defeat cosmic forces. Time and the inevitability of death fell even the greatest champion. Samiilo Kishka successfully escapes Turkish captivity, rescues fellow galley slaves, and kills many enemy combatants, yet his song too tells of his ultimate death. Hubris, especially defying divine will, as heroes like Gilgamesh tend to do, does not go unpunished. A self-confidence bordering on arrogance may be necessary if a man is to venture into foreign territory, if he is to face impossible odds. Yet dumy heroes, if they defy God's will, if they do not honour their parents and show respect for the church, will just as surely be punished as ancient heroes who defy the gods or express disdain for divine order. Like Roland and also Kriemhild, Beowulf and other heroes, duma heroes face impossible choices. Should they choose the militarily prudent option or do they sacrifice themselves like Koroghlu? When they choose death, do they really serve the wives, children, and parents whom they ostensibly protect? Duma heroes invariably choose glory, as do Roland, Beowulf, and heroes from other traditions. And like other traditions, Ukrainian epic songs are a powerful artistic testimony to the difficult situations that give rise to epic.

Duma Collecting and Scholarship

Perhaps an even more important trigger to the burst of folklore collection and scholarship which characterized the nineteenth century was Jacob and Wilhelm Grimm's *Kinder- und Haus Märchen*, or *Children's and Household Tales*. The first edition of this seminal work came out in 1812 and a second volume was printed in 1815. The collection was reprinted again and again, with each edition bigger than the one before, and the tales were so popular that, during the Grimms' lifetime, a total of seven editions appeared. The Grimms were not the first to publish folktales. In fact, collections of tales now recognized as important, such as those by Giovan Francesco Straparola, Giambattista Basile, and Marie-Catherine d'Aulnoy, had been published in previous centuries, but it was the Grimms who impacted intellectual life in Europe and beyond. Their work defined the folktale and the only earlier collection which most non-specialists know today is the one composed by Charles Perrault. One of the main reasons for the tremendous impact of the Grimms' work was its fortuitous timing. The intellectual climate of the nineteenth century was perfect for the emergence of folklore scholarship. Romantic nationalism was characterized by emphasis on the local. It worked against the perceived homogenization of peoples and sought to find traditions that were particular to each specific ethnos. As the Grimm brothers had provided German material to define and assert German identity and to consolidate the German peoples living in a plethora of separate principalities into one nation, so collectors in other world areas rushed to find what was specific to their cultural group.

The Grimm brothers collected tales, but their work was equally influential in the area of other folk narrative, specifically epic. MacPherson's *Ossian* may have preceded the publications produced by the Grimms, but it was their folktale books, more than earlier publications of epic, that prompted the recording of epic poetry. One issue was that epic poetry was seen as a written, not an oral, genre. Even *Ossian* was based on a purported manuscript. With its historical content and its description of important battles and heroes, epic was certainly recognized as central to national identity. The origins of Western literature were thought to be in Classical Greece and perfect proof of national legitimacy was to have one's own Homer and a national equivalent of the *Iliad* and the *Odyssey*. It is perhaps ironic that Charles Perrault had used his specifically French folktales to oppose people who insisted that Greece should serve as the model for all writing, whereas in the nineteenth century people who wanted to assert national distinctiveness searched for their own equivalent to Homer. Some nations had old manuscripts with epic poems such as the English Beowulf and the German Nibelungenlied. As manuscripts, they were the closest to our records of Classical literature. But what about nations where no such old manuscripts existed? Were they less legitimate and less civilized because they had no written epic texts? The collecting boom of the nineteenth century soon produced the answer, for, in some areas without manuscripts, there were living epic traditions. Bards were singing epic songs about the heroic deeds of times gone by. If a nation lacked an epic tradition in manuscript form, then it could establish its cultural legitimacy through oral epic.

In Russia the need for a national epic was met by an enigmatic collection called *Ancient Russian Poems Collected by Kirsha Danilov*. It first appeared in 1804 and was then published in another, better known, version in 1818.[6] Considering the dates, the latter publication, prepared from the manuscript original by a different editor, might well have been encouraged by the success of the Brothers Grimm. Almost immediately after the publication of the Russian collection, a Ukrainian book followed. *An Experiment in Collecting the Ancient Songs of Little Russia*, compiled by Nikolai Tsertelev, was published in 1819.[7] Was this publication prompted by the appearance of the Kirsha Danilov collection? Was it inspired by the Grimms' folktale books and the general atmosphere of the time? We do not know. Kateryna Hrushevska, writing in the introduction to her compendium of dumy, speculates that Tsertelev had begun collecting spontaneously, as had many people influenced by Romanticism.[8] But the idea to publish his materials, she suggests, came when he learned of the success of the Russian collection through a circle of gentlemen with whom he met to discuss literature and culture. Tsertelev's publication opened a floodgate of sorts and collection after collection followed. Mykhailo Maksymovych published one work in 1827,[9] another in 1834,[10] and a third in 1849.[11] Izmail Sreznevskyi put together three volumes which appeared between 1833 and 1838.[12] Panteleimon Kulish prepared a book of songs which was published in 1843.[13]

In the nineteenth century folk texts were viewed differently from the way they are seen now. The assumption was that oral texts functioned very much like written ones: there was an original and there could be reproductions of that original, but, while written texts could be copied and thus reproduced with a high degree of accuracy, oral texts, because of the absence of writing, necessarily deteriorated over time. Dumy were oral and they were recorded from illiterate performers long after the events that they described. This being the case, collectors assumed that what they heard were corrupted versions of some more perfect original. Dumy verse is unusual. It is not structured line-by-line, like most epic poetries, nor does it exist in stanzas, like ballads and historical songs. It is rhymed, but the rhymes come in uneven clusters of lines called tirades. Furthermore, the length of the lines of verse is uneven. Some lines are quite short: just a few words long, and others can be quite lengthy, going on for sixteen syllables. Early collectors took the peculiarities of duma verse as further proof of deterioration.

Tsertelev, discussing the irregular lines of Ukrainian epic poetry, felt that this was a dying genre and that he had found "the ruins that testified to the beauty of the collapsed building."[14] Maksymovych, writing in the introduction of his 1827 collection of dumy, speculated that these songs had "gradually departed from their original form."[15] Because the early publishers of dumy saw them as defective texts, they took it upon themselves to modify what had been collected and to bring it closer to what they assumed the original to be. Kulish compared his editing of his dumy texts to clearing the underbrush from a forest, making it into a grove in which one could walk with pleasure and without difficulty.[16] In short, people who prepared dumy for publication took folk texts and made them into verse that came closer to the standard with which educated readers were familiar. Sometimes editors put texts together to create something they considered more perfect. Maksymovych, in the later editions where he had access to several variants of a song, says that he compared these variants and made them "agree," often using what was in one text to fill out what was missing from the other.[17] While the approach to texts used by early collectors and publishers of dumy is considered unacceptable today, a violation of the integrity of a folk performance, it was common practice in the nineteenth century. Furthermore, the editing of folk texts was not something that was done to dumy alone. As many scholars have shown, Wilhelm and Jacob Grimm, while urging others to be as faithful to folk originals as possible, edited their own texts extensively. They even changed texts that they themselves had previously published, bringing the material closer and closer to their patriarchal world view.[18]

A change in attitude towards folk texts came in the second half of the nineteenth century as more and more scholars listened to actual folk performances. As recognition of the artistry of the folk performer grew, so did respect for the text produced by that performer. Hryhorii Bazylevych should be credited with being the person who first brought attention to Ukrainian dumy singers. Bazylevych was a priest in a village called Oleksandrivka, in the Chernihiv region. He wrote down dumy, like other collectors, but he also recorded the names of his sources and gave some biographical information about each performer.[19] Andrii Shut, the kobzar who caught the attention of Bazylevych, was a remarkable man and an outstanding artist who would go on to be recorded by other important collectors. But it was not just Shut's personality that caused the priest to deviate from previous practice and include biographical information in his essay. There was a growing interest in ethnography. Bazylevych saw his work as an ethnographic study of the village of Oleksandrivka, as the title of his article attests. Dumy and their performers were not his primary focus, for Shut was featured as an important citizen of the village which Bazylevych sought to describe. Whatever the reason for the attention to Shut, the tide had turned and more and more collectors and other scholars gave information about performers.

Kulish was so intrigued by Bazylevych's work that he went to Oleksandrivka and the surrounding region and recorded Shut and also the kobzar Andrii Beshko and the lirnyk Arkhyp Nykonenko.[20] Other collectors followed suit. The artist Lev Zhemchuzhnikov found Ostap Veresai and made him famous by having him perform at the Archaeological Congress in Kyiv in 1873, where he caught the attention of several prominent figures, including the Frenchman Alfred Rambaud. Rambaud published an article about this kobzar in his home country, thus making Ukrainian epic and its performers known in the West.[21] Veresai was even invited to St Petersburg to perform in front of the tsar, making him known in Russia. Porfyrii Martynovych recorded minstrel biographies and was able to collect information about the secret lives of minstrels such as their guilds and their initiation rites.[22] Other important collectors included Mykhailo Speranskyi,[23] Mykola Sumtsov, Oleksandr Malynka, Valerian Borzhkivskyi, and Vasyl Horlenko.[24] Mykola Lysenko transcribed the music of a minstrel performance.[25] His attention to music is indicative of growing scholarly awareness of the fact that a duma is more than a verbal text. By the beginning of the twentieth century, Opanas Slastion and Hnat Khotkevych, in addition to collecting and publishing data about performers, sought to learn minstrel art themselves. Both learned to play the bandura and acquired a sizable repertory of songs.[26]

The emphasis on performance in the second half of the nineteenth century signalled a change in the direction of scholarship. Epic song came to be appreciated in a different way. The idea that there had existed some original and more perfect text which then deteriorated over time was replaced by the understanding that each performance constituted a creative event that affected the tradition. The importance of the singer in determining the structure and content of his text was recognized. What was not fully appreciated was the role of the audience and their effect on the performer and his duma. The singer, as we shall see, was trying to earn money with his song and so he adapted his material to please his audience, trying to make his song as meaningful and affective as possible. If we today are to understand dumy, we must take into consideration, not only the events that gave rise to them, but also the circumstances in which they came to be recorded. We must look at the lives of minstrels in the late nineteenth and early twentieth centuries and we must also understand the people for whom minstrels sang, the audience who shaped the texts that were then recorded by collectors. In the second half of the nineteenth century scholars and amateur collectors provided descriptions of performance situations, but did not fully consider how these might impact duma texts. My own work, both my book on Ukrainian minstrels and the discussion of performers and performance in the chapter which follows, makes up for the lack of attention to the audience and uses collector observations of minstrels in action to provide a fuller description of how performance situations impacted duma texts.

The reason that the impact of the performance situation on the text was not fully appreciated was the persistence of the belief that the historical events which dumy recorded were the same as the ones that scholars and other members of the elite considered important. According to this approach, the heroes of dumy were leading political and social figures, the sorts of men (and most duma heroes were male) whom historians would choose to describe. This led to efforts to try and identify the important historical figures and battles to which any particular text might be linked. The belief that there was only one history which all members of a society would recognize came from the view that there was only one path of human development. The work of Edward Burnett Tylor said that mankind went through predictable stages, only not all peoples went through these stages at the same pace.[27] Thus, some cultures were more advanced than others and, even within a culture, certain strata developed rapidly while others remained backward. The folk were held to be the less "developed" stratum of a culture and they could, therefore, be expected to retain survivals of beliefs and practices that other levels of the society had forgotten. It was in folk memory, especially in folk historical material like epic poems, that one could find survivals of old practices and a memory of events long past. Folk memory could be used as a historical source if one took into account the text deterioration that was taken for granted at the time. Using folk texts as a source of historical information was especially tempting in the Ukrainian case because there were so few official documents that could be used as sources for information on the fourteenth to sixteenth centuries, and dumy were one of the few places where this period was reflected. As a result, many of the collectors of dumy presented their texts as a historical record. This was true of Sreznevskyi's three-volume work[28] and of two of Kulish's publications.[29] Perhaps the most interesting use of dumy as historical record was Platon Lukashevych's *Folk Dumy and Songs of Little Russia and Red Russia*, which arranged its texts by historical figure.[30] The collection tried to provide at least one song for every major historical personage: dumy where these existed and other folk songs where they did not. The idea that folk texts were a historical record, but an imperfect one, corrupted by the poor memory of illiterate performers, can also be seen in the behaviour of some collectors. Kulish, for example, "reminded" some of his performers of songs that he felt they should know, such as the dumy from the Khemlnytskyi cycle.[31] The understanding of dumy as historical records continued through the late nineteenth century and on into the early twentieth. This can be seen from the title of Volodymyr Antonovych and Mykhailo Drahomanov's 1874 *The Historical Songs of the People of Little Russia,* a massive work which sought to publish all duma variants ever recorded.[32] In keeping with the idea that folk art captured and preserved history, the Antonovych and Drahomanov volumes included all songs with historical content. It also did not stop with the seventeenth century and the Khmelnytskyi Uprising and included songs that were not dumy, but reflected and could be used as a source for more recent times. The historical basis of dumy continued to be important into the time of Hrushevska and her foreword to each set of duma variants seeks to trace all links between the texts that follow and historical fact.

In the twentieth century, attention to the dynamics of performance created a more nuanced view of the relationship between epic song and history. Milman Parry and Albert Bates Lord developed the oral theory and paid careful attention to the way a text is created by a singer in performance.[33] This led to performance studies and to examination of the synergy between singer and audience.[34] Such developments in the understanding of epic had little impact on Ukraine. Ukraine came under Soviet rule and the Iron Curtain sealed it and the other Soviet republics off from the rest of the world. Scholarly contact ceased and Ukrainian folklorists lost touch with their colleagues outside the Soviet Union; they no longer took part in international discussions and were limited to interaction with academics in the Soviet sphere, interactions that were under the strict oversight of Soviet central authority. Kateryna Hrushevska was able to publish volume 1 of her collection of dumy in 1927. By the time the second volume was printed in 1931, however, the political situation had changed to such an extent that publishing dumy was not possible. Existing copies of this volume were confiscated and destroyed. Only a few copies survived and they were in academic and private collections. Kateryna Hrushevska's father, the famous historian and political figure Mykhailo Hrushevskyi, was accused of bourgeois nationalist tendencies. When he was exiled to Moscow, Kateryna followed him there. Upon his sudden and suspicious death in 1934, she returned to Kyiv and worked on preparing some of her father's writings for publication. She herself was arrested in 1938 and sent to Vladivostok where she died in 1943.[35] Important folklore work, including work on dumy, was done in Western Ukraine, where the suppression of scholarly activity was not as severe. Filaret Kolessa, an ethnomusicologist, made recordings of dumy on wax cylinders and transcribed music along with text.[36] Volodymyr Hnatiuk collected ethnographic information, which included a great deal of data on performers.[37] Kyryl Studynskyi and Ivan Franko were also important as collectors of both texts and information about performers and as authors of scholarly studies.

In Eastern Ukraine the publication of dumy virtually ceased. Precisely because dumy were associated with national identity, their publication was suppressed and their performers harassed, if not actually executed as popular belief maintains.[38] Klement Kvitka put together a questionnaire and fieldwork guide for collecting information from kobzari and lirnyky, but he was the only person to make use of it.[39] Volodymyr Kharkiv did a great deal of collecting but it remained in manuscript form.[40] Book publication of dumy did not resume until the 1950s and, when it did, dumy were presented in a very different light. Instead of being seen as part of bourgeois nationalist expression, dumy were reinterpreted and now presented as a step in the development of Soviet socialist folk art. The 1995 publication prepared by Pavlii, Rodina, and Stelmakh, for example, presented dumy as part of the grand scheme of Ukrainian historical verse, one that started in the remote past and pointed to the Soviet Socialist future. This book, entitled *Ukrainian Folk Dumy and Historical Songs*, began with dumy about the fourteenth to sixteenth centuries.[41] It featured a long section on the Khmelnytskyi period since Khmelnytskyi was revered by Soviet historians for signing a pact between Ukraine and Russia. The bulk of the book, over four hundred of its six hundred plus pages, was devoted to later periods. In this latter part there were sections about the First and Second World Wars, about the building of socialism, and, of course, dumy about Lenin and Stalin. To what extent dumy about Lenin and Stalin and other songs about socialism might be considered folk creations will be discussed immediately below. What is important here is that Pavlii, Rodina, and Stelmakh selected and published material that they considered representative of historical events. Furthermore, their definition of what constitutes a historical event is one that involves leading political personages. In keeping with this view, great Soviet leaders are memorialized in dumy. Important events such as the construction of the Kharkiv tractor factory where no single political figure plays a leading role are also remembered in songs, but these songs are not in duma verse.

Folk performers were rethought and reimagined in a manner similar to the reconfiguring of dumy. In the studies of kobzari and lirnyky written by Omelchenko and Lavrov, minstrels are pictured as freedom fighters. They are portrayed as proto-revolutionaries and those who lived at the time of the Soviet socialist revolution are described as the supporters and helpers of revolutionary partisans, aiding them by carrying secret messages hidden inside either their musical instruments or their clothing.[42] The traditional performers who lived into the post–Second World War period, when living conditions began to improve, were brought into the Folklore Institute of the Academy of Sciences, where they were recorded and photographed. But now folklorists had a new job in addition to recording existing texts: they were supposed to help kobzari and lirnyky create new dumy about Lenin and Stalin, and this they did.[43] In books like *Ukrainian Folk Dumy and Historical Songs*, discussed above, folk performers are credited as the creators of songs about Soviet leaders, but this creation probably occurred with the help of academic professionals who also made sure that the songs conformed to political imperatives.

In the second half of the twentieth century smaller collections of dumy were published. Dumy were also typically included in folk-song readers intended for use in schools. Here, as in the *Ukrainian Folk Dumy and Historical Songs* book, dumy are presented as part of Ukrainian history. They were grouped into categories such as "dumy of the feudal period," "dumy about the class struggle of workers," and "dumy of the capitalist period." As for the scholarship of this era, while it was not free of Soviet constraints, it often managed to produce some interesting and useful work. Borys Kyrdan, for example, did text comparisons which showed how a singer changed his dumy over time, partially reacting to audience demand and partially guided by his own sense of what made for artistic excellence.[44] In 1972 Kyrdan also produced a good collection of duma texts entitled simply *Ukrainian Folk Dumy*.[45] This book was devoted to dumy alone; it did not seek to mix dumy with other song genres that contained historical subject matter. It provided multiple versions of texts, acknowledging the variation that is typical of oral tradition, and each text was accompanied by notes giving the source of all variants. There was information about important performers, a dictionary, and transcriptions of music. A very useful list of place names explaining the terminology used in dumy and giving the current names of the locations in question was included. The collection includes the requisite dumy about Lenin, though Stalin is not represented because his regime had been discredited by the time of publication. The inclusion of the Soviet texts, however, does not overwhelm this volume, as it did in early Soviet duma collections. Moreover, it is the volume's scholarly apparatus that makes this publication distinctive.

Expanding freedom also allowed for increased contact with scholars outside the Soviet Union. When Pritsak set out to smuggle volume 2 of Hrushevska's collection from the Soviet Union to the West, he was on an official trip. In the 1970s, contact between the West and the Soviet Union expanded. Student groups were allowed in on educational tours and student and scholarly exchanges began. Western publications were brought in by scholars and given to their contacts, becoming available to at least a limited circle of individuals. This was the beginning of a renewed scholarly dialogue.

With the independence of Ukraine, things changed more rapidly and more dramatically. Classic studies such as Kulish's *Notes about Southern Rus* were reprinted.[46] Reprints of other classics that had been suppressed and were hard to get soon followed. This was not the case with dumy and, because dumy were emblematic of Ukrainian identity, a struggle over the right to be the first to print a full collection of all known dumy texts ensued. At the time when Omeljan Pritsak set out to bring volume 2 of Kateryna Hrushevska's collection to the West, there was a sense that publishing all duma variants that had ever been collected would be a powerful assertion of Ukrainian independence. As Pritsak told us graduate students and as many believed, publishing all the dumy, in all available variants, would reveal the truth and enable the Ukrainian people to free themselves from the constructed history forced on Ukraine by Soviet authorities. In addition to the two volumes in the possession of the Harvard Ukrainian Research Institute, there were rumoured to be additional volumes, dumy that had been prepared for publication but never sent to press. The hope was to secure and publish these also. In 1970 the institute announced plans to publish all known dumy texts. While the grand collection was being prepared, a collection of selected texts, a dual-language Ukrainian/English edition, was to be made available. I was given the job of writing the introduction to this work and the poets George Tarnawsky and Patricia Kilina were asked to provide English translations of the Ukrainian song texts. The book appeared in 1979.[47] The grand collection did not materialize, however, even as Perestroika (Perebudova in Ukrainian) eased Soviet era restrictions and allowed scholars at Harvard to work with scholars in Ukraine. While I cannot be certain why the grand edition was not produced in the West, I can attest that there was friction between the Ukrainian Diaspora and Ukrainians in their home country. There was a sense of competition between the two groups as each sought to produce the full set of dumy more quickly. This competition was a manifestation of conflict over the right to define Ukrainian national identity. The debate was not over the propriety of using dumy to make that definition; rather, it was over the right of the Diaspora to define identity for native Ukrainians. While many in the Diaspora felt that it was they who had preserved true Ukrainian culture, their former homeland being corrupted by Russification and imposed Sovietization, many people in Ukraine resented this self-righteous attitude and felt that they themselves should determine who they should be. They felt that it was their prerogative to publish the texts that define their history.

Dumy are emotionally powerful texts because they provide engrossing artistic expression of struggle, painting an intimate and moving picture of the burdens and sorrows of individuals caught in conflict. Dumy are descriptive rather than prescriptive and they need to be studied and their complexities understood. Publishing them alone does not have the effect of a talisman which magically effects a transformation. Yet there was an overwhelming belief in the transformative power of publishing dumy. Still, nothing other than the dual-language edition of selected texts appeared as East and West struggled over issues of possible collaboration and yet continued to compete. In 2004 the Rylskyi Institute of Folk Art, Folklore, and Ethnology at the Ukrainian Academy of Sciences published a facsimile edition of the two-volume Hrushevska collection. I have a copy along with the Xerox of the original edition and a print-out of the microfilm. Outside the Academy of Sciences Volodymyr Kushpet published a book on minstrelsy.[48] It is detailed and richly illustrated and provides information on musical instruments and a dictionary of the secret language of minstrels, as well as other details of minstrel life. In 2009 the Rylskyi Institute put out an edition of dumy that contained all known musical transcriptions. This book did not have as many verbal texts as the Hrushevska collection, but it did add the important dimension of music. I own this book as well.[49] In 2008 the institute also produced an enormous tome that claimed to be what Harvard had planned and was never able to accomplish: a book containing all known variants of all dumy ever collected. I have seen this book only once when it was ceremonially displayed at the International Congress of Slavists held in 2008 in Ohrid, Macedonia. It was enormous and so heavy it was hard to lift. It struck me as an artefact rather than a scholarly resource and it remains virtually inaccessible. Our library at the University of Alberta does not own it, even though it owns the other books described above. But this complete collection needed to be published even if it is not something that would ever be used. Assertion of national identity and the belief in the talismanic powers of a complete collection of dumy demanded its publication. The Ukrainians needed to say that they possessed all known texts of the songs that they considered emblematic of their nationhood.

Dumy were not just a scholarly concern: performers and their audiences also revived and enjoyed their traditional songs. Dumy had started to become very important during the period of Perestroika/Perebudova, and Pavlo Suprun, a minstrel friend of mine, a nationalist, and an activist, used these songs to teach school children about their Ukrainian past. With the independence of Ukraine in 1991, Pavlo became a champion to many as he joined the ranks of performers spreading the national idea. Believing that dumy are the vehicle through which important historical events are carried forth into the future and disseminated to posterity, Suprun composed a duma about the disaster at Chornobyl, based on a poem by Mykola Chychkan. This song received a fair amount of attention and an article about it appeared in the magazine *Socialist Culture*.[50] Suprun then composed a duma about the disappearance and presumed murder of the journalist Heorhii Gongadze. This composition, perhaps because of its highly controversial subject matter, was not successful, and Suprun no longer includes it in his performances. Dumy are important now as Ukraine struggles with the Russian annexation of Crimea and the threat to its independence posed by the conflicts in the eastern regions of Donetsk and Luhansk. Dumy are a part of the repertory of young, sighted minstrels such as Taras Kompanichenko and Jurij Fedynskyj, and can be heard at large national festivals such as Kraina Mrii.

As for Ukrainian scholarship, with independence, not only were suppressed scholarly works reissued, but collections of folklore texts which had been unavailable in Soviet times were rediscovered and published. Ukraine also began re-entering the scholarly world. For a while, those Ukrainian scholars who had been to the West and had developed an interest in Western approaches to folklore were criticized. Investigation of topics such as graffiti, urban folklore, children's sadistic rhymes, and other genres that had not been part of the folklore canon was considered to be the study of the trivial and not worthy of serious researchers. With time, tolerance for topics and approaches introduced from the West has grown and folklorists now collect and study all the folklore forms listed above and more. Personal narratives, as well as traditional folktales and legends, are now recorded and analysed. In fact, there is more work on topics such as accounts of people's actual experiences of resettlement because of the construction of the Kremenchuk Dam than there is recording of the genres collected and studied in the past, such as folktales, lullabies, and ballads. Collections of Diaspora folklore such as Robert Klymasz's work among Ukrainians in Canada have been translated into Ukrainian.[51] The divide between East and West is rapidly closing.

The study and collection of translated texts which follows, while cognizant of the history of Ukrainian work with dumy, is written for a Western audience. It is aimed at the members of the Ukrainian Diaspora who need to understand the genre that they consider emblematic of identity; it is intended also for all those interested in epic poetry in all its many forms. Ukrainian dumy are relevant to all peoples everywhere. The scholarly approach used here grows out of current trends in folklore scholarship in the West. Looking at folksong in context captures the lived experience of the common man, the folk, and it is, after all, the folk who composed these songs. It is for and to the folk that these songs were sung. Looking at songs in the context of the historical period which they reflect is an approach that characterizes the work of Joanna Brooks[52] and can be found in some of the writings of Natalia Khanenko-Friesen.[53] It is an approach that I find both timely and productive and one that may, at some point in the future, have an impact on scholarship in Ukraine.

Historical Memory in Dumy: New Approaches to Epic and History

Connecting folk songs to life in the period that the songs describe is a new approach. Early collectors of dumy, like other scholars working with folk genres, did believe that songs reflected the circumstances of their composition, but their approach was different from that now coming into vogue. In the nineteenth century and well into the early twentieth, people working with dumy assumed that these songs were composed shortly after the events described and that any disparity between them and historical reality was caused by attrition: singers forgetting words or pieces of a text that they had learned from a master. They saw only the possibility of material being lost and did not think that dumy could accrue new images or new text to keep the songs current and relevant. Their job as scholars, they believed, was to identify any historical personages, places, or events that the songs might reflect. With the advent of performance studies, the approach changed and the emphasis switched to studying the moment when a text was sung. Scholars looked at performers as creative individuals, not simply repeating something they had memorized, but reacting to their audience and modifying a text to suit the people listening to a song, composing it anew with each singing. My own earlier book on minstrels and minstrelsy was precisely an attempt to characterize the situation in which dumy were performed and to use that situation to explain duma content.[54]

One problem with a strictly emergence-in-performance approach to dumy is the presence of content that pertains to institutions that had ceased to exist long before the nineteenth century. Dumy sing about Tatar slave raids and about the pain of captivity, even though such raids had stopped centuries earlier. They describe a type of warfare, both on land and on sea, that existed at the time of the Kozak Sich, an institution destroyed by Catherine the Great in 1775. According to a strict emergence-in-performance approach such content should not be present because it was no longer a part of the lives of minstrels and their audiences. In my book on minstrels and minstrelsy I propose that this subject matter was meaningful in the nineteenth and early twentieth centuries because both minstrels and their audiences saw parallels between what was being described in dumy and the situations that they themselves experienced. Yet the drawing of parallels does not explain all duma content. There was a great deal that people living in the nineteenth century could not have understood, material that did not parallel their lives – and that was preserved regardless. We can offer reasons for preservation such as the supposition that subject matter distant in time offered emotional distancing and thus allowed treatment of painful topics. Yet it seems inevitable that we must admit that much of what is in dumy simply cannot be explained by nineteenth-century circumstances. We must accept that part of the reason for the existence of material that made little or no sense to a nineteenth-century audience is fossilization.

Our most recent work shows that a certain degree of fossilization does exist precisely in song texts. These are more stable than performance studies would have us believe. My own crowd-sourcing experiment confirmed this in a surprising way.[55] For the study, volunteers were asked to transcribe and translate recordings that I had made in Ukraine. The recordings were of three types: folktales, accounts of beliefs, and folk songs. As builders of the site, we chose tales and beliefs because my retellings of these in English were very popular with the Ukrainian Diaspora. Folk songs were included, but members of the project team feared that no volunteers would work on these because deciphering sung words is far more difficult than making out the words of a spoken text. To our surprise, members of the Diaspora, people who were insecure in their knowledge of Ukrainian, transcribed and translated songs. Of all the Ukrainian material that they had been exposed to, songs were what they remembered best. Furthermore, they did not know the meaning of all the words that they had transcribed and needed to turn to the site master (this author) for help. Recognizing the power of songs to retain information about situations that no longer exist takes us to the next step beyond performance studies and to the recognition that folk songs need to be examined not only in the context of performance, but also in terms of the historical situations which prompted their composition.

My approach to making connections between the times when dumy were composed is not a return to the historical reference-seeking of nineteenth- and early-twentieth-century scholars. On the contrary, it is drastically different from their approach. Earlier scholars assumed that what the songs preserved would be the same as the material written in the history books: the names and deeds of leaders, and the locations and descriptions of decisive battles. Famous leaders and important historical events, however, were not the concern of either the composers of dumy or nineteenth- and early-twentieth-century performers and their audiences. It was the inadequacy of this type of connection that contributed to dissatisfaction with early efforts at finding historical relevance in epic and led to the turn to performance studies. What needs to be done now is not to reject performance studies, but to add historical context. And, when looking at history, we need to recognize that dumy are precisely folk songs. They are the songs of ordinary people; they are about ordinary people, and they were consumed by the folk. Folklore is for the folk and it is about the folk. The only dumy to which this does not apply are the songs of the Khmelnytskyi cycle; their special position will be discussed in both the chapter on minstrels and minstrelsy and in the one devoted to dumy from this cycle. Because of the need to understand historical context in terms of the lived experience of the folk, the pages which follow try to reconstruct the folk experience of Tatar raids and Ottoman slavery. They examine life on the steppe and the gradual militarization of the people who had to both farm and defend themselves. They look at military operations from the point of view, not of the regiment commander, but of the ordinary fighting man. The goal here is to give a picture of the life of the people who experienced the events recounted in dumy. It is about them that dumy were originally composed. It is for ordinary people that dumy were performed.

2 Kobzari and Lirnyky – The Singers of Dumy

All the dumy texts that we have today were collected from blind mendicant minstrels called kobzari or lirnyky, depending on the instrument they played. These men did not begin the duma tradition; the events about which dumy sing occurred several centuries before the recording of the songs took place. Nonetheless, kobzari and lirnyky are the source of our information and, as this chapter argues, they did not simply transmit poetry created by others; they were instrumental in making dumy what they are. This chapter is dedicated to them. It looks at the scholarship which gave us information about the performers of dumy and it presents what we know of minstrel life. Understanding the circumstances of performance and the performers themselves is crucial to understanding the texts translated here.

Early collectors of dumy ignored the minstrels from whom they wrote down their texts. They thought of dumy as songs with historical content and assumed that they were composed at a time close to the events that they describe. Scholars tried to identify the people mentioned in dumy and the deeds which these songs described, but they paid little or no attention to the performers and audiences of dumy. Information on minstrels began to be collected only in the second half of the nineteenth century. But dumy, like all texts, were sung by people who reacted to their circumstances and could not help but reflect their own concerns and views in their performances. They were people who responded to their audiences and modified their songs to correspond to the needs and interests of their listeners. Oral texts do not exist except in performance and so we need to look at performers and their audiences if we are to appreciate dumy. These songs are indeed powerful and magical – but they did not appear out of nowhere. Dumy do indeed retain a great deal of historical information but, because they continued to be sung for a long time, the circumstances in which they were performed over the centuries did affect their content.

Hypotheses about the Origin of Dumy

It is tempting to assume that the original singers, and thus the composers of dumy, were kobzari, military musicians who were affiliated with the Kozaks. As men who worked with the military, they would be sighted and they would have first-hand knowledge of the events about which they sang. The image of a military man who is also a singer is widely known from a very popular folk painting which can justifiably be called iconic because it was found alongside religious icons in many homes. This is the picture of Kozak Mamai, a work of folk art that exists in many variants. Among the variants, the most typical ones show a man sitting cross-legged and playing a kobza, a fact that is sometimes underscored by a caption which reads "here sits Mamai, playing the kobza." The man wears rich clothing and almost always has a *chupryna*, a Kozak hairstyle borrowed from the Tatars and Nogais: his head is shaved except for one forelock that is allowed to grow long and is then draped across the forehead and in back of the ear. In the Kozak Mamai painting, the central figure is surrounded by various Kozak attributes: a horse, a sword, a rifle, and a powder horn; this is a military man with his instruments of war close at hand. Sometimes the Kozak Mamai painting pictures a bottle and a goblet, indicating what the Kozak might want in times of relaxation and rest. In a few paintings we see other Kozaks in the background preparing a meal around a campfire or torturing a prisoner by hanging him from a tree by his feet. In a few pictures a girl stands off to the side. Kozak Mamai sits apart from the others, however. He seems to be engrossed in thought and in his music.[1]

The original kobzari might well have been men like Kozak Mamai. They might indeed have accompanied Kozak forces into battle or been Kozaks themselves who, in the evening, would sit apart from the others, composing dumy about their comrades who had fallen in battle. The problem is that we cannot establish this with any degree of certainty. What we do know is that, in the nineteenth and twentieth centuries, minstrels were nothing like Kozak Mamai. They were not warriors in any sense; rather, they were beggars, blind mendicants who were affiliated with the church rather than with the military. Furthermore, their instruments were different. The ones who were called kobzari played an asymmetrical lute called the bandura, an instrument that likely evolved from the kobza. But within their ranks and belonging to the same professional guilds were also men who played the lira, an instrument that bore no resemblance to the kobza. The lira is a hurdy-gurdy which looks and sounds quite different from the kobza and requires a very different playing technique. In addition to the difference in instruments, or rather the addition of the rather unexpected lira, there was also great disparity between the beautifully clothed and equipped Kozak Mamai who appeared in pictures and the indigent mendicant musicians whom nineteenth-century collectors encountered in real life. This likely contributed to scholars' inability to see the men from whom they were writing down dumy as anything other than imperfect carriers of someone else's creativity. They could not imagine any other connection between the beggars who sang before them and the noble warriors whom they envisioned as the creators of dumy. A connection can be made, however, and there is even some documentary evidence to support an evolution from Mamai-like Kozak-kobzari to blind beggars.

By the nineteenth century, all men who wanted to perform dumy in public had to be blind. A requirement of being a kobzar was membership in a guild and these admitted only handicapped individuals because performing was a profession and a social welfare institution, a way to support those who could not do normal farm work. To protect their financial interests, guilds forbade public performance of dumy by people who were not members. Sighted people could sing dumy in private locations such as the home, but public performance was not permitted and there is at least one documented case of a sighted man who wanted to be a kobzar but was prohibited from performing. His story will be discussed in more detail below. With blindness being such an absolute requirement for minstrelsy, we need to find evidence that sighted kobzari did, in fact, exist in the past if we are to make a connection between blind nineteenth-century singers and kobzari who served with the Kozaks. Such evidence is scarce. There are a few historical records, specifically court cases, which do speak of sighted kobzari. One documented sighted performer was Danylo Bandurko, a man arrested for banditry and theft in 1761.[2] He had trained with a master and, upon completion of training, became a court poet of sorts in the service of the governor of Kyiv. After the governor died, he went home to his mother. He then sought employment again and ended up with the Kozaks in the Zaporozhian Sich, again as a performer. He also took odd jobs as a handyman, but he was not a Kozak.[3] He did not stay in the handyman position long, however, and soon started joining various raiding parties, an activity that led to his apprehension and arrest. The surviving court document contains only Bandurko's autobiographical

A Mamai-themed painting with a Kozak encampment showing men cooking and drinking and an enemy combatant being tortured by being hung upside down. Unknown artist, nineteenth century. Courtesy of Rodovid Press.

deposition; the outcome of his trial is unknown. We do know, however, that he was sighted, that he was a performer, and that he worked as such in the company of Kozaks, at least for a time.

The fate of three other banduristy, or bandura players, is more certain. As documented in the *Kodenskaia kniga* (*The Book of Koden*), they were executed somewhere between 1769 and 1772.[4] While there is no mention of their physical condition, the crimes of which they were accused, including robbery and murder, imply that they must have been able to see. The eighteenth century seems to have been a period of transition between sighted minstrels and blind ones because the scant evidence of sighted kobzari affiliated with Kozaks is balanced by documentary evidence of blind performers from the same period. An arrest warrant dated 1730 was issued by Empress Elizabeth of Russia for the blind kobzar Hryhorii Mykhailovych Liubystok.[5] The empress had imported this performer to Moscow from Ukraine to satisfy her taste for Ukrainian music. Liubystok apparently did not care for life in the capital and fled, making it all the way to Kyiv, in spite of his blindness, before he was arrested and brought back to Moscow in 1731. From what we know, he did not try to escape again.

Because extant court documents speak of both sighted performers and blind ones, we can suppose that, in the eighteenth century, sighted and blind kobzari existed side by side. The evidence is slight and cannot be called solid proof, but existing court documents might well point to a transitional period between sighted military kobzari and blind beggars affiliated with the church. Sighted performers would then predate the eighteenth century and be contemporaneous with Kozaks, while blind musicians would come later and dominate the tradition completely by the 1800s.

The Church and Minstrelsy

The church likely played a pivotal role in the transition from sighted military kobzari to blind mendicants. Prior to the Khmelnytskyi Uprising of 1648, much of Ukraine was part of the Polish-Lithuanian Commonwealth, a polity that was beginning to slip into a period of decline. Economic hardships hit the non-Polish citizens of the Commonwealth the hardest, leading to great resentment: bitter feelings eloquently expressed in the dumy of the Khmelnytskyi cycle. Economic problems were compounded by threats to religion. In 1596 a group of Orthodox clergy signed the Union of Brest, an agreement that allowed them to keep the Eastern rite in their services, but accepted the governance of the Catholic Church. With this union, the defence of Orthodoxy fell to the laity, primarily church-affiliated brotherhoods, most of which consisted of tradespeople. Tradesmen and their guilds did have an enormous effect on kobzari, but they were not the only influence. In 1620 Petro Sahaidachnyi had the entire Zaporozhian Kozak Host join the Kyiv Epiphany Brotherhood. With this, the connection between the Kozaks and the church was sealed and, when the Khmelnytskyi Uprising took place, defence of Orthodoxy was its rallying cry.[6]

Churches in the seventeenth century were complex institutions which served a number of functions in addition to providing a place of worship.[7] They ran schools, training not just seminarians, but all children who wanted an education, girls included. Churches also took care of the handicapped and the indigent through a system of hospices called *shpytali*. Both the schools and the hospices were run, not by the church hierarchy, but by the lay brotherhoods affiliated with the church. These philanthropic efforts may well have been part of their work in support of Orthodoxy because similar institutions did not exist in neighbouring countries where Orthodoxy was not under threat. While the brotherhoods and some wealthy individuals did provide support for the hospices, this was not sufficient, and the people who lived in such places were expected to contribute to their upkeep by begging under the banner of the brotherhood. Begging with the sanction of the brotherhood might have given church-affiliated beggars an advantage over those without such an affiliation, and this may have forced independent mendicants into the church system. Within the church system, the people living in hospices needed to be organized in order to function and, not surprisingly, the organizational system that they used was patterned on the trade guilds of the men who were their sponsors.

Kozak regiments were affiliated with churches as lay brotherhoods. They contributed to the support of the church with which they were affiliated and undoubtedly used its services. Those of their number who were too old to fight and had no family to take care of them most likely ended up in the hospice system. At least some of the Kozaks who came to live in church hospices must have been kobzari. There they met another type of instrumentalist, the lirnyk. Their instruments, as already noted, were dramatically different. The bandura, the instrument that developed out of the kobza, is an asymmetrical lute with a distinctive appearance. The body protrudes to one side and on this part of the instrument the strings are of varying length. They are plucked and strummed, somewhat like the way a harp is played and, in fact, one of the ways of holding this instrument is between the knees, like a harp. The melody is played on these shorter strings. The neck has a set of bass strings, usually played with the left hand, and these produce the accompaniment. There are two ways to hold and three ways to play the bandura. One is as described above. The other way of holding the instrument is flat against the body. In this position, the hands typically cross over so that the right hand reaches across to play the melody on the shorter strings that form the harp-like part of the instrument and the left reaches over to play the bass strings on the neck. It is also possible to play the melody with the left hand and the bass strings with the right; this method of play is called the Kharkiv style.[8] The bandura played by folk minstrels in the nineteenth century had a limited number of strings, typically in the twelve to twenty-two range. When bandury began to be commercially manufactured, the number of strings grew, but the ones that concern us here were not that complex or elaborate; they were of the simpler and handmade variety. The other type of professional minstrel allowed to perform dumy in public was the lirnyk. His instrument bore no resemblance to the bandura. It was a hurdy-gurdy with three strings, a crank, and a set of keys which are depressed to produce the melody. A person playing the lira turns a crank with the right hand to make the wheel spin. The wheel rubs against the three strings and produces a continuous drone. The melody is played with the left hand and is produced by the keys touching one of the strings, varying its length and thus its sound.

As the church was the likely catalyst for bringing all beggars into the guild system, indigent Kozaks included, so it was also the place where kobzari and lirnyky became one. Prior to this amalgamation of minstrels, kobzari were associated with the Kozaks and probably played in other secular settings, the way Danylo Bandurko entertained the governor of Kyiv. Lirnyky were probably always affiliated with the church and always mendicants rather than musicians connected to other professions such as the military. The geographical distribution of kobzari is very limited. Until recent times and certainly in the late nineteenth and early twentieth centuries, the period which yields most of our information about this profession, kobzari were restricted to areas roughly coincidental with the Hetmanate, the Kozak state that came into being after the Khmelnytskyi Uprising. In other words, they were found primarily in the Kyiv, Poltava, and Cherkasy regions. The correspondence between the geographical distribution of the kobzari and the last Kozak state makes it appear that kobzari were indeed closely linked to Kozaks. Lirnyky, by contrast, had a much wider distribution. They are attested on the entire territory of Ukraine and also in Russia, Poland, Hungary, and even France.[9] One series of paintings by Georges de la Tour, a famous French painter from the seventeenth century, features lirnyky. Lirnyky are thus a more common type of musician, probably always connected to the church and the life of a mendicant. If, on the territory of Ukraine, lirnyky lived in the church-supported shpytali, then that is a likely place for them to come in contact with kobzari. When those members of Kozak regiments who could play and sing and who needed social support went to reside in hospices, they encountered lirnyky and the two groups learned from each other, with lirnyky acquiring dumy and historical songs and kobzari learning folk psalms and other songs with non-military subject matter which we will discuss below. Both lirnyky and kobzari had an advantage over other beggars because they could play a musical instrument. This increased their earning potential and made them feel that they were not simply begging, but working and providing a service that was in public demand. Being able to call oneself a professional rather than a simple beggar was extremely important to many performers, as a number of the interviews conducted with them attest.[10]

The importance of the church is reflected in dumy. We do not know what duma content was like prior to its being recorded in the nineteenth century, but in the texts that we do have, religion plays a pivotal role. Heroes held in captivity express ardent longing for Christian surroundings and song after song concludes with wishes to return to "happy lands, to Christian lands." The conflict with the Turks and the Tatars is pictured in religious terms and the most unacceptable affront is an insult directed at the Christian faith. Some of the actors accept life in captivity and even marry Muslims. Nonetheless, they can never give up their emotional tie to Christianity. Ivan Bohuslavets marries a Turkish woman and seems quite happy with her until she makes light of his faith, an action which prompts him to kill her and to lead all the Kozaks held captive in Kozlov (present-day Evpatoria) out to sea and away to freedom. Marusia Bohuslavka is also married to a Turk. In fact, she tells the Kozaks whom she sets free that she has become "Turkified" and that there is no point in her going back to her homeland. When Easter time draws near, however, she thinks of her Christian home and frees her countrymen, an action that could have serious negative consequences and, in one cartoon version of this epic, does get her killed.[11] The story of Samiilo Kishka and

Liakh Buturlak is quite striking. Samiilo is the leader of a group of Kozaks who are galley slaves, kept in chains and exploited for their labour. Liakh Buturlak is a Christian who has converted to Islam and now works as the overseer of the men in chains. In fact, Buturlak may be interpreted as a corruption of Poturnak, a Pole who has "turned Turk." He displays the zeal of the convert when he has the slaves whipped and otherwise tortured. Nonetheless, he longs to discuss the Christian faith with some-one and chooses Samiilo Kishka. Kishka seizes the opportunity which Buturlak's longing provides. He gets Liakh Buturlak drunk and liberates his fellow Kozaks. Love of the Christian faith is shown as irrepressible in song after song. Furthermore, proper Christian behaviour, or lack of same, is the determining factor when it comes to victory on the battlefield and survival at sea. Ivas Konovchenko is victorious as long as he remem-bers to request a blessing before riding out to confront the enemy; when he forgets and rides out without first being blessed, he is surrounded and killed. In any number of dumy, men who are dying say that what has killed them is not the mortal wounds inflicted by their enemies, but their own misdeeds: failure to respect their parents, failure to remove their hats when riding by a church. When it is not a parent's curse that leads to the hero's downfall, it is nature executing God's will, and in several songs the waves at sea punish men for misdeeds similar to those listed above.

The other probable effect of the church on the Ukrainian epic tradi-tion was the introduction of songs about Khmelnytskyi. Khmelnytskyi dumy are very different from other texts. While their verse structure is not distinctive, their subject matter is dramatically different from any-thing else in the duma canon. Many, if not most, dumy are about suf-fering on the field of battle or during a campaign at sea. The death of the hero is a common topic and the song often serves as a memorial to the courageous fallen Kozak. In Khmelnytskyi dumy the heroes do not die. In fact, very few Khmelnytskyi texts focus on an individual hero; most deal with the Kozaks en masse and their enemies, also en masse. Typically, a Khmelnytskyi text begins with a description of the myriad injustices inflicted upon the Ukrainian people, most often by the Jew-ish agents of the Poles, men hired by them to do their dirty work. The Jewish *arendari*, a word that can be translated as leaseholders, collect taxes from the local Ukrainian population and do so in an exploitative manner. They are insensitive to human needs and prevent people from using their own churches for weddings and baptisms. After cataloguing the injustices committed by the enemy, the duma goes on to a descrip-tion of the Jews, and sometimes the Poles, either fleeing Kozak might or begging for mercy, or both. In the Khmelnytskyi songs no valiant

Ukrainian hero dies a glorious death. There is no longing for Christian lands to which the Kozaks hope to return. With all these differences, the Khmelnytskyi dumy stand out against the background of the rest of the genre. They seem not to belong and, indeed, this cycle of songs was not popular with the folk audiences for whom the kobzari and lirnyky normally performed. The only people enthusiastic about these songs were the elite collectors of dumy who saw in them known historical figures, place names that they could identify, and events that were also attested in historical records. It was collectors and other members of the elite who likely helped this cycle of songs live on into the twentieth century.

Because the Khmelnytskyi dumy are so different from other epic songs, it is tempting to see them as originating outside the milieu which generated the rest of this genre. That source was probably the seminarians studying in the schools adjacent to the hospices which housed the kobzari and lirnyky. Like nineteenth-century collectors, seminarians were educated and they too likely prized material about known historical events. Furthermore, like others who had no personal experience of military life and learned about it through formal instruction in history, seminarians were likely to see fighting forces as units, not as individuals. They too might well have thought in terms of leaders and the armies they commanded. Not having been on the field of battle, they, like nineteenth-century historians, viewed conflict from a distance rather than seeing the struggles of the individual Kozak. The fact that seminarians had multiple incentives to compose songs about the Khmelnytskyi period also suggests that these songs might be the products of their work. The events of this period were better known and thus easier to describe with historical accuracy and Khmelnytskyi subject matter was likely to appeal to church hierarchs and to the brotherhoods which supported church schools. Khmelnytskyi, as already noted, presented himself as a champion of Orthodoxy and his uprising as an act in defence of the church. Praise of a defender of Orthodoxy and the presentation of his uprising as successful would indeed appeal to men who supported the church and its philanthropic institutions. Similar praise for a leader has in fact been documented. Hrushevskyi[12] notes that when Sahaidachnyi, a Kozak hetman who championed the Orthodox brotherhoods, passed away, "so many memorials to him [were] composed by students that the educational organization to which he belonged published them in a book praising his heroism." If so much could be written about a less successful, though no less dedicated, champion of Orthodoxy and the Ukrainian lands, the likelihood of written compositions about Khmelnytskyi is great.

If Khmelnytskyi songs were indeed composed by seminarians rather than kobzari or lirnyky, they could easily have been transferred to the latter. The schools where seminarians studied were literally adjacent to the hospices where minstrels lived. They were founded and supported by the same church brotherhoods that organized and ran the hospices, and the two types of structures were typically built simultaneously. Thus, if a church was large enough to have a hospice as part of its complex, it was likely to have a school as well. Furthermore, there was extensive interaction between hospice and school. Pupils studying in a particular school who did not live locally would be housed in the hospice and would thus be in regular contact with its residents, Kozaks and minstrels included. The children in the schools were expected to behave in ways similar to hospice residents. Pupils were required to contribute to their support, and the form which these contributions took varied a great deal. When students first arrived at a school in the fall, they usually brought food from home, often large donations such as an animal which would then go to feed those living on church grounds. But many could not afford so substantial a contribution and, besides, funds were needed the entire year, not just at the beginning. Apparently students generated such funds either by begging under the banner of the brotherhood, just like hospice residents, or they sold their services. Offering services for a fee was typical of older students, especially the ones who were seminarians and had training in the arts. Seminarians, being literate, could earn a few coins by penning a document for a villager who could not write himself. Students who were artistically adept drew and painted on demand and those with verbal gifts wrote poetry and songs.[13] There is concrete evidence that some of these songs entered the repertory of minstrels. Hryhorii Skovoroda was a seminarian who became a poet, and we know for a fact that at least one of his compositions, "To Every City Its Rights and Mores" (Vsiakomo horodu nrav i prava) became a song quite popular among minstrels because it was recorded from them by several nineteenth-century collectors. Might it not have been possible that seminarians, especially pupils studying in a school supported by a Kozak brotherhood, composed the songs of the Khmelnytskyi cycle and that these were then adopted by the minstrels affiliated with the same church? With pupils, Kozaks, and kobzari all living and working together, they could easily have cooperated, exchanging information and musical and literary talents for the greater benefit of all. Khmelnytskyi songs might have had great appeal at the time of the Hetmanate, only to die out as their subject matter became less meaningful. It is noteworthy that Khmelnytskyi songs do not include the church-related subject matter found in the songs from the other duma cycles, and it is tempting to speculate that church-related topics were not introduced because the Khmelnytskyi dumy were already of church origin. In any case, in this cycle of dumy there is little mention of sins such as failure to show respect for the family and the church, sins that retained their meaning in the nineteenth century when minstrels were performing in homes and outside churches. We will look at nineteenth- and early-twentieth-century minstrel life in the next section.

Becoming a Minstrel: The Causes of Blindness

The church was enormously influential in making dumy what they are. The daily life of the performers of dumy was also important in shaping the texts as we now know them. By the nineteenth century the men who sang dumy were not employed by the Kozaks, nor were there disabled Kozaks living in hospices. When scholars and other members of the gentry started documenting the lives of minstrels, kobzari and lirnyky were men who lived in villages, like other peasants. They were not romantic loners like the figure of Perebendia described by Taras Shevchenko; they were married and had families and lived lives similar to those of other peasants, at least in their own villages. Usually the women willing to marry minstrels were widowed, or had a physical defect of their own, or they were spinsters.[14] Still, this did not preclude happy marriages and successful families. Between the sighted members who could do the farm work and the income which the kobzar or lirnyk brought in by begging, a family could survive and even prosper to the point of affording an education for some of the children.[15]

A person became a kobzar or a lirnyk as a way to deal with blindness. Blindness in the late nineteenth and early twentieth centuries was far more common than it is today. Children could be born blind or they could become blind as the result of injury or disease. In villages especially, babies were delivered at home with the assistance of a midwife or no assistance at all. All sorts of things could go wrong with such deliveries, including infection and physical damage to the cranium. Some babies were born under circumstances even more threatening to health than delivery in the home. Kushneryk told the folklorists who interviewed him that he was born when his mother was working in the field. She apparently delivered the infant, laid him down until she finished her work, and only then took him home.[16] Many children went blind as the result of illness. The illnesses attested to in kobzar biographies include measles, cholera, smallpox, and the common cold. An especially common cause of blindness was scrofula, a disease which was virtually eradicated until it returned with the spread of HIV/AIDS. Scrofula is a tuberculosis-type illness that affects lymph nodes and mucous membranes and often produces growths on the neck. When it affects the eyes, blindness is almost invariably the result. Some minstrels attributed their blindness to the evil eye and other malevolent magic. The famous kobzar Ostap Veresai gave magic as the reason for his loss of sight, although disease or a genetic predisposition to blindness, a condition Veresai shared with his blind father, were more likely causes. Injuries could also lead to blindness.[17] The lirnyk Doroshenko was a serf on a nobleman's estate when he was kicked in the head by a horse and rendered blind.[18] Ivan Kravchenko-Kriukovskyi's story is especially poignant. As he told the folklorist and ethnographer Porfyrii Martynovych, his family, whose name was Kravchenko, were serfs on the estate of the Kriukovskyis. The estate owners offered to take Ivan into their home as a companion to their son and the peasant boy's parents gladly accepted because such an arrangement meant better nutrition and medical care for Ivan and possibly even access to an education. The semi-adoption implied in this agreement is reflected in the fact that the noble family's name was added to the name of Ivan's birth family. But the arrangement proved disastrous. The panych (nobleman's son) was sadistic and took every opportunity he could find to beat and torture Ivan. Things became really bad when the panych went to boarding school and Ivan was sent along as his companion. Without constant adult supervision, the panych was free to torture his servant boy as he pleased. He hit him and pinched him and did everything that he could. Ivan's eyes began to water; soon they were tearing uncontrollably. By the time that the two boys returned home, it was clear that Ivan was seriously ill. His family tried to cure him, but it was too late. He was blind.[19]

Becoming a Minstrel – Apprenticeship and Training

Living in a village meant working the land and that was not something that a blind person could easily do. Because everyone in a family had to contribute to its survival, blind people, if they could not perform farm labour, needed to do something that would generate an alternate income. From what we know of minstrel biographies, the blind could plait ropes and some performers did indeed take on such work in addition

The Pokrova Icon – the Mother of God of the Protection. The Mother of God of the Protection was the patroness of Kozak regiments. The request for a piece of cloth, like the one with which the Mother of God shields the Kozaks, was a prominent part of minstrel begging songs. Unknown artist, Chyhyryn region, early nineteenth century. Courtesy of Rodovid Press.

to minstrelsy. Most blind children, however, became the apprentices of professional beggars, learning how to make a living by asking for alms. Apprenticeship was a formal arrangement where the established mendicant accepted the child as his charge in return for income from the begging that the child would do while in the master's care.

Begging was a profession and beggars belonged to guilds. In fact, it was almost impossible to beg without securing guild approval through apprenticeship leading to membership. Blind children, both boys and girls, could be apprenticed to any beggar. Being apprenticed to a kobzar or lirnyk meant that the child would have the opportunity to receive the most extensive training available and thus have the best earning potential. The first step in training was to teach the child how to deal with blindness, how to find things, how to travel, how to survive in the world. As one minstrel eloquently put it, this was teaching the child to see with his or her "third eye, an eye of the spirit rather than a physical eye."[20] After basic survival skills came the fundamentals of begging. These included a song that asked for alms and a corresponding song of thanks. The songs appealed to the generosity of the listener, praising him or her. They reminded the audience that almsgiving was considered a religious duty and assured listeners that anything they might give would not be an undue sacrifice or cause deprivation. By learning begging songs, the apprentice learned which folk beliefs held particular appeal. In addition to the claim that generosity to beggars would ensure the well-being of one's soul in the afterlife, begging songs emphasized beliefs also found in dumy. They stressed the unhappy situation of those who died violently and before their time: people killed in war and in accidents, people who, if not prayed for, would become unquiet dead. Begging songs taught the apprentice to underscore the power of words and especially the efficacy of prayer. They stressed that giving money on behalf of a child who had died unbaptized or even someone who had taken his or her own life, the most serious violation of the natural order and the one most likely to damn the deceased, would help that person rest in peace.[21]

A good example of a begging song is the one recorded from the kobzar Pavlo Hashchenko by Volodymyr Kharkiv. It is the work of a mature and accomplished performer. An apprentice would be unlikely have this degree of complexity and expressiveness in his singing. The song here shows the level of mastery that could be achieved.[22]

God's greetings to you,
Most merciful mother,

Most merciful mother, my nanny,
May you behave in this righteous world,
So that Christ in Heaven …
So that you may be beloved by God.
Please cut me a piece of towel,
For the sake of Christ,
So that I may collect [cloth] towards a shirt,
As one needs to in this world,
As was done by two poor brothers,
In the name of Christ.
And it will be apparent, it will be clear,
What you give on this damp earth for the sake of your soul.
I ask you, my nanny, my mother,
Not for silver and not for gold and not for costly clothing,
I ask you for a scrap of towel in the name of Christ,
Because we will gather scrap upon scrap,
And we will remember those of your relatives who have been sinners,
Those who have died before their time,
And those who were killed by falling trees,
And those who drowned in waters,
And those who were burned in fires,
And those who laid down their heads in battle,
And those who shed their blood for the Christian world.
For their sake you should allot us, you should provide us,
A scrap for cloth in the name of Christ,
He will cover you with the holy mantle that does not decay,
    with the protective hem of his coat,
And protect you from eternal torment and from the most horrible fear,
From the inextinguishable flame,
The Lord will protect you and have mercy upon you.
Don't place your trust, merciful father,
And you, my merciful nanny, oh my mother, in your neighbors,
    in your siblings,
Or in beautiful, multicoloured clothing,
Or in this bright, in this appealing world.
Because this world is like the flower of a poppy,
It blooms and it blossoms and then it falls to the damp earth.
Therefore know, my merciful father,
And you, my merciful nanny, oh my mother,
That we live and we dwell in this bright world,

And we do not know when the hour of our death will come,
Perhaps we will be alive in the evening,
And in the morning we will have to lie in a coffin,
And we will be able to take nothing with us.
The only thing that we will be able to take, that we will be able to bring
     along,
Will be a deep, deep measure of earth,
A measure of earth deep and wide,
And that will be our only wealth.

According to Kharkiv, Hashchenko then added: "and if the above doesn't work, if you don't get alms having sung the above, then you can add the following":

Oh my nanny, oh my mother,
Did you never have a child that died,
Did you never have a small child,
That you need to have remembered,
That you can afford not to give alms?
Cover, oh my mother,
Cover my sinful body upon this earth,
Like the Lord Himself covers,
The tree with leaves,
The earth with grass,
The fish with scales,
The birds with feathers,
The sky with clouds,
And the sinful person with the blankets of Christ.

Besides emphasizing the power of prayer and the need to help the souls of the unquiet dead, Hashchenko's request for alms makes it clear that cloth would be a particularly welcome donation. The reason for this is partially practical: a cloth could be sold for money, whereas the other type of non-cash alms typically given to a minstrel, namely food, would spoil and be more difficult to sell. But the reason for the emphasis on cloth in general and towels in particular is again part of a belief system that apprentices learned during their training. A most important icon, both to the public at large and to Kozaks in particular, was the Mother of God of the Protection, the Pokrova figure. This portrays the Mother of God with a cloth, either a cloak or a ritual towel, called a *rushnyk*, which she holds above the multitudes gathered at her feet, sheltering them and literally offering protection. The appeal of this icon was enormous, partially because of its inherent meaning, and partially because of its connection to the Kozaks. The Pokrova, or the Mother of God of the Protection, was their icon, and October 1 (October 14 according to the old calendar) was their sacred holiday. Because of the special significance of the Mother of God of the Protection, many minstrels explicitly linked their request for a piece of fabric to this figure, as this excerpt from a begging song recorded from a lirnyk by Valerian Borzhkivskyi shows.[23]

> Behave, my mother,
> Like the Mother of God behaved,
> She had but one cloak,
> But she divided it into three pieces
> And the first piece, my mother,
> And the first piece, my mother,
> She gave to St Basil to protect him,
> With the second piece she covered the poor,
> And the third piece, my mother,
> And the third piece, my mother,
> She gave to the churches and the chapels,
> She inherited the Kingdom of Heaven.

The request for alms and the song of gratitude were the basics of professional begging, and a person who knew this much could survive as a mendicant. Once a child had learned these basics, he or she could go out in public and beg. And the child was expected to do just that, bringing back the proceeds of his or her work to the master. Because the basic begging songs were sufficient for survival, some pupils, presumably the least adept or gifted, stopped at this point and, after fulfilling their financial obligations by serving for the time period of their contract with the master, they left his service and went to work on their own. A typical period of apprenticeship was three years.[24] We also have information that some performers entered apprenticeship not as children, but as teenagers or young adults. These were people who wanted to improve their lot and their earning potential through specific performance skills such as the ability to play a musical instrument or knowledge of specialized, complex songs such as dumy. Typically these were people who had already served an apprenticeship, only their master had been a regular beggar who was not a kobzar or a lirnyk and could not offer musical instruction. Those who became apprentices when they were older did not need to be taught how to deal with blindness; all they needed was instruction in how to play a musical instrument and how to sing the songs they were missing from their repertory. Their period of apprenticeship was correspondingly shorter, usually one to two years.[25]

Those who received advanced training spent some time out begging and earning money and some of their time acquiring new knowledge. The type of knowledge that typically followed begging songs was knowledge of folk psalms called *psalmy*. These are religious verses with apocryphal content. Ostensibly based on biblical figures, they are narratives that offer dramatic accounts of good and bad behaviour, similar to the behaviours described in dumy. Failure to help family members in need was one such issue, as can be seen from the song about Lazarus, sometimes also called "The Two Lazaruses." A variant recorded from the lirnyk Adrian Kravchenko goes as follows:[26]

Oh, there has been more than one rich person,
Who always lived in luxury.
He had enough gold and silver,
And never admitted any of the clergy into his household,
He did not recognize his brother Lazarus as a brother.
Oh, in that household there was not a single soul,
Who would approach the sickly Lazarus,
And bring him food and drink.
Only the rich man had two fierce dogs,
They would always go under the table,
They would gather tiny crumbs,
They would bring them to the sick Lazarus, sitting in filth,
They would drip water on his parched lips,
They would lick his painful wounds,
They would lighten and support his body and soul.
Oh, when the rich man caught sight of the two fierce dogs,
He ordered his servants to chain them with iron chains,
To punish them with iron whips,
So that they would not go to the sickly Lazarus,
So that they would not use up his possessions,
Would not carry away his gold and his silver …
"Oh, my brother, you are rich and powerful!
But it looks like you think you won't die,

Because you do not care to make preparations for the hereafter."
"If I start to die, then I will buy my way out of it;
If I can't buy my way out of it, then I will fight my way out,
I will not submit to all of the Holy ancestors in Heaven
And I am not afraid of the Lord God Himself ..."
"Oh, Lord, God, Saviour, divine mercy is Yours!
Lord, hear my prayers:
Accept my body and soul, according to Your divine mercy!"
And the Lord listened to his prayer,
"Go, Angels, go fetch his soul.
Descend, Angels, go very quietly,
And gently take Lazarus' soul into your hands.
And seat him to the right of Abraham,
In the heavenly Lord's bright Paradise!"
Then the Angels and the Archangels sing a song,
They cheer up the sickly Lazarus.
Oh, after some time, after an hour, after a little bit,
A desire to go out, to ride in the open field seized the rich man ...
Oh, the rich man rode out from his household, from his new gates,
And his entourage followed him, his sumptuous troops,
And they saw that there was no more brother Lazarus and nothing to
    worry about.
The rich man rode past the second set of gates,
And a black illness came out after him:
It took the rich man and started to beat him against the earth ...
It finally occurred to the rich man to pray to God:
"Oh, Lord God, Saviour, divine mercy is Yours!
Oh, Lord, do not be angry with me now!
Did I not eat, did I not drink, did I not walk,
That I have angered the Lord God onto eternity.
Oh, Lord God, divine mercy is Yours!
Oh, Lord, hear my prayer:
Take my body and my soul, take them to where Lazarus is!"
And the Lord heard his prayer,
And he sends the servants of Hell to fetch his soul:
"Go, servants of Hell, go quickly to the earth,
And take the soul of the rich man into your hands ..."
And the servants of Hell had not yet reached his household,
And yet they have already turned his wealth into ashes, scattered far and wide:
They chased away his ready entourage,

They took away his gold and silver,
They took the rich man's soul out with a hook.
They hung the rich man from his left rib:
"Tell us, oh rich man, where is your wealth,
Your ribbons, your towels and your fine carvings,
Your gold, your silver, your ancient coin?"
Oh, they carried the rich man high into the sky,
And they dropped the rich man into Hell, way below:
"Swim, swim, oh rich man, there is plenty of room here,
Look up at Heaven, see how high God is!"
The rich man looked up to heaven with his eyes,
And he cried with his voice unto his brother Lazarus,
He pleaded and cried and he even called him his dear brother:
"Oh, brother, my own dear brother!
Couldn't you please exercise your will,
Couldn't you dip your pinky finger into the sea,
Couldn't you quench the fires of Hell just a bit?"
"Oh, brother, my own dear brother!
I could exercise my will,
But I do not want to anger the Lord God;
Even if I dip my pinky finger into the sea,
I can never quench these fires of Hell."
"Oh, brother, my own dear brother!
One mother bore us, she carried us under the same heart,
But she did not give us the same fate:
She gave you, my brother, great poverty,
And she gave me, my brother, great wealth.
You earned the heavenly kingdom with your poverty,
And I inherited Hell through my wealth.
Oh, brother, my own dear brother,
Pray to God for me once more;
Ask Him to let me return to the world once more;
If I have gold and silver, I will hand it out to the poor,
Every Sunday, every holiday, I will go to God's temple
And I will pay for the services and the reading of the Psalter,
And I will always recognize you, brother, as my kin;
I have five more brothers, and I will teach them [I will say]: ...
That in the world there are sacred spiritual writings:
Let them read the sacred writings,
And may you, my five brothers, come to understand."

This is vernacular religion which shares little with the biblical story of Lazarus aside from the name of the main protagonist and the unpredictability of the hour of death. What it expresses are not biblical themes, but the issues that dominated the repertory of minstrels and were important to their audiences, such as the misery of poverty and the obligation of family to help each other. As the apprentice learned to sing folk psalms and effectively narrate the problems faced by his listeners, his earning potential grew.

Other folk psalms include "The Song about St Barbara." It tells about a Christian woman who refuses to marry a pagan prince. To force her to accept the union, she is tortured by being boiled in oil, made to walk on broken glass, and finally by being immured in prison for thirty years. When Barbara's tormentor asks to see her bones after the thirty-year period has elapsed, she emerges fresh and beautiful. Again, both protagonists die, with Barbara ascending into Heaven and her tormentor going to Hell. The appeal of this song lay not only in its assertion of the power of Christian belief, but also in its dramatic treatment of a problem actually faced by women in the minstrel's audiences, namely, pressure to marry against their will.[27]

Many of the folk psalms describe the sinful soul and its fate after death. Tensions between parents and children are a prominent topic and apprentices learned that this was a good way to appeal to their audiences. In one such song, the prodigal son is transformed, following folk etymology of the Ukrainian word for "prodigal," into a son given to fornication and debauchery. The version recorded by Mykola Lysenko from Ostap Veresai goes as follows:[28]

Oh, he who comes into the world,
In this day and age,
Every such person must sin,
Oh, this miserable age.
And as he sins, he thinks to himself:
"Oh, I am still young,
I will have time to repent before I die,
And I will not go to Hell!"
But on Sunday, in the morning,
Do not drink wine:
There is much sin in wine, –
It will make you lose your senses.

A group stopped by an inn,
To have a drink and a bite,
And, having done so, they lost their senses,
They had to sin.
The prodigal son's father and mother come to him
They try to teach him some sense, for they pity their child;
And he flees from them like an animal,
He despises their words;
And, drunk, he sits there naked,
And shakes his fist,
And evil faith follows him,
And evil faith seduces him,
And leads him,
To sin, to fornication, to theft.
"When I stop sinning,
God will forgive me."
God gave the prodigal son,
God gave him an early death:
The sinner lies in his coffin,
He is plagued with misfortune.
The sinner races through Hell and through fire,
He is confused;
He spies his father and his mother,
He begs them to save him:
"Rescue me, I am your babe, oh, father, oh, mother!
How long will you let me scream and cry in these flames?"
"Run, son, run through Hell and through fire:
That is what you deserve;
I tried to lead you to your senses, –
But you did not like it.
Run, son, run through Hell and through fire,
Run night and day,
Because you did not heed your father and your mother,
Nor righteous people!
Son, your soul will perish in Hell,
Until Jesus Christ Himself comes
To save all souls."
Rescue God, rescue, oh Creator,
Save this soul from torment,
Hand not this body and soul into the Devil's grasp.

In some versions of this song, when the son dies and prays to his parents for rescue, God grants the mother and father permission to try and pull their son out of Hell by the one thing that he had given to the poor during his lifetime: a green onion. The parents try their best, but the onion breaks and the sinful man falls back into the torments of Hell. The song focuses not only on the behaviour of the son, but also on the relationship between parents and children – a topic found throughout the repertory of minstrels. Alcohol plays a prominent role in this song, and the belief that it can ruin a life is articulated in both psalms and dumy. As we will see later, alcohol is the downfall of not only Kozaks, but also Muslims who, according to their religion, should abstain from drink.

Folk psalms were the largest part of a minstrel's repertory and their subject matter covers much of the same topics as dumy, in addition to more specifically religious concerns such as preparing for the Last Judgment. Folk psalms, more than the other genres in a minstrel's repertory, warned listeners that people who do not go to church on Sunday, who do not give alms to the poor, and who count on getting around to doing all those good deeds at some future date might suddenly find themselves being called by Death. These songs describe sins and human failings and list the torments found in Hell. Their use of narrative structure, presented through colourful vocabulary, made psalms an audience favourite and even a beggar who knew psalms only could be quite successful.

Both begging songs and psalmy could be sung without musical accompaniment. When the master first taught these to his apprentices, they sang a cappella. This is the level of training at which female beggars, even the most gifted among them, had to stop. Women were not allowed to achieve high professional status. They were not taught how to play musical instruments, either the lira or the bandura, and they were not allowed to sing epic poetry or other verse narratives with historical subject matter. According to statements collected from kobzari and lirnyky in the nineteenth century, the reasons for this had to do with money. Supposedly, and probably this is indeed the case, the ability to play a musical instrument and perform dramatic epics and historical songs would bring the performer more public attention and more money. Women were considered less in need of money than men because they had fewer dependents. This meant that guilds tried to ensure that they would receive a smaller share of the alms that the public was likely to give. Women, the kobzari and lirnyky also stated, had nicer, more pleasant voices and this gave them an advantage in terms of attracting listeners and earning money. To even out access to available monies, women were deprived of the additional advantage of musical instruments and a more complex and interesting repertory. It is also likely that the Kozak legacy played a role in imposing gender restrictions on minstrelsy. If the original kobzari were musicians who lived and rode with the Kozaks, then only men could have become kobzari and it is possible that this gender restriction stayed even as kobzari went from being military bards to church-affiliated mendicants.[29]

Singing benefited from musical accompaniment and those male apprentices who were gifted enough to proceed were then taught the playing of a bandura or a lira, depending on what the master himself played. Because the boys could not see, masters had to teach the instrument by touch. The descriptions of this process are interesting and include one account which tells how the master tied his pupil's fingers to his own to give him the feel of the proper technique.[30] The last thing learned was the genres that have received the most scholarly attention, namely, dumy and historical songs. Dumy were the most complex and the most difficult songs to learn because they have uneven line length, groups of rhyming lines rather than stanzas, recitative sections that are spoken rather than sung, and complex musical accompaniment. Few kobzari and even fewer lirnyky knew dumy. Translations of dumy and historical songs will be presented in the context of the historical events which they describe in the next section of this book.

We have records from collectors such as Porfyrii Martynovych which show that women, too, knew dumy and that they could play musical instruments, the bandura included, even though they could not learn these skills through apprenticeship. This was knowledge that they acquired on their own, often from family members, but it was something that they could display in private settings only; they could play in the home, but not in public and not for money.[31]

In addition to begging songs, psalmy, dumy, and historical songs, kobzari and lirnyky knew quite a variety of other verse. Many performers were both musically inclined and quite enamoured of music. They picked up all sorts of songs and performed them for each other and for audiences outside the guild-sanctioned begging situations which will be discussed shortly. There were also certain typical minstrel songs which do not fall into the broader categories listed above, but were very popular with minstrel audiences. These include "The Orphan Girl" (Syritka), a narrative that tells about a girl whose mother dies. The girl, who is mistreated by her stepmother, asks the dead birth mother to take pity and to accept her into the land of the dead. The song lists both the various types of abuse that the orphan suffers in her life and the horrors of death, which the dead birth mother recites to discourage her child from seeking eternal rest.[32] The song "There Is No Justice in This World" (Nema v sviti pravdy) lists the forms of injustice that exist in life on earth.[33] Minstrels, because of their musical abilities, could learn and perform songs that were known by all villagers. They would not do so as part of their mendicancy, but nothing stopped them from singing these songs to entertain others. In fact, minstrels would perform at weddings and at dances and would earn money for doing so. The lira was an especially useful instrument at dances because the keys, when returning to their normal position, would make a clicking sound and thus add a bit of percussion to the performance.[34]

The context of a minstrel's repertory is crucial to understanding dumy and how they functioned. Because scholarly interest focused specifically and almost exclusively on dumy as a historical record of the Ukrainian past, genres other than dumy did not receive much attention. Only historical songs, precisely because they are historical and close to dumy in content, sometimes even being confused with dumy, were recorded in any significant numbers. Even folk psalms, the most important and requested songs in actual performance settings, were published only sporadically and only as individual items in journal articles until the work of the Demutskyi in the early twentieth century. But folk psalms share a great deal of imagery with dumy and the list of sins which dumy give as the cause for mortal wounds on the battlefield bears a great deal of resemblance to the list of sins in Last Judgment songs. Marriage to a foreigner, especially a foreigner who is not a Christian, appears in folk psalms, dumy, and historical songs. Songs like "The Orphan Girl" share with dumy accounts of female suffering, and songs like "There Is No Justice in This World" talk about social inequities, just like the dumy "Khvesko Andyber" and "Kozak Holota." Again, we cannot know if the religious subject matter and the imagery of suffering and injustice in dumy was taken from folk psalms and other popular minstrel songs or simply reinforced by them, but the overlap between the genres is clear.

An important part of minstrel training had nothing to do with performance, but was essential to life as a beggar and guild member. At some point close to the completion of their apprenticeship, kobzari and lirnyky were taught a special language called the *lebiiska mova*. This was a secret language, known only to minstrels and other mendicants, although dictionaries of it were compiled late in the nineteenth century.

It was a language that minstrels used to greet each other and to communicate among themselves, especially when they were on the road or in public. There has been debate about the purpose of this language, with some claiming that it was used by minstrels to conceal from the public those of their activities that were less than pious. Others claim that the language was a calling card of sorts, a proof of legitimacy that would assure other minstrels that the person speaking to them was indeed a guild member, someone who had gone through all the proper stages of apprenticeship and training. In all likelihood, the lebiiska mova served both of these functions. Because minstrels could not see, they did need a way of identifying who they were talking to, a way of distinguishing friend from foe. Similarly, minstrels did need to maintain a godly appearance at all times, concealing any discussions of mundane matters that might arouse suspicion.[35] Any person who is different from others tends to be viewed in extremes and opposites, and this was as true of blind mendicants as of any other liminal group. Minstrels were seen as the emissaries of God, the successors of the apostles – and they were suspected of shameless licentiousness. There is an interesting document which describes a gathering of minstrels and other beggars as a festival of debauchery, one "capable of destroying one's physical and moral sensibilities." The author, Jozef Dzierzkowski, paints a grotesque picture of people shedding their appearance of suffering and meekness for carnivalesque, even lewd, festivities far from the eyes of ordinary villagers. The document is unique, but it does reflect the widely held suspicion that the disabled were deformed not only physically, but also morally, and that their piety was a pretence used to bilk the tender-hearted out of their money.[36]

Apprenticeship ended in a formal initiation rite called the *vyzvilka*. This conferred upon the initiate the status of minstrel and allowed him to make a living as a kobzar or lirnyk. The initiation rite tested proper behaviour as much as, if not more than, knowledge of songs. It also constituted a formal request for permission and a ritual purchase, from the master and from the other guild members, of the right to perform. When the apprentice had fulfilled his contractual obligations and when the master deemed his apprentice ready to set out on his own, he called an assembly of minstrels. The apprentice bought food and drink for those present and ritually requested permission to join their ranks. The procedure required addressing each member in turn, according to his rank, and requesting his permission and his blessing. The initiate also treated all those present to drinks, again in a ritual manner, first requesting permission to do so and then serving each in turn. The initiation rite was considered secret and closed, although, towards the end of the nineteenth century, scholars were able to record several detailed descriptions which now serve as our sources of information.[37]

More about Learning Songs

There are many additional interesting details connected to schooling which are not as widely attested to as the ones given in the description of apprenticeship above. One such detail is the existence of entire schools of minstrelsy. In the late nineteenth and early twentieth centuries, the period from which we get most of our information, individual minstrel masters were the norm. They usually had several apprentices living with them at any one time, boys and perhaps girls, in different stages of training. However, on the territory of Western Ukraine, entire schools, probably patterned on church schools for the sighted, seem to have existed in the past. These were distinctive in that they had a number of masters and a sizable body of pupils. We have only hearsay evidence of minstrel schools, word-of-mouth accounts about bygone institutions plus one reference to a large building which had supposedly housed such as school. These large training facilities existed for lirnyky only. Kobzari seem to have always trained in one-to-one situations.[38]

Some accounts of minstrel life refer to several stages of professional competency. According to these, a man who passed his initiation rite was allowed to perform, but not to take on apprentices. Only after he had worked for a significant length of time (the number usually given is ten years) was a minstrel given the right to teach others. That right was conferred in a second initiation ceremony which very much resembled the first. At the conclusion of this second ceremony, the performer had the title of master added to his designation as kobzar or lirnyk and was allowed to accept pupils. Having apprentices was advantageous not only because a minstrel's income would improve, but also because his quality of life became better. With apprentices doing at least part of the begging, a minstrel did not need to travel and endure the hardships of the road as often.[39]

Formal learning of the minstrel's art occurred in the context of apprenticeship, but many, if not all, minstrels continued to learn after initiation. Many say that this was a necessity because masters did not teach all the songs that they knew to their pupils to reduce competition. Thus, to fill out their repertory, kobzari and lirnyky would need to pick up songs by listening to other minstrels perform in places which attracted a large number of performers such as bazaars and fairs or large church events such as *vidpusty* or *khramy*. Sometimes they would pick up songs in a more intimate setting such as a tavern or a church hospice where minstrels stopped on their journey. Minstrels could request permission to learn a specific song and then pay the person who already knew it so that he would teach the desired music and lyrics. Such teaching might well require a number of tedious repetitions of a particular text, as some documents attest. Gifted musicians could pick up new material by simply listening to others perform and then practising on their own, either out loud or in silence. When a song was acquired without payment it was not tactful to then go and perform that song in the presence of the man to whom it originally "belonged." The best of minstrels also worked on the songs that they already knew, improving them so that they would be more emotionally effective. Both comparison of different performances of the same song by a single performer over time and the words of the minstrels themselves attest that the most dedicated minstrels worked on their repertory, trying to achieve the greatest possible artistic excellence. In addition to learning orally from other minstrels, it is possible and even likely that kobzari and lirnyky acquired new material from written sources. We know that some collectors taught minstrels the songs that they thought they should know. But minstrels might have had access to written sources before the interference of collectors. As noted in the discussion of Khmelnytskyi dumy, minstrels learned songs written by the seminarians with whom they shared the church complex of school and hospice and the songs of the Khmelnytskyi cycle might have been among such written compositions that entered the minstrel repertory and were then transmitted orally, like other minstrel texts.[40]

Minstrel Guilds – Life as a Professional Kobzar or Lirnyk

Teaching kobzari and lirnyky the skills that they would need was not the only function of the guilds: these organizations controlled all aspects of the professional lives of minstrels. When a minstrel went out to sing and beg, he did not do so in his own village. Begging is an awkward situation. It is embarrassing to the person doing the begging and minstrels often insisted that they were not beggars, but persons who offered a service in exchange for pay. Still, they recognized that turning to people and asking them for money was not an ordinary commercial transaction: it was a form of begging and required a special relationship. To reduce awkwardness and to keep mendancy professional, minstrels begged outside their own villages only; they did not approach people whom they would encounter on a day-to-day basis. While at home, kobzari and lirnyky were ordinary villagers, just like their neighbours, and this allowed them to have neighbourly relations with the people around them.[41] When they did go out to beg, where they might travel was determined by their guild. According to the work of Mikhail Speranskii, the guilds were territorial, with hegemony over a certain area and a formal affiliation with a church. Each guild controlled its region by excluding from its territory the members of other guilds and people with no guild affiliation. Any infringement could be punished and a man caught begging in a guild's territory without its permission could be subject to a beating.[42]

The guilds were democratically governed. The officers of the guild were elected by the entire membership and they could be ousted from office if they displeased their fellows. Each guild had its own treasury into which all members paid dues and the office of the treasurer was an important one. Several records show that, in addition to the treasurer, there was also a guild key-keeper, a person who ensured that the chest holding the guild's funds could be unsealed only when the guild assembled for a meeting. This arrangement prevented the treasurer from being tempted to help himself to guild monies. Guild funds were used to support an icon, a candle, or an icon-lamp in the church with which the guild was affiliated. They were also used to help members in need. While the private lives of minstrels were outside guild jurisdiction, if someone suffered a catastrophic loss, such as having a house burn down, the guild would come to his aid. Similarly, misbehaviour, especially if directed against a fellow guild member, would be tried by an assembly of the guild, which could then levy a fine or administer physical punishment.[43]

The beggars' guilds were arranged by region and a particular guild worked in a particular territory, one in the proximity of the church which sponsored the guild. Guilds were also arranged by specialization, and kobzar and lirnyk guilds were distinct from guilds of other beggars. At the same time, the various types of beggars' guilds were affiliated with one another. They recognized each other; they respected each other's territory; they helped each other in times of need, and there are indications that they met in large "conventions" of multiple guilds, not just guilds of kobzari and lirnyky, but guilds of all kinds of beggars, on a regular, perhaps annual, basis. It is probably just such a meeting that was described by Dzierzkowski in his effort to expose the lack of piety among mendicants.

As travelling was difficult for a blind person, kobzari and lirnyky routinely hired a sighted guide, a boy, or more rarely a girl, called a *povodyr* to accompany them when they went out to beg. Children who accepted such a position were typically in a financially difficult position. They were orphans, or the children of families that were large and poor and could not support all their members. Some were sickly and less capable of farm labour than their siblings, though still able to travel. A povodyr or his parents would enter into a verbal agreement with the minstrel. The child would agree to serve for a specified length of time. In exchange, he received support in the form of food, shelter, and clothing. He was also given a portion of the minstrel's earnings. Though this was never a substantial amount of money, it was still enough to allow the child to return home at the end of the term of service with some cash, thus improving his or her lot.[44] We know little about povodyri because they were not artists, and so of little interest to scholars, but apparently at least some liked the work. Valerian Borzhkivskyi recorded the story of one boy who worked as a guide and who came to like the life of a minstrel so well that he wanted to become one himself. Of course he was sighted and that excluded him from joining a guild and becoming a professional. He tried performing, but his potential audience would simply not accept him, despite his musical abilities, because he was not blind. He tried various ways of working around the problem, including marrying a blind wife, but this did not help. Eventually he learned to roll his eyes back so as to look blind. When he did so, those who did not know his true physical condition did accept him as a performer; those who knew that he was really sighted did not.[45]

Travelling with their sighted guides, kobzari and lirnyky went to public events in urban as well as in rural areas. Fairs, especially in cities, were a good place to encounter many people and earn some cash or other donations. Especially profitable were church holidays such as the *khram*, *praznyk*, or *vidpust*. A khram (Orthodox) and praznyk (Eastern rite Catholic) is a celebration of the day of the saint or religious holiday after whom or after which the church is named. People come from outside the village or town where the event is being held: those who had left return home if they can and friends and relatives come to visit. The event is a joyous one with plenty of food supplied by local residents, which puts attendees in a generous mood. Since the celebration was a religious one, people were also more aware of the religious obligation to support the poor and this further encouraged almsgiving. A vidpust is a more sombre event, one where people seek to expiate sins through pilgrimage and prayer. As described by Borzhkivskyi, at vidpusty people offered all sorts of religious services in exchange for alms. There would be people who read religious texts aloud and there would be plain beggars who presented only the opportunity to do a good deed. Performers such as kobzari and lirnyky would typically stake out an area on the church grounds or on the road leading to the church so that they could play and sing without interference from others.[46]

A great deal of the work that minstrels did was on a smaller scale, and the audiences that they drew in these venues likely influenced the content of their repertory, dumy included. In the villages where minstrels would travel to beg, they would simply go from house to house. Arriving outside a home, a minstrel would begin with the begging song, the sort of song that he had learned at the beginning of apprenticeship. The residents of the house could give the minstrel something at the conclusion of the song. This could be cash, but it was more often a product of some sort, perhaps a prepared food such as bread, perhaps a food ingredient such as flour. Clothing or even a length of fabric was a desirable donation, as seen from the begging songs translated above. The residents of a house could also excuse themselves and tell the singer that they had nothing to give. If this was the case, the minstrel would walk to the next home and try his luck there. If the residents of the house were interested, they could invite the minstrel into the yard or into the house itself. This implied a more substantial donation and it allowed listeners the opportunity to request whatever songs they wished to hear. These could be folk psalmy, or dumy and historical songs, or songs like "The Orphan Girl." The people who would typically be at home when a minstrel came by were women. Men would be out in the fields either planting, or working the crops, or harvesting. Women would be at home tending the kitchen garden, doing household chores, and minding the children. There would be a number of them together in one place, unlike the men, who would be scattered across the fields. This made women a good target audience.[47] The importance of women as an audience and thus as a determining factor in the repertory of minstrels is manifested in many ways. For example, a number of the begging songs that have been collected and preserved are specifically addressed to female listeners, as in the texts translated above. As for the other songs, some, like folk psalms, deal with religious issues that are gender neutral. Many, however, are clearly aimed at women. A good example is "The Orphan Girl." This is a narrative that would appeal to any woman. Even if she had not lost her mother like the orphan of the song, many a woman could identify with the plight of the title character. Upon marriage, a woman moved in with her husband's family and often had to live with her mother-in-law, a "second mother" who could be less than kind and who might well mistreat her like the stepmother abuses the orphan. Thus, "The Orphan Girl" offered the opportunity for a bit of indulgence in self-pity and a good cry. And, as Varion Honchar and other performers noted, getting the audience to cry was a good way to ensure a more generous donation.[48]

Perhaps some of the most significant adaptations to a female listening audience can be found within dumy themselves. Dumy may well have originated on the battlefield or in Kozak encampments and, during the time they were sung to an all-male audience, they may have contained military subject matter only. By the nineteenth century, however, they were full of topics that would appeal to women; they voiced the concerns of women and dealt with family and gender issues. In the song about Ivas Konovchenko, for example, one of the central plot elements is the struggle of wills between a mother and her son. The son wants to heed a call to arms and join the military. The mother, having lost all the other men in her family, wants him to stay home and be a farmer. The son disobeys his mother and does what he wants to do behind her back: while she is in church, he enlists with a colonel who is recruiting men to join the Kozaks and leaves for the front. When the mother returns home, she discovers what has happened and curses her son. The narrative then follows two parallel lines. Back home the mother has a change of heart and decides to make the sacrifices that her son had requested and to buy him the horse that he had wanted. On the field of battle young Ivas successfully engages the enemy until he becomes too drunk to remember to ask for a blessing before riding out to fight. As soon as he does so, the mother's curse takes effect and he is killed. The song does not clearly favour the son's decision to put his desire to prove himself ahead of his mother's equally strong desire to keep him at her side. Rather, it presents a complex and nuanced picture that acknowledges the merits of both positions. The song speaks to a generational conflict that could occur in times of peace as well as in times of war, the sort of conflict that must have been experienced by many people in the minstrel's audience. By focusing on the mother and her legitimate desire to keep her son by her side, it speaks to women who might well have had their own contests of will with their offspring or with other family members. The version of Ivas Konovchenko published by Pavlo Zhytetskyi goes as follows:[49]

In glorious Ukraine, in the city of Korsun,
There lived a Korsun colonel named Pan Filon ...
When he started to assemble a volunteer army,
He put out a call for volunteers,
He called, and he shouted, to the winemakers and the beer brewers,
To the drunkards and the men playing knucklebones,
"He who does not want to distil horilka [vodka] in the winery,
He who does not want to brew beer in the brewhouse,
He who does not want to play knucklebones and waste his time,
Let him come with me, the Korsun colonel, and join the volunteer army
And go to the city of Tiahynia,
To the Cherken Valley,
To stand in defence of the Christian faith,
To win knightly renown for himself!"
Speaking these words,
He hurries to the city of Cherkasy on Friday,
And on Saturday, early in the morning, he raises his colourful banners.
He calls and he shouts to the lieutenants and the colonels,
To the hetmans and the captains,
To the young Kozaks,
To the military servants:
"Oh, you lieutenants and colonels,
You hetmans and captains,
Come with me, the Korsun colonel, and join the volunteer army,
To go to the Cherken valley
To the city of Tiahynia
To stand in defence of the Christian faith,
And we will win knightly glory for ourselves,
We will wear out our Moroccan leather boots!"
In the city of Cherkasy there lived a widow,
She was an old woman
By the name of Hrytsykha,
And she was called Konovchykha,
She had a son Ivan Konovchenko,
Her only widow's son.
She kept him beside her until he was grown,

She did not let him become a hired hand,
She didn't let the hands of others wear him down,
She was counting on his remembering her and praising her after she died.
Well, Ivan Konovchenko went out to the market,
And he hears the Korsun colonel Filon speaking with words,
And calling people to join the volunteer army.
Well Ivan Konovchenko goes to his elderly mother,
And he speaks with words,
"My mother, my elderly one,
If you would do the right thing,
You would take four oxen and two raven horses and separate them
   from the herd,
You would drive them to the Jewish merchant's
And you would also give him 100 zloty coins
And you would buy me a fine horse.
My youthful and manly Kozak soul would like that very much.
I'll go, Mother, to venture into the Cherken valley,
I'll stand up for the Christian faith,
I will win knightly glory for myself,
And I will learn Kozak customs well."
The widow, the old woman, she heard these words,
And she spoke in answer:
"My son, my son Ivas Konovchenko,
Don't you have enough to drink and to eat,
Don't you have nice clothes to wear,
Don't the local elders respect you,
Does the company of Kozaks look down upon you?
It would be better if you took the four oxen and the two raven horses
   and harnessed them to a plow,
You would plow and sow grain,
You would invite the Kozaks and the men to break bread –
And the Kozaks would teach you military ways and Kozak customs."
Ivas Konovchenko heard this,
And he spoke saying,
"My mother, elderly lady,
I don't want, my mother,
To call to the oxen with a Kozak voice,
I don't want to soil silken cloth with dust,
Even if I invite the Kozaks into my house,
They will call me a homebody and a buckwheat-sower,

It is much better, Mother, that I
Go to the Cherken Valley,
To stand steadfast for the Christian faith."
On Sunday, early in the morning,
The widow, the old woman, set off for God's church,
She took all the weapons that were in the house and locked them up,
All she left out was the seven span long rifle, –
Well, Ivan Konovchenko gets up out of bed,
And he goes out to the market,
And there the Korsun colonel, Pan Filon, is speaking with words:
"Whoever waits for a meal with his father and his mother,
That person will need to catch up with me for I will be eight miles
    from Cherkasy."
The neighbours were going to church,
And they said to the widow:
"Widow, you are standing here in church and you realize nothing,
You do not know that your son Konovchenko is no longer home."
The widow came home from church,
And she did not find Ivan Konovchenko at home.
She berated him and cursed him:
"May you, my son Ivan, find neither luck nor good fortune,
Because you have left me, an elderly widow, to care for the
    homestead alone."
Early on Monday the widow awoke from sleep,
And she spoke saying:
"Oh my poor, my foolish widow's head,
I should not have berated and cursed my son,
I have ruined his Kozak fate and good fortune."
Then she took heed,
And she took four oxen and two raven horses and separated
    them from the herd,
And she added some money,
And she bought her son a fine horse,
So that his brave young Kozak heart would rejoice and be glad,
And she gave seven measures of cloth to a Kozak,
So that he would deliver the horse to her son.
The Kozak saddles the horse
And catches up to the Korsun colonel twelve miles outside Cherkasy;
He caught up to the colonel quickly,
And he went among the foot soldiers,

And he recognized Ivan Konovchenko among the infantry,
And he handed the fine horse over to him.
Ivan Konovchenko mounted the good horse,
And he spoke, saying,
"Brothers, I thought that my mother had forsaken and foresworn me,
And here she is doing me a great service,
For she has bought a fine horse for me,
So that my Kozak soul would rejoice and be glad.
If merciful God allows me to return from this campaign,
Then I will know,
How to honour my elderly parent,
I will send her twelve Turks-janissaries to be her servants!"
As the Korsun colonel Pan Filon started to arrive in the Cherken
    Valley, near the city of Tiahynia,
He started to speak to the Kozaks, saying,
"Kozaks, brave gentlemen!
Who among you will volunteer to mount his horse,
And to go battle the Crimeans and the Nogais at the crossroads?"
All the Kozaks fell silent,
Ivan Konovchenko alone answered,
Only he, the widow's son:
"Bless me, Pan Filon, so that I may mount my good horse,
And meet the Crimeans and Nogais in single combat!"
Then the Korsun colonel spoke, saying:
"Ivan Konovchenko!
You are but a young child:
You have had no experience either on land or at sea
You have never seen Kozak blood,
When you see Christian blood being spilled,
You will become afraid."
Ivan Konovchenko spoke, saying:
"Korsun colonel, Pan Filon!
Go to the river and catch a young duck and a mature one,
Then set them back on the water to see if the young one does not
    swim like the old."
The Korsun colonel answers:
"Ivan Konovchenko!
Since you have managed to pose such a riddle,
I bless you that you may mount your good horse,
And battle the Crimeans and the Nogais."

Konovchenko mounted his horse,
He accepts the blessings of the Kozaks,
And he rides out among the Crimeans and the Nogais,
He knocks sixty-six Crimeans and Nogais off their horses,
He cuts their heads off from their shoulders,
He lassos fourteen Turkish knights with his lariat,
And drives them back alive to the Kozak encampment.
The Korsun colonel, Pan Filon, sees all this,
And he speaks,
He calls Konovchenko his brother:
"Ivan Konovchenko, my dearest brother,
Since you have managed to win true knightly renown,
I bless you and ask you to join me and to rest in my tent."
And Ivan Konovchenko hears this,
And he is greatly pleased,
Because the Korsun colonel has referred to him as a brother.
So he speaks, saying:
"Korsun colonel, Pan Filon,
Bless me that I may drink distilled horilka,
Then I will fight the Crimeans and the Nogais better still."
The colonel speaks, saying:
"Ivan Konovchenko!
I have heard old people say,
That this distilled horilka is very potent,
More than one person has left this world because of it."
At that time and in that hour,
The Korsun colonel was distracted,
And Ivan Konovchenko drank his fill of horilka.
He mounted his good horse,
He let his sword fall from his hands,
And he rode amidst the Crimeans and the Nogais,
He knocks seventy men off their horses,
And he cuts the heads from their shoulders.
The godless Turks started to sense that the Kozak was drunk,
And they began to drive him away from the Kozak encampment,
They surrounded him on all sides,
And there they chopped him and they hewed at him,
There they inflicted mortal wounds,
Only they were not able to capture the Kozak's horse.
The Kozak's horse prances back into the encampment,

Like a bright falcon flying,
The Korsun colonel notices this,
And he speaks:
"It is not without reason that Konovchenko's horse is prancing
	about the encampment.
It means that he is no longer alive,
You, gentlemen, did not behave well,
Because you let a drunken man out of your hands,
Now do the right thing, my brothers,
Mount your Kozak steeds,
And gather the Kozak's body,
And bring it to the Kozak tents."
Then the Kozaks did as they were told,
They gathered up the Kozak's body,
They dug the dry loam with their swords,
They carried the earth with their hats and with the skirts of their coats,
And fired their weapons,
And they proclaimed the Kozak's glory,
They built up a burial mound seven spans high.
In the city of Cherkasy.
The widow, the old woman,
Called Hrytsykha,
And nicknamed Konovchykha,
Had a dream, a strange and marvelous dream,
Very strange and curious …
The widow awoke from her dream,
And she went to the marketplace,
And she consulted with her neighbours:
"I had a dream strange and marvellous,
I saw that my son got married while he was away at war,
And that he took a Turkish woman, proud and haughty, as a wife,
She dresses in a green dress with white braid,
And she does not serve any lord,
And she does not pay any tribute,
No one pushes her into a corner,
The only lord that she acknowledges is the righteous judge God in Heaven."
The neighbours heard this,
They guessed the meaning of the widow's dream,
Only they did not tell her the truth:
"Widow, you poor woman!

Your son will come back from the war,
And he will give you gifts of Kozak brocade."
Then the widow was not stingy,
She set out four kegs of horilka and six of mead at her gate,
On holy Sunday she awaited the return of the Kozaks from their campaign.
The Kozaks return from their campaign,
The troops hum like bees,
The first division walks up,
And the widow inquires about her son Ivan Konovchenko,
The Kozaks knew what had happened all too well,
But they did not tell the widow the truth,
The second division came along,
And the widow asked about her son there also,
And the Kozaks there also knew what had happened,
But they did not tell the widow the truth:
"Widow, poor widow, don't worry,
Your son got married while at war,
He took a Turkish woman proud and haughty as a bride."
The widow heard this,
She toasted every single Kozak,
And she spoke, saying,
"I praise you, oh Lord, that I have been granted a quiet and cheerful
    daughter-in-law!
Even if I have to sweep out the chicken coop for the Kozaks,
At least they will keep me by their side in my old age."
And then the third division came along,
The Korsun colonel is leading the horse by his reins.
Then the widow, the old woman,
As soon as she saw this,
Then she became as if paralyzed,
She could no longer stand on her feet,
And she fell prone to the damp earth,
She raised her hands on high,
And she cursed the colonel:
"Oh, colonel, Pan Filon,
May you know neither luck nor good fortune,
Since you have lost my son from amongst your ranks."
The colonel himself was not proud,
He dismounts from his horse,
He picks the widow, the old woman, up from the ground,

And he says:
"Widow, poor woman!
Don't curse me,
Don't ruin my fate and my Kozak fortune:
You yourself did not behave properly,
Because you sought to keep your son out of the volunteer army,
You ruined his luck,
Because you cursed him ..."
Then the widow behaved in a way that was not stingy,
She invited forty thousand Kozak soldiers into her yard,
For three days she gave them [as much] food and drink as they wanted,
And she gave all the Kozaks gifts that would be fit for noblemen,
She gave them rushnyky that were woven and embroidered,
She celebrated a funeral and a wedding all in one,
And she proclaimed the glory of the Kozaks.

This is a long and complex duma which explores many issues including the power of words, be they blessings or curses, the importance of a horse to the style of combat in which Kozaks engaged, and the problem of violent death, which is often pictured as a death-wedding. But one of the central issues is the conflict between a mother and her son over what constitutes proper and honourable behaviour. The powerful artistic articulation of this topic which this song provides would surely have appealed to the women in the minstrel's audience.

One of the dumy from the everyday life cycle speaks to women's concerns even more directly. This song, usually referred to as the "Duma about a Widow and Her Sons," tells of a mother who does everything she can for her three boys in spite of the hardships imposed by her status as widow. The woman, who presumably lost her husband in battle, does not let her sons become hired hands, as would normally happen in a family without a father. Rather, she sacrifices her health so that her boys can have the best. The sons grow to manhood and prosper; in fact, they become quite wealthy. As they entertain rich guests, they become embarrassed by their sickly mother. They eventually kick her out of the house so that they can entertain without interruption, showing total disregard for everything that their mother has done. A neighbour takes pity on the woman and takes her in. As soon as the brothers get rid of their mother, their fortunes begin to decline. In due course they realize that their problem is their mistreatment of their mother and they ask her to return. The mother does return in some versions of this duma, though not in others. But, regardless of the ending, the song articulates precisely the sort of feelings of being unappreciated, or under-appreciated, that might well have been held by many women listening to a minstrel. A version of this song published by Pavlo Chubynskyi goes as follows:[50]

It was not the grove rustling,
As it was the elderly widow,
Lamenting in her home over her dear children!
She had three sons – bright as young falcons,
She nurtured them until they were grown,
She did not let them become hired hands,
She ruined her head [her health] for their sake,
She hoped that she would be able to live with them.
They themselves [the sons] started to reach maturity,
They began to marry young wives,
They started to make fun of their mother,
They started to speak to each other.
The youngest said to the middle brother,
And the middle brother says to the oldest,
The oldest says to their mother:
"Go, mother, go away from me,
Mother, I will host rich guests,
They will be lords and princes dressed in gilded caftans,
They will drink and they will make merry,
And you, my elderly mother, will stand by the entryway,
And I won't know how, in my pride, I should address you,
How I can possibly call you 'mother'?
I'll call you a hired woman or a servant –
And that will be a sin,
Because you are neither my hired woman nor my servant,
But my own birth mother!"
Well, the widow heard this,
And she left the household,
She stumbles down the street, she falls,
She can't see God's world for her copious tears.
Oh, there is a great pain in the widow's heart,
As if someone is piercing it with a knife.
Soon the close-by neighbours saw this,
And they spoke to the widow:

"Oh, widow, you elderly woman,
Come to our house to live and to dwell,
We will feed you with bread and with salt."
Well, the widow heard this,
And she goes into a stranger's house,
And she lives, and she dwells,
She has no rest either at dusk or at dawn,
She blames her sons.
Those people who were drinking and making merry at their house,
As they left, they blamed them [the widow's sons],
"Dear brothers, fair as turtledoves,
For all the time that we have been drinking and making merry
    at your place,
We have not, for some reason, seen your elderly mother.
Did you sell her or did you trade her,
Or did she eat up all the bread and salt at your house,
Or is she cursing you in your old age?"
The oldest brother hears this,
He goes to the morning service at church,
He listens to the whole service,
He becomes close to God.
And he speaks to his brothers, saying:
"My dear brothers,
Fair as turtledoves,
We need to think and we need to ponder,
How to get our elderly mother back into our house,
It seems that the Lord is punishing us,
He is diminishing our sustenance in the field and in the home,
We have no order in our home without our elderly mother."
Those were not eagles calling,
Those were three brothers, widow's sons, looking for their mother
    and asking after her.
When they came to the third house,
The oldest brother walked into the home,
He removes his hat, he bows low:
"Oh, widow, our elderly mother,
Come to our house to live and to dwell,
We will take care of you in your old age,
It seems that God has started to punish us,
To diminish our sustenance in the house and in the field."

My sons, bright falcons,
It is one thing to ask for your father's and your mother's prayers,
And it is another thing to anger your mother.
As the widow had cursed and reviled her sons,
So she thought and she pondered,
And she saved their souls from the sea,
And she ransomed them from their sins,
She led them to the heavenly kingdom.

Dumy which speak about the tragic lives of women are most common in the cycle called the songs about everyday life. They tell of the plight of a Kozak's wife who must care for her children on her own while her husband is away; she is a woman who must suffer herself and also somehow explain this hard life to her children. In some versions of this particular text the woman endures physical abuse from her husband when he returns on top of the misery that was her lot while he was gone, and to make the song more poignant still, she must lie to her neighbours about her bruises. Songs tell of a sister's plight when a brother must leave home either because of poverty or to avoid conflict with his stepfather. But women's issues are found throughout dumy and historical songs and, in many, women do not suffer passively. In one of the dumy about captivity, Marusia Bohuslavka takes action and releases her fellow Ukrainians from prison. In historical songs women help other women either bear the burden of enslavement or escape from it.

Minstrel songs, dumy included, that did not appeal specifically to women still dealt with issues that were relevant to the nineteenth- and early-twentieth-century audiences listening to kobzari and lirnyky. Even dumy that sing about death on the battlefield and the dilemma of finding a worthy successor to take one's place, even songs that talk about escape from captivity and the hardships of languishing in prison contain family-centred subject matter. In "The Escape of Three Brothers from Azov," for example, the relationship between the three brothers is as much of an issue as the strategies they use to ensure successful flight from captivity. The way the brothers interact with their parents is important. Inheritance, an issue as real in times of peace as in times of war, is a motivating factor for the two older siblings. In several texts, even battlefield outcome is contingent on behaviour towards kin and fellow villagers. In these songs, religious subject matter, motivated by the minstrels' affiliation with the church, blends with family-life themes. Kozaks who are threatened by a deadly storm at sea or who are dying of mortal wounds on the field of battle address each other and say that the cause of their plight was not lack of military prowess, but misbehaviour on the home front. As they explain, when they left home to go to war, they did not honour their parents, they roughly shoved their brother aside, they did not take their hats off as they passed the church, and they rode arrogantly down the street, trampling small children and the elderly. It is these sins in the civilian sphere, or parental curses provoked by these sins, that cause downfall on the field of battle. Again, disrespect and improper behaviour in the village setting are not problems limited to times of war. The arrogant behaviour of youthful community members troubles society at all times and it would have been a real issue for civilians in the nineteenth and twentieth centuries.

The song about Khvesko Handzha Andyber speaks about people being fooled by appearances. When the hero of this song, a hetman, appears in a tavern dressed as a common soldier, he is treated as such, in other words, not very well. When he shows up in his finery, everyone present treats him with the utmost courtesy. While the song deals with military rank, failure to recognize true worth in the absence of external signs is a perennial issue, valid in any context, and one that would have been meaningful to the village audience of a minstrel.

Subject matter that touches on the life of the village audience is present in all known dumy. Even the songs from the Khmelnytskyi cycle, where family problems such as conflicts between parents and children are absent, recount the bad treatment of the ordinary peasant and give it as the reason for the action that follows. It is because Jews collect impossibly high tolls, and because they demand payment for the use of the church that Ukrainians must rebel against the Poles whom the Jews serve. Did dumy contain non-military subject matter from the beginning or was this material added as the audience listening to these songs switched from a military to a civilian one? It is indeed possible that family life was treated in these songs all along. After all, Kozaks, like anyone else, would have had personal problems such as difficulty reconciling family loyalties and military obligations. Many would have been peasants themselves before joining the Kozak Host and thus affected by the same issues as other villagers. Besides, as noted above, many problems, such as the tendency to go by appearances and to fail to see the true worth of a human being are perennial issues, affecting all people at all times. Their relevance is eternal. If issues such as conflicts with parents, the temptation to look down upon family and village, and the conflicting pulls of military and familial loyalty were articulated in early dumy, then it is likely that these were the songs that continued to be performed even as songs with strictly military subject matter were forgotten because they did not resonate with the concerns of the village audiences for whom kobzari and lirnyky performed in the nineteenth century.

It is also possible that dumy were modified to bring issues connected with civilian and family life to the fore or to introduce such topics where they had not been previously treated. After all, dumy are oral literature. They exist in variants and, from what we know of the artistic practice of the best of kobzari and lirnyky, performers did modify their texts to increase artistic integrity and to enhance audience appeal. Finally, it is possible that certain dumy are new creations, songs that came into being after the Kozak era. There is very little military subject matter in a song such as the "Duma about a Widow and Her Sons," or the songs in the everyday life cycle of dumy. These may be post-Kozak era creations in duma style, songs that came into being in order to address the issues of the mostly female audience that minstrels typically encountered. They may also be extensively modified songs that took the description of an earlier historical reality and changed it to suit the situation of the new, civilian listeners. Some versions of the "Duma about a Sister and a Brother," for example, describe a woman married to a man in a distant and foreign land. Such a situation could occur at any time, especially to a woman whose family was poor. It is also possible that this song was once a narrative about a Ukrainian slave, taken as a captive, and later married to her owner. This song and other dumy from the cycle about everyday life will be discussed in the last chapter of this book.

The Decline of Traditional Minstrelsy

Towards the end of the nineteenth and the beginning of the twentieth centuries, minstrelsy as a formal structure with an organized guild system and requisite apprenticeship and initiation began to fall apart. Public interest in minstrel song, historical songs and dumy included, decreased and the only real clientele for these was the intelligentsia. Khmelnytskyi songs were kept alive almost solely by the elite, who were interested in them for their historical value. There were concerts organized by scholars which showcased minstrels. Hnat Khotkevych organized one in Kharkiv in 1902. It is noteworthy that even as knowledgeable a man as Khotkevych and one as dedicated to folklore as he was saw fit to adapt the music of the kobzari and lirnyky to elite taste. He organized minstrels into ensembles instead of allowing them to play solo as they typically did in the village setting. He tried to improve their voices with lemon and honey. He even retuned their bandury.[51]

The Soviet socialist revolution brought the institution of minstrelsy to an end. Minstrels who were trained through apprenticeship and belonged to guilds did survive the revolution and, when Gorky's speech at the Congress of Writers made it acceptable to study folklore again, they were recognized and received their due as artists. Performers like Yevhen Adamtsevych, Yehor Movchan, and Fedir Kushneryk were treated in scholarly literature, but they were redefined to fit Soviet perception of what a folk artist should be. Instead of being described as pious mendicants, minstrels were presented as proto-revolutionaries, supporting the Soviet socialist movement and even acting as couriers for partisans. In keeping with Soviet policies towards folklore, minstrels were encouraged to compose new songs on new topics appropriate to Soviet ideology, the "Duma about Lenin" being one example. They were trained in the composition of these new, Soviet texts by professional folklorists.[52] While dumy with Soviet subject matter were a requisite part of every minstrel performance, they were not accepted by either minstrels or the listening public and did not become part of the tradition. These were songs forced upon minstrels and their audiences, not something generated by them and, as soon as the Soviet Union fell apart and Ukraine became independent, the performance of Soviet dumy ceased. Yehor Movchan had an even more strongly negative attitude towards dumy on Soviet topics. Towards the end of his life, his fingers swelled to the point that he could no longer play the bandura and give himself the pleasure and the solace of his beloved instrument. As he told Pavlo Suprun, this was God's way of punishing him for composing the duma about Lenin. Because he had caved in to the pressures of Soviet officialdom and written a song on a topic alien to the duma tradition, he said, he was deprived of the ability to participate in that tradition when he needed it most.[53]

With the Soviet period, the guild system, apprenticeship, and training with a master disappeared. The decade of the 1930s is often given as the time when minstrelsy ended completely. Some say that the demise of traditional minstrelsy came with the Holodomor, the famine that gripped Ukraine and was especially severe in the area where kobzari practised their craft. As the poorest members of society, the ones forced to rely on the handouts of others, minstrels could not survive when their fellow villagers were themselves impoverished and had nothing to give. Another version of the end of minstrelsy ascribes it to an edict to eliminate minstrels issued by Stalin. As noted in the introduction, rumour has it that another conference, one analogous to the event organized by Khotkevych, was called in 1939. Minstrels did go to this gathering – and then they were rounded up and executed as purveyors of nationalist ideas and a threat to the Soviet state. There are references to the conference in places like Kushneryk's autobiographical statements, but conclusive documentation is yet to be found. A copy of an order to execute Ivan Kuchuhura-Kucherenko, dated 1937, has recently appeared online.[54] Otherwise, all we have is the controversial Shostakovich *Testimony* published by Solomon Volkov (see Introduction).

Kobzari and lirnyky did continue to exist during the Soviet period, with kobzari being considerably more popular. Many were concert performers, schooled in conservatories and performing classical music on the bandura. Many sang and played in ensembles rather than as solo performers, the mode traditional to Ukraine. Some, like the blind kobzar Pavlo Suprun, even though he trained in a school rather than with a master, did try to revive the tradition by singing old songs and performing solo in small group settings. Hryhorii Tkachenko, a sighted artist, tried a different approach to reviving the tradition by playing a handmade rather than a factory-produced bandura and singing in the old style. In the late 1980s and early 1990s, just as the Soviet Union was falling apart, a few men made an effort to use dumy for the nationalist purposes that metafolklore ascribes to them. Suprun, once an ardent supporter of the Soviet system, became disenchanted with the Soviet idea and started singing dumy to the young, both university students and pupils in elementary schools. His intention, as he stated in an interview, was to help the young understand Ukraine's true past and to arouse their nationalist feelings. He turned traditional songs from other genres into dumy because he considered this genre to be especially powerful. Specifically, he took historical songs that he thought were particularly relevant and performed them in "duma style," reciting certain portions instead of singing them. He even composed new dumy. He rightly understood that the collapse of the Soviet Union was as momentous a period as any in Ukraine's past and tried to memorialize it in song. His best-known effort is "Duma about Chornobyl," an ode to the nuclear reactor disaster that likely did indeed contribute to the downfall of Soviet power. While this duma was popular for a time and was written up in magazines, it did not enter the repertory of other minstrels; Suprun was its only performer. The duma canon was closed and new nationalist compositions were no more accepted into the tradition than dumy about Lenin and Stalin. Suprun's "Duma about Gongadze," a song dedicated to the journalist who was kidnapped and murdered in 2000, received less attention than "Duma about Chornobyl" and even Suprun himself soon stopped singing it. Needless to say, it too did not enter the tradition.[55]

With the independence of Ukraine, kobzari, and to a lesser extent lirnyky, have become popular again, but now as icons of Ukrainian nationhood, not as singers of popular verse. In their efforts to revive the past, contemporary kobzari address each other with lebiiska mova formulas; they form organizations which they call guilds or brotherhoods. They sing a variety of songs, just as kobzari and lirnyky did in the nineteenth century; they do not focus on dumy to the exclusion of other genres. Some have started making instruments using old techniques such as hand-hewing and hand-carving the wood, and a particularly active craft school is run by Jurij Fedynskyj. The revival of old, pre-Christian religions, with its focus on the uniqueness of the Ukrainian ethnos, has also encouraged interest in minstrelsy.[56] The dumy that today's mostly young and sighted kobzari and lirnyky sing are the traditional ones recorded in the nineteenth and early twentieth centuries. The trend now, be it in the realm of song or in the construction of instruments, is to revive and explore the past. The traditional canon is the one performed now, especially at festivals and other venues where Ukraine, its history, and Ukrainian nationhood are celebrated. As of the writing of this work, the dumy canon is the same as it was when Hrushevska's book was published.

3 Turko-Tatar Slavery

Slavery – Life as a Domestic Slave

Human labour is extremely valuable. Today's world sees everything from illegal human trafficking to Canada's Temporary Foreign Workers program. In the fourteenth through sixteenth centuries and beyond, labour shortages were solved through a complex and highly evolved system of slavery. Much of the prosperity of the Ottoman Empire depended on the use of slave labour. Slavery was of several types. In the period described in dumy, some captives became galley slaves and were essentially worked to death; they were used for their manpower only. Other slaves worked for a certain period, usually six or seven years, and then were manumitted. People who provided skilled labour, such as a craftsman, were especially likely to fall into this category. After manumission, slaves could return home, taking their earnings with them, or they could remain within the empire and become part of Ottoman society. Most chose to remain precisely for the economic opportunities afforded. The closest analogue might be today's temporary foreign workers, some of whom return home while most try to stay. The third category of slave was intended for integration into the Ottoman world: men who would become janissaries (*yeni cheri* in Turkish),[1] women who would become domestic servants and possibly the mothers of Turkish children and sometimes, though not always, the wives of their fathers. Slaves who became part of Ottoman society could rise to high positions and become quite wealthy. Roksolana, the wife of Sultan Suleyman the Magnificent, is the most famous Ukrainian among them. Many, if not most, slaves ended up in Turkey proper, with the majority of them bought by the wealthy in urban centres like Istanbul. The suppliers of slaves, however, were often non-Turks. The Ukrainian lands were subject to raids primarily by the Tatars of the Crimean Khanate.[2] This polity extended quite far into what is now Ukrainian territory, and geographic proximity led to incursion for profit. Slavery is the subject matter of a number of dumy and will be examined below.

According to Islamic law, the enslavement of non-Muslims was legal. As Bernard Lewis states: "The law [the Sheria] is clear. An unbeliever may be enslaved, a Muslim may not; but adoption of Islam by an unbeliever after his enslavement does not automatically set him free."[3] The sources of slaves were various.[4] People taken into slavery could be captured in warfare or they could be kidnapped, as long as it was from a non-Muslim land. They could be acquired from others as tribute or tax payment. People who were in debt could be forced into slavery and slavery could be imposed as a punishment for a crime. The children of slaves could become slaves, as could children who were abandoned or sold into slavery by their parents. The latter means of enslavement were rare in the Ottoman world, and the chief means of generating new slaves was through a combination of raids and warfare. According to Clarence-Smith, "A compilation of estimates indicates that Crimean Tatars seized 1,750,000 Ukrainians, Poles and Russians from 1468 to 1694."[5] Hrushevskyi gives similar figures.

The Crimean Khanate and the Ottoman Porte had an insatiable appetite for slaves. As Madeline Zilfi writes: "Gifts of cloth, furs, and gold were relatively sterile in comparison to the rich, lifelong potential afforded by wealth in people. More formally in the period of expansion, the institutional commitment to male slavery reflected the empire's increased manpower needs for its broadened institutionalization and sovereign protection. Male slaves also met the ruling classes' voracious appetite for male dependents to serve in private militarized households."[6] In addition to expansion, the practice of manumission meant that the supply of slaves needed to be continuously replenished. As Clarence-Smith writes: "Obligatory emancipation after a fixed time was praiseworthy in both Shii and Sunni Islam, and may have derived from the Jewish precedent of freedom in the seventh year. In the nineteenth century Balkans and Anatolia, the seven year rule was reserved for Blacks, cheap and adversely affected by cold weather, whereas more resilient, and expensive, white slaves completed nine years. Manumitting a couple when they married was another norm in Anatolia. In the wider Turkic world a similar custom prevailed. Crimean Tatars freed most of their slaves after six years."[7] Slave owners would often free their slaves when they themselves were about to die. Slave owners, when they approached death, would often free their slaves because this charitable act was considered a good way to atone for one's sins.[8] Freed slaves were of great importance to Ottoman society, for most did not return to their country of origin but stayed in the Muslim world, fulfilling many needed functions and maintaining a client relationship with their former master.[9] They worked as artisans, as farmhands, and in a number of other capacities, often rising to the position of managers. According to Erdem, with time, entire business dynasties came out of the ranks of slaves. The Ottoman slave system was an open one in which slaves were continually integrated into society as full members.[10]

Manumission was not the only way that former slaves joined Muslim society as full members. Children were particularly desirable slaves. In the Balkans, a levy called the *devshirme* produced a regular supply of boys for the army. These could be trained in the capital and become part of the sultan's troops or they could undergo a double period of training, working first for eight years as labourers, and then going on to military training and induction into the janissaries.[11] Ukraine was not subject to the devshirme, but when children were captured along with adults, desirable boys were selected out and placed in the service of the Porte. One fifth of all captured slaves or the equivalent of their value belonged to the sultan, and this allowed him or his staff to choose the most desirable captives, young boys being one such category.[12] The jobs assigned to boys were various. The most prestigious and the one with the greatest possibility for advancement was military service. Boys could, however, be taken into the Porte and other palaces to work as staff where the services they provided could include the personal pleasure of the sultan and other nobility. Zilfi says that such practices were attested to in the seventeenth and eighteenth centuries, when sultans were known for their "attachment to male favorites and lack of zeal for female company."[13] This period is slightly beyond the period covered by the dumy, but the practice described is one that might well have prevailed earlier.

Understanding the nature of slavery in the times of the Ottoman Empire and the Crimean Khanate is crucial to appreciating the behaviour of characters in dumy. Concentrating on male figures for the moment, we see that quite a few of them participate in Turkish society. They do not behave the way our North American experience with the slavery of Blacks would lead us to expect. Liakh Buturlak is a convert to Islam in charge of Ukrainian Kozak captives in the duma about Samiilo Kishka. He still has feelings for his homeland and especially for the

Christian faith. Nonetheless, until he runs into Kishka, he enjoys his high position as overseer of the galley slaves who provide the manpower for the ship belonging to a Turkish pasha. He tries to get Kishka to convert also and promises that the Turkish ruler will reward him with a similarly high office, if not an even better position. Kishka rejects the offer, but the song attests that the practice of conversion leading to advancement in society was widely known. The version of this song recorded from a bandura player whose name is given only as Strichka and published by Platon Lukashevych goes as follows:[14]

> Oh, a galley left the city of Trabzon,
> With three colours it was bedecked and painted;
> The first colour with which it was bedecked
> Was blue and with gold plates on its sides
> And the second colour with which it was decorated
> Were the canons [it had] on its decks
> And the third colour with which it was decorated
> Was the Turkish white gabardine of its sails.
> On that galley walks Alkan Pasha
> Strolls the young prince of Trabzon.
> He has his chosen men at his side:
> He has seven hundred Turks and six hundred janissaries,
> And a hundred and fifty poor captives,
> This is not counting their military leaders.
> The most senior man among them
> Is Kishka Samiilo, the Zaporozhian hetman,
> The second [in line] is Marko Rudyi, the military judge,
> The third is Musii Hrach, the military trumpeter,
> The fourth is Liakh Buturlak, the galley's keeper of the keys.
> He had been a lieutenant in Pereiaslav
> And now he was a traitor to Christendom.
> He had been in captivity for thirty years,
> And it had been twenty-four years since he had been freed.
> He had become Turkified and Islamicized
> For the sake of great wealth,
> For the sake of miserable luxury.
> Well that galley sailed far away from its mooring,
> And they [the men] wandered across four seas,
> And they came to the city of Kefe
> Where they rested well and for a long time.

Then Alkan Pasha,
The prince of Trabzon, the young lord,
He had a dream, a very strange and wondrous dream.
Then Alkan Pasha, the young prince of Trabzon,
Called to the Turks and the janissaries and to the poor captives,
"Turks," he said, "Turks and janissaries,
And you, you poor captives,
Whichever Turk or janissary can interpret my dream,
He will receive three Turkish cities as a reward,
And whichever captive can interpret my dream,
For him I will write a letter of manumission,
So that no one will dare touch him again."
The Turks heard this, but no one said a thing;
The poor captives, although they knew [the meaning], they kept silent.
Only one person among the Turks answered,
It was Liakh Buturlak, the keeper of the galley keys,
Who had been a lieutenant in Pereiaslav
And now was a traitor to Christendom.
"How," he said, "oh, Alkan Pasha, can we interpret your dream
When you won't tell us what it was?"
"This, you faithless ones, is the dream I had,
May it never come to pass:
I saw that my decorated and painted galley
Had been stripped, had been set afire,
I saw that my Turks and my janissaries
Were all hacked to pieces,
I saw that my captives,
The ones who had been enslaved,
Were now liberated,
I saw that Hetman Kishka,
Had chopped me into three pieces,
And had thrown me into the Black Sea ..."
As soon as Liakh Buturlak heard this,
He spoke to him, saying,
"Alkan Pasha, prince of Trabzon, young lord,
This dream will not happen and it will not come to pass,
Order me to keep a closer eye on the poor captives,
Tell me to walk from row to row,
Tell me to affix two or three shackles, old and new,
To their hands and to their feet, to seat them row by row,

To take red willow twigs in bunches of two,
To whip them across the backs of their necks,
To shed Christian blood upon the earth."
As soon as they heard this,
They released the galley from its moorings,
The poor captives laid their hands upon the oars,
They dipped their oars deep into the sea.
And when they heard this,
They sailed far away from the dock,
To the city of Kozlov,
To the maiden Sandzhakivna, to a meeting, they hastened.
They arrived at the city of Kozlov,
And the maiden Sandzhakivna came out to greet them,
She invited Alkan Pasha into the city,
Along with all his troops,
She took Alkan Pasha by his white hand,
She summoned him to her drawing room, to her fortress,
She seated him upon a white bench,
She treated him to costly liquors,
And she hosted his troops in the marketplace.
Well Alkan Pasha, the prince of Trabzon,
Did not so much enjoy the costly liquors,
As he took care to send two Turks to eavesdrop,
To see whether Buturlak would unlock Samiilo Kishka,
And seat him next to himself.
Quickly the two Turks arrived at the galley,
Kishka Samiilo, the Zaporozhian hetman
Was speaking and saying,
"Oh, Liakh Buturlak, elderly brother,
At one point you were in the same sort of captivity
As we are now.
Do a good deed,
Release at least the men amongst us who are of senior rank,
Let us walk around the city a bit,
Let us experience the wedding of our rulers."
Liakh Buturlak said,
"Oh, Kishka, Samiilo, Zaporozhian hetman,
Father of the Kozaks, do a good deed,
Trample the Christian faith beneath your feet,
Break the cross that you are wearing.

If you trample the Christian faith beneath your feet,
Then our young master would accept you as if you were his kin,
As if you were his own blood brother."
As soon as Kishka Samiilo heard this [he said],
"Oh, Liakh Buturlak, traitor to Christendom,
May you never see the day
When I trample the Christian faith beneath my feet!
Even if I have to spend the rest of my life in captivity,
I will still want to rest my Christian head in the Kozak lands;
Your faith is vile,
Your land is accursed."
As soon as Liakh Buturlak heard this,
He struck Kishka Samiilo across the face,
"Oh," he said, "Kishka Samiilo, Zaporozhian hetman,
If you will reproach me for abandoning the Christian faith,
Then I will torment you more zealously than the other captives,
I will hobble you with shackles, old and new,
I will bind you thrice with chains."
Well, those two Turks heard this,
And they went back to Alkan Pasha,
"Alkan Pasha, Prince of Trabzon, you can celebrate in peace,
You have a good and faithful keeper of the keys.
He strikes Kishka Samiilo across the face,
He tries to convert him to the Turkish faith."
Then Alkan Pasha, the Prince of Trabzon, felt great joy,
He divided the costly liquors into two portions,
He sent one half to the galley,
And he enjoyed the other half with the maiden Sandzhakivna.
Alkan Pasha drank the costly liquors and he sipped them
(And so did Liakh Buturlak).
Then thoughts began to trouble the key keeper's head,
"Oh, Lord, I have drinks to drink and the means to celebrate,
But I have no one with whom I can discuss the Christian faith."
Then he went to Kishka Samiilo,
He seated him at his own side,
He poured him costly liquors
Two and three goblets at a time.
Well, Samiilo Kishka took the goblets two and three at a time,
And some he poured down his sleeve and some down the front of his shirt.
And Kishka Samiilo had anticipated well,

He put Liakh Buturlak to bed as if he were a young child,
He himself pulled eighty-four keys out from under his [Buturlak's] head,
He gave every fifth person a key:
"Kozaks, gentlemen, take heed,
Unlock each other's shackles,
But do not remove them from your hands and your feet,
Wait until the midnight hour."
Then the Kozaks unlocked one another,
But they did not remove the shackles from their hands and their feet,
They waited for the midnight hour.
And Kishka Samiilo had great foresight
And he bound himself with chains thrice around,
Waiting for the midnight hour.
The midnight hour approached
And Alkan Pasha and his army returned to the galley;
As they were approaching the galley, he said,
"Turks and janissaries, please be quiet,
Do not awaken my faithful keeper of the keys,
And you yourselves walk from row to row,
Examine each captive,
Make sure that, when he got drunk,
He did not release anyone."
The Turks and the janissaries took candles in their hands,
They walked from row to row,
They looked each person over,
God came to the rescue and they did not touch any of the shackles.
"Alkan Pasha, you can be carefree and relax,
You have a good and faithful keeper of the keys
He has seated the poor captives row by row,
He has put two and three shackles upon them, both old and new,
As for Kishka Samiilo, he has bound him thrice with chains."
Then the Turks and the janissaries boarded the galley,
They lay down to sleep without a care.
And the ones who were drunk and especially sleepy,
They lay down to sleep on the Kozlov docks.
Then Kishka Samiilo felt that he had waited long enough,
He stood up among the Kozaks,
He cast the shackles from his hands and his feet into the Black Sea,
He walked about the galley and awakened the Kozaks,
He chose the best steel sabres,

And he said to the Kozaks,
"Kozaks, brave men, do not rattle your shackles,
Don't let on [to what we are doing]
Do not wake a single Turk on this galley."
Then the Kozaks did as they were told,
They cast off their shackles,
They threw them into the Black Sea,
They did not awaken a single Turk.
Then Kishka Samiilo spoke to the Kozaks,
"You, Kozaks, brave men, take heed, my brothers,
Move away from the city of Kozlov,
Hack the Turks and the janissaries to pieces,
Or throw them alive into the Black Sea."
Then the Kozaks departed from Kozlov,
They hacked the Turks and the janissaries to pieces,
And some they threw alive into the Black Sea.
And Kishka Samiilo took Alkan Pasha out of his fine bed,
He cut him into three pieces and threw him into the Black Sea.
He spoke to the Kozaks, saying,
"Gentlemen, lads, take heed,
Throw everyone into the Black Sea,
Just do not attack Liakh Buturlak,
Let him remain to keep order in the army,
Leave him to serve as our vizier."
Then the Kozaks did as they were told,
They threw all of the Turks into the Black Sea,
Only Liakh Buturlak they did not attack,
They left him to serve as vizier among the troops,
To serve and to maintain order.
Then they sailed the galley away from the docks,
They sailed far into the Black Sea.
On Sunday, early in the morning,
It was not the grey cuckoo who was cooing,
It was the maiden Sandzhakivna who was walking by the docks,
She was wringing her white hands and speaking these words,
"Alkan Pasha, Prince of Trabzon,
Why were you so angry with me
That you left me today so early?
I will be disgraced before my father and my mother,
My parents will scold me.

You should have let me spend at least one night with you."
As she was speaking, the galley sailed far from shore,
It sailed far across the Black Sea.
And on Sunday, at midday,
Liakh Buturlak awoke from his sleep.
He walked throughout the galley and saw that there was not a single
   Turk on board.
Then Liakh Buturlak got up from his bed,
He goes to Kishka Samiilo and falls at his feet,
"Oh, Kishka Samiilo, Zaporozhian hetman, Father of the Kozaks,
Don't behave towards me,
As I behaved towards you these last days,
God helped you defeat your enemies,
But you don't know how to make it back to the Christian lands.
Heed me well: put half of your Kozaks in chains and at the oars
And dress the other half in fine Turkish clothing.
Because as you travel away from the city of Kozlov,
You will travel by the city of Tsarhrad [Constantinople,
   present-day Istanbul],
And from the city of Tsarhrad twelve galleys will sail forth,
They will congratulate Alkan Pasha and the maiden Sandzhakivna
Congratulate them on their nuptials.
How will you respond in such a case?"
As Liakh Buturlak taught him,
That is how Kishka Samiilo, the Zaporozhian hetman, behaved;
He put half of the Kozaks at the oars in chains,
And he dressed the other half in fine Turkish clothing.
As they travelled from Kozlov to Tsarhrad,
Twelve galleys departed from Tsarhrad to meet them,
They started firing their cannons,
They were congratulating Alkan Pasha and the maiden Sandzhakivna
Congratulating them on their nuptials.[15]
Liakh Buturlak himself walked out on deck,
He waved a white Turkish flag,
And he spoke once in Greek
And a second time in Turkish,
He said, "Turks and janissaries, be quiet, my brothers,
Move away from our galley,
Because they [the married couple] have celebrated and are resting,
They are incapacitated from drink,

He [Alkan Pasha] won't be able to raise his head and arise,"
And further he said, "When we return this way,
I will not forget your kindness."
Then the Turks and the janissaries turned back from the galley,
They sailed back to Tsarhrad,
They fired twenty-one cannons,
They gave their salute.
Then the Kozaks did the right thing,
They fired seven cannons,
They gave their salute.
And they went to the River Liman
And they travelled on to the Dnipro.
"We thank you God and praise you,
We were in captivity fifty-six years,
May God now grant us some time to live freely."
And on the Island of Tendrov stood Semen Skalozub,
He was camped there with his reserves,
He saw the galley,
And he spoke to his Kozaks saying,
"Kozaks, young lords, why is this galley wandering here?
Has it grown world-weary,
Does it have many of the King's people aboard;
Is it seeking great booty?
Now you take heed,
Take two cannon balls
Greet that galley with shots from our fierce cannon,
Give it a big present!
If there are Turks and janissaries on board, then hack them to pieces
And if there are poor captives on board, then give them aid."
Then the Kozaks spoke,
"Semen Skalozub, Zaporozhian hetman, .
Father of us Kozaks,
Are you yourself so afraid
That you are scaring us Kozaks?
What if this galley is not lost,
What if it is not world-weary,
What if it does not have many of the King's people on board,
And what if it is not seeking great booty?
Maybe it is poor captives, long imprisoned,
Who are fleeing captivity."

"Don't be too trusting,
Take at least two cannon balls,
Fire upon that galley from our fearsome cannon,
Give that galley a 'treat' from us.
If there are Turks and janissaries [on board], then hack them to pieces
If there are poor captives [on board], then give them aid."
Then the Kozaks misbehaved like children,
They took two cannon balls,
They greeted the galley by firing upon it from the cannon,
They knocked three planks out of its side,
They let in the waters of the Dnieper.
Then Kishka Samiilo, the Zaporozhian hetman,
He figured out what was going on, he went up on deck himself,
He took the old red banners with a cross out of his pocket,
He unfurled them,
He lowered them down to the water,
And he himself bowed low.
"Kozaks, gentlemen! This galley is not lost,
And it is not world-weary,
It does not have many of the King's people on board,
And it is not seeking great booty,
These are poor captives, captured long ago,
This is Kishka Samiilo fleeing captivity.
We were in captivity for fifty-four years,
Now we are hoping that God will grant us a few years of freedom."
Then the Kozaks jumped into their skiffs,
They took that galley by its painted panels,
They dragged it to the docks,
They pulled it from oak tree to oak tree,
Up to where Semen Skalozub was.
They tied that galley to the pier.
They took the blue cloths and handed them to the Kozaks,
And the gold cloths they gave to the hetmans
And the white gabardine they divided among the plain folk;
As for the galley, they burned it.
They took the gold and silver and divided it into three parts,
They reserved the first part for the church,
For the church of Christ the Saviour in Mezhyhirria,
For the Terekhmet [Trakhtemyriv] Monastery,
For the church of the Protection of the Mother of God,

Which was built long ago with Kozak monies,
So that the monks and the clergy, as they got up and as they went to bed
Would pray to God to have mercy upon them.
And the second part they divided amongst themselves.
And they took the third part
They sat down together
And they drank and they celebrated
And they fired off their long-barrelled rifles,
They congratulated Kiska Samiilo on gaining his freedom,
"You, Zaporozhian hetman, did not die in captivity,
You will not die living in freedom with us Kozaks."
And in truth, gentlemen, Kishka Samiilo lay down his head
In a monastery in Kyiv,
But his fame will not die and will not perish,
His fame will be great,
Amongst the Kozaks,
Amongst his friends,
Amongst the knights,
Amongst all good men.
Oh God, watch over, the people of the King,
Over the Christian people,
Over the Zaporozhian army and the army on the Don,
And over the common people on the Dnipro, the poor people,
For many years,
Until the end of time.

Liakh Buturlak, the galley master in charge of the Kozak rowers in this duma, is a conflicted character. He treats the Kozaks in his charge with exceptional cruelty, partially to please his Ottoman lord, but partially out of hatred for his former compatriots. At the same time, he longs for the Christian religion, something that he shares with the Kozaks he beats so brutally and something that he gave up when he converted to Islam. He tries to convince Samiilo Kishka, the leader of the Kozaks, to behave as he did and become a Muslim also. Yet when Kishka defeats his Ottoman masters, Buturlak has no problems siding with the Kozaks and even using his linguistic abilities to help them escape. According to Madeline Zilfi and other scholars of Muslim slavery, this sort of mindset was precisely what characterized slaves who had entered the Ottoman system. As she states, "Surviving records suggest the deep involvement of former slaves, whether or not compatriots, in perpetuating Ottoman

Villagers resting after a day in the fields. Ivan Doroshev, "The Sun is Setting," late nineteenth century. Courtesy of Rodovid Press.

slave culture."[16] They knew from personal experience what being a slave was like and, sharing the culture of the slaves under their command, they also knew precisely how to appeal to their charges and how to work on their emotions. The extreme trauma of becoming a slave created a mindset which fostered both extreme hatred for the men who were like what the slave-turned-master had once been and an overwhelming nostalgia for the culture and identity that was lost. The duma about Samiilo Kishka captures this aspect of Ottoman slavery. This song also gives a remarkably accurate description on what being a galley slave was like, as will be discussed in the section on that form of Ottoman slavery.

Ivan Bohuslavets, the main character of the duma which bears his name, is a different sort of captive. Although he is kept in prison along with his fellow Kozaks, he is singled out because of his high status and offered a prominent position in the Turkish hierarchy without being asked to convert to Islam. In this song, Ivan and his men are being held in Kozlov (present-day Evpatoriia). When Alkan Pasha, the ruler of the city, dies, his widow proposes marriage to Ivan and he accepts. This is a happy union until Bohuslavets's wife insults his Christian faith – at which point he rebels and kills her. We can speculate that Alkan Pasha's widow chose Bohuslavets because of his military prowess and high rank (and possibly also his good looks, although these are not mentioned), much as Buturlak tries to recruit Samiilo Kishka on the basis of his rank and promise as a warrior. Whatever the reason, Alkan Pasha's widow wants Ivan Bohuslavets badly enough to offer the bonus of freedom to all the Kozaks in the young man's charge, should he accept her marriage proposal. Bohuslavets does consent to the union on the condition that he be allowed to keep his faith and that his wife respect his religion and his wishes. All goes well until the wife gets drunk. What she says insults Ivan himself more than his faith and she accuses her husband of giving up Christianity for the many benefits of living as a Muslim lord. At this point Ivan becomes enraged. When night fall, he abandons his wife and joins his Kozaks who, by now, are far out to sea. He then leads them back to Kozlov and allows them to sack the city and kill its inhabitants. Ivan himself kills the woman who had been his wife. The version of this duma published by Pavlo Zhytetskyi goes as follows:[17]

In the city of Kozlov there was a prison built of stone,
And it was set into the earth seven fathoms deep,
And in the prison were seven hundred Kozaks,

Poor captives.
But they were not without their Kozak leaders,
There was one leader in particular, Ivan Bohoslavets,
     a Zaporozhian hetman.
The Kozaks were in captivity for ten years,
And Ivan Bohoslavets sat among them and thought and pondered,
Then he speaks to the Kozaks, saying:
"Kozaks, gentlemen, brave lads,
Today, this day, is Holy Saturday,
And tomorrow it will be Easter, the Great Day,
Our parents will arise early in the morning,
And they will go to church, to God's house,
They will listen to God's word,
And they will remember us, us poor captives."
Well, the captives heard all this,
And they began to shed copious tears,
And they cursed Ivan Bohoslavets and reviled him:
"May you, Ivan Bohoslavets, know neither luck nor good fortune,
For you have reminded us of this holiday."
Ivan Bohoslavets heard this,
And he spoke, saying:
"Don't curse me, brothers, and don't revile me,
Perhaps merciful God will help us, brothers,
Maybe He will lead us out of bondage."
Well, on Sunday, early in the morning,
Alkan Pasha's wife, the Turkish woman, was left a widow,
She buried her husband,
She went to the prison,
She unlocked the prison,
And she began to walk among the captives,
She took Ivan Bohoslavets by his white hand,
And then she spoke, saying:
"Ivan Bohoslavets!
If you would break with your Christian faith,
And if you would accept our Muslim faith,
Then you could rule in the city of Kozlov …
I would let all your prisoners out of the dungeon,
I would carefully escort them to the Christian lands."
Ivan Bohoslavets hears this,
And he speaks, saying:

"Widow of Alkan Pasha, young lady,
If you don't fault my Christian faith,
Then I will take you as my wife."
Well, Alkan Pasha's widow, the young woman,
She did not taste any alcoholic beverages for seven weeks,
And she said nothing against the Christian faith;
She let all the prisoners out of the dungeon,
She escorted them carefully to the Christian lands.
When, in the eighth week, she began to use spirits,
Then she began to celebrate with young Turkish men,
She began to belittle the Christian faith before Ivan Bohoslavets:
"Look, gentlemen,
See what a handsome husband I have,
He has become one of us for the sake of Turkish luxury."
Ivan Bohoslavets heard this,
And he quickly went down to the Black Sea,
He got into a boat,
He caught up with the Kozaks on the Black Sea.
And joined them on their ship.
Alkan Pasha's widow, the young woman, went down to the Black Sea,
And she saw Ivan Bohoslavets on the Kozak ship
She shed bitter tears:
"Ivan Bohoslavets,
May merciful God punish you in this world,
Because you have betrayed me, a young woman!"
Dark night settled in,
And the Kozaks started to return to the city of Kozlov,
They started to attack the sleeping Turks,
They started to strike them and cut them,
And they attacked the city of Kozlov with fire and sword,
They started to destroy the Turkish store houses,
And to take gold and silver and fine fabrics.
And Ivan Bohoslavets stabbed Alkan Pasha's widow, the young woman.
Then they hurried to the docks of the city of Kozlov,
And they made it back to the Kozak Sich before daybreak.
In the Sich they began to divide up the Turkish treasure,
And the Kozaks spoke, saying:
"Ivan Bohoslavets, Zaporozhian hetman,
You spent ten years in captivity,
And you did not lose a single one of your men!"

Free, oh God, free the prisoner from captivity,
Let him return to the happy lands,
To the world of the Christians!

Ivan's marriage to the widow of Alkan Pasha may not have been a happy one, but many marriages between Muslim women and their Christian slaves did work well. In fact, the institution of the former slave as *damad* (Turkish for son-in-law) was popularized by Mehmed the Conqueror, who became known for marrying high-ranking women to male members of the slave elite, many of whom would then go on to become trusted counsellors, some rising to the position of vezir.[18] Former slaves who were granted high positions, because of their gratitude to their masters, were deemed to be the best advisers and administrators.[19] In the time of Suleyman the Magnificent, Ibrahim Pasha, a man who chose to remain Christian, rose to the highest ranks possible and served as grand vezir.[20] It should be noted that the marriage of free women to slaves was not limited to the elite; Yvonne Seng found court records which show that ordinary Muslim women could and did marry slaves.[21]

Recruiting especially accomplished captives and offering them a position of honour and prestige within Turkish society appears clearly in historical songs, a genre closely related to dumy and sometimes confused with them.[22] The song about Baida, a character based on the historical figure Dmytro Vyshnevetskyi, describes its hero as a valiant fighter who is offered the sultan's daughter in marriage and the high position that would go with such a union. The offer is made on the basis of Baida's military prowess and his reputation for unparalleled courage and daring. It is an effort to secure the services of a particularly adept combatant. But Baida refuses the offer, an act which the sultan finds insulting and which leads him to order the Kozak's torture. Baida is suspended from a meat hook inserted under his ribs and thus made to suffer a slow and painful death. He endures his agony for three days, but eventually convinces his servant to give him his bow and arrow which he uses to kill the Turkish ruler and his family, thus exacting revenge just moments before he himself dies. The text translated below was published by Antonovych and Drahomanov.[23]

In Istanbul, at a market,
There Baida drinks mead and horilka [Ukrainian for vodka];

Oh, Baida drinks not a day and not two,
Not one night and not one hour;
Baida drinks and then he nods,
And he looks at his squire,
"Oh, my squire, my young one!
Will you be faithful to me?"
The Turkish king sends for him,
He calls Baida to his side:
"Oh, you, Baida, you fine young man!
Be my faithful knight,
Take my daughter as your wife,
And you will rule over all of Ukraine!"
"King, your faith is accursed,
And your daughter is a pagan."
Oh, the king screams at this servants:
"Take Baida, seize him well,
And hang him by his rib from a meat hook!"
Baida hangs not a day and not two,
Not one night and not one hour.
Oh, Baida hangs and Baida ponders,
He glances at his young squire,
He glances at his black horse.
"Oh, my squire, my young one,
Give me a tightly strung bow,
And a handful of arrows!
I see three doves,
And I want to shoot them for his [the Turkish king's] daughter.
If I have hope, then I can survive,
Here I hang heavy; with arrows I can fight."
Oh, he shot and he hit the king,
And he hit the queen in the nape of her neck,
And he shot the princess in the head.
"Those shots, oh king,
Are in retaliation for Baida's punishment,
So that you will know,
How to punish Baida:
You should have severed Baida's head,
And buried his body,
And ridden on the black horse,
And won the affection of his servant."

Songs do not picture marriages between Ukrainian men and Muslim women as happy or enduring unions. In fact, in both dumy and historical songs, marriage to a foreign woman is used as a metaphor for death. Ivan Konovchenko dies in battle in the song that bears his name and his death is presented to his mother as precisely such a marriage. The variant of the song translated here and presented in the section on minstrels and their predominantly female audiences (see chapter 2) has a short rendition of this metaphor. In other variants of the Konovchenko duma, the comparison between marriage and death is developed more fully. In these songs, when the hero's fellow Kozaks return from combat and go to tell his mother what has happened, they do so by describing a marriage to a rich Turkish woman. The mother is pleased that her son has made such a good match and found himself a wealthy bride. As the men go on to say that the couple's matchmaker was the sharp sword, their pillow the hard rock, and their coverlet the green grass, she finally understands the symbolic meaning of the Kozaks' words and realizes that her son is dead. An almost identical passage appears in the historical song about a Kozak and his horse, where a man dying on the battlefield instructs his mount to go and describe a similar sort of wedding to the man's family, a task which the horse fulfils. The man in this song is already married and yet his death is described as marriage to a foreign woman. This underscores the association between dying on the battlefield and the death-wedding. The text published by Antonovych and Drahomanov, entitled "The Dying Kozak and His Horse," goes as follows:[24]

Three years and three weeks
Have elapsed in Ukraine,
Since the Tatars mortally wounded a Kozak,
And placed him beneath a sycamore tree.
Under the green sycamore tree
Lies a young Kozak;
His body has turned black,
It has become covered with scabs from the wind,
His horse, standing over him, pines in sorrow,
He has stamped his feet [so hard] that he has sunk into the earth
    up to the knee.
"Don't stand over me, my horse,
I see your true devotion!
Run through the steppe and through the groves,

Through the valleys and through the ravines,
To my dear family,
To my faithful wife!
Strike the gate with your hooves,
Jingle your harnesses.
My brother will come out and be sad,
Then my mother will come out and be sorrowful,
My beloved will come out and rejoice,
Then she will stop and look and swoon!"
"Oh, horse, where did you throw you master?
Tell me, horse, has he perished?"
"The Turks caught up with me,
They took my master off my back.
They shot him and they chopped him,
They celebrated near the Dniester River."
Oh, Mother, don't be sad!
Because your son has married:
And as a wife he took
The green valley,
And the steep grave ...
Take, Mother, a handful of sand,
Sow it upon a stone:
When that sand sprouts and grows,
Then your son will come home from battle!

Equating marriage to a Muslim woman with death speaks to the fact that a man who did enter Ottoman society, as he would through marriage, was essential lost to his Ukrainian kin. In many senses he was as good as dead: the chances of his returning to his birth family were nil. This imagery also has a great deal to do with Ukrainian beliefs about untimely death. As Dmitrii Zelenin explains in his seminal work, all people were believed to have a *srok*, an allotted amount of time they were to spend on this earth. If they died before this time was complete, then they would become unquiet dead, revenants who haunted the living.[25] Minstrels made use of this belief in their requests for alms. Begging songs often assert that people should give alms because those who died before their time and especially those who died violent deaths need the prayers of minstrels to help them rest in peace. Another way to care for the souls of those who died prematurely was to celebrate their funeral as a death-wedding. A death-wedding quite literally combines ritual elements from the wedding with those of the funeral. Typically, a wedding bread or *korovai* is prepared and topped with a *hiltse*, a ritual branch used at weddings. The deceased wears wedding clothes and a ring made of beeswax is placed on his or her finger. Such a combined ritual was considered essential for those who died unwed. Adding wedding symbolism to a funeral is supposed to grant peace to the departed, to set his or her life right by providing the crucial, but missing, element of marriage. With a wedding worked into the funeral, a person's life was complete and he or she was believed to be at peace.[26] Such a person did not need to haunt the living. The death-wedding is still practised in many parts of Ukraine, though it is becoming less common. During the time that dumy were recorded, the death-wedding was an obligatory practice, one that was known by all. We can then theorize that, for those men who died in battle, whose bodies were not returned home for burial, describing their death as marriage to an enemy woman was a way to provide ritual requisites and necessary closure. Of course, equating marriage to a Turkish or Tatar woman with death did not make such a union attractive. It is possible that Baida refuses the offer of a princess's hand precisely because he sees it as akin to dying. Had he been a Turkish captive, already integrated into the Ottoman system and cut off from his home, such an offer would have been much more attractive. In short, even though there were many successful marriages between Christian men and Muslim women, people on Ukrainian soil were not witness to them and happy unions are not presented in Ukrainian song.

Marriage to the widow of a pasha like the one Ivan Bohuslavets is said to have entered, or rising to the position of slave overseer as Liakh Buturlak is said to have done, was not something that most captives were able to achieve. Still, many slaves were able to succeed in captivity and even earn money while working for a master. Slaves could negotiate a contract with their owners called the *mukatebe*. "The mukatebe was the self-purchase of the slave by his own labor."[27] It was advantageous to the slave owner because it allowed him to justify his investment in his purchase in a relatively short amount of time, and it was attractive to the captive because he could secure his freedom more quickly. Slaves fulfilled the terms of the mukatebe by practising a trade and turning over their earnings to the master or through performing specified labour for pay. The possibility of earning money in Ottoman captivity explains the situation found in the duma "About the Escape of Three Brothers from Azov." The two elder brothers who are on horseback not only have fine mounts, they have costly clothing and other goods. Their coats are lined with silk, as we find out when the song tells of the middle brother ripping out the lining so that he can leave markers for the youngest brother to follow. Apparently, the goods are so fine and desirable that the two are unwilling to discard them in order to give their youngest brother, who is without a horse and travelling on foot, a ride back to Christian territory. Two captives owning great wealth is so hard to imagine in today's world that Oles Sanin, in his film based on this duma, had the two older brothers escape with nothing and steal the horses that became their mounts.[28] The dumy themselves give a different picture. The text translated below was recorded by Panteleimon Kulish from the lirnyk Arkhyp Nykonenko:[29]

Oh, from the land of the Turks,
From the faith of the Muslims,
From the city of Azov, it was neither dust nor fog that arose,
It was just a small band,
Little and insignificant,
Three brothers, all related,
Three companions, all dear,
Two on horseback and one foot, an infantryman,
He runs after the horses and chases them,
He tramples the black fire with his white feet,
He drenches his footsteps with blood,
He grasps the stirrups,
And he speaks with words:
"Oh my dear brothers, my beloved brothers,
Do me at least one kindness,
Take that fine clothing, take your booty and throw it off your horses,
And take me, your foot soldier brother, upon your horses instead,
Carry me for at least a verst [3500 feet], at least a mile,
And show me the way,
So that I may know,
How to follow you, how to escape harsh captivity and flee to Christian cities."
Then the eldest brother speaks, saying proudly,
"Would it be proper, my brother,
For me to cast aside Turkish goods and leave them by the road,
And then take you on my horse instead?
If I do that, then we ourselves won't escape,
And we won't be able to save you either.
The Crimeans and the Nogais, the godless Muslims,

Will pass by you, a foot soldier, as you rest,
They will pursue us [who are] on horseback,
And they will force us to return to Turkish lands."
So the brother on foot, the infantryman, runs after the horses
    and chases them,
He tramples the black fire with his white feet,
He speaks with words:
"My dear brothers, my beloved brothers,
Do me at least one kindness,
Turn your horses around,
Take your sabres out of their sheaths,
And take my head, the head of a foot soldier, an infantryman,
    off my shoulders,
Bury me in the open field,
Don't let my body fall prey to animals and birds."
Then the eldest brother speaks, saying proudly,
"Would it be proper, my brother, to hack away at you?
Our sabres could not possibly rise up to do this,
We could never lift our arms to do such a thing,
And our hearts would never have the courage
To hack away at you.
If you are alive and well,
You will reach the Christian lands on your own."
Then the youngest brother, the infantryman on foot, runs after
    the horses and chases them,
He speaks, saying:
"Do me at least one kindness,
When you pass the blackthorn bushes and the gullies,
Turn aside just a bit,
And chop a few branches off the bushes,
And leave them on the path,
Leave them for me, your infantryman brother, the one on foot, as a sign."
When the oldest brother and the middle one approached the blackthorn
    bushes and the gullies,
They rode to one side,
And they chopped off green branches,
And they left them for their youngest brother, the infantryman on foot.
When the youngest brother, the infantryman on foot, ran as far as the gullies,
He started finding the blackthorn branches,
He picked them up with his hands,

And he pressed them to his heart.
He speaks, saying,
He cries, shedding tears:
My dear Lord, Heavenly Creator!
I see that my brothers, as they fled from harsh captivity, rode by here,
They made a big effort on my behalf.
If God were to help me escape this bitter Azov captivity,
Then I would be able to honour my brothers in their old age and respect
    them.
Then the oldest brother and the middle one came out onto the fields,
They found themselves in the high steppe, on the wide road,
And there were no more blackthorn bushes to cut.
Then the middle brother said to the oldest one:
"Let's, brother, take off our green overcoats,
Let us tear up the red silk and the yellow lining,
Let us leave it by the road as a marker for our brother on foot, the
    youngest one,
So that he, poor fellow, may know where to follow us, who are on horseback."
Then the oldest brother spoke, saying proudly:
"Is it proper, my brother, that I should tear my Turkish goods to shreds
That I should leave them for my youngest brother as a sign?
If he is alive and well,
Then he will make it to the Christian lands on his own, without
    all our markers."
Then the middle brother took pity,
He ripped the red and yellow silk lining from inside his overcoat,
He left it by the path, by the roadside,
To give his youngest brother a sign.
When the youngest brother, the infantryman on foot, came out onto
    the fields,
Onto the high steppe, onto the wide roads –
There were no gullies or blackthorn bushes there,
There were no markers or signs.
Then he started to find the red silk and the yellow.
He picks it up with his hands,
He presses it to his heart,
He speaks, saying,
He cries, shedding tears:
"This red silk and this yellow is not scattered here by the road
    without a reason,

Perhaps my brothers are no longer in this world,
Perhaps they have been cut with sabres,
Or perhaps they have been shot,
Or perhaps they have been taken into harsh captivity.
If I knew for sure that they were shot or cut with sabres,
Then I would look for their bodies in the field,
I would bury them in the open field,
I would not let them become prey for animals or birds."
Well, the youngest brother, one thing he suffers from is lack of water,
And the second thing is lack of food,
And the third is the fact that the wind knocks him off his feet.
He arrives at the Savur-mohyla,
He ascends to the top of the Savur-mohyla,
And there he rests for nine days,
For nine days he hopes for weather and water from the heavens.
After he had rested a little, rested for a while,
Grey-maned wolves started to approach him,
And black-winged eagles started to fly near,
They perched above his head –
They wanted to celebrate his dark funeral while he was still alive.
Then he said, speaking with words:
"Grey-maned wolves and eagles with black wings,
My dear guests,
Wait just a bit, a little bit,
Until the Kozak soul leaves the body,
Then you can pull my black eyes out from under my forehead,
You can pluck my white flesh off my yellow bones,
And cover it with reeds."
He rested for a while, he rested a little bit,
He could not raise his arms,
His feet would not move,
His eyes could not look up to the heavens …
He glances heavenward,
He sighs pitifully:
"My head, my Kozak head,
You were in the Turkish lands,
In the land of the Muslim faith,
And now it is your fate to die of hunger and thirst.
It's been nine days since I've had food on my lips,
I'm dying of hunger and of thirst!"

He spoke thus … it was not a black cloud that flew by,
It was not a fierce wind that blew,
It was the soul of a Kozak, a brave man, that parted from his body.
Then the wolves with grey manes approached,
And the eagles with black wings flew nigh,
They perched above his head,
They plucked his black eyes out from under his forehead,
They picked his white flesh off the yellow bones,
They carried the yellow bones and deposited them under the green maples,
They covered them with reeds.
The eldest brother and the middle one came upon the River Samarka,
Dark night caught up with them,
The eldest brother said to the middle one:
"Brother, let us stop here and pasture our horses,
The kurgans here are high,
And the grass is good,
And the water is fine.
Let's stop here and wait a while,
Until the sun turns,
Perhaps our infantryman brother, the one on foot, will arrive.
If he does, I will show him pity,
I'll throw away all my booty,
I'll take him, the infantryman, on my horse."
"You should have taken him when I told you to, brother!
Now nine days have passed,
Since he ate bread and salt,
Since he had anything to drink,
He is no longer in this world!"
Then they let their horses graze freely,
They spread their coats beneath them,
They hid their rifles in the reeds,
They lay down to sleep with no fear,
They were going to wait until the dawn of light.
God's day began to dawn,
And they began to saddle their horses,
They fled across the Samara River and into the Christian lands.
Then the oldest brother started to say to the middle one:
"Brother, when we get home to our father and our mother,
What will we tell them?
If we tell them the truth, brother,

Then our father and our mother will curse us;
And, brother, if we lie to our father and to our mother,
Then merciful God will punish us, sending us punishment seen and unseen.
So what if, brother, we do this,
What if we tell them that we did not serve the same master,
That we were not in captivity together,
That we fled harsh imprisonment in the middle of the night,
That we stopped by to see him,
That we called him to join us, saying,
'Get up, brother and come with us Kozaks to flee harsh captivity!'
Let us say that he answered:
'Go ahead, brothers, and flee,
And I'll stay behind,
I'll see if I can improve my fate here.'
And when Father and Mother die,
Then the land and the livestock will be divided between two people,
There won't be a third person to get between us."
And as he said all this,
It was not grey eagles who were calling,
It was Turks, janissaries, who attacked from behind a kurgan.
They shot them and they wounded them with swords,
They took their goods from their horses and took them back to the
    Turkish land.
Two brothers laid down their heads by the River Samarka,
And the third at the Savur-mohyla.
But their fame will not die and will not perish.
From now until the end of time.
And may all of you be granted many years.

This text underscores the possibility of earning money in captivity in two ways. First, the goods the two brothers had amassed and taken with them were substantial indeed – they are attractive enough for the Turks to take and carry back to their own homeland. The ending is meant to be ironic, of course, with the brothers losing precisely that for which they sacrificed the life of their sibling. Second, when the two older brothers discuss how they should explain the absence of the youngest brother to their parents, they agree to tell them that the youngest brother stayed behind by choice, wanting to earn more money before leaving captivity.

The work of a slave and the services he provided could take many forms and the practice of using captive boys for a ruler's pleasure is reflected in dumy as well, although far less frequently and in more cryptic form. In the song about a baby falcon, a father goes to seek his fortune and leaves his son unprotected. The child is kidnapped and taken to Constantinople (present-day Istanbul), where he is arrayed in jewels and "amuses" Ivan Bohoslovets.[30] Probably because homosexual contact was an uncomfortable topic in the nineteenth and early twentieth centuries when our dumy texts were recorded and because it was a topic that would be taboo in a group affiliated with the church, this is the most metaphorical of dumy, presenting the events by speaking not of humans, but of birds. One of the most puzzling aspects of this text is the name of the ruler: Ivan Bohoslovets. This name is clearly not Turkish or Tatar, but Ukrainian. The use of this name seems to stem from an association between names derived from the city of Bohuslav and incorporation into the Muslim world, the song about Ivan Bohuslavets translated above being but one example. The use of a Ukrainian name here may also be motivated by the need to explain why the ruler gives up his captive so easily. Perhaps the singer thought that a Ukrainian, even one who has entered the Ottoman sphere, would be more sympathetic to other Ukrainians, as is the case with Marusia Bohuslavka, whose song is presented later in this chapter. The text of the duma "About a Falcon," which is translated below, was published by Mykola Kostomarov:[31]

The falcons flew in from a foreign land,
And they alighted, they came to rest on a magnificent oak tree,
And they built themselves a nest, a rich one, a fine one,
And they laid themselves an egg of pearl,
And they hatched themselves an ill-fated child.
The elder falcon flew off to a foreign land to seek a living,
And he could not find a way to prosper,
But he did lose his child, his fatherless, ill-fated child, his bright falcon.
Riflemen, warriors, were coming from Tsarhorod [Constantinople/Istanbul]
And they spotted the fine nest,
And they chopped down the oak tree,
And they took the fatherless, ill-fated baby falcon with them,
And they carried him to Constantinople,
And they turned him over to Ivan Bohoslovets for his amusement.
He bound his legs with silver tethers,
And he placed a pearl-studded cap over his eyes,
He strolled around Constantinople,

And his heart was merry,
His soul was comforted by the baby falcon.
The elder falcon returned from the distant land,
And he met a grey-winged eagle in his home county:
"Greetings, greetings, grey-winged eagle!
How have you been living here and dwelling here,
How have you been flying about your country?
Have you heard, have you been listening, have you seen, have you
    witnessed,
Have you any idea if my fatherless, ill-fated bright child is still wandering
    about this land?"
"Oh, hey, you bright falcon, your child is in this country no longer,
Your child, your fatherless, ill-fated child, your bright falcon,
Is in the land of the Muslim faith,
He is in Turkish captivity,
He lives in the city of Constantinople,
And he lives to amuse Ivan Bohoslovets."
Then the old falcon spoke to the grey-winged eagle saying,
"Tell me what I need to do to see my child, my fatherless, ill-fated child, my
    bright falcon,
Tell me how I can cheer my heart."
The grey-winged eagle spoke, saying,
And he cried bitterly and wept,
"Don't you know what to do, old falcon?
Fly to Constantinople, and cry most mournfully,
Entertain the Muslim faith, the place of Turkish captivity, with your voice,
And tell the whole truth to your ill-fated child, your bright young falcon:
Tell him not to gaze upon his silver tethers,
Or to admire his pearls,
Or to think that his life there is good
Because he has his fill of food and drink,
Tell him that he needs to know Kozak ways.
Tell him that when Ivan Bohoslovets goes for a walk about Constantinople,
Carrying him, the falcon, with him,
Comforting his heart with the sight,
Tell him to tilt his head in great sorrow,
So the Ivan Bohoslovets will be moved to great pity,
So that he will hand over the falcon to his servants,
And speak to his servants thus:
Oh, you servants, my dear ones,

Take the silver tethers and remove them from the legs of this fatherless,
   ill-fated falcon,
And take off the pearl cap from his head, from over his eyes,
Take him to the outskirts of the city of Constantinople,
Set him atop a high embankment,
See if a gentle wind might not blow,
Might not bring health to the fatherless, ill-fated bright falcon."
And lo they heard this,
And they went outside the city of Constantinople,
And they set the fatherless, ill-fated bright falcon on a high embankment.
The old falcon lowered his wings to the ground.
He lifted his child, the fatherless, ill-fated bright falcon on his wings,
He carried him high in the sky.
And he spoke to his child, the ill-fated, fatherless bright falcon, saying,
"Well, my child, my bright falcon, is it better to live in Constantinople with
   Ivan Bohoslovets,
Or is it better to race about the wide world?
Oh, it is better, my ill-fated, fatherless, bright falcon, to wander about the world,
Than to live with Ivan Bohoslovets in Constantinople, in Muslim, Turkish
   captivity."
Oh, the old bright falcon flew across the city of Constantinople,
And he cried mournfully and he wailed,
He cursed the city of Constantinople and reviled it,
"Although you, oh city of Constantinople, lack for nothing, neither silver
   nor gold,
Although it is good to live there, and people have clothes to wear,
And they have food to eat and drink to imbibe,
Still a man can find no happiness there!"

The choice of bird symbolism comes from a combination of Ukrainian symbolism and Turkish practice. The Ukrainians used a system of bird symbols to indicate humans of various genders and at various stages in their lives. Thus, a young woman was a *lastivka* or lark, because, as a lark weaves its nest under the eaves of a house, so the young woman would be expected to create her domicile under a new roof, that of the household of her husband. A young man was a falcon because, like a falcon, he needed to be a hunter. At the same time, falconry was a favourite pursuit of the Turkish nobility and good falcons were highly prized. Thus, the falcon in this song could be both a young man and a prized possession of a Turkish magnate.

In the Ottoman Empire, both in Anatolia and in the Crimean Khanate, a vassal state, young girls were also desirable captives. They could be sold or traded but, as often as not, they were kept by the people who bought them and were raised as future brides for the sons of the family or for other young male relatives. As Zilfi explains, this practice had many advantages.[32] It allowed the family to meet the requirement of exogamy, while procuring a bride whom they themselves had reared and who had become knowledgeable of the family's customs and its likes and dislikes. In addition, a slave bride was one who had no contact with kin; there was no one who might interfere on her behalf, a situation which permitted the family into which she married to do with her as they pleased. The practice of using female slaves as brides for upper-class males might help explain not only the presence of Ukrainian women among the Turkish and Tatar elite, but also the need for upper-class Turkish women to look to Kozaks as potential husbands and could be the motivation behind the behaviour of Ivan Bohuslavets's wife. She is young and probably eager for male companionship and she is a widow in a high position. Her status as a widow might make it harder for her to find a Turkish husband and also give her more freedom to choose a man who was to her liking.

Girls reared from childhood were not the only source of foreign brides for the Turkish upper classes. All women who were taken as slaves were the sexual property of their masters and had no right of refusal. Owners were not allowed to use their slaves as prostitutes and to sell their services, but that was the only restriction on the sexual availability of slaves.[33] As Zilfi points out, the presumption has been that young women were subject to concubinage, while older women were used primarily as workers and were free from the imposition of unwanted sex, but this was not necessarily the case. All women, no matter of what age or status, were subject to exploitation.[34] Sexual contact with the master had its advantages, however. Closeness to the slave owner provided opportunities to gain favours and improve one's position and becoming pregnant with the master's child was an almost certain path to advancement.[35] If the master recognized paternity, such recognition would mean good opportunities for the child; for the slave-mother, it meant possible manumission or at least an increase in status as *umm-i veled* or mother of the master's child.[36] Up until Sultan Suleyman married Roksolana, also known as Hurrem Sultan, the mothers of all rulers were slaves who were the concubines of the sultan. When such a concubine became pregnant and delivered a male child, she was allowed to bear no more male children; all subsequent male infants were strangled at birth. When the male child of the sultan reached maturity, he was sent to serve as governor of a municipality within the Ottoman Empire and his mother went with him. In such a position, she held high status, even though she had originally been a slave. Upon the death of the sultan, the various half-brothers were expected to fight it out, using the armies of their respective municipalities. The victorious son of the sultan would then ascend to the throne and take his father's place, his ex-slave mother assuming a position of great power as Valide Sultan. Slave women could advance to the highest ranks of society.

The value of adult women, especially if they were young, of pleasant appearance, and not pregnant, was great. In fact, records indicate that the price of desirable captives ran parallel to that of real estate.[37] Women were desired precisely as potential bedmates and foreign observers noted that buyers at slave markets would examine women's sexual attributes, such as their breasts, albeit surreptitiously.[38] These records date to the nineteenth century, but presumably describe practices that existed not only at that time, but earlier as well.

The capture of adult women and their incorporation into the household is reflected in the duma about Marusia Bohuslavka, a woman who, if she is not the wife of her Turkish master, is his trusted concubine. The household where she lives is substantial, large enough to include a prison with male slaves, and Marusia is close enough to the master to be the keeper of the keys in his absence. Although she claims to have accepted her new culture and become a Muslim, she, like Liakh Buturlak, displays strong feelings for Christianity and cannot help but be emotionally affected by Christian holidays. Unlike Liakh Buturlak, she pities the Ukrainians held in captivity. This leads her to violate the trust placed in her by her Turkish lord and she liberates the Kozaks on Easter. Her story, as performed by kobzar Ryhorenko and published by Panteleimon Kulish, goes as follows:[39]

Oh, in the midst of the Black Sea,
On a white rock,
There stood a stone prison.
In that prison seven hundred Kozaks languished,
Seven hundred poor captives.
They had spent thirty years in captivity,
And during that time they did not see either God's light or the righteous sun.
To them comes the captive maiden

Marusia, the priest's daughter from Bohuslav,
And she speaks with words, saying:
"Oh, Kozaks,
Oh, you poor captives!
Guess what day it is today back in our Christian land."
Well, then the poor captives heard this,
They recognized the captive maiden,
Marusia, the priest's daughter from Bohuslav,
Recognized her by her speech.
And they spoke, saying,
"Oh, captive maiden,
Marusia, the priest's daughter from Bohuslav,
How can we possibly know
What day it is today back in our Christian land?
We've been in captivity for thirty years,
We haven't seen God's light or the righteous sun with our own eyes.
And so we cannot know
What day it is today back in our Christian land."
Then the captive maiden,
Marusia, the priest's daughter from Bohuslav,
When she heard this,
She spoke to the Kozaks, saying,
"Oh, Kozaks,
Oh, you poor captives,
Today, back in our Christian land, it is the Saturday before Easter,
And tomorrow is the great holiday, the annual celebration of Easter."
Well, when the Kozaks heard this,
They fell with their white faces to the damp earth,
And they cursed the captive maiden,
Marusia, the priest's daughter from Bohuslav,
They cursed and reviled her,
"Oh, captive maiden,
Oh, Marusia, the priest's daughter from Bohuslav,
May you never have luck or good fortune,
For you told us about the great holiday, the annual celebration of Easter."
Then the captive maiden,
Marusia, the priest's daughter from Bohuslav,
Then she heard this,
And she spoke, saying,
"Oh, Kozaks,

Oh, you poor captives,
Don't curse me and don't revile me,
For when our master, the Turkish lord, goes to the mosque,
Then he will give me, me the captive maiden,
Marusia, the priest's daughter from Bohuslav,
He will give me the keys, place them in my hands;
Then I will come to the dungeon,
And I will free all you poor captives, I will let you escape."
Then on the great holiday, on the annual celebration of Easter,
The Turkish lord set out for the mosque,
And he gave the captive maiden,
Marusia, the priest's daughter from Bohuslav,
He placed the keys in her hands.
Then the captive maiden,
Marusia, the priest's daughter from Bohuslav,
She took great care,
And she went to the dungeon,
And she unlocked the dungeon;
All the Kozaks,
All the poor captives,
She releases them and sets them free,
And she speaks, saying,
"Oh, Kozaks,
Oh, you poor captives,
I say unto you, please do the right thing,
Flee to the Christian cities,
But I ask one thing – do not bypass the city of Bohuslav,
Let my father and my mother know,
Let them heed my words,
Tell them not to sell their possessions or their lands,
Tell them not to amass a great treasure,
Tell them not to ransom me,
The captive maiden,
Marusia, the priest's daughter from Bohuslav,
Tell them not to buy my freedom from captivity;
Because I have become Turkified and Moslemized,
For the sake of Turkish luxury,
For the sake of unfortunate pleasures!"
Free us, oh God, all us poor captives,
From harsh captivity,

From the Muslim faith,
And let us go to bright dawns,
To quiet waters,
To the happy land,
To the Christian world,
Listen to us, oh God, to our sincere requests,
To our earnest prayers,
Listen to us poor captives.

On the surface the story of Marusia seems simple enough. She releases her fellow Ukrainians from captivity and they escape. She chooses not to go with them because she has done very well for herself within the Turkish realm. As the mate of a Turkish lord, she holds a position of prestige and power. Because she is doing well, she chooses to remain among the Turks rather than return home. She does, however, want her parents informed of her situation so that they will not trouble themselves on her behalf. We have documentary evidence, albeit from the eighteenth century, of women making the same choice as Marusia. Lady Mary Wortley Montagu, wife of the English ambassador to Constantinople, writes of a Christian Spanish lady who was taken captive and raped by a Turkish admiral during a Mediterranean raid. Her brothers paid ransom for her and her master released her, telling her that she was free to go. But her choice was to stay. As quoted in an article on Lady Montague by Danielle Haase-Dubosc, the Spanish captive "very discretely weighed the different treatment she was likely to receive in her native country." She concluded that, back in Spain, the best that she could hope for was living out the rest of her life in a nunnery. On the other hand, her "infidel lover" was "very handsome, very tender, fond of her, and lavished at her feet all the Turkish magnificence." Furthermore, when she asked him to, "he married her, and never took another wife." In short, she never had any reason to regret the choice that she had made.[40]

Marusia's choice may appear logical and straightforward on the surface, but folk poetry is seldom simple. It thrives precisely because it does have multiple meanings. In this particular text, Marusia's hint at her conversion to Islam is problematic. If she were so thoroughly a Muslim, would she still keep track of Easter, the most holy day for Orthodox Christians? Would she bother to go share her Easter thoughts with her compatriots? Marusia's attachment to Christian holidays indicates that her Ukrainian sentiments remain strong. She has not forsaken her heritage for the sake of luxury as she claims. Furthermore, if she is the person to whom the Turkish lord gave the dungeon keys, then surely it will be obvious that it was she who released the captives. If Marusia could not simply request that the lord free the Kozaks, if she had to release them at a time when he would be away, then one can assume that he would be angry upon discovering their escape. Would he not take out his anger on Marusia? Captives were worth a great deal of money. Because these men are being held in prison, they are probably galley slaves and the numbers given in this text (seven hundred captives held for thirty years) are surely exaggerations for effect. Still, losing a large number of slaves is suffering serious financial damage. This reading implies that Marusia has not really chosen "Turkish luxury" over her allegiance to her homeland. Rather, she is sacrificing herself so that her fellow Ukrainians, the Kozaks, can escape. The probability that the text wants to present Marusia as a heroine who sacrifices herself is high. Many dumy showcase courage in the face of death. In them, the male protagonist, a Kozak, acts bravely even as he knows that he will die. Because this is such a common theme in dumy, Marusia Bohuslavka might well have been the female equivalent of these courageous men.

Marusia as heroine is an image that is especially appealing to Ukrainian intellectuals who see her as the folk equivalent of the historical Roksolana, wife of Sultan Suleyman the Magnificent. Roksolana was born as Oleksandra or Anastasia Lisowska. She is said to have been a priest's daughter, just like Marusia Bohuslavka. She was born in Rohatyn, a city which was then part of Poland. Her birth date is calculated to be somewhere between 1502 and 1504. Although she was from an area under Polish rule, her father was Orthodox, which would make her almost certainly Ukrainian and the name by which she is known, Roksolana, indicates her Ruthenian origins. She was captured in a Crimean Tatar raid at age twelve and made the journey to Istanbul, likely by way of the slave market in Kefe on the Crimean peninsula. She entered the sultan's harem, some say as the gift of Ibrahim Pasha, and worked her way up the harem hierarchy to eventually hold a position of enormous influence over the sultan and the Ottoman Empire as a whole. Roksolana had the reputation of being vastly clever and frighteningly ruthless. She is said to have tricked the sultan's favourite concubine, Mahidevran, also called Gulbahar, into attacking her. Then, when Suleyman summoned her to his bed, she complained that she was too disfigured by the attack to be worthy of the sultan. Using this strategy, she succeeded in demoting Gulbahar, an action that allowed her to herself assume the position of the sultan's favourite. Suleyman is said to have been truly in love with her, charmed by her cheerful nature and musical abilities. She was also called Hurrem Sultan in recognition of her pleasant personality. This personality apparently did not reduce Roksolana's ability to manipulate the sultan. She converted to Islam and then, when the sultan again called her to his bed, she claimed that, as a Muslim woman she needed to be married to comply with this request. Suleyman did marry Roksolana and, unlike sultan's consorts before her, she was allowed to bear four sons, none of whom was killed. Furthermore, Roksolana was allowed to remain in Istanbul; she was not sent with one of her sons to a provincial city. Roksolana is said to have influenced Suleyman's foreign policy. During her reign, wars with Poland were few. In terms of domestic politics, she was rumoured to be ruthless and enormously destructive. Mahidevran/Gulbahar had borne a son named Mustafa, who was reputed to be the most capable of all of Suleyman's offspring. Roksolana is said to have worked in collusion with Rustem, the husband of her daughter, and started rumours that Mustafa was plotting a coup. The rumours convinced Suleyman to have Mustafa executed, thus clearing the path to the throne for Roksolana's children. Roksolana is also blamed for the execution of Ibrahim, Suleyman's friend since childhood, his grand vezir and, according to some accounts, the man who had brought Roksolana into the imperial palace in the first place. Ibrahim was then replaced by Rustem. Roksolana died in 1558 in Istanbul and is buried in the garden behind the Suleymaniya Mosque. The image of Roksolana varies a great deal, depending on the source. An entire book on literary, historical, and cultural portrayals of her was published in 2010.[41] As the book details, Europeans tend to see Roksolana as vicious and conniving, an exotic and dangerous Oriental "Other." Ukrainians see her in a much more positive light. Oleksander Halenko, writing in this book, argues that the favourable Ukrainian view of Roksolana owes much to her being conflated with Marusia Bohuslavka, the priest's daughter who liberated Kozaks in the duma translated above.[42]

Returning to folk poetry, we find that the plight of women in captivity appears more frequently in historical songs than in dumy. Perhaps because the prohibitions against women singing dumy were so strict, historical songs were the genre where women's experiences were more often told. In one such song, a mother and a daughter are held together in the same household. The mother wants to flee and return home. The daughter, however, because she has children with her master, is not willing to leave and prefers to stay with her family. In another song, a

The women slaves in the folk imagination. Unknown artist, "The Harem," early twentieth century. Courtesy of Rodovid Press.

young woman who has children with her Turkish master is surprised when an older woman, newly captured and brought into the household, sings a lullaby to the younger woman's babies and calls them her grandchildren. As it turns out, this is the woman's own mother, but someone whom she has not seen for so long that she was incapable of recognizing her. Here the young woman has enough power and status to grant her mother's wish to return home and helps her make that journey.[43]

What is it that gleams white in the valley,
Is it geese or is it swans?
Geese do not fly at this time [of year]
And swans do not swim.
It is Tatars with their convoy of captives,
And one part is made up of women,
The other is made up of girls,
And the third consists of children.
They stopped and camped by the Yarysh,
And they started to divide their bounty,
A girl became the property of a young man,
And a woman became the property of her son-in-law.
He tied her to his horse,
His horse runs along the road,
And she runs through the brambles;
She looks behind her,
And blood is flooding her footprints,
A black crow comes flying
And drinks that blood.
He [the Tatar lord] arrives at his household:
"Come, come out, my Tatar bride,
I have brought you a slave,
Who will work for you until her death."
She took her and led her inside,
And she gave her three tasks:
To pasture the flock with her eyes,
To spin flax with her hands,
And to rock the child with her feet.
The mother-in-law rocks the baby,
And she sings to the child:

"Liuli, liuli, little Tatar,
My grandchild on my daughter's side,
May the entire flock die out,
May the spindle burn to ashes,
May the child turn to stone."
A faithful servant heard this,
"Mistress, did you hear
How your servant cursed you:
May the entire flock die out,
May the spindle burn to ashes,
May the child turn to stone!"
The Tatar woman came running,
Running barefoot and without her girdle,
And she struck [her] across the face,
She struck her own mother.
"Oh, my daughter, oh, my daughter,
All I did was feed you,
I never struck you across the face."
"Mother, oh my elderly mother,
What sign did you see,
That you are calling me your daughter?"
"On Sunday you were cutting periwinkle
And you cut off your pinky finger,
That is how I recognized you."
"Mother, my dear mother,
Cast off these rags,
Take these fine garments,
And you will rule along with us."
"I prefer my rags,
To your costly garments,
And I do not want to rule here,
I want to go to my homeland to die."
"My servants, my faithful ones,
Saddle the raven-black horses,
Take my mother to her homeland."

One poignant song tells of a gentleman who buys a lovely girl at the slave market. She is apparently quite beautiful because he gladly pays a great deal of money for her. The gentleman wines and dines the slave that he has bought, then sends her to make the bed where, presumably, he will have her sexually. As it turns out, the woman to whom he is so attracted is his own sister.[44]

A Turk walks through the market, oh, the sea foams!
[Refrain] He leads a girl along, oh, my heart!
He asks silver for her [refrain repeated here and after each line below],
He asks silver without measure,
He asks gold that is beyond weighing.
One gentleman is found,
He pours out silver without measure,
He puts out gold without weighing it.
Oh, he [the man who bought the girl] held her around the waist,
He led her under his roof.
Oh, he took her by the hand,
He led her to his house.
Oh, they sat down for supper,
After supper they played cards.
He tells her to make the bed,
She made that bed,
And she began to weep quietly.
The gentleman came into the room,
He began to talk to the girl,
"Oh, Marusia, Marysenko!
What sort of family do you have?
Do you have many relatives?
Why is it that you are perishing in captivity?"
"Oh, I had three brothers,
Three brothers, my own kin,"
"Where did they disappear?
Your three brothers, your kin?"
"One went to Vologda,
The second one went to Hungary,
The third one went to Turkey."
"Would you be able to recognize them,
Your brothers, your own kin?"
"I would no longer be able to recognize them,
Because I perish in captivity.
What kind of world do we now have,
That a brother does not recognize his sister,

What sort of hour is this,
That a person cannot recognize his kin?"

This song attests to the value placed upon attractive female captives. It confirms what Zilfi says about the presumed sexual availability of all slaves. It also shows that a man who was not a Turk could achieve wealth and high standing in Ottoman society.

Galley Slaves

Household slaves were but one category of captured and enslaved peoples. Perhaps the greatest manpower need of the Ottoman Empire was for galley slaves, men who would row the Turkish war and merchant vessels. Big warships could require as many as three hundred oarsmen and the conditions on all vessels used in battle were so brutal that galley slaves seldom lived long; they needed to be replaced on a regular basis.[45] As Zilfi notes, "Both Ottoman and European calculations are prone to overlook the thousands of (male) galley slaves consumed by the great Mediterranean navies and the murderous sea battles of the 16th and 17th centuries."[46] Her statements are based on earlier work by Inalcik where he concluded that the Turkish ruling class, in addition to being "the single major group keeping the slave market alive" in fact disposed of more military slaves that any other category of slave.[47] The horror of galley slavery is the topic of many dumy. The captives whom Marusia releases are galley slaves. Held in dungeons in large cities such as Istanbul and its suburbs of Galata and Uskudar, such slaves would be released only in chains and they were the men used in shipbuilding and other hard labour. When the ships were seaworthy, they were the ones who were forced to propel the vessels.[48] While the exploitation of household slaves was bad enough, the worst possible fate that could befall a captive was life as a galley slave. Called "a living hell" and "an unspeakably wretched existence," galley slavery offered next to no opportunities to better one's lot and the only thing that lay ahead for most rowers was an early demise.[49] There was no chance of integrating into Muslim society. The men who rowed the ships of the Ottoman Empire essentially worked themselves to death.

The least desirable of captives became galley slaves, although Davis does mention that the men were tested for strength before being purchased for work on a galley and that their teeth were checked to make sure that they could eat the dry food that would be their sustenance while at sea.[50] Slaves were chained by their wrists to the oar that they were supposed to manipulate and anywhere from three to five men were assigned to each oar. The number of men per oar depended on the size of the ship, but even the smallest galleys required four rowers for the big stern oars. There was a chain on the floor of the galley that ran the length of each bench and was bolted to the ship's ribbing, and the men were shackled to it by their ankles. The system of double chains meant that movement was possible only along the length of the bench and that, when a man needed to relieve himself, he had to move the length of the bench to the hull of the ship. Some were too exhausted to do so, especially when they were made to row full-out, either in pursuit of an enemy ship or when being pursued by one. As a result, some befouled themselves and the stench in galleys was reputed to be next to unbearable. Men were sometimes given only shorts to wear and were thus subject to sunburn, a fact reflected in the captives' plea for rain in one of our duma texts. Sometimes there was not enough water to drink and men resorted to drinking seawater in desperation. But the worse aspect of galley slavery, according to the few who did survive and return home, and were educated enough to write accounts of their experience, was sleep deprivation. Men were chained to their oars day and night and lying down to sleep was not possible. Because of sleep deprivation, slaves suffered from hallucinations, along with the exhaustion caused by lack of sleep. Antonovych and Drahonomov, in their commentary to the "Samiilo Kishka" duma, claim that galley slaves slept in shifts, but they too underscore the suffering inherent in galley slavery.[51]

The number of slaves who died on galleys cannot be overestimated. According to Davis, ships returning from a campaign would be met by priests with holy oil because at least some of the men would be either already dead or expected to die shortly.[52] In Algiers, galley slaves, when they were not at sea, lived in structures called bagnos. These were large barracks, built in a square shape with a courtyard in the middle. Slaves were locked inside the bagno at night but, in the daytime, they could go outside and try to earn a little money. Bagnos were also the place where liquor was sold. Since alcohol is prohibited in Islam, only Christian areas such as the bagno could trade in alcoholic beverages. Those Muslims who wished to partake of spirits did avail themselves of bagnos, bringing in money for the slaves running such establishments.[53] No such opportunities existed for galley slaves held in Istanbul and cities further to the East, where most Ukrainian slaves were located.

Here galley slaves were confined to dungeons and not permitted outside except to do the work forced on them by their masters, such as ship building.[54]

The horrors of galley slavery are central to two dumy that focus on captives' laments and also feature prominently in the "Samiilo Kishka" duma. Even though the songs were recorded several centuries after the abolition of slavery, they all picture the suffering of a galley slave quite accurately. In these songs, as in the eastern parts of the Ottoman Empire, the captives are kept in prison until they are used to man the oars of Turkish galleys. They are shackled hand and foot and pray to nature for rain presumably because they are suffering from sun exposure. They are not unshackled even at night, prompting Samiilo Kishka to ask that at least the higher-ranked men among them be given a respite, and yet this bit of mercy is denied. The "Samiilo Kishka" duma and one of the songs where the captives are nameless state that the Turkish and Tatar masters of the Ukrainian galley slaves, not satisfied with the pain and suffering inflicted by living constantly in shackles and rowing the galley, increase the men's torment with beatings and by adding chains or secondary shackles. Their motivation seems to lie somewhere between the need to beat slaves into submission when they begin to protest and the desire to take sadistic pleasure at the expense of helpless slaves. Such incidents surely occurred in real life as well as in songs about captivity, but any urge to abuse one's slaves was held in check not only by Sheria law but also by economic considerations: slaves were expensive and damaging them meant damaging valuable property. Reducing a slave's ability to work meant reducing the value of one's investment.[55]

There are two dumy that are called captives' laments. The first is a text where the galley slaves speak as a group. They list the torments that they must endure – the shackles, the sun exposure – and they ask for God's help. As in the song about Samiilo Kishka, this enrages the Turkish pasha, who takes the Kozaks' words as a sign of rebellion. He calls on his henchmen and has them punish the galley slaves. The punishment – whipping with thorns and with meadowsweet, a plant that has especially thin, strong, and pliant stalks – is meant to cause maximum pain with minimal long-range damage. Thus, the Pasha seems intent on beating his captives into submission, while still preserving their ability to row. The text translated below is usually entitled "The Lament of the Captives." It was published by Filaret Kolessa, who recorded it from Opanas Slastion, a scholar who learned it from a minstrel in the Poltava region.[56] Because it is a relatively recent transcription of an oral text, it preserves many performance features, including the use of ornamental words such as the "Hey-hey" line, with which the text begins.

Hey-hey, hey-hey, hey-hey, hey-hey, hey!
Oh, on that holy day, on Sunday,
Very early, early in the morning,
Oh, those were not the grey eagles calling,
It was the poor captives,
Crying in harsh Turkish captivity, hey.
They raised their hands to the heavens,
The clanged their shackles,
They called upon God and they begged Him:
"Oh, God, give us, give us soaking rain from the Heavens,
And send up a powerful wind from below,
So that a fast-moving wave might form on the Black Sea,
And so that it might break the Turkish anchors, hey-hey.
For we have grown weary of this Turkish penal servitude,
The iron of our shackles has torn our ankles,
It has taken our white flesh, our Kozak, young men's flesh,
And worn it down to the yellow bone, hey-hey."
At that time the Turkish ruler, the Muslim pasha,
The one who did not believe in Christianity,
He climbs on up to the rafters,
And he hears what the Kozaks are saying,
And he angrily summons his servants, the Turkish janissaries,
"Oh, I say, I say unto you, Turks, janissaries, hey,
That you should behave properly,
That you should guess my meaning well,
That you should take three bunches of thorns,
And four bunches of black meadowsweet,
That you take them in your hands,
And walk through row after row,
Strike each of the poor captives three times in the same spot."
Oh, then they, those servants,
The Turks, the janissaries,
Well, they did as they were told,
They guessed what was wanted of them,
They took three bunches of thorns,
And four bunches of black meadowsweet,
And they took them in their hands,

They walked from row to row,
And they struck each poor captive thrice in the same spot,
They shed innocent Christian blood, hey!
Oh, when those Kozaks, those young men,
When they saw Christian blood on their own bodies,
Then they began to curse the land of the Turks,
The faith of the Muslims,
They cursed and they blamed it, hey!
"Oh," they said, "land, land, oh, Turkish land,
Faith, oh, accursed Muslim faith,
Oh, separation from all things Christian,
Oh, you have separated far more than one person,
You have separated brother from sister,
And men from their faithful wives,
And true friends from their true friends, hey-hey, hey!
Oh, liberate us, oh save us, Lord,
Save all us poor captives,
Save us from harsh Turkish captivity!
Bring us to quiet waters,
And to bright dawns,
To a happy land,
To where the baptized people dwell,
To where the Christian cities lie,
To our father, our dear mother,
To our beloved family,
And give us many years,
Until the end of time! Hey!
Oh, I bow first before the Lord God,
And then before the hetman, our military leader,
And before our entire company, blood kin, beloved people,
And before all those who are listening,
And I wish them many years,
Until the end of time."

The other duma which speaks from the point of view of a captive gives the voice of a single man rather than a group. It is called "The Lament of the Captive." The speaker here also seems to be a galley slave because he complains about his shackles and about spending all his time on the Black Sea. The reference to rawhide is somewhat puzzling. When wet rawhide dries, it tightens and would indeed cut into flesh. This would be extremely painful, like being whipped with thorns and meadowsweet. It would cause greater damage than a whipping, however, unless it was quickly removed and slave masters wanting to preserve the value of their captives presumably did not let the rawhide cut too deep. But what is important about the song translated below is the discussion of ransom and the slave trade. Captives could indeed be ransomed and the cities with slave markets listed in the duma that follows were indeed places where slaves were bought and sold. The text which follows was published by Antonovych and Drahomanov, who took it from a manuscript compiled by Novytskyi.[57]

> Oh, it is not a bright falcon calling and crying,
> It is a son sending his respects to Christian cities, to his father and mother;
> He addresses the falcon and calls him his brother:
> "Bright falcon,
> My dear brother,
> You fly high,
> You see far,
> Why don't you ever visit my father and my mother?
> Fly, bright falcon,
> Fly, dear brother,
> To the Christian cities,
> Alight at my parents' home, in front of the gate.
> Then call out mournfully,
> Remind them of my Kozak adventures.
> So that my father and my mother may know what happened to me,
> So that they may sell their goods and possessions and amass a great
>   treasure,
> So that they may ransom my Kozak head and free me from captivity.
> Because when the Black Sea begins to storm,
> Then neither a father nor a mother will be able to tell,
> Where, in which Turkish prison, they should look for their son,
> Whether it be in the Port of Kozlov, or in Constantinople [Istanbul] at the
>   market.
> Then the men with uskufs [a type of headgear worn by the janissaries],
>   the Turks, the janissaries, will arrive,
> They will sell us beyond the Red Sea, they will sell us into a country of slavery,
> They will collect more gold and silver for us than can be counted,
> They will get fine fabrics in bigger bolts than can be measured.
> Hey, hey, hey, hey, hey!"

A companion, a friend who is like a brother, hears this,
He speaks to his friend, his companion, saying:
"My friend, my dear brother, we should not be sending respects to the
    Christian cities,
We should not be compounding our father's and our mother's grief,
Because even if our father and our mother did take great care,
Even if they did sell land and possessions and amass a great treasure,
They would never be able to determine in which Turkish country,
    in which place of captivity, they should seek their sons.
Because no one comes here,
And baptized people do not travel through these parts,
And only bright falcons come this way,
And they alight on our prison,
And they call mournfully and cry.
They wish good health to all us poor captives who are in harsh bondage."
Then the poor captive experienced Turkish imprisonment in full,
His shackles dug into his arms and his legs,
And the wet rawhide ate through his white flesh and cut it to the bone.
And the poor captives looked at their flesh, at their blood,
They thought about their Christian faith,
They cursed the Turkish land, the faith of the Muslims, and reviled it:
"Oh, you Turkish land, you Muslim faith,
You are filled with gold and silver,
But you deprive poor captives of their freedom;
Poor captives spend their time living in this land,
And they can experience neither Christmas nor Easter,
They spend all their time on the Black Sea in accursed penal servitude,
They recall the Christian faith,
And they curse the Turkish land, the Muslim faith, and revile it.
You, Turkish land, you Muslim faith,
Oh, separation from all things Christian;
You have separated more than one person from another with your seven
    years' war,
You have parted husband from wife,
And brother from sister,
And little children from their father and their mother.
Free, oh God, free the poor captive,
Let him reach the holy shores of Rus
Let him reach the land that is happy,
The Christian land!"

In this song, the companion of the man whose voice we hear convinces him of the futility of ransom and this duma, like the other captives' lament, ends with a curse of the Turkish land and the Muslim faith. Words are the slave's only recourse. While ransom at the point when a man was already a galley slave might have been futile, ransoming captives was a regular part of the practice of enslavement. The best time to ransom prospective slaves, both from the point of view of the attackers and from that of those captured, was shortly after a raid. However, opportunities for ransom came at many stages of the enslavement process, a system that was highly developed and complex, as will be described below.

Capturing Slaves

The acquisition of slaves through warfare is a complex topic and it is difficult to describe it to a contemporary audience, especially since films with purported historical subject matter often present the army defeated in battle as captives in chains. The warfare in which Ottoman slaves were captured was not like the warfare of today. Armies did clash and enemy combatants who were taken captive could become slaves as long as they were not Muslims. The prohibition against enslaving Muslims was not always adhered to, but many times it was and Mehmed II is said to have killed 6200 captured enemy soldiers because they would continue to pose a threat if freed and yet, as Muslims, they could not be enslaved.[58] Many of the people captured during campaigns were not combatants; women and children taken as captives were not acquired on the field of battle. Ostapchuk describes the military endeavours of the Crimean Tatar khan Sahib Gerey. Most of the captives taken by his forces were acquired after the campaign, on the army's journey home, when the khan would allow his men to raid the civilian population so that they could recoup their expenses and make some money from their participation in his expedition.[59]

In the geographical area described by dumy, during the course of the fourteenth through sixteenth centuries, there were few organized campaigns where large-scale armies engaged each other. Rather, captives were taken in raids by bands of armed men, usually ten to thirty in number. Such attacks on Ukraine, Muscovy, Poland, southeastern Europe, and the Balkans were the main source of slaves in the early sixteenth century.[60] The raiders would attack a village, relying on surprise as much as they could, and capture what they could: people, horses, cattle and other farm animals, movable goods. Almost everything was of value. In the duma about Kozak Holota, the hero is presented as bedraggled and poor, but the Tatar who rides out to capture him still sees great potential in taking him captive. He will profit, he says, from Holota's weapons and his horse, but most valuable is the Kozak himself, for he will fetch a most handsome sum on the slave market. Raiding one's enemy was a way of keeping the opposition subjugated, or at least in check. It was also an economic enterprise, a way of earning money, and was much like the foraging done on the steppe, where men would fish as a group, or collect honey, or hunt game. Raiding meant banding together to collect booty, only it was done in settled areas rather than on the open steppe. Once the people, animals, and goods had been captured, the raiding party would withdraw and wait for a few days. It would then return to the village that had been attacked and offer to return the captured people in exchange for the payment of a certain sum of money. Villagers were given a limited amount of time to raise the funds needed to ransom their relatives. The ransom collected in the village was a far smaller sum than what a captive might fetch if sold in the market. Still, ransoming was profitable because it was guaranteed income, whereas the process of delivering a person to the point of sale had many risks, including the escape of the captive, injury to him or her, and even the captive's death.[61] While the sum requested as ransom was relatively small, it still imposed an enormous burden on the relatives of the captured person. Far from all captives were ransomed. Even if relatives succeeded in amassing the needed cash and goods, they were left so impoverished that their ability to function as an economic unit was almost certainly destroyed and they were forced to become indentured servants or worse.[62] Antonovych and Drahomanov give a touching example of a father who does not ransom his daughter, but tries to pursue the raiding party taking her to market.[63] The reason for not ransoming the daughter is not clear: perhaps the father could not afford to pay the amount requested; perhaps he was not given the chance because the daughter was too valuable a catch. In either case, he does not offer payment to his daughter's captors, but sets off in pursuit. Unfortunately, his efforts are in vain. The text, first published by Metlynskyi, goes as follows:

> Oh, from the mountains, from the mountains, from the black forest,
> The Tatars come, leading Volynochka.
> Volynochka's braid is of golden hair,
> It lights up the whole forest,
> And also the green grove and the gravel road.

Behind her, in pursuit, runs her father.
She nodded and she waved her white hand:
"Go back, father, go back, dear one!
You won't be able to free me and you yourself will perish,
You will leave your head in a foreign land,
And your eyes will be on the Turkish border [i.e., the father
    will always look with longing toward Turkey]."

Antonovych and Drahomanov devote an entire section of the first
volume of their collection of dumy and historical songs to Tatar raids
and slave capture.[64] A description of life in the territory that became
Ukraine will be given in the next chapter. This will help to further
explain the nature of Turkish and especially Crimean Tatar raids.

Once taken, the captives were driven to market. Although slaves were
very valuable, they were transported under horrible conditions. As Zilfi
states, "Captives on route suffered forced marches, scant food, bad
water, exposure, filth, disease, and raw fear. Outsiders who had occasion to view Black Sea captives in transit were struck by their deplorable
state. In the seventeenth century, Sir John Charkin described a shipment
'of women and children, half-naked or covered with rags and filth'
loaded onto a vessel for the voyage south."[65] Part of the reason for treat-
ing slaves badly during their journey to market was economic, the desire
to increase one's profit margin by spending as little as possible on the
upkeep of captives. Part of the reason was psychological. Slaves were
prepared for a life of submission by this brutal treatment and they were
"seasoned" by giving them nothing to do except worry.[66] They were further readied for their new position in life by having older, trusted slaves,
preferably of the same ethnicity as the captives themselves, mingle
with them, talk to them, and prepare them for what lay ahead. As Zilfi
says, "Particularly insidious was the role of ex-slave compatriots in the
mechanics of enslavement. Their own firsthand experience made them
especially valuable in priming their co-ethnics for the path they themselves had traveled. Surviving records suggest the deep involvement
of former slaves, whether or not compatriots, in perpetuating Ottoman
slave culture. Former slaves identified vulnerable targets. Many were
the small-time and big-time brokers and traders without whom there
would have been no slave labour for urban customers."[67] These older
slaves also served the purpose of ascertaining the status of the various
captives and their abilities. The possibility of ransom continued even
as slaves moved into Ottoman territory and were held for sale in major

trading centres such as Kefe, now called Feodosiia. A larger ransom could be demanded for a captive of higher social status, which gave the captives incentive not to reveal who they were so that their ransom would not be set higher than their relatives could afford and gave their captors reason to send in people who might surreptitiously ascertain a captive's true worth. At the same time, a slave did not want to seem like an ordinary person because that would increase the probability of his being assigned to work rowing a galley. Davis gives some interesting material on nationalities, the prices set for them, and their reactions to these prices. The French were not desirable captives because their relatives were believed to be poor and incapable of paying a high price. The Spanish were judged to be peculiar because they became enraged when their price was set low, feeling that this was an insult to their dignity and that of their relatives.[68] People who knew a trade were valuable because the master could sell their expertise or the products of their labour and they would fetch a higher price on the market. Such men might also enter into a mukatebe contract with their owners.

Ransoming slaves was widely practised. The subject of ransom comes up again and again in dumy and historical songs. As seen in the text translated above, Marusia Bohuslavka asks Kozaks whom she liberates to stop by her hometown and tell her parents that she is alive and well. She adds that her parents should not try ransoming her because she now has a life in the Muslim world and cannot go back. In a duma about a captive given earlier, a slave asks an eagle to send the exact opposite message to his parents: they should "sell their goods and possessions and amass a great treasure" so that they can buy his freedom. A fellow galley slave tells him not to trouble his family because captives are shipped all over the empire and the parents will never be able to find him. Begging relatives to buy one's freedom appears frequently in historical songs. These picture captives writing home to their relatives and asking them to pay for their release. The first letter is written to the father and he refuses, saying that the price requested would ruin the family. The second letter goes to the mother and gets the same response. Only the captive's sweetheart is willing to risk all and, in one song, a young woman declares her willingness to give up everything for her man, while in another it is a man who will do anything to free his beloved.[69] The song about a sweetheart willing to ransom her Kozak goes as follows:

Oh, what is that smoke in the field?
A Kozak sits in captivity.

He sits and he breathes with difficulty,
And he writes letters to his father:
"Father, please have pity,
And buy me out of here."
"What am I supposed to give for you, my son?"
"[Give] eight oxen from our household."
"Oh, I can't give that, my son,
You will have to perish."
Oh, what is going on in the field?
It is a Kozak sitting in captivity,
He sits and he breathes with difficulty,
And he writes letters to his mother.
"Oh, mother, please pity me,
Please purchase my freedom."
"What do I need to give for you?"
"Eight cows with their calves."
"Oh, I can't give that much,
Son, you will have to perish."
Oh what is going on in the field?
It is a Kozak sitting in captivity,
He sits and he breathes with difficulty,
And he writes letters to his beloved.
"Oh, my darling, have pity on me,
And purchase my freedom."
"What should I give for you, my beloved?"
"Seven hundred ducks from your household."
"Oh, my darling, I am willing,
To sacrifice all that I own,
Rather than to let you perish."

Those slaves who were not ransomed and remained in captivity had
to undergo a major psychological shift. As Zilfi points out, a slave's
chances of improving his or her life depended on the ability to repress
memory, since "most of the enslaved had surely witnessed the killing or
other abuse of relatives and friends in the days of their own capture."[70]
Yet the process of capture and transport, one that had been developed
and perfected over time, helped make this shift in mentality possible.
In songs we see captives who have become so much a part of their new
world that getting them to remember their former identity is difficult.
This is the case in the duma about the young falcon who comes to live

in Istanbul. In the poem "Yevshan zillia," written by Mykola Vorony and based on the story about Khan Otrok, it is a Turkish youth who becomes so used to his new life that his father cannot get him to remember his origins until he has him smell the herb of the poem's title. Abused persons do come to identify with their abusers and, in the period we are dealing with, there was often no recourse but to accept the situation and make the best of it. Apparently the mental shift that slaves made in order to survive made them the most loyal of dependents. Ibrahim Pasha, the vezir and confidant of Sultan Suleyman the Magnificent who has already been mentioned, is but one example. In medieval Egypt the rulers had to be Mamluks, or ex-slaves, and the children of Mamluks became ordinary citizens rather than members of the Mamluk category; the ranks of Mamluks were replenished by the capture of new slaves. Why slaves were considered particularly loyal is difficult to answer. Perhaps it was the process of capture and the extreme psychological trauma inflicted on the slave that made him or her so attached to his master. Some writers speculate that it was gratitude to the master for giving the former slave freedom and a chance to succeed.[71] Perhaps the financial and social success available to at least the fortunate few among former slaves far exceeded anything that that they could hope to achieve back home. Many dumy talk about the temptation of Turkish luxury or curse the Ottoman Empire for being a land of wealth – and also bondage.

The issue of language is seldom mentioned, but it needs study as a factor in helping the slave make the needed mental shift. During capture and transport, the slave probably had no idea what his captors were saying. Not knowing what was being said and what was going on surely increased isolation and fear. As the slave was integrated into Ottoman society, his or her language capacity likely grew. Certainly, slaves who had been in captivity for a time learned Turkish and knew it well. Roksolana's letters to Sultan Suleyman show an increasing mastery of the Turkish language and progressively greater sophistication in terms of language knowledge and use.[72] Did the process of language acquisition parallel the acquisition of a new identity as a member of the Ottoman realm?

Today language is connected to ethnic, if not national, identity. In the period about which dumy sing, this may not have been the case. Knowledge of Turkish was probably widespread, at least among the elite. Dashkevych, an early leader of the Ukrainian Kozaks, was bilingual if not multilingual. He is said to have dressed like a Tatar and been so fluent in the language that he could infiltrated Tatar camps and learn

The Kozak and his beloved. Panas Plinik, "Courtship," 1889. Courtesy of Rodovid Press

of military plans and movements, thus gaining great strategic advantage in conflicts with his enemy.[73] Former slaves who had risen to positions of leadership were certainly bilingual or multilingual. In the duma "Samiilo Kishka," Liakh Buturlak, the convert to Islam who is assigned to supervise the galley slaves, speaks in Turkish and in Greek, providing the diversion that allows the escaped Kozaks to pass by guard ships as if they were still a Turkish galley. Presumably Buturlak speaks to the Kozak galley slaves in Ukrainian and, since Liakh is a word used to indicate Polish identity, it is probable that he knew Polish as well. The trusted slaves who were sent to supervise new captives, both to break their will and assimilate them into their new status and to discover their true identity for the sake of setting the highest possible ransom, were surely at least bilingual. Did their bilingualism make them feel superior to the new captives? Did it foster the strange combination of hatred for former compatriots and nostalgia for the homeland that is ascribed to Liakh Buturlak in the "Samiilo Kishka" duma?

St John the Russian is an interesting example of a different approach to accepting captivity. John was apparently not a Russian at all but a Ukrainian Kozak who fought with the Russians. Nonetheless, he was called Russian by Western observers, who tended to lump all Slavs together under the Russian rubric, something which happened with Roksolana as well. John was captured in battle and became the slave of the Aga of Procopion, a town near Caesarea in Asia Minor. Some accounts say that he, like other Christian captives, was tortured in an attempt to force him to renounce his faith. In all accounts, he is pictured as a person who perseveres in his belief in Christianity no matter what happens. He is also consistently pictured as being assigned to the lowly position of stable hand and forced to sleep in the stable, along with the animals. John, it is said, accepted all the trials and humiliations to which he was subjected and maintained his faith in God, always behaving towards his Muslim masters with kindness and always keeping his own faith and persisting in his prayers and devotions. Impressed by John's piety, his master the Aga offered him better quarters and, eventually, manumission. John refused both offers, saying that it was God's will that he suffer and accept his destiny to be a slave. John performed miracles while alive and his tomb is also the site of miracles, emitting a marvellous light and helping women with difficult pregnancies. His relics are now in Euboia and are the destination of pilgrims. While figures like John do not appear in dumy, this man does help us understand how, once captured, people came to accept their lot as destiny and learned to make the best of slavery.[74]

Escape from Slavery

John may have come to accept his position as a slave, and a few extraordinary slaves may have risen to high positions, but they were the exception rather than the rule. We know about them precisely because they were worthy of note for being different from other slaves. Accounts of successful slaves survive into the present because records of people in high places were the ones that were kept, whereas the lives of ordinary citizens went unrecorded, except in their songs. These tell us that slavery was hell. In the song about three brothers dying by the river Samara, the mortally wounded siblings debate playing a musical instrument to let others know their location. They decide against revealing their whereabouts. As the youngest says, it may be that their own comrades will find them – but then again they may be found by the Turks and the janissaries. If the latter is the case, then they will be taken into captivity. Since the men are on the verge of death, it would seem that enslavement need not be a concern. And yet the song proclaims that captivity is more frightening than being found and further shot or otherwise wounded.

Captivity was horrible and, for all those slaves who did not follow in the steps of St John, one response was to attempt to escape, just like the three brothers fleeing Azov in the duma of the same name. Male slaves were more likely to take this route than females. One reason was motherhood: women, if they had children, found it difficult to abandon them and run. The other was opportunity: a woman out alone in public would arouse suspicion; a man would not. Apart from galley slaves, men were allowed far greater freedom of movement than women. They could go outside. They might be working at a site where they would be under limited supervision or observation. This allowed them to run, and run they did. Slaves would sometimes travel with their master and many found this to provide an excellent opportunity for escape. Some slaves fled when their master died. What does not seem to have happened is mass escape from captivity such as described in the "Marusia Bohuslavka," "Samiilo Kishka," and "Ivan Bohuslavets" dumy. The control that masters had over slaves, both logistic and psychological, did not permit escape in large groups and what we see in dumy seems to be a combination of wishful thinking and exaggeration for effect. Escape by individuals, by contrast, was so common that there were regular procedures for recapturing slaves and returning them to their masters or selling them to new owners.[75] When slaves did flee, the fugitives often travelled with one or more companions, as in the "Three

Brothers Escaping from Azov" duma.[76] Their fate was likely similar to that of these three brothers. In other words, some would escape and others would not. In the Azov dumy, sometimes the two brothers on horseback do make it home, while in other versions they let down their guard, are ambushed, and return to captivity, as in the text translated above. Of course, a person travelling on foot, like the youngest brother in this duma, while he might have a better chance of hiding, would suffer extreme want in the steppe and be likely to die of exposure. The necessity of having a horse to ensure survival will be discussed at length in the next chapter. Here it is enough to note that the lack of food and the physical demands on an escapee with no mount are pictured accurately in our duma texts. It should also be noted that the elder two brothers, the ones who are on horseback, when they do make it home, are banished by their parents for abandoning the youngest sibling in the steppe, making their escape virtually meaningless. In one version, the middle brother curses his elder sibling and the latter ends up living as a beggar instead of enjoying his inheritance.[77]

The fact of escape, attested in songs and in the established procedures for recapturing and returning slaves, runs counter to evidence of slaves being the most loyal of servants. This seems to have been true of manumitted slaves as well as those men who ran while still enslaved. What slavery did to the mental makeup of people who became captives is difficult to fathom and the picture of reactions in opposites and extremes, given in the dumy presented in this chapter, because it is a picture generated by the folk themselves, is almost certainly an accurate reflection of the emotional upheaval caused by enslavement.

The End of Ottoman Slavery

Ottoman slavery gradually collapsed and disappeared. According to most authors, it was Western pressure that led to the repudiation of this institution by discrediting it and labelling it as inhumane. As we will see in the next chapter, much of the behaviour of the Kozaks resembled that of the Turks and Tatars against whom they struggled – except for practising slavery on a larger scale. Kozaks did take captives in war, but mostly to use in prisoner exchanges, a human form of ransom that could be used to secure the freedom of their countrymen. An example of a prisoner exchange as a performance meant to affect both sides of the transaction is given by Koray Durak, albeit the period which he describes precedes the one covered here.[78] Why did the Kozaks use captives for prisoner exchanges only? Why did they not keep slaves? Was it just a matter of religion and custom or did economic considerations come into play? All these factors likely played some role in creating the situation which existed, the economic one needing more attention than it has received. In spite of the great richness of the steppe lands that became Eastern Ukraine, the political situation in the area, especially in the fourteenth to sixteenth centuries, was so unstable that it allowed foraging only.[79] Large-scale operations which could profit from slave labour were not an option. As dumy tell us, families lived at close to subsistence level and the loss of adult males, such as the loss of a father in battle, would have serious economic impact, typically requiring children to be sent away to work as hired hands. Labour of this sort was difficult, even brutal, and widowed mothers who resisted the temptation to send their sons to work as hirelings are presented in dumy as especially praiseworthy. This is the case in the "Widow and Her Three Sons" duma translated in the previous chapter and one that will be given again in the section on everyday life songs. Similarly, Ivas Konovchenko's mother, also a widow, refuses to send her son to work as a hireling in the hope that he will recognize her sacrifice and care her for in her old age. If Kozaks and other Christian dwellers on the territory of Ukraine could barely support children, there was little chance of their being able to take on the task of feeding slaves, even if the slaves could be forced to work. Records show that non-Muslims who were integrated into Turkish society and lived within the Ottoman Empire did keep slaves, much like their Ottoman former masters.[80] On Ukrainian soil, however, the economy was too fragile to allow for slavery. There are indications that Ukrainians, like their Turkish and Tatar neighbours, did exploit the labour of others. In the duma "Ivas Konovchenko," the hero, when he learns that his mother has sent him the horse that he had asked for, vows to repay her by capturing twelve Turkish janissaries and sending them to be her servants. Such allusions to the use of Turkic captives as servants are relatively rare.

Clarence-Smith argues against the hypothesis that Western aversion to slavery eliminated this institution in the Ottoman realm, and shows that the roots of the drive for emancipation lay in Islam itself. Islam, he argues, never really condoned slavery, even though it did not prohibit it. Dumy and their performers support Clarence-Smith's assertion, not by talking about Islam, but by reminding us that slavery was indeed practised in the lands of the neighbours and enemies of the Ottoman Empire, only under a different name. Dumy about captivity, about the terrible burden of working for a master, survived well into the nineteenth century because, as their performers themselves noted, the conditions described by dumy were much like those imposed by serf-dom. The Ukrainian lands did not have slavery, but serfdom was not abolished until 1861. Serfs could be sold. They could be beaten without justification, as happened to the kobzar Ivan Kravchenko-Kriukovskyi, whose account of going blind is given in the preceding chapter. Sexual exploitation was also a likely occurrence. The desire to profit from the labour of another without offering compensation for that labour is an ever-present problem.

4 The Rise of the Kozaks – Battles on Land and on Sea

Serfdom was not a part of life in Ukraine in the fourteenth through sixteenth centuries. It would come to the region much later. In the period reflected in dumy, bondage and servitude were something that befell a person living on the territory of what became Ukraine only if he or she was captured by Turks or Tatars. Serfdom, like slavery, required much greater social organization and government control than was available at the time with which we are concerned. During that period, life was characterized by a unique social order, one which, according to Hrushevskyi, lacked the "formulas of the legal, economic, and cultural life" of a state.[1] The territory that would eventually become southeastern Ukraine was a wild land, both very attractive and very dangerous. After the collapse of Kyivan Rus in the thirteenth century, the territories to the east and south of Kyiv were a no-man's land, marvellously rich in game, fur-bearing animals, fish, and honey, as travellers such as Michael the Lithuanian would attest.[2] And yet this was a lawless area, under constant pressure from nomadic tribes. People who ventured into this territory could amass great riches – but only at commensurately great risk. Marauding nomads could attack at any moment, and a person or a group of people out foraging could lose not only the bounty they had gathered, but also their lives. The soil in the area was also fantastically productive. When uncultivated, it was described as covered with lush growth. When cultivated, it was said to yield superior and plentiful crops with little effort. Communities did settle this land and did work it, using the surrounding areas for grazing livestock and as a source of honey, game, and fish. But even the existence of settled communities was precarious. The region was controlled by Tatars and its stability would vary depending on the degree to which central authority could keep marauding bands in check. As Tatar power weakened and tribute collectors became the only Tatar officials to interact with settled communities, as raids became more frequent, settlements became largely self-sufficient. From what we know, they were led by a person called an *otaman*, who was expected to organize his group so that they could protect themselves. The otaman was also responsible for interacting with Tatar officials and, when tribute collectors came, he was the one who gathered and paid the necessary monies.[3]

An interesting historical song published by Antonovych and Drahomanov describes a leader name Kovalenko, perhaps an otaman, taking a group of young men and women outside the village to do necessary farm work and falling victim to a raid. It is spring, and they plan to harvest the winter wheat that is now ready for reaping. The leader cares for his team and appears to be very proud of them, for he gives them not ordinary equipment, but sickles of gold. Unfortunately, he also seems a bit too self-confident, perhaps even arrogant, and leaves his crew to work without supervision and protection while he goes home to eat and relax. This is a fatal mistake, for he is captured and blinded. Considering the practice of raiding for the sake of capturing slaves, we can assume that the entire crew, both Kovalenko and his young workers, will be taken and sold on the slave market. The text, which Antónovych and Drahomanov took from Novytskyi's manuscript, goes as follows:[4]

Oh, on Sunday, early in the morning,
Kovalenko gathered a company of select reapers,
Boys and girls, they were all young,
And he made them sickles, all made of gold.
He led the reapers through the dale and through the valley,
To the meadow with winter wheat,
"Oh, reap my reapers, do reap well,
But keep an eye on the black cloud,
I will go home and have breakfast,
I will go and have my early Sunday meal."
Oh, not much time passed
And they [the Turks] come leading Kovalenko, having caught him.
They lead Kovalenko through the village and down the street,
They have tied his hands with rawhide,
They have tied his white hands,

And they have shackled his legs,
And they have ruined his dark eyes.
"Oh, wind, blow from the north,
[Blow] on my white face and my dark eyes,
Oh let me just look [once more]
At my reapers, my young ones,
At the sickles, the golden ones.
Oh, it seems that God has punished me,
Because I sat down to eat early on Sunday,
Oh, it seems that God has struck me down,
Because I drank horilka [vodka] on a Sunday."

The blinding of captives was not a common practice because a useful slave was one who had all of his physical abilities. Yet leaders may have been blinded to make them incapable of resuming their position, and this is apparently what happens to Kovalenko. In some versions of this song the tortures to which Kovalenko is subjected are given in more detail and we learn that his eyes were "ruined" with hot pitch, a common method of rendering people blind.

In the second half of the fourteenth century Eastern Ukraine became part of the Lithuanian state while Galicia belonged to the Kingdom of Poland and efforts to colonize the rich and tempting land began in earnest. But the area was still wild and the success of attempts to impose order and establish settled communities would vary with the quality of the leader.[5] Documentary material for this period is scant and yet it may well have been the era when institutions and approaches to life and to politics that would come to characterize the Ukrainian Kozaks were formed. The nature of the administration of Ukrainian territories by the Lithuanian state was such that it encouraged self-sufficiency and independence. The state seemed to promise protection, but defence of its subjects from raids was seldom forthcoming. Thus, the population armed itself and became skilled at using its arms effectively. The people learned to defend themselves from raids. When they could not put up an effective defence, they learned to hide, shielding themselves, their families, and their goods. They also developed the practice of launching preventative attacks to weaken their enemies and make them less capable of launching a raid.

Settlement and administration by a central government required the construction of fortifications. Referred to as castles, these were population centres governed by an administrator called a *starosta* or a *hospodar*. Castles were supposed to protect the local population from attack by outsiders such as the marauding Tatar bands. The promise of shelter was, of course, attractive to people dwelling in the area. Regrettably, the castles were often small, with the interior space measuring about the size of a courtyard. They were built of wood and susceptible to fire. A layer of mud over the wood was used to prevent the wood from burning but, as often as not, this layer was not applied. The builders of fortifications took advantage of natural barriers such as rivers, cliffs, and bogs whenever they could. Unfortunately, in some cases, the natural barriers actually prevented the population from using the castle for shelter. At Zhytomyr, an argument between the starosta, or head official of the town, and the townspeople over who should pay for the construction of a bridge meant that no bridge was built at all and the peasants living outside the fortress could barely enter the protective walls on foot; driving carts in to safeguard any possessions was completely out of the question. As a result, in most instances of attack, the castle provided no protection, and the peasants fled into the forest.[6] The forest was not the only potential hiding place. One historical song describes a raid on a settlement in which almost all the inhabitants are taken captive. Only the speaker of the text manages to escape, and Antonovych and Drahomanov explain that he or she does so by hiding underwater and breathing through a hollow reed.[7]

Across the rivers fires burn
There the Tatars are dividing their captives.
They have set our village on fire,
They have stolen all of our wealth,
They have struck the old granny and killed her,
And they have taken the young woman as their captive.
In the valley drums are sounding,
Because people are being led to slaughter,
About their necks there is a rope
And around their feet chains clang.
And I, the poor sufferer, with the children,
Will go through the forest and along the paths,
Let my fate be in water
While a gull flies above me.

Although the song states that the speaker's fellow villagers are being led to slaughter and speaks of ropes around their necks, what he or she is actually describing is the preparation of captives for transport, a description that is consistent with the methods used to lead captives to the slave market discussed in the previous chapter. The reference to slaughter should be taken to mean that slavery is akin to death.

Even castles with good access were useless unless the people working out in the fields were given advanced warning and sufficient time to withdraw. But guard posts were not always manned and the necessary alarms were often not sounded in time. Thus the potential benefits of living near a fortified castle were simply not realized in many instances, prompting the locals to resort to their own measures. As travellers to the area noted, the villagers were most adept in the use of firearms and carried their weapons with them constantly. As late as the sixteenth century, farm work was done "with arms in hand."[8] Foraging in the steppe, which meant moving away from the potential protection of the castle, required even more serious protection. Men who would go out on such expeditions did so in groups of ten, each one of them armed, so as to have sufficient firepower to resist attack.[9]

The colonization of Eastern Ukraine was done for financial gain. Peasants were to deliver a certain percentage of their crop to the starosta or hospodar of their settlement and foragers were required to surrender a certain percentage of their catch of fish, a certain quantity of honey or of the mead brewed from the honey, and so forth. When such levies were perceived as excessive, a situation that would typically occur when fees were raised to pay for a push to acquire additional territory, resentment would grow among the castle's subjects. When the burden of heavy taxation was accompanied by a lack of protection from marauders, the people living in an area could simply leave and move further east to as yet unsettled lands. Moving to an unsettled territory meant putting one's self at even greater risk and necessitated even better self-defence. Thus, those peasants who settled new areas were doubly motivated to take up arms and to organize so that they could safeguard their families and their property.

The exact sequence of developments is hard to reconstruct. In all likelihood, things happened contemporaneously. It is clear, however, that many factors encouraged the people living on the territory that would become Ukraine to form semi-organized, quasi-military units. Whether it was because the castles near where they lived offered little protection or whether they needed to fend for themselves in newly settled lands, the local population gradually became militarized. With the people already armed, with the practice of gathering small companies to go on foraging expeditions, with the constant threat of Tatar raids, units of armed men stood ready to act. Thus, if a settlement was raided and people and goods were captured by a Tatar band, a unit of local men would react by setting out in pursuit. Since the raiding parties were relatively small, often just ten in number, a force of ten Ukrainian men on good horses would have a good chance of catching up to the raiders, defeating them, and recovering what had been captured. With the likelihood for raids being great and with time being of the essence when it came to responding to an attack, units that would be prepared to immediately defend a settlement or pursue the Tatar enemy came to have a more or less established existence. The group of guardians was set and ready to go; there was no need to discuss, deliberate, and select a volunteer force. It is probably no coincidence that the size of the units ready to defend the local population against Tatar attack was approximately the same as the size of the marauding bands that raided settlements in the Ukrainian area and the same as foraging parties.

The existence of established quasi-military units encouraged a new type of defence: the launching of preventative raids on Tatar cities and villages. Thus, by the early sixteenth century the groups of armed men who had originally been organized for purposes of protection were being used for aggressive, as well as defensive, purposes. We do not know if the attacks were originally seen as pre-emptive, or whether they were for revenge. Perhaps they were for the sake of booty, much like Turkish and Tatar attacks on Ukrainian settlements and somewhat akin to the foraging already practised on the steppe. The duma "Death of a Kozak in the Kodyma Valley" talks explicitly about a raid for the sake of booty. Kodyma is quite far south, near present-day Mykolaiv. In the period to which the dumy of this cycle refer, it was well inside the Crimean Khanate. Thus, although the text focuses on a single individual and his suffering, this person must have been part of an organized party, for no single person, no matter how brave, could undertake such an expedition alone. The supposition that the dying man was someone who perhaps became separated from his fellows is supported by the fact that, as the young man lays dying, an entire expedition of Kozaks arrives in ships and assumes the duty of burying his body and honouring his memory. The text translated here was first published by Mykola

Setting out on a campaign. Unknown artist, mid-twentieth century. Courtesy of Rodovid Press.

Kostomarov, who took it from a manuscript in the collection of Mykola Bilozerskyi.[10]

On one side of the valley, next to two black poplars,
A Kozak, shot and cut to pieces, is succumbing to mortal wounds,
And he calls upon the righteous judge in heaven;
He has by his side neither his father nor his mother,
His bullet wounds have filled with blood,
His sabre wounds have penetrated to his heart.
Then the Kozak curses the Kodyma Valley with three curses:
"May you, Kodyma Valley, be swamped by mosses and marshes,
So that you will not shine or glow in God's springtime,
This is the third time that I have ventured out upon you,
And not once have I been able to win Kozak booty here;
The first time I ventured here, I lost my raven horse,
And the second time I came here, I lost my closest friend,
Now I am here for the third time and I have to lay down my
    own Kozak head."
Then the black-winged eagles,
They who keep vigil over Kozaks,
They flew nigh,
They watched over the Kozak's soul.
Then the young Kozak remembers his father and his mother:
"Help me, oh father's and mother's prayer, help me get on my knees,
And pick up my rifle, seven spans long,
Help me pour in three measures of powder,
And ram in three lead bullets,
So that I may send the black-winged eagles,
Those who keep vigil over Kozaks,
Send them a great gift."
Well, then, the young Kozak,
The military companion,
Pours in three measures of powder,
And he rams in three bullets,
And he sends the black-winged eagles,
Those who keep vigil over Kozaks,
He sends them a great gift.
And he himself falls upon the earth with his noble heart,
He throws aside his rifle, suitable for a commander,
And he gazes at the sea one last time,

There he sees that the waters are abloom with three colours:
The first is colourful islands,
And the second is bright ships,
And the third is young Kozaks.
Then the Kozaks, the good young men,
Came to the Kodyma Valley,
They gathered much gold and silver,
They found the Kozak who had been shot and cut to pieces,
They dug a hole with their own sabres,
They fired off their rifles, seven spans long,
And they paid their respects to the Kozak,
Using their hats they piled up a burial mound, as high as seven mounds
    [would be],
And they set up a flag on top,
They celebrated the Kozak's glory.

The use of the word "Kozak" in the text above needs clarification. During the time when raiding parties were still quasi-military units, the men who took part in them were not called Kozaks. The term "Kozak" would evolve gradually, as will be discussed below. The text here is given as an example of attempts to collect booty. Such attempts did continue during the Kozak period, but they began early, long before the Kozaks became an organized force. Raids well into Tatar territory would seem to promise riches, but securing booty is not the fate of the hero of the song above. Quite the contrary, he experiences progressively greater losses with each foray and now all that he can hope for is proper burial. The main character's hopes are realized for a water-borne expedition, such as will be discussed later in this chapter, arrives and inters his body as custom demands.

Proper burial is extremely important to Ukrainian belief and features prominently in several duma texts. The idea that a body must be whole was, and still is, part of Ukrainian belief. When the Last Judgment occurs, people are supposed to arise in the flesh, as well as in spirit, and, while that flesh decays after death, all bones need to be preserved. This is one of the reasons that beggars who are missing arms or legs keep their bones and display them as they request alms. Seeing the bones along with the person of whom they were once a part stimulates sympathy and generosity, but that is not the only reason for preserving body parts – a major reason is to preserve all parts for burial. Because of the great importance of retaining all bones, being attacked by animals after death and having one's body parts scattered over the steppe becomes even more threatening than the horror of animals eating one's flesh. This is why the Kozak dying in the Kodyma Valley makes a special effort to chase off the birds gathering to feast on his body. A similar scene occurs in the duma "The Escape of Three Brothers from Azov." In some versions of this song, the youngest brother, as he succumbs to thirst and hunger, tries to chase the gathering animals away. In others, as in the version translated in the chapter on slavery, the young man asks the animals to bury his bones once they have feasted on his flesh. This they do by covering his remains with reeds, the only burial of which they are capable. Burial by one's fellow Kozaks is, of course, the most desired option, and this is what happens to the the man who dies in the Kodyma valley. He is fortunate to receive not only proper burial, but also a celebration honouring his life and death.

The proper interment of the body needed to be accompanied by the proper dispatch of the soul. Ukrainian belief holds that laments must be sung to help the soul leave this world and journey to the next.[11] It is possible that dumy originated as special laments that took care of special situations: the violent death of a young man well before his time.[12] While we cannot ascertain how and why Ukrainian epic poetry came to be, there is no doubt that dumy share many images with laments, as will be discussed in the section of everyday-life songs. Some dumy are called laments, such as the songs of men in captivity translated in the previous chapter. There are also songs that use bird symbolism to provide a man dying on the steppe with a substitute singer of laments. As noted in connection with the song about a falcon, a set of bird symbols or associations equates young men with falcons, young women with larks, and older women with cuckoos. In some versions of "The Escape of Three Brothers from Azov," such as the one published by Mykola Tsertelev, when the youngest brother dies, a cuckoo comes and laments over him, performing the function that a mother would have done had the man died at home. There is also a separate duma called "The Cuckoo's Lament," which is an extended version of the scene in "The Escape for Three Brothers from Azov." Here too a cuckoo takes the place of a female relative and performs the lament required to help the soul of the deceased make the transition into the afterlife. Kateryna Hrushevska found the text given here in the Revutskyi archives.[13]

On Sunday, very early in the morning, early at dawn,
A grey cuckoo came flying
And she alighted on a burial mound,

And she cooed mournfully,
"Oh, Kozak's head, oh, head of a brave youth,
Do you have a father or a mother in the lands of Rus,
Or do you have a younger sister?
If your father or your mother saw you,
They would send a white shroud for your death,
Or if your youngest sister would know,
Then she would get up early in the morning on Sunday,
She would lament mournfully over you,
She would coo like a cuckoo bird.
Oh, Kozak's head, oh, head of a brave youth!
You have been in foreign lands,
You have pranced on expensive horses,
And now you have no need for rich raiment,
No need for jet black horses;
All you need is God's salvation!"
Oh and the Kozak died!
But his glory will not die and will not perish,
From now and until eternity.

While songs, dumy included, sing of threatening or even tragic events, raids by people living on the territory that would become Ukraine were often quite successful. Many were lucrative, in fact. Armed groups from Ukrainian territory attacked Turkish and Tatar foragers, caravans, and other traders, and even settled areas. Hrushevskyi calls this situation "small-scale guerrilla warfare," and says that the "robbing of Tatars was becoming … a sport, and at the same time a source of income for the vanguard of Ukrainian colonization."[14] In the duma called "Ataman [Otaman] Matiash the Elder" a group of young men out on a such a foray do treat their expedition as sport – and come precariously close to meeting the same fate as the Kozak who died in the Kodyma Valley. There is some confusion as to their location because the Samara River is a tributary of the Dnipro and thus in the southeastern part of what is now Ukraine, while the Bug is to the northwest, in the direction of Poland, and Semen may refer to a local leader in the Savran area. The only place with the name of Kainar is in Moldova, which would indeed be under Tatar control at that time. As for Bravoslav, it may refer to Bratslav, but with the distortion of place names over time it is hard to place the city that is supposed to be the home of this expeditionary force. Whatever their geographic location, the company has ventured away from home and the young men are carefree.

When they camp for the night, they do not take proper precautions and are admonished by their older and wiser leader, Matiash. Exhibiting the bravado of youth, the young men turn the tables on Matiash and admonish him for being too much of a worrier. In their arrogance, they even imply that he lacks knowledge of proper Kozak behaviour. The territory where the men find themselves is a dangerous place and the elderly leader's precautions prove justified. The company is attacked at night and only Matiash, having kept his horse and his armaments by his side, is able to offer resistance. He proves successful, although the number of enemy that he is said to conquer is surely exaggerated. In the end, the young Kozaks acknowledge Matiash's wisdom and good advice. They even manage to acquire some "gold and silver" to justify the risk of undertaking their expedition. The version of this duma translated here was first published by Pavlo Zhytetskyi in 1893. He attributes it to a Kobzar Ivan living in the Myrhorod area.[15]

> At the mouth of the Samarka, the Bug,
> At the Semen fork in the river,
> There all the Samarka fields had been scorched by fire,
> Only two valleys full of thorns had not burned,
> Because they sheltered important guests.
> There twelve Kozaks stayed, men from Bravoslav, inexperienced men,
> They were under the command of Ataman Matiash the Elder.
> When evening came,
> The Kozaks started making fires with the brambles,
> They let their Kozak horses graze in the fields,
> They threw their Kozak saddles far to the side,
> They hid their seven-span rifles in the bushes.
> Ataman Matiash the Elder observed all this,
> And he spoke, saying:
> "Kozaks! Gentlemen! Sirs!
> Don't behave as if you haven't got a care,
> Don't let your Kozak horses go untethered,
> Don't take your Kozak saddles out from under your heads,
> Because this is the Kainar Valley
> Not far from here the Tatar lands lie."
> Then the Kozaks made fun of Ataman Matiash:
> "Maybe you, Ataman Matiash, old man, have not spent time among the
>   Kozaks,
> Maybe you have not eaten Kozak porridge,

Maybe you don't know the ways of the Kozaks,
Maybe that's why you are trying to scare us Kozaks, us young men from
    Bravoslav."
Then Ataman Matiash went far away from the other Kozaks,
He built a fire of brambles,
He saddled his horse,
And kept the horse nearby.
Then in the night, in the middle of the night, in the wee hours,
What came was not a fierce wind blowing,
It was Turks-janissaries riding into the valley from the field,
They took the twelve Kozaks from Bravoslav, the inexperienced men,
    prisoner.
Then Ataman Matiash, the old man, mounted his good horse,
He conquered six thousand Turks-janissaries,
He freed the twelve Kozaks from Bravoslav, the inexperienced men,
And he spoke, saying:
"Come to my aid, to the aid of an old man!"
Then the Kozaks mounted their horses,
They defeated four thousand godless Ottomans,
They took away their silver and their gold,
They rode quickly to the city of Sich,
In the city of Sich they were safe,
There they divided the silver and gold amongst themselves,
And they prayed to God on Ataman Matiash's behalf:
"May your mother be blessed in Heaven,
For having given birth to you!
For you spent time in the open field,
And you did not lose a single man from among us, the men from Bravoslav."

By the sixteenth century attacks on Tatars were such a regular activity that the booty captured in raids on caravans, settlements, and even Tatar cities was subject to a levy, similar to the levies imposed on the fish, animals, and honey collected on the steppe. Records from this period are better and, as might be expected, profit is never presented as a motive for attack. Rather, expeditions against Tatar camps and fortifications are justified either as a response to attacks already committed by the enemy or as preventative measures. The justification in the duma about "Ivan Sirko" is finding lost family members. The head of the family disappears and leaves his wife alone to care for their children. As the boys grow, they start asking questions about their father and, when they hear

that he disappeared while on an expedition, one of them, Petro, goes in
search of his parent. He heads for the city of Tor, present-day Slaviansk
in eastern Ukraine. While waiting to get news of his father, Petro and
his men camp for the night. The older Kozaks warn Petro to be cautious, but he too is overly confident and entrusts his page with the job
of looking after the horses while he himself goes to sleep. In the night
the page, who is presumably without weapons and on foot rather than
on horseback, is captured and buys his freedom by promising to kill his
master. The page fulfils his promise and beheads Petro Sirchenko. The
elderly mother is then left to mourn the disappearance of her husband
and the death of her son. This version of the "Widow of Ivan Sirko"
duma was also first published by Pavlo Zhytetskyi.[16]

In the city of Merefa there lived a widow,
An old woman,
Sirchykha, Ivan's wife.
She lived for seven years,
Without setting eyes on her husband.
All she had was two sons,
The first son was called Petro Sirchenko
And the second was called Roman Sirchenko.
She cared for them until they grew up,
What she hoped for was that they would remember and honour
    her after her death.
As Petro Sirchenko started to grow up,
He began to ask his elderly mother:
"Oh, Mother, elderly woman,
In all the time that I have been with you,
I have never laid eyes on my father, Ivan Sirko.
I want to know,
Where I can search for my father Ivan Sirko."
"Your father went to the ancient city of Tor,
And there he laid down his kozak head."
When Petro Sirchenko heard this,
He asked Pylyp Merefianskyi to join him,
And Holub Voloshyn was his page.
They journeyed to the old city of Tor,
They hailed the Ataman of Tor, Yatsyk Lokhvytskyi.
The Ataman of Tor, Yatsyk Lokhvytskyi, comes out of his house,
He speaks, and says,

He acknowledges Petro Sirchenko:
"Petro Sirchenko, why have you come here,
Are you perchance looking for your father?"
And Petro Sirchenko answers and says,
"Ataman of Tor, Yatsyk Lokhvytskyi,
I've been living for the past seven years,
And I have not seen my father, Ivan Sirko"
Then Petro Sirchenko and his Kozaks take their leave,
They arrive at the green thorn thicket.
The Kozaks speak to Petro Sirchenko and they say:
"Sirchenko, Petro, don't be careless,
Don't let your kozak horses wander away from you."
But Petro Sirchenko does not believe this,
He lies down by the bushes and the thicket and rests, .
He lets the horses wander as they please,
He just sends Holub Voloshyn to look after the horses.
The Turks see this,
And they run out from the bushes, from the thickets,
And they captured Holub Voloshyn and imprisoned him,
And they spoke, saying:
"Holub Voloshyn, we do not want your raven horses,
We want the sort of information
That will enable us to kill your young master."
And Holub Voloshyn spoke, saying:
"Turks!
If you will set me free,
Then I myself will take his head off his shoulders."
The Turks heard this information,
And they let Holub Voloshyn go.
Holub Voloshyn approaches Petro Sirchenko,
And he speaks, saying:
"Sirchenko, Petro, young sir,
Mount a fine steed,
And hurry to ride amongst the Turks"
No sooner had Petro Sirchenko ridden out amongst the Turks,
Then Holub Voloshyn took his head off from his shoulders.
Then the Turks surrounded Pylyp Merefianskyi,
And they took his head off of his shoulders,
Then chopped his Kozak body and they hacked it.
The elder Kozaks became aware of this,

They mounted their fine horses,
They defeated the Turks,
They gathered the Kozak's body,
And they brought it back to their ancient fortress,
They dug the soil with their sabres,
And they carried the soil with their hats and the skirts of their coats,
And they buried the Kozak's body.
The Ataman of Tor, Yatsko Lokhvytskyi, hears about this,
He sends a letter to the old widow, to Sirchykha, Ivan's widow
    in the city of Merefa,
Sirchykha, Ivan's widow, reads the letter,
And she speaks, saying,
As she falls prostrate upon the damp earth,
"Three great sorrows have befallen me,
The first is that I have lived seven years
Without setting eyes on Ivan Sirko,
The second is that Petro Sirchenko is no longer alive in this world,
And the third is that Roman Sirchenko is dying."

The text here presents Roman, the other Sirchenko son, as also on his deathbed. Why he is about to die is not explained. Perhaps the impending death of this young man is meant to underscore the suffering of the mother.

There are several other dumy about men on foreign territory. Some of these expeditions are motivated and others are not. No reason is given for the excursion to the region of the Samara River in which three brothers lose their lives. All we see is the aftermath of what appears to have been an armed conflict, one undertaken by a volunteer army that resulted in a military engagement large enough to devastate the landscape with fire. Who started the battle is not clear, but the song tells us that it was disastrous for the young men from Ukraine venturing into a territory beyond the Dnipro River. There are many things going on in this text. The threat of slavery looms large even though the men are mortally wounded. Fear of captivity was certainly great. The belief in the power of parental prayers, a motif that reflects the influence of the church on minstrels and minstrelsy, also figures prominently. The text translated below was recorded by Filaret Kolessa from the kobzar Mykhailo Kravchenko.[17]

Oh, all the Samara fields have turned black,
They have been burnt by bright fires,

The only thing that has not burned
By the River Samarka,
Are three small plots,
Three green ravines.
The only thing that has not been burned are three brothers,
Three fair turtledoves,
They are wounded and they are shot and they rest,
And the reason that they rest
Is that they are succumbing
To the wounds, made by cuts and by shooting.
Oh, and then the oldest brother calls out,
He speaks to the middle brother with words,
He sheds copious tears:
"Oh, brother, my middle brother,
Brother, do the right thing,
Either from the river Samarka,
Or from the well Saltanka,
Draw some cool water,
Sprinkle my wounds, my wounds from cuts and from firearms,
Cool them with the water."
"Oh, my dear brother,
Fair as a turtledove,
Brother, don't you know me;
Brother, are you trying to make fun of me,
Were we not cut by the same sabre,
Were we not shot with the same bullets?
I have on my body,
Nine wounds from cuts that are wide,
And four wounds from bullets that are deep …"
"Oh, brother, let's do the right thing,
Let us ask our youngest brother,
Let our youngest brother,
Let him take heed,
Let him get up, let him at least get on his knees,
Let him take his military trumpet,
Let him play it, play it well.
Then other Kozaks will hear us,
They will ride up to where we are,
They will attend to our death,
And they will bury our Kozak bodies, our young bodies,

They will bury them in the open field."
The youngest brother hears what they say,
And he speaks to his brothers, saying:
"Oh, brothers, dear brothers,
Fair as the turtledoves,
It was not the janissaries' bullet that shot us,
It was our father's and our mother's prayer that cursed us.
When we were riding to join the volunteer army,
Riding away from our father and our mother,
We did not ask our father, our mother, or our kin,
We did not ask them for their blessing.
Oh, when we rode past the church, past the house of God,
We did not remove our hats from our heads,
And we did not ask merciful God,
We did not request God's protection.
Even if I play the Turkish trumpet,
Even if I play it mournfully,
Then only the Turks and the janissaries,
Only the godless Muslims,
Only they will hear us,
Only they will hear our Kozak music,
And they will ride to where we are,
And they will attack our bodies,
They will chop our bodies and cut them,
Or they will take us into harsh captivity.
Brothers, dear brothers, let us,
Let us brothers, fair as turtledoves,
Let us die here.
We will never see our father, or our mother, or our dear relatives,
We will never behold them with our eyes."
Oh, in the sky,
A black cloud began to approach,
And in the open field,
The young Kozaks began to die.
They died in the open field, by the River Samarka.
May their memory be eternal, oh God,
And may God send to all who are listening,
To this dear company, this beloved group,
May God send them many years,
And until the end of time!

The duma "Three Brothers by the River Samarka" and the other texts translated above artistically express the reality of life in what would become Ukraine. In the period of small-scale expeditions, the Ukrainian units were heavily dependent on their leader and his wisdom and experience. A wise leader like Matiash could save his men; an overly confident man like Kovalenko could expose his charges to capture and enslavement. Expeditionary units were small and heroes could easily become separated from their comrades. Success was possible, but the threat of failure loomed large. The horse was of paramount importance and making sure that one's mount was ready at a moment's notice was crucial. Ukrainian fighters had no uniforms and their weapons were not standard issue. Good weapons gave their owner an important advantage, but any equipment that a fighter might use had to be provided by the man himself. His arms were his personal property: no starosta or hospodar issued equipment. A man acquired his arms, his clothing, his horse as best as he could, often through capturing them on the field of battle. An enemy's clothing was fair game and we are told that, if sumptuous clothing was found on a deceased combatant, the victor would take it and don it himself. Men were not squeamish about putting on other people's garments and clothing was used to intimidate the enemy rather than to visually distinguish one group of combatants from another.

Kozak Holota is the quintessential rag-tag fighter who, despite his shabby appearance, proves to be a most adept warrior, able to defeat his enemy and acquire the adversary's rich clothing. When we encounter him, he is riding alone near the city of Kiliia, an Ottoman stronghold which is quite far south, near Odesa. Because Holota is so deep into enemy territory, he is most likely a member of a raiding party. Why he ventures out alone is not stated. We do hear that he forgoes possible attacks on villages and that his goal is Kiliia itself, presumably because it is a far richer target. We also learn that Holota looks terrible. Every item of his clothing is worn to the point of being nearly useless and its bad condition is underscored by irony: the item, be it the hat or the footwear or the cloak, is first described as' being very fine – and then its true state is revealed. As Holota rides along, he is spotted by a rich Tatar who sees in him a chance to make some money: he will capture the Kozak and sell him as a slave, taking his horse and his weapons and selling those as well. The Tatar, probably misled by the young man's shabby appearance, thinks that Holota will be easy prey. He himself dresses for battle in splendid clothing, presumably to intimidate his adversary. The Tatar rides out and the two men size each other up verbally. As it turns out, it is the Tatar who is easy prey and Holota shoots and kills him handily. In the end, Holota is the one to profit for he acquires the Tatar's sumptuous outfit. The text here was recorded by Panteleimon Kulish from the lirnyk Arkhyp Nykonenko.[18]

Oh, along the field, along the Kilian field,
Along the well-worn path to Horodynsk,
There a Kozak named Holota was riding.
He feared neither fire, nor the sword, nor the viscous swamp.
As it happens, the Kozak was dressed in fine clothing.
He was dressed in three stunning garments.
One was bad and the other was no good,
And the third was not suitable for wearing in a pigsty.
And as for his footwear – it is shoes of fine leather,
And footcloths of silk –
They are like women's washcloths,
And the shoes are like women's felt boots.
And the Kozak wears a stunning hat,
With a hole on top;
It is sewn with grass
And lined with the wind,
Where the wind blows, it wafts on through,
It keeps the young Kozak cool.
Well, the Kozak rides and he wanders,
He attacks neither city nor village,
While he eyes the city of Kiliia.
In the city of Kiliia there sits a Tatar, a bearded one,
He walks through his chambers,
And he speaks to his Tatar wife:
"Oh, wife, oh Tatar wife,
Are you thinking what I am thinking?
And do you see what I see?"
And she said, "Oh, my Tatar husband, grey-haired and bearded,
I see only that you walk before me through our chambers,
I have no idea what you are thinking and contemplating."
And he said, "Oh Tatar woman,
What I see is that in the field, it is not an eagle that is soaring,
It is Kozak Holota riding about on his fine horse.

I want to capture him alive,
And take him to the city of Kiliia,
And show him off before the great gentlemen and the pashas,
And sell him for an untold number of gold coins."
And saying this, he dons his fine clothing,
He pulls on his boots,
He puts a velvet cap on his head,
And he mounts his horse.
And he chases after Kozak Holota without a care.
Well, Kozak Holota knows Kozak customs well,
He looks at the Tatar askance, as a wolf would,
And he says, "Tatar, oh, Tatar,
What are you after?
Is it my shining weapons,
Or is it my raven horse,
Or do you want me, the young Kozak?"
"I," he answered, "want your shining weapons,
And even more so your raven horse,
And most of all I want you, young Kozak.
I want to capture you alive,
And sell you in the city of Kiliia,
I want to show you off before great lords and pashas,
And I want to sell you for many gold coins,
For costly garments without number."
Well, Kozak Holota knows Kozak customs well,
And he looks as the Tatar askance, as a wolf would,
"Oh," he says, "Tatar, you grey-haired and bearded one,
It seems that wisdom is not your strength.
You haven't taken a Kozak captive
And already you are counting the money that you will earn for him.
You have not been amongst the Kozaks,
You haven't eaten Kozak gruel,
And you do not know Kozak customs."
Having said this,
He raised himself up in the saddle,
He poured in gunpowder without measure,
And he sent the Tatar a gift right into his chest.
Even before the Kozak could properly take aim,
The cursed Tatar has already fallen off his horse.

The Kozak does not trust the Tatar,
He rides up to him,
He strikes him with his mace between the shoulders,
And when he takes a good look – his [the Tatar's] spirit has departed.
Then he heeds well,
He pulls off the Tatar's boots,
He puts them on his Kozak feet;
He takes off the Tatar's clothing,
And he puts in on his own Kozak shoulders;
He takes off the velvet hat
And puts it on his Kozak head;
He took the Tatar horse by the reins,
And he took it to the city of Sich,
And there he drank and celebrated,
And he praised and lauded the field by the city of Kiliia:
"Oh, Kilian field,
May you be green in summer and in winter,
Because you have aided me in the hour of my misfortune,
May God grant that all Kozaks drink and celebrate,
That they have pleasant thoughts,
That they take even better booty than I did,
That they trample their enemy underfoot!"
Glory will not fade and will not perish,
From now and through the ages!
God grant us many years!

As Hrushevskyi writes, in this period "a small-scale border war in forage areas and small expeditions and attacks carried out by the population itself, with the friendly neutrality or even encouragement of the local administration, and the practice of pursuing Tatars after they attacked turned imperceptibly into military campaigns against the Tatar lands organized by the local administration."[19] Slowly but surely the groundwork was being laid for the establishment of the Kozaks as a distinct social entity. The progressive organization of the population for military purposes also led gradually to the formation of a rudimentary national identity. People living on the territory of what would become Ukraine began thinking of themselves as a unit. They looked beyond small village forces organized for self defence and saw a polity.

The Development of a Kozak Identity

The development of the Kozak identity is complex and its history hard to trace. In dumy, the term "Kozak" is consistently used for Ukrainian combatants. This is a retrospective view, one characteristic of the nineteenth century, when the songs were collected. During the period of small-scale forays and campaigns, the term was just coming into use and was applied, not to heroic fighters, as Kozaks are presented in dumy, but to marginal elements, involved in undesirable, if not outright criminal, behaviour. The term first appears in Lithuanian letters to Tatar leaders, where it is used to mean men outside of civil authority, vagabonds, lawless individuals. Lithuanian officials in charge of Ukrainian territories, when they received complaints from Tatar rulers about attacks on caravans and others misdeeds, would typically dismiss them by blaming Kozaks. Trying to maintain good relations with their neighbours, they would say that any transgression was the responsibility of "Kozaks," persons outside the law, for whom they could not be responsible.[20] Such excuses were usually accompanied by promises to catch the perpetrators of the attack and punish them for their illegal behaviour, promises which were not always kept. According to Hrushevskyi, while many explanations for the origin of the term "Kozak" exist, and we cannot determine the etymological source of the word with certainty, we do know that in the late fifteenth and early sixteenth centuries "Kozak" meant a landless and unsettled person, in other words, steppe riffraff. A Kozak was "a robber of the steppe, a taker of booty,"[21] and the name "Kozak" was a pejorative term, making it easy to label anyone who misbehaved, such as the perpetrator of an unauthorized raid, a Kozak. The image of Kozak Holota from the duma which bears his name may be a remnant of the idea of a Kozak as a vagabond. While it turns out that Holota is a most able fighter and his appearance belies his true abilities, there is no doubt that he is dressed like steppe riffraff. He is far into enemy territory, perhaps precisely on an unauthorized raid. It should also be noted that his name, Holota, could be a proper name and it could also refer to rabble. As a collective noun, *holota* translates literally as "the naked ones" and was used to refer to the poorest of the poor, the dregs of society.

Whether the men to whom the label "Kozak" was applied were truly as lawless as Lithuanian authorities claimed is another matter. They may indeed have been lawless at first, especially when made desperate by economic circumstances, but by the time they appear in surviving documents, they seem to be more organized. Furthermore, there is fairly ample evidence that various government officials such as border starostas would make use of Kozaks for both defensive purposes and for manpower in their own raids on Tatar territories.[22] The process by which rag-tag bands became an organized force was slow and the border starostas might well have played a role in the creation of a structured Kozakdom precisely by employing these men in organized combat missions. The documentation of this process is meagre and political exigency seems to have determined whether Kozaks were seen as rabble or as defenders of the land. By the end of the sixteenth century, however, Kozaks were indeed an organized force who saw themselves as such. Their basic unit was the squad of ten men, each lead by an *otaman*, the term once used for leaders responsible for local defence. The squads were grouped into companies of one hundred men called *sotni*, each lead by a *sotnyk*. These, in turn, came under regiments or *polky*, each with a colonel in command. By this point the Kozaks had a headquarters on Bazavluk Island in the mouth of the Chortomlyk River and they were ruled by an elected leader called a *hetman*.[23]

The particulars of Kozak organization help us understand the more formal call to battle that we see in texts such as the duma "Ivas Konovchenko," presented in the chapter on minstrels and minstrelsy. This song starts with an account of the assembling of a military force. By this point the Kozak army is big enough to be commanded by a colonel who is gathering men for an expedition that will venture quite a distance from Cherkasy, the home city of the hero of this song. Tiahynia, present-day Bender or Bendery, is currently a part of Moldova and far to the east and south of the hero's place of origin. While the number of men assembled for the raid, like the number of enemy whom the hero fights, is surely exaggerated, the song confirms that, by this point, Kozak expeditionary forces could be quite large. Historical records also confirm that, by the end of the sixteenth century, Kozak attacks had become campaigns. They also attest that Kozaks did indeed travel considerable distances.

It is also significant that this song presents being a Kozak as prestigious. By the time reflected in this song, being a Kozak is not equivalent to being a vagabond; quite the contrary, a Kozak is someone whom others respect and look up to. A man who has served in a Kozak expedition is not a highwayman and a robber; he is the defender of the Christian faith. In the first part of this duma, the colonel assembling his forces uses the prospect of winning glory in battle as a way to encourage men to

The dying Kozak and his horse. P. Shtorm, "A Fire Burns on the Hill," mid-twentieth century. Courtesy of Rodovid Press.

enlist, and it is glory and paths to glory that cause an argument between the hero and his mother. Ivas Konovchenko insists that he wants to do as the colonel suggests: he wants to establish his prowess on the field of battle, thereby winning honour and social prestige for himself. The mother offers the counterargument that being a farmer and feeding Kozaks is just as respectable and just as valid a path to a position of honour in society. Of course, Ivas chooses the military option and this prompts his mother to curse him which, in turn, leads to his downfall on the field of battle. While Ivas sees joining the Kozaks as a way to achieve honour and glory, it should be noted that many of the men to whom Colonel Filon addresses his call are not respected members of society. Quite the contrary – they are riffraff, the men who are wasting time drinking and playing knucklebones. Beer-brewers and wine-makers are also called to drop what they do and join the expedition. Beer brewing and wine making may have been decent occupations but, since alcohol is so closely linked to trouble in Ukrainian song, perhaps they were not seen as such. In short, all the men addressed by occupation – or lack thereof – are not upstanding citizens. The colonel tells these men that becoming a Kozak will allow them to overcome their lowly position and make a useful contribution to society. His words seem to mark the period of transition when Kozaks switched from being riffraff to being men admired by others.

The Kozak and His Horse

A pivotal figure in the duma about Ivas Konovchenko is his horse. Horses deserve special attention in terms of the nature of steppe warfare. In the Konovchenko duma, the Kozak forces consist of both cavalry and infantry. This is a characteristic of the later, more developed fighting style, when Kozak forces consisted of large numbers of men, some of whom would be foot soldiers. But having a good mount provides a considerable advantage over fighting on foot, which is why Ivas's first request to his mother is for a good and, as it turns out, very expensive horse. If horses provided an advantage during the period reflected in the Konovchenko duma, they were an absolute necessity in the conditions that characterized earlier forms of combat. If a settlement was attacked by a Tatar raiding party, the only way to give chase was on horseback; trying to pursue mounted raiders in any other way was pointless. Foraging in bands required horses, both to transport the proceeds of the work in the steppe back to the settlement and to escape attack, should the foraging party encounter Tatars. Raids on Tatar caravans or settlements had to be made on horseback, both so the attackers could quickly escape once they had secured their prize and so that they could carry away their booty. The Kozak dying in the Kodyma Valley names his raven horse as one of his great losses, and the Tatar looking to capture Holota views his horse as a valuable prize. In both the duma "Otaman Matiash the Elder" and the one about Petro Sirchenko looking for his lost father, letting horses roam free at night rather than keeping them saddled and ready proves disastrous. The horse was crucial to being a Kozak and the iconic image of Kozak Mamai always features Mamai's horse as a prominent part of the painting. Other attributes may be optional, but the horse is obligatory to the picture of Mamai. With the crucial role that the horse played in the lives of people living on the Ukrainian territories in the fourteenth through sixteenth centuries, it is no wonder, then, that horses feature prominently in many dumy.

The horse was the hero's constant companion and virtually his alter ego. This is true not only of the Ivas Konovchenko song, where the horse becomes so much a part of the hero's military identity that no one will ride the animal after the hero's death, leading Ivas's mother to immediately recognize the meaning of the riderless animal. Historical songs also speak of the horse as the Kozak's most trusted companion. The song entitled "A Dying Kozak and His Horse," translated in conjunction with death-wedding beliefs, presents the horse keeping vigil over the young man's last moments. The hero himself, even though he is dying, expresses his appreciation of the horse's dedication. He then dispatches the animal to tell his family of his tragic fate. The horse does as told and is pictured as delivering the message in a human voice. Other historical songs also feature horses who can speak to their masters. While horses could not literally talk, ascribing this ability to them underscores the closeness between animal and human. Kozak and horse surely did communicate, though not in words. The song translated below is an eloquent testimony to the importance of horses. It was published by Antonovych and Drahomanov and taken from a Kyiv manuscript collection:[24]

Oh, in Vilhov, at the market
A young Kozak walks the stalls,
He walks through the market, and leads his horse,
He leads his horse and he speaks to him:

Horse, oh, my horse, I will sell you,
I will sell you for a hundred gold pieces,
For a hundred gold pieces and a barrel of wine."
"Master, oh, my master, don't sell me,
Don't sell me, just think about me,
How Turks and Tatars were chasing us,
How I jumped and leapt across the whole of the Danube,
Jumped across the entire Danube, and didn't even get my hooves wet,
Didn't let the sharp sword [wound you] young man."

The speaking horse makes it clear that, if he did not exist, the young man would be dead, or at the very least a Turkish captive. Why the horse is so dedicated to his foolish young master is not clear, but other versions of this song do give Kozak's motivation for selling the animal. In these, the young man admits to having spent all his money on liquor. This is what is forcing him to sell his most prized possession – his horse.

The horse is part of the hero's identity in the duma "Khvedir the Man without Kin." Here, as in the song "The Three Brothers by the River Samarka," the narrative begins with a description of the sad outcome of a conflict. We do not know if conflict was part of an expedition by a large force or a foray by a small raiding party, although the involvement of the tsar and the mention of a hetman does make this seem like an organized campaign. In any case, we are told that the devastation that resulted from a battle that preceded the action of the song was enormous, and as a result, the hero of the song lies dying. Everyone around him is already dead and only his horse, his faithful companion, keeps vigil over his final moments. Suddenly the hero's page approaches and, of course, it is the horse that points out to him where Khvedir lies. The hero seeks to ensure his own legacy by having his page take his place in battle. The servant is of small stature and the hero seems concerned about the young man's ability to take on the role of a combatant. To see if the page can be a Kozak, Khvedir asks him to take his armour and his clothes and to put them on. Most important, of course, is the test of mounting the hero's horse and proving that he is a worthy rider. The page does what is requested successfully and the hero instructs his servant on the manner in which he should ride out to join the Kozaks. Again the page does as he is told. When the Kozaks see him, the first thing they recognize is Khvedir's horse, a virtually intrinsic part of the hero, and they accuse the young man of acquiring the horse by illegitimate means. When they learn what has happened, they bury

Khvedir's body with honour. The text below was recorded by Porfyrii Martynovych from Ivan Kravchenko-Kriukovskyi.[25]

At the behest, at the behest of the tsar,
Many troops were destroyed,
They were cut and they were smitten with mortal wounds.
Among the corpses, there is not a soul left alive,
Only Khvedir the man of ill fate,
The one without kin and without a clan,
Injured with fatal gunshot wounds,
Wounded with deep cuts,
Only he remains barely alive.
There is no one at his side,
Just his raven horse with the spiky mane who stands at his head and keeps
    vigil over his dying moments.
Through the corpses the page Yarema comes walking.
He catches sight of the raven horse with the spiky mane,
And he rushes to that spot,
Catching Khvedir the man of ill fate still barely alive,
He dismounts from his horse,
And he speaks with words, to Khvedir the man of ill fate, the man
    without kin,
He weeps bitterly and he cries,
He sheds copious tears:
"Hail to you, oh hail Khvedir, man of ill fortune, man without kin and
    without clan,
Are you asleep, are you dreaming?
Are you succumbing to your mortal wounds?"
"Oh," he says, "my page, you who are small and short in stature,
I am not asleep and I am not dreaming,
I am succumbing to my mortal wounds.
Oh, my page, you who are small and short in stature,
If you were to know Kozak customs well,
You would saddle my raven horse and mount him,
You would prance before me,
And demonstrate your Kozak valour, your manliness."
When the page, the small one, short in stature, hears this from Khvedir the
    man of ill fate, the man without kin,
He immediately mounts the horse,
And he prances before him.

Then Khvedir the man of ill fate speaks to the page Yarema saying,
"Oh my page, you who are small and of short stature,
I bequeath you, upon my death, my red armour,
And my caftan, embroidered with gold from the hem to the collar,
Don my clothing,
Then mount my good horse with the spiky mane,
And prance before me,
So that I may determine,
If you are worthy of riding amidst the Kozaks."
Then the page, the small one, short of stature, hears this,
He takes the red armour,
And the caftan embroidered with gold from the hem to the collar,
And he removes them from Khvedir,
And he puts them on himself,
And he mounts the raven horse with the spiky mane,
And prances before him,
He salutes him as Kozak custom requires.
Then Khvedir the man of ill fate, the man without kin, speaks, saying,
"I thank you, oh Merciful God,
That my animal with not fall into hands of a worthless man.
He will pray to God for me and ask for mercy,
And Merciful God will favour him always."
And then Khvedir the man of ill fate, the man without kin, addressed the
    page Yarema saying,
"Oh, my page, small and short of stature,
Take your own horse by the reins,
And mount my raven steed,
And ride quickly,
And ride with haste,
Ride along the Bazavluh Meadow and along the Dnipro Slavutych River.
When you hear swans call, then answer,
If you hear the sound of river pirates, then hide,
And when you see Kozaks coming along Dnipro Slavutych, then show
    yourself,
Take off your cap,
And execute a low bow,
Prance before them on your good horse,
Do all the things that Kozak custom requires."
And the page Yarema paid good heed,
He mounts the horse,

He rides quickly and he hurries along the Dnipro, through the Bazavluh
    Valley,
He emerges for the Bazavluh Meadow,
He looks at the Dnipro carefully,
And he sees that a Kozak vessel is sailing on the Dnipro;
When he catches sight of that vessel,
He removes his cap,
He executes a low bow.
And the Kozaks catch sight of him,
And they approach the shore.
Then the leader of the Kozaks, the Zaporozhian hetman,
Sees Yarema with his eyes,
And says to him with words:
"The horse on which you prance before me is not yours,
You have the horse that belongs to Khvedir the man of ill fate, the man
    without kin.
Perhaps you have killed him, perhaps you have sold him,
Perhaps you have surrendered him alive and allowed him to be taken
    prisoner?"
"Well," he said, "leader of the Kozaks, Zaporozhian hetman,
I neither killed him nor did I sell him,
And I did not surrender him alive to be taken prisoner.
It was at the behest, at the behest of the tsar,
That many troops were destroyed,
And they were shot full of mortal wounds,
And they were cut with deep wounds,
And I was there amongst all those corpses,
And I came upon Khvedir the man of ill fate,
The man without kin,
With mortal gunshot wounds,
And with deep sword cuts,
I found him barely alive,
And he bequeathed to me his horse,
And then he gave up his life,
Saying that I should give a low bow on his behalf to all the Kozaks, the
    Zaporozhians."
Then the father of the troops, the Kozak leader,
The military hetman,
He did the right thing,

He selected fifty men from amongst the Kozaks,
And he sent them through the Bazavluh Meadow,
So that they would find that body,
So that they would locate Khvedir the man of ill fate, the man without kin.
And the Kozaks heeded well,
They rode through the Bazavluh Meadow,
And they looked for the body of Khvedir the man of ill fate, the man
    without kin.
On the third day they found him,
And they lifted up his body on red silk,
And they washed his mortal wounds,
And they dug the soil with their spears,
And they buried the body of the brave Kozak properly,
And they carried the earth in their hats,
And they built a high burial mound,
And they erected an oaken marker at the head,
Then they celebrated his memory,
With that which they had:
It was dry military crackers that they ate.
Therefore, even though Khvedir, the man of ill fate, the man without kin,
Lay down his Kozak head by the Dnipro River,
His Kozak fame will not die and will not perish,
Neither amongst the noblemen,
Nor amongst the Kozaks,
Nor amongst all the Orthodox Christians.
Oh Lord, give strength to all the people,
All the tsar's people, all the people of the Empire,
And, Lord, please grant long life to all those who are listening,
Grant them many years, until the end of time.

There is an inconsistency in this song which speaks to the importance of the horse. At the very beginning, the page Yarema is pictured
as walking across the field of battle, looking among the wounded for
his master. When he does find Khvedir, the text says that he dismounts
and attends to the dying Kozak. Needless to say, Yarema cannot both
walk and dismount. As a page, the young man probably did not have a
horse but, in the duma world view, leading actors are so closely associated with horses that the singer automatically pictures Yarema as getting off one.

The Kozak and His Clothing

Kozaks had to supply not only their own mounts, but also their own clothing, so when Khvedir the Man without Kin succumbs to his wounds on the steppe, he bequeaths to his page not only his horse, but also his attire. While not as prominent on the emotional landscape of dumy as the horse, clothing does deserve comment. Kozaks did not have uniforms even when they became an organized military force. As they themselves evolved from groups of armed villagers, so their clothing evolved from village attire. There were certain consistent features to Kozak dress, as books on the history of costume have noted.[26] The need for comfort influenced what men wore. Desirable clothing consisted of garments that were practical and suitable for riding horses, engaging in armed conflict, and enduring prolonged exposure to the elements out on the steppe. Beyond practicality, what was desirable was fine and sumptuous clothing. Portraits of hetmans, or Kozak leaders, show striking garments. Fine clothing could be purchased, it could be received as a gift, and it could also be won in battle, either as one's share of booty or by removing the clothing from a fallen adversary, as was the case in the "Kozak Holota" duma translated above. The quality of one's garments indicated status because, during the distribution of clothing as booty, better garments were given to those in higher office. Since clothing could be removed from one's foe, fine garments indicated success in battle and could serve to intimidate the adversary. According to Seng, clothing was an important indicator of status in the Ottoman world, and this would further contribute to how a combatant might be assessed.[27] Thus, having opulent array was not just something that provided personal pleasure: it offered a distinct advantage on the battlefield. Kozaks did not use uniforms to mark the fact that they were a military unit, but they did use clothing to indicate status and prowess and to intimidate their enemies.

Because so much importance was assigned to lavish clothing, the minstrels who performed dumy and possibly also their predecessors, the dumy's composers, could use clothing to talk about appearances and to question what determines the true worth of a man. The best example of a duma that shows how people tend to judge a man by his dress rather than by his qualities as a person is the song about Khvesko Handzha (sometimes given as Fesko Khanzha) Andyber. In this text, the hero shows up at an inn poorly dressed. Three noblemen referred to as dukes, men with Ukrainian surnames but prosperous enough under Polish rule to be more than able to buy a poor man a drink, react to the Kozak with disdain and refuse to buy him anything precisely because he looks shabby. One of the dukes does feel a touch of compassion for the bedraggled man and asks the barmaid to get the Kozak some cheap beer. The hero accepts the beer, downs it in one gulp, and gets slightly tipsy. This causes him to reveal his true nature. He bangs his beer mug on the table with such force that his physical strength becomes apparent. He takes out a money pouch and orders his own drinks. He then summons his men and has them dress him in his fine clothing. When he appears in garments that correspond to his true position in the Kozak hierarchy, the noblemen and the barmaid grovel before him, offering him liquor and their companionship. Andyber accepts the drinks and pours them on his clothing, saying that the garments deserve the alcohol because it is they that are being honoured and not he himself. The text which follows was translated from a version first published by Amvrosii Metlynskyi.[28]

Oh, along the fields, along the Kilian Fields,
Along the path well-trodden by the Horde,
A poor Kozak was riding, was riding for seven years plus four,
In those years he had lost three mounts, three raven-black horses.
And the Kozak, the poor wretch,
He wears a cloak woven out of bast,
And a waist sash made of hops,
He has on Saffiano leather boots,
Through which you can see his heels and his toes,
Wherever he steps, he leaves bare footprints;
And the Kozak also has on a conical hat –
Which has a hole on top,
It is sewn with silk,
And lined with the blustery wind,
As for its sides – they are long gone.
Well, the Kozak, the poor wretch, arrives at the city of Kiliia,
And he does not ask where he can camp,
Where he can pasture his horse,
He enquires about the new inn,
And about the young innkeeper,
Nastia, the tavern maid:
She is the one who looks after us Kozaks, even though she gets mad at us.
As he walks along the streets of Kiliia,
He listens and he pays attention,

To see if anyone is preparing to go to Zaporizhia to party,
But the only ones who are preparing to go
Are three dukes, three rich men,
They are planning to go to the tavern,
To drink mead and distilled horilka [Ukrainian for vodka].
Well, then the Kozak took great care,
He went and rented himself a room in that tavern;
Then he went and sat by the stove,
Went to warm his Kozak shoulders.
Then the dukes, the rich men entered the tavern,
They sat down at the table,
They ordered a pail of mead and one of distilled horilka.
The first rich duke was Havrylo Dovhopolenko of Pereiaslav,
The second was Voitenko of Nizhyn,
And the third was Zolotarenko of Chernihiv.
They don't greet the Kozak, the poor wretch,
They don't offer him a glass of mead,
And they don't offer him a shot glass of horilka;
Well, the Kozak, the poor wretch, he looks askance at the dukes.
One duke, one rich man, was more cautious,
That was Havrylo Dovhopolenko of Pereiaslav,
He took a small coin from his pocket,
He handed it over carefully to Nastia the tavern maid,
And he said, speaking quietly,
"Hey," he said, "young innkeeper, Nastia, the tavern maid,
You get mad at the poor Kozaks, but you look after them,
If you would please do a good deed,
You would accept this coin,
You would go down into the cellar
And bring up at least some cheap beer,
And give it to this Kozak, this poor wretch,
So that he could get a bit of alcohol in his stomach."
Well then Nastia the tavern maid took the coin,
She poured out some mead and some distilled horilka,
And she put a mug into the poor Kozak's hands.
Well, the Kozak, the poor wretch, took the mug by the handle,
And before you could blink, the bottom was dry.
Well, then the Kozak, the poor wretch,
As he started to feel the effects of Kozak intoxication,
He took his mug and started to bang it on the table,

And the dukes' glasses and shot glasses,
They started to fly off the table;
Well, as the Kozak, the poor wretch,
As he started to feel more intoxicated,
He took a solid gold axe out,
Out from under his cloak,
And he offered to give it to the innkeeper as surety for a pail of mead.
The dukes, the rich men,
Started to speak to each other quietly, to whisper,
And they spoke softly to the tavern maid,
"Nastia, young tavern maid,
Nastia, young woman,
Don't let this Kozak, this poor wretch,
Try to buy back this surety, this pledge from you,
Let him work instead for us, the rich dukes,
Let him pasture our oxen for us,
And let him fire up your oven for you."
When the Kozak, the poor wretch,
When he started to hear these words,
Then he sat down at the end of the table,
He took out his money pouch,
And then for Nastia the tavern maid,
Nastia the young woman,
He started to cover the whole table with gold coins.
Then the dukes, the rich men,
When the saw the gold coins in his possession,
Then they started to greet him,
And to toast him with a glass of mead,
And a shot glass of horilka.
And the tavern maid, the young woman,
Nastia the innkeeper,
She spoke to him in a whisper,
"Oh, Kozak," she said, "Kozak!
Did you have breakfast today and did you have your dinner?
Let us, you and me, sit down together and have breakfast,
Or let us have our dinner."
Then the Kozak, the poor wretch,
He walked about the tavern,
And he opened the door to his room,
And he looked at the swift rivers,

And he called out, he called well,
"Oh, rivers," he said, "oh you tributary rivers,
You helpers of the Dnipro,
Either help me out,
Or take me with you!"
Well, then one Kozak appeared,
And he carries expensive garments,
He puts them on his [Andyber's] Kozak shoulders;
And a second Kozak comes and he carries boots of Saffiano leather,
And he puts them on his Kozak feet;
And a third Kozak comes,
And he carries a Kozak hat,
And he puts it on his Kozak head.
Then the rich dukes,
They started to speak quietly and to whisper:
"Brothers, this is not some Kozak,
This is not some poor wretch,
This is Khvesko Khanzha Andyber,
The hetman of the Zaporozhians!"
[Realizing who he was] they said to him – "Move over closer to us
And we will bow low before you.
And we will discuss,
Whether life is good in glorious Ukraine."
Then they started to toast him
With a glass of mead,
And a shot glass of horilka.
As for him, he accepted the drinks from the rich dukes,
But he did not drink them himself,
He poured them out on his garments:
"Oh, my clothes, my garments,
Drink and be merry,
It is not I who am being honored;
It is you who garner respect.
If I were not wearing you,
No one would take me for a hetman."
Then Khvesko Khanzha Andyber,
The hetman of Zaporozhia,
Spoke quietly, saying,
"Hey, Kozaks," he said, "my children my friends, young men,
I ask you to heed my words,

Take these rich dukes by their foreheads
And lead them out from behind the table like a herd of oxen,
Place them down in front of the windows,
And whip them with three birch twigs."
Well, the Kozaks, the children, the friends, the young men,
They did as they were told,
They took the rich dukes by their foreheads
And led them out from behind the table like a herd of oxen,
And placed them down in front of the windows,
And whipped them with three birch twigs.
As they did so, they spoke quietly, saying,
"Oh, dukes," they said, "you dukes,
You own all the fields and the byways,
There is not a single place where our brother, the poor Kozak,
Can even pasture his horse."
Well then, although Khvesko Khanzha Andyber,
The hetman of Zaporozhia,
Although he died,
His Kozak fame will not die and will not perish.
As for now,
Lord support and help your people,
The people of the Tsar,
The Christian people,
For many years.

The location of Khvesko Khanzha Andyber's adventure is hard to pin-point. He is said to have gone to the city of Kiliia, which is near present-day Odesa and, in the period in question, would be in Tatar territory, yet he is pictured in an established tavern and talking to dukes. The use of the term "duke" would imply that he is dealing with Polish gentle-man and this latter interpretation makes more sense in terms of the content; Kiliia is probably imported into this narrative from the "Kozak Holota" duma, since both texts describe men who are poorly dressed. Hrushevska's work also supports the interpretation that Andyber is dealing with Poles.[29] She states that there was a historical Khanzha who was a contemporary of Bohdan Khmelnytskyi, the leader who rebelled against the Polish-Lithuanian Commonwealth and the subject of the next chapter. If this song does refer to the conflict between the Kozaks and the Poles, the question of appearance would indeed be important. The Poles did their best to intimidate the opposition with their dress. The winged hussars, known from the late sixteenth and seventeenth centuries, wore wooden frames on their shoulders to which feathers were attached. The wings made their wearer look considerably taller than he really was and, thus, more imposing. The feathers also made a noise when the hussar charged the enemy, thus adding another intimidation factor. The "Khvesko Khanzha Andyber" song says that appearances can be misleading. Perhaps this is a statement that was once directed at Poles, asserting that their elaborate costumes were for nought and did not have the desired effect of dispiriting their adversaries.

Sea Campaigns and Dumy about Storms at Sea

The people who colonized the area that would become Ukraine were adept at water travel. From their earliest arrival on the Ukrainian steppe, fishing was a significant source of income and waterways were important for transportation and for defence from attack. When Kozaks became an organized stratum of society and began to mount large-scale campaigns, they used their knowledge of vessel building and navigating the waterways of their territory to add sea warfare to their arsenal. Kozak expeditions ranged far and wide, often reaching the western shore of the Black Sea and cities that are now in Moldova. Some of the forays into these territories were by land, as in the song about Ivas Konovchenko, but many were by sea. The Kozaks were known as extremely effective maritime combatants. The boats that the Kozaks used for their voyages were different from the galleys used by most men who sailed the Black Sea and the Mediterranean. Understanding what these boats were like and how they were used in combat helps us better appreciate the dumy that describe maritime events. A Kozak boat, called a *chaika*, was approximately sixty feet long, about ten or twelve feet wide, and twelve feet deep. It had no keel to increase manoeuvrability. Essentially, either end of the chaika could be the bow and the boat did not have to make a circle when it wanted to switch directions; all the men had to do was turn around in their seats and then row the opposite way. The boat had two rudders, one at each end, to assist in the process of steering and thus either end of the boat could also serve as the stern. Sixty men could make a boat in about two weeks. Kozaks were good at many trades. Among them, there was a sufficient number of men skilled in boat building to manufacture eighty or a hundred boats whenever they were needed for an expedition.[30] The chaika was considerably smaller than a galley and it was low in the water.

This meant that a Kozak fleet could get quite near its target before it was spotted. A Kozak fleet could sneak up on a galley or the city that it wanted to attack and approach within a short distance from its target without being detected. Kozak boats were quite buoyant. A layer of tightly bound reeds as thick as a barrel was secured to each boat on all sides. This allowed the boat to stay afloat even when it was filled with water. Inside the boat were ten to twelve oars, four to six light cannon called falconets, and several containers with provisions. A mast allowed the boat to hoist sail in good weather. A single chaika could hold fifty to seventy men, each armed with two rifles and a sabre. As fighters and rowers were the same, Kozak forces did not rely on captives to propel their ships.

The ships belonging to the adversaries of the Kozaks, the Turkish and Tatar galleys, operated on an almost diametrically opposite set of principles. They were large and formidable – and not as manoeuvrable as Kozak chaiki. They were manned by captives and their fighters were freemen. Their effectiveness in battle depended a great deal on intimidation. Galleys were built and decorated so that they would look fearsome and frighten the sailors on the boats with which they fought. To that end, the fronts of galleys were often fitted with huge battering rams and painted to look like mythical beasts, with the battering ram made to look like a nose above a fearsome mouth with pointed teeth. Atop a galley were sails and other decorative features used to impress the opposition with their opulence and to serve the same purpose of intimidation as luxurious clothing. A very fancy and colourful galley is described in the duma "Samiilo Kishka." It is not only lavishly painted, it has blue and gold plates attached, and the sails are of finest gabardine, further adding to its rich appearance. It is perhaps especially elaborate because it is taking Alkan Pasha, the young master of the vessel, on a mission of courtship, and the many colours and decorations of the ship are meant to impress Sandzhakivna, the Pasha's intended. The vessel's striking appearance plays a role at the end of the song when Kishka sails it towards Kozak shores and the Kozaks fire upon him and his men because they believe that a ship that fancy could only be a Turkish galley, and one manned by Turkish troops.

The effectiveness of the Kozak fleet had nothing to do with show. As with their clothing, the Kozaks trusted more to function than to appearance. The Kozaks relied on speed, for the small chaika could travel much faster than a galley. They made use of the manoeuvrability of their boats. They took advantage of the fact that the chaika was low in the water and could long remain undetected. When it came to fighting the Kozaks, the psychological and physical might of galleys was of little use. The battering rams, while effective against other galleys, were too high to cause harm to a Kozak chaika. Furthermore, the Kozaks were well aware of the advantages of their chaiki and were thus not intimidated by their opponents' show. In a sense, the success of seemingly unimposing boats, like the fighting prowess of seemingly bedraggled men, had its own ability to intimidate.

Some of the advantages of the chaika, namely, small size and the fact that the boat could easily go in either direction, were also drawbacks. While size could be used to great advantage when sneaking up on enemy ships, it was disadvantageous in a storm. Manoeuvrability made the chaika less stable than other craft and rough seas could easily carry the small Kozak boats off course and even overturn them. This is what we see in dumy which tell, not of Kozak triumphs at sea, but of the perils they faced. In these songs, Kozaks are in danger, not from Turkish galleys, but from storms which develop on the Black Sea. Storms toss the small and light boats about. They separate the boats one from the other, leaving the Kozaks in one boat without the support of the rest of the Kozak fleet. This is what happens in the song "Duma about Oleksii Popovych." Moreover, in the version of the Oleksii Popovych text translated below, the problem of rough seas is exacerbated by snowy skies. The almost surreal threat posed by the forces of nature is indeed an extraordinary phenomenon. While the younger men may not understand what is happening or why they are in such peril, their older and experienced leader suspects that the storm is a form of divine retribution and calls upon his men to confess their sins. To the surprise of all present, Oleksii Popovych, the company's scribe and the man who reads Holy Scripture to his fellows, comes forward with a confession. It is he, the hero explains, who brought on this calamity. The storm is punishment for the sins he committed against family, village, and church. These sins cause nature to attack the fleet, and so Oleksii proposes that his shipmates sacrifice him to the stormy sea so that it will be satisfied and calmed and so that the rest of the men might not share the hero's fate. As it turns out, the confession of sins alone brings miraculous results and the fearsome sea becomes calm. In fact, the waves that threatened to drown the men carry them to safety instead. It should be noted that, before Oleksii calms the waters with his confession and while the sea is still angry, one of the punishments it inflicts on the Kozaks is delivering them into the hands of their enemy. We are told

An imperial galley of the tsar's fleet. This is not a Kozak chaika. Rather, it is one of the grand ships against which the small and manoeuvrable chaika was so effective. Unknown artist, nineteenth century. Courtesy of Rodovid Press.

that the sea takes one of the ships away from the fleet and delivers it to a Muslim port, where the men will be captured and sold as slaves. The text translated below was recorded on a wax cylinder by Filaret Kolessa. The performer was Hnat Honcharenko and the transcription was done by Lesia Ukrainka.[31]

Oh, on the Black Sea,
Oh, on a white rock,
There a bright falcon perched,
And he called and wailed mournfully,
And he gazed intently at the Black Sea
Because something bad was starting to transpire
A huge, mean wave, a defiant wave was rising,
And it took the ships of the Kozaks, the brave lads,
And it broke the flotilla apart into three groups.
It grabbed the first group [of ships]
And carried them to the lands of the Turks,
And it took the second group
And forced them into the mouth of the Danube,
As for the third part, that group was here,
In the middle of the Black Sea,
Atop a high, fast-moving wave,
Sinking in the middle of a fierce snow storm.
Oh, on that third group [of ships] there was a large army;
And who was their leader?
It was Hrytsko Kolomyichyn,
Respected and hailed by the entire army.
It is he who speaks to the Kozaks saying,
And he cries, shedding tears,
"Oh, Kozaks, gentlemen, brave lads,
Listen and take heed,
Do not conceal any sins that you might have,
Confess your sins,
First before All-Merciful God,
And then before the Black Sea,
And then before the Koshovyi hetman."
Well, the Kozaks heard this,
And all fell silent,
The only person who responded
Was Oleksii Popovych,

The hetman, the man from Zaporozhia.
And he spoke saying,
"Do a good deed,
Take me, Oleksii Popovych,
Seize my person,
And tie a white stone to my neck,
Take my Kozak eyes, my brave lad's eyes,
And blindfold them with red silk,
And take me and lower me into the Black Sea.
It is better that I sacrifice my head to the Black Sea,
Than that I take many souls, many Christian believers,
And let them perish,
Perish in the Black Sea."
The Kozaks heard this,
And they addressed Oleksii Popovych
And they spoke, saying,
"Oh, Oleksii Popovych,
Glorious knight, our scribe,
You are the one who takes the Holy Scripture
And [you] read it three times a day.
And [you] teach us, ordinary Kozaks,
All that is right and proper,
How can you have sins that are greater than ours?"
Oh, Oleksii Popovych hears this,
And he speaks, saying,
And he sheds copious tears,
"Oh, Kozaks, gentlemen, brave lads,
Indeed I am the one who reads the Holy Scripture,
Reads it three times a day,
And I teach you ordinary Kozaks,
All that is good and proper,
But I still have sins that are worse than yours.
When I was leaving for the volunteer army,
I did not behave as I should,
My father and my mother –
I did not ask for their blessing,
My older brother – I treated him as if he were not a brother to me,
My older sister – I did not respect her,
I kicked her in her breast with my spur,
And Kozaks, gentlemen, brave lads,

I committed sins that are worse still,
As I was riding out of the city,
The littlest children –
I trampled them with my horse,
I spilled Christian blood,
I spilled innocent blood.
And young women ran out of their gates,
They picked up their little children,
And me, Oleksii Popovych,
They cursed me and reviled me.
And then I rode past forty churches,
In my arrogance, I did not remove my hat,
I did not cross myself,
And I did not remember my father's and my mother's prayers.
Well, Kozaks, gentlemen, brave lads,
There is yet another sin that weighs upon me:
As I rode by the tsar's people,
I did not remove my hat because of my arrogance,
The peasants and the Kozaks,
I did not greet them and wish them a good day,
I did not offer them holiday greetings.
And Kozaks, gentlemen, brave lads,
These are the sins that are my ruin …
It is not the Black Sea which is causing me to drown,
I am being punished by my father's and my mother's prayers!
If only my father's and my mother's prayers,
If only they could save me from death,
Save me from drowning in the Black Sea,
Then I would go to my father and my mother,
I would go back to my family,
I would honour my father and my mother,
Honour them and respect them.
I would go to my older brother,
And treat him as if he were my father,
As for my neighbours,
I would treat them as if they were my brothers."
As soon as Oleksii Popovych,
As soon as he started to speak the whole truth,
As soon as he confessed his sins to God,
Then quickly the big and defiant wave,

The enormous and destructive wave,
Started to die down on the Black Sea.
The wave on the Black Sea subsided
As if a wave had never arisen.
And it took all the Kozaks,
And carried them alive to an island.
Then all the Kozaks walked out on the island
And they marvelled at what had happened,
And they spoke, saying,
And they cried, shedding tears,
"Just now we were on the Black Sea,
Atop a fast-moving wave,
In the midst of a fierce snowstorm,
And, because of Oleksii Popovych,
We did not lose a single Kozak from amongst us."
Oleksii Popovych walks out amongst them,
He takes the Holy Scripture in his hands,
And he reads it three times a day,
And all the Kozaks,
He teaches them what is right and proper:
"Kozaks, gentlemen, brave lads,
Listen to what the Holy Scripture reveals,
What all prayers indicate:
Whoever heeds his father's and his mother's prayers,
Heeds them and honours them and respects them,
Then the prayers of his father and his mother
Will aid him in business and in his trade,
Will aid him in the field and on the sea,
Will aid him and will help him.
The prayers of one's father and one's mother
Can pull one out from the bottom of the sea,
Can ransom one's soul from grievous sins,
Can lead one to the heavenly kingdom."
We must always remember
Whose prayers were there when we first partook of bread and salt.
Grant, oh God, grant to the tsar's kingdom,
To the Christian people,
Grant them health from this day forward,
And for many years,
For many years.

The song about Oleksii Popovych contrasts the hero's pious behaviour aboard ship to his misdeeds back at home. As in many epic traditions, hubris does not go unpunished; Oleksii's arrogant treatment of his family and his fellow villagers causes the storm at sea. In some versions of this text, such as the one published by Tsertelev, confession of sins is not sufficient to stop the storm and an actual blood sacrifice is required. Oleksii's pinky finger is chopped off and his blood is allowed to flow upon the waters; only then does the storm subside.[32] The Oleksii Popovych duma is a complex song which, like the texts about Kozaks and clothing, contrasts appearance and reality. This song also speaks about the power of words. As the hero points out, the prayers of one's parents and the curses of fellow villagers can doom the object of their rage. But parental prayers also have the tremendous power of support and salvation. It should be noted that Oleksii's own words are enormously powerful because, in most versions, his confession alone is enough to calm the stormy sea. In all probability, the minstrels who sang songs such as this duma wished to imply that their words could be powerful as well; they wished to let their listeners know that their words could effect the salvation of souls which begging songs promised.

The duma "The Storm on the Black Sea" is very similar to the song about Oleksii Popovych. The difference is that the men whose fates the text narrates are actually tossed into the waters. The two men are brothers and they confess their sins to each other. Here too confession calms the storm and the men swim to shore. After they escape the storm at sea, the two men travel to their parents' home and, when asked about their adventures, they contrast what happened to them to the fate of a man who had no relatives to whom he could pray and from whom he could beg forgiveness. This man, unlike the two brothers, drowned as a result of the storm. The version translated below was recorded from the famous kobzar Ostap Veresai and was first published by Panteleimon Kulish.[33]

Oh, on the Black Sea,
On a white rock,
There sits a bright falcon, a falcon with clear eyes,
And he bows his head low,
And he screeches and cries mournfully,
And he looks at the light-coloured sky,
And at the dark sea,
And he gazes vigilantly,

Because in the sacred Heavens
And on the dark sea, something bad is about to happen:
In the bright sky all the stars have grown dim,
And half of the moon has been hidden in darkness,
And on the dark sea, something is going wrong,
Because, from the bottom of the sea, a powerful wave is rising,
And it breaks apart the Kozak fleet, separates it into three parts,
It separated out one group [of ships]
And carried them to the quiet Danube,
And it separated out another group
And carried them to the Arabic lands,
And into Turkish captivity,
And it separated out a third part
And started to sink the ships in the dark sea.
Oh, among the men on the third group of ships were two brothers,
They were fair as turtledoves,
And they were drowning,
And they saw no hope of aid from anywhere,
And they swam one towards the other,
And they spoke with words,
And they cried bitterly,
And they begged each other for forgiveness,
And they confessed their sins,
Confessed them before merciful God.
Well, those brothers spoke saying,
And they shed bitter tears,
"Oh, brothers, it is not a powerful sea wave that is killing us,
It is our father's prayer, and our mother's
Which is punishing us,
Because we set out for the volunteer army,
And we did not ask our father and our mother for their blessing,
And we pushed our elderly mother away from us with our stirrups,
And we were overcome by arrogance,
We did not recognize our elder brother as our kin,
And our middle sister – we treated her with disrespect.
And we were so full of pride,
[That] we deprived our neighbour of his bread and salt,
And we were so arrogant
That, as we rode past God's churches,
We did not take our caps off of our heads,

And we did not cross ourselves,
And we did not call upon our merciful Creator for help.
And as we were riding through the streets,
We didn't greet anyone that we met,
And we let our horses trample small children,
We spilled Christian blood upon the damp earth!
Oh, brothers, if only our father's and mother's prayers could save us,
Then we would know what to do,
We would know how to honour our father's and mother's prayers,
And respect our elder brother as if he were our father,
We would know how to respect our middle sister,
And treat our neighbour as if he were our kin."
Well, as they spoke these words,
As they heeded their father's and mother's prayers,
Then merciful God began to help them,
And the dark sea began to grow calm,
And it became so calm,
That you would never guess that it had been stormy.
The two brothers began to swim to shore,
They began to grasp the white rocks with their hands,
And they began to climb out onto land,
They walked out on the happy shores,
Among the Christian peoples,
Into the Christian cities,
And they came to their father and their mother.
Their father and their mother came out to greet them,
And they asked their sons,
"Oh, sons, brave lads,
Did things go well in your travels?"
"We had a good time, father and mother, on the Black Sea,
But what was bad, father and mother,
Was that a stranger drowned in the dark sea.
He had no one whom he could ask for forgiveness,
And to help him out while he was in a foreign land."
Hear, oh God, hear our prayers and our requests,
Hear the voice of the tsar's people,
The Christian people,
And grant many years to all who are listening,
Have mercy upon them for many years,
Until the end of time!

The success of Kozak sea campaigns also depended on the ability to hide from pursuit. The Kozak Sich, or headquarters, was on an island in the middle of a river. The best known Zaporozhian sich is the one on Khortytsia Island in the Dnipro, but there were also others constructed on the same principle. A headquarters up a river was accessible only to small craft such as the chaika. A large galley simply could not navigate the rapids and occasional shallow waters of a river. A chaika could and, when it could not, it was small and light enough for the men who rowed it to be able to lift it and portage it beyond the impassible point. Legend has it that Turkish and Tatar forces would try to stop the Kozaks from fleeing upstream by stringing chains across the Dnipro. Even if they did, the Kozaks could carry their chaiki beyond the chains as easily as they could carry them past river rapids. Turkish and Tatar efforts to stop Kozak sea forays were of little use. One historical song describes a successful attack on Varna, a port city on the Bulgarian Black Sea coast. The text translated below is from a manuscript found in the Staro-Samborsk castle and published by Antonovych and Drahomanov.[34]

A queen, a powerful lady, cursed,
She cursed the Black Sea:
"May you, oh sea, may you not flourish
May you forever dry up,
Because you have taken my son, my only son,
My only son, you have taken him.
Did I not pay the armed forces
With golden coins,
And with white thalers,
Did I not clothe the forces,
Clothe them in red silk,
So that they would oppose the Kozaks."
But on Sunday, early in the morning,
A force gathered,
They gathered for a Kozak council,
They started to talk and to consult,
About how best to take the city of Varna:
Would it be best from the land or from the sea,
Or by means of a small river?
An envoy was sent to Varna,
And he captured a Turk,

A Turk, an old warrior;
And they started to question him,
How to best take the city of Varna,
Would it be best from the land or from the sea,
Or by means of a small river.
"Not from land and not from the sea,
But from that small river."
Well, on Sunday, early in the morning,
Boats come floating and come sailing;
Their oars flashed,
And they shot from their guns,
They fired fifty-seven rifle shots,
And half a hundred cannon shots.
The Kozaks began to approach
And the Turks began to curse;
They [the Kozaks] reached Varna,
And the Turks began to flee,
They started to curse that river:
"May you, oh river, never flourish,
May you dry up forever,
Because you took [the lives of] us Turks!"
Varna was famous from long ago,
But the Kozaks were more glorious,
Because they reached the city of Varna,
And they chased the Turks out.

Unlike many historical songs, this text tells a rather cheerful tale. The tale may be one of woe for the Turks, but the outcome for the Kozaks is a good one. Rivers are often presented as something positive and here the Kozaks take advantage of the small size of the chaika and its ability to sail on rivers to achieve their goal. But, in reality, sailing on rivers was not always easy. Travelling in a chaika down the Dnipro or the Danube could be quite perilous, and this is acknowledged in a duma. The song where the rivers Dnipro and Danube converse with each other and discuss the Kozaks has a happy ending where we see the Kozaks celebrating successful campaigns and dividing booty, but it too starts by describing the threats that water-borne campaigns posed. The two rivers ask each other why no Kozaks have sailed upon their waters for several years and the Dnipro accuses the Danube of causing catastrophes like the ones in the dumy "Oleksii Popovych" and "Storm on the Black Sea." As it turns out, the Kozaks have not been sailing the two rivers because they have been on land campaigns and these have been quite successful. The text below, usually entitled "The Conversation between the Dnipro and the Danube," was first published by Pavlo Zhytetskyi.[35]

The Dnipro asks the quiet Danube,
"Quiet Danube,
Why don't I see my Kozaks upon your waters?
Did your river mouth devour my Kozaks,
Did your Danube waters claim my Kozaks?"
And the quiet Danube answers Dnipro-Slavutych,
"Father Dnipro, Slavutych,
I myself am thinking and wondering
About the fact that I don't see Kozaks upon my waters,
Already a quarter of a year, already three months have passed,
Since the Kozaks have been upon my waters,
My river mouth has not devoured them,
And my Danube waters have not claimed your Kozaks,
And the Turks have not shot them or hacked them to pieces,
They have not taken them to Istanbul as captives.
All my field flowers and valley basins have wilted,
Because they have not seen your Kozaks upon them.
Your Kozaks are spending their time on the Cherkes mountain,
They are scooping up cold water into their kegs,
They have been marking the paths and the roads,
They have been plundering the Muslim cities,
They have been fighting with fire and sword,
They have been collecting gold and silver,
And they have been arriving on the River Khortytsia,
And they forded that river,
And they hurried to the old sich,
Where they seated themselves by rank,
And divided the Turkish gold and silver into three parts,
Where they drank mead and distilled horilka [Ukrainian for vodka],
Where they prayed to God for the whole world,
Whichever Kozak has wandered through the open field,
They know the tributaries, the helpers of the Dnipro well.

Conclusion

The fourteenth through sixteenth centuries were the time when Kozaks became an institutionalized force. The term "Kozak" originally designated steppe vagabonds, men without a specific and established domicile and without stable social ties. They were among the many types of people who lived in what later became southeastern Ukraine, a wild and dangerous land, but also a place of great riches that lured people to seek their fortune. Because the steppe was such a dangerous place, its inhabitants needed to defend themselves and each other. As the defensive measures became more coordinated, as raids on neighbouring Tatar encampments and even cities became, not just of a way of preventing future attack, but a path towards capturing rich booty, the Kozaks became more and more organized. The Lithuanian nobility who blamed Kozaks for any misdeeds that might draw the ire of the neighbouring Tatar Khanate, also employed them as a fighting force, possibly helping their progressive institutionalization. The battles in which the Kozaks engaged occurred on sea as well as on land. All of this is reflected in dumy and the fact that this was the formative period for Kozakdom may well explain why this period is the one that became the subject matter of the majority of duma texts.

The historical background given here is purposefully geared to what is found in dumy. It does not present the history of Kozakdom as it is typically treated in scholarly works. What we see here is history as it would have been seen by the common man, not by the elite. This is not the view of Kozak leaders or of men who left their mark in historical records; it is the perspective of the rank and file and their relatives and friends back home. It is history as experienced by the folk and it is the history immortalized in dumy.

5 The Khmelnytskyi Period

The Distinctive Characteristics of Khmelnytskyi Cycle Songs

The dumy about the Khmelnytskyi Uprising are the same as other dumy in form, but quite different in content. In many senses they more closely resemble the presentation of history that is found in historical writing and contain more facts than typically found in folklore. One reason for this may be the availability of better documentation. More complete records exist for this period than for the periods which preceded it, when life on the steppe had little government control and official records were scant. The other possible reason may be that Khmelnytskyi dumy did not start out as oral poetry, but as texts written by seminarians in duma style. The possibility that Khmelnytskyi dumy were composed by seminarians living in the same complexes as church-supported minstrels was presented in the chapter on minstrels and minstrelsy. In his discussion of the image of the Jews in Khmelnytskyi dumy, Zenon Kohut also notes the similarity between these songs and written histories.[1] He proposes that the similarity arose, not at the time when the songs were created, but later, when nineteenth-century collectors, having at their disposal more Khmelnytskyi facts than information about earlier periods, inserted the names of known leaders and other historical references into this duma cycle. As noted in the chapter on minstrels, Khmelnytskyi dumy were less popular than other minstrel songs, both with the minstrels themselves and with their audiences, and thus were not as well remembered by minstrels as their other material. Dealing with more fragmentary texts, collectors might well have tried to flesh them out with what they themselves knew. Panteleimon Kulish admitted in print that he "reminded" performers of material that he felt they had forgotten. In fact, he prided himself on his knowledge of this subject matter and claimed that minstrels were impressed by his erudition.[2] Whether Khmelnytskyi dumy were composed on the pattern of historical works to begin with or came to resemble written histories later, under the influence of collectors, they are nonetheless different from other dumy. The focus is on Kozak leaders, and more names of known historical figures appear in these songs than in any other set of dumy. Khmelnytskyi himself is an especially important actor, while ordinary Kozaks are presented, not as individuals, but as a group; the rank-and-file act as a unit and no individual who is not a leader is ever named. The concerns dealt with in these songs are the issues that leaders face, namely, making military and political decisions. There is no examination of struggles within families, or conflicts between generations. The motif of the arrogant young man who mistreats kin or fellow villagers and is then punished for his hubris, so common in other dumy, is present only in the duma entitled "The Death of Bohdan Khmelnytskyi," in which the young man, Khmelnytskyi's son, is shown as more foolish and pleasure-seeking than arrogant. What Khmelnytskyi texts do share with other dumy in terms of content is emphasis on economic issues as a stimulus for action. The Poles ruling Ukrainian lands, through their Jewish agents, exploit the population to such a degree, the dumy tell us, that there is no choice but to rebel.

As different as Khmelnytskyi dumy are from other songs of this genre and as influenced as they may have been by seminarians or highly educated collectors of folklore, they are still not the history of historians. What they share with historical writing is facts. The battles and campaigns described did indeed occur and were indeed important. The personages who appear in these dumy are indeed known figures. But as historians differ in their interpretations of the motives of historical actors, so the performers of Khmelnytskyi dumy, and presumably also their composers, offer their own reasons for the behaviour of Khmelnytskyi and the other persons who appear. The motives presented in these dumy, as in other folk narratives, are issues of concern to the folk. Khmelnytskyi becomes hetman to protect rank-and-file Kozaks and prevent them from being cheated of their rights. He breaks the treaty that he had signed at Bila Tserkva because he learns of the suffering that Poles inflict upon peasants. Complex diplomatic negotiations are not the subject of dumy the way that they are in historical writing about this period. Military strategy is not based on the relative size of armies or the availability of cavalry or cannons. Khmelnytskyi gets others to act by appealing to their thirst for alcohol. Outside of famous people like Khmelnytskyi and Pototskyi, the only people referred to by name are the Poles and Jews who get their just deserts for oppressing the Ukrainian people, and the names used are generic first names, the sorts of names that Ukrainians might use in everyday references to hated others. In sum, the songs of the Khmelnytskyi cycle are a hybrid of historical fact and folk interpretation. This approach to history is precisely what provincial seminarians would be likely to produce, which gives further support to the theory that Khmelnytskyi dumy were composed by them. With time, the folk element would have been maintained by the nature of duma performance, namely, the fact that these songs were sung by mendicant minstrels for a folk audience. In the second half of the nineteenth century historical names and places could well have been corrected or added by collectors and scholars.

The Historical Background behind the Khmelnytskyi Uprising

The Khmelnytskyi Uprising was the most successful of the Kozak uprisings, but it was not the first. Starting in the late sixteenth century, uprisings occurred almost one right after the other. In 1591 Kryshtof Kosynskyi led the first such uprising. He acted against the state because of an injustice that he himself had suffered, but anger at exploitation by the Polish nobility was so great that he had no trouble rallying the Kozak Host to fight on his behalf. Also indicative of the unrest in the country and the wide-spread resentment of Polish rule is the fact that his uprising was supported by the peasantry, who felt the abuse of the Poles too. Kosynskyi was defeated and received light punishment, but died not much later under mysterious circumstances.[3] In 1594, Severyn Nalyvaiko led a group of Kozaks against the Polish nobility. They were joined by disgruntled peasants and campaigned successfully, penetrating Galicia, Volhynia, and Belarus, but eventually succumbed to superior numbers, hunger, and disease. In a bid to save their own lives, the Kozaks surrendered Nalyvaiko to the Poles. He was taken to Warsaw, where, in 1596, he was tortured and executed.[4]

The reasons for the volatility of the Ukrainian lands and the anger directed against the Poles were many. The situation developed gradually. As described in the previous chapter, in the fourteenth through sixteenth centuries, most of the territory that would become Ukraine was under the control of the Grand Duchy of Lithuania. Nobles and appointed officials such as the starosta had little government oversight and commensurately scant government support, forcing the people who settled these lands to be largely self-reliant. To run their castles and to meet their administrative expenses, starosty collected a certain percentage of the wealth that foragers gleaned from the steppe and promised protection in return, a promise that was not always fulfilled. The balance between the duty collected and the services provided was not perfect but, if the population found it acceptable, they continued to live on the lands where they had settled. If, however, the taxes became too high, peasants simply left and moved further east or south, to more unsettled, more dangerous territory. Moving was not easy. Relocating a household is difficult enough, but moving in this period also meant accepting the burden of living in a wilder, less hospitable environment where the chances of Tatar raids were great and where fellow Ukrainians who might come to one's aid were few. Still, the option of escaping from an unjust master was always there.

With time, the situation changed. Just as the Kozaks gradually moved from being opportunists to forming an organized force, one with progressively increasing self-awareness and commensurate organizational structure, so the administration of civilian life became more firmly established, more orderly, more structured. Important to the tightening of government control was the formation of the Polish-Lithuanian Commonwealth at the Union of Lublin in 1569. In the period described in the previous chapter, Ukrainian territory was administered largely by Lithuania. During that same period, Lithuania and Poland vied for hegemony and fought a series of wars. Attempts at cooperation led to several proclamations of union named after the cities in which they were negotiated. None of these was lasting until the Union of Lublin, which created the Polish-Lithuanian Commonwealth. This polity was unique for its time because it was governed by an elected monarch and not a hereditary one. The monarch was elected by the nobility, or *szlachta*, and he served at the nobility's pleasure; he was not elected for a fixed term. The system of governance which administered the Commonwealth gave the nobility an enormous amount of power and a commensurate degree of privilege with respect to other social classes.[5]

As the nobility gained power and as administrative structures became more complex and more firmly established, the ordinary person's freedom of movement was imperceptibly, but increasingly, curtailed and serfdom became a reality. Serfdom was something that developed gradually, but this did not make it any the less onerous. At the same time, the opportunities for escape from serfdom became fewer, that is, the areas where peasants could relocate shrank. As Subtelny points out, the Kozak uprisings occurred where "some of Europe's most exploitive feudal lords confronted some of its most defiant masses."[6] The most volatile areas were the recently colonized provinces of Kyiv, Bratslav, and Chernihiv, where nobles distant from the Polish centre and unable to rely on government support held enormous tracts of land and exploited them as much as they could, trying to get the most out of peasants who had just recently shown their resistance to domination by colonizing new territories. Although this was a powder keg ready to explode, rebellion was far from the only approach that the Ukrainian masses and their Kozak leaders used to deal with their situation.

After Nalyvaiko, the next important leader was Petro Konashevych-Sahaidachnyi, born in 1582. His genius was not as a leader of insurrections, but as a powerful negotiator on behalf of Kozak and Ukrainian peasant interests. Sahaidachnyi tried his best to achieve a working compromise between the Kozaks and the Polish throne, using his enormous success as a fighter on behalf of Poland to leverage his demands. Most prominent among the causes that Sahaidachnyi championed were better treatment of the Orthodox Church and the expansion of the Kozak registry.[7] The registry is important for understanding Khmelnytskyi dumy and it appears as a contentious issue in several songs. Registered Kozaks first came into being in the middle of the sixteenth century when the Polish kings Sigismund August, Stephen Batory, and Sigismund III tried to rein in the Kozaks, who were demanding freeman status, the removal of the obligation to pay taxes, and the ability to requisition supplies from the civilian population when these were needed for war. The compromise was that a limited number of Kozaks would be registered and assigned the privileges requested, while the rest were to return to the status of serfs. Being a registered Kozak also meant receiving a salary from the Polish crown, something that, from the beginning, was seldom paid and yet was repeatedly offered to lure Kozaks into service.[8] When Sahaidachnyi assumed the post of hetman he at first tried to appease Poland and agreed to lower the number of registered men. He also punished Kozaks who went on sea raids without authorization. Subsequently, whenever the Polish king called upon the Kozaks to fight on behalf of the Poles, Sahaidachnyi pressed for an increase in the number of registered Kozaks and for recognition of Orthodox bishops.

Sahaidachnyi is known for several important military victories. He led campaigns against the Crimean Tatars, overpowered the fortress at Varna, and destroyed an enormous Turkish fleet. The historical song about the capture of Varna translated in the previous chapter is probably based on this military encounter. Sahaidachnyi attacked and captured Kefe, releasing the captives who had been brought there for sale at the slave market. The most notable conflict was the one at Khotyn, where Polish forces would surely have been defeated by the Turks had not Sahaidachnyi broken through enemy lines and held out against the enemy, even as some of the Polish fighters fled. Realizing the role that the Kozaks had played in this victory, Sahaidachnyi requested an increase in pay for his men, compensation for the losses they had sustained, the right to settle on land belonging to the crown, and again support for the Orthodox Church. The Polish king, however, feeling that he would have no need for the Kozaks in the immediate future, denied the requests and actually reduced the number of registered men to two thousand, promising to raise the registration limit to three thousand in times of war. Recognizing the injustice of his actions, he tried to mollify Sahaidachnyi by offering him gifts and physicians to cure the wound he had suffered while breaking through enemy lines to lend support to the Poles at Khotyn. Attempts to heal the wounded leader came too late, however, and he died in 1622, leaving his fortune to his favourite cause, the Orthodox Church brotherhoods.[9] As noted in the chapter on minstrels and minstrelsy, Sahaidachnyi is credited with forging the link between the Kozaks and the church. It is he who led the Zaporozhian Host to join the Kyiv Epiphany Brotherhood, thus laying the groundwork for the merger of kobzari and lirnyky and giving shape to minstrelsy as it was described and recorded by scholars in the nineteenth century.

As for the rank-and-file Kozaks, after the confrontation at Khotyn, they returned either to the Sich or to their towns and villages, but their resentment over the way they had been treated was enormous, ready to flare up at the slightest provocation. Their hetman, Mykhailo Doroshenko, attempted to direct their animosity away from the Poles and authorized raids against the Ottomans, even though the Polish crown was officially at peace with the Porte.[10] The change in attitude of the rank-and-file Kozak can be seen in a historical song recorded by Poznanskyi and published by Antonovych and Drahomanov.[11] In this song, "The Crimean Campaign," the young hero does not look forward to his military service. There is no possibility of honour and glory or of returning with rich booty. All he sees before him is exposure to the elements and the suffering that goes with it. When he reaches his destination, he sees his Turkish enemy and the possibility of death.

A falcon became sad:
"Oh, my poor and troubled head,
[I am sorry] because I left my winter quarters early,
Because the snow still lay on the mountains,
And because the snow still lay on the mountains,
And the waters were still [frozen] in the valleys,
While poppies were blooming in the cities."
Oh, those were not poppies, they were Kozaks,
They were Kozaks marching on Crimea,
And they were Kozaks marching on Crimea,
They raise dust along the gravelled roads.
A mother comes out to meet her son,
She tries to get him to come home.
"Oh, son, return on home,
I will wash your hair for you."
"Oh, mother, wash your own hair,
Or wash the hair of your daughter,
Because my hair, mother, will be washed by the rains,
And it will be dried by the tempestuous winds,
It will be dried by the tempestuous winds,
And my hair will be combed by the dense brambles.
Oh, mother, don't make me sad,
Because I myself know sorrow,
Oh, I myself know sorrow,
Because my hetman is sending me to the Danube,
And I myself don't know the Danube,
Perhaps I will ask people.
Oh, I arrive at the Danube,
And I look across to the other bank,
I look across to the other bank,
And there is a Turk there, cutting cloth,
Is it for a Turkish woman, or for our leader,
Or is it [a shroud] for a young Kozak."

This song presents a striking contrast to the "Ivas Konovchenko" duma. In both songs the mother tries to dissuade her son from going on a campaign; in both she fails. But while Ivas goes willingly and eagerly looks forward to fighting his Turkic enemy, the Kozak in this song expresses none of this positive anticipation. By the time of the Crimean Campaign described in this song, going off to battle is drudgery, not adventure. The Kozaks are an organized force and the hero of the song, presumably a registered Kozak, does not have the option of not joining the campaign on which his unit has been sent. The young man must go and he must expose himself to the elements and the threat of death.

Doroshenko had many unhappy men on his hands and tried to divert them by sending them into military action. The fact that he undertook campaigns without Polish authorization, however, meant that the Kozaks were acting as an independent state within the Commonwealth. This infuriated the Poles and led them to attack Ukraine. When peace was concluded, the Kozak register was increased to six thousand. Other attempts at controlling the Kozaks followed, including the construction of a fortress at Kodak and a further increase in the number of registered Kozaks. A pattern of sorts was developed where whichever state wanted to make use of the military might of the Kozaks would offer them legal status – meaning registration – and an increase in pay, only to renege on those promises once peace was achieved. As often as not, the Kozaks received little or no pay for their sacrifices.[12]

After Sahaidachnyi and Doroshenko, Polish attempts at subjugating the Kozaks were countered with resistance or Kozak attacks, including the destruction of the Kodak fortress.[13] In 1638 the Poles felt that they had finally defeated the restless insurgents and a period of relative calm followed, only to explode in the Khmelnytskyi Uprising, a massive revolt that changed the history of Ukraine and of all the polities in that part of the world. Bohdan Zynovii Khmelnytskyi was a quiet and well-educated man who inherited his father's estate in Subotiv and lived a life in harmony with the government until he, like so many people at all levels of society, became the victim of the greed and acquisitiveness of a Polish magnate. The nobility in the newly colonized areas of Ukraine exploited the land with impunity and peasants were not the only people to suffer in the process. In 1646 Daniel Czaplinski laid claim to Khmelnytskyi's estate, attacked and raided it, killing Khmelnytskyi's youngest son and abducting the woman whom the widowed Khmelnytskyi was planning to marry. Khmelnytskyi, being an upstanding citizen, used legal channels to appeal for redress of his grievances; he was fifty years old at the time and well established and did not seem like a man who would be willing to do anything other than act through formal channels. Yet, when his attempts to secure justice proved futile, he took action. Khmelnytskyi, like his father before him, was a registered Kozak. When the Poles took no notice of his grievances, he turned to the other group with which he was affiliated, the Kozaks. He fled to the Zaporozhian Sich, was elected hetman, expelled the Polish garrison from the sich, and began the revolt that would bear his name.[14]

The duma entitled "Khmelnytskyi and Barabash" is usually given as the first song in the Khmelnytskyi cycle and explains his rise to the position of hetman in a manner dramatically different from the historical account given above.[15] In the duma, Khmelnytskyi acts because of the injustices inflicted upon his men; his motivation does not come from the personal wrongs that he suffered. In this song, Khmelnytskyi is presented as initially very friendly to those who support the Poles. In fact, he and Barabash and Klysha all act according to the dictates of their Polish lord. But Khmelnytskyi suspects that there is something wrong with the administration of the Kozak register. Presumably, the number of men listed is not the same as the number who are actually allowed to assume the position of registered Kozaks. Barabash, who is serving as hetman at that point, is the one keeping the Kozaks from claiming what is rightfully theirs. Fearing that something is amiss, Khmelnytskyi tries to get Barabash to let him see the actual registers. Barabash tries to dissuade him from pursuing the matter, warning him that this might anger the Poles. Khmelnytskyi takes advantage of the human proclivity to alcohol. He uses the technique employed by Samiilo Kishka and gets Barabash drunk. Removing tokens from Barabash's body, he sends his servant to retrieve the critical register letters. Barabash's wife suspects that something horrible is about to happen, but she honours the tokens and turns over the registers as requested. Sure enough, Khmelnytskyi's suspicions were justified and a battle ensues. The Poles supporting Barabash are defeated and Khmelnytskyi himself kills Barabash, even though he is his sworn kin. Furthermore, Barabash's family is surrendered to the Turks to be sold as slaves. The text below was recorded by Kulish from Andrii Shut and first published by Metlynskyi.[16]

Oh, on a certain day and at a certain hour,
Great wars took place in Ukraine,
But no one could be mustered,
To stand up honourably for the Christian faith,
The only ones who came forward were Barabash and Khmelnytskyi
And Klysha Bilotserkivskyi.
Then they wrote letters with their own hands,
And sent them to King Radyslav.
Then King Radyslav read the letters,
And he wrote back,

And he appointed Barabash to be hetman in Cherkasy,
"Barabash, you be hetman in the city of Cherkasy,
And you, Klysha, you be a colonel in the city of Bila Tserkva,
Khmelnytskyi, you be the military scribe in the city of Chyhyryn."
Well then, young Barabash, did not serve as hetman for long,
It was only one year and a half.
Then Khmelnytskyi took great care,
He called the young hetman his kin and invited him over,
And he treated him to costly liquors,
And he spoke quietly, saying,
"Oh, sir, Barabash, my sworn kin, my dear young hetman,
Would it be possible for us both, you and me, to read the king's letters,
So that we could issue the proper orders to the Kozaks,
So that they would honourably defend the Christian faith?"
Well then, Barabash, the young hetman,
He spoke quietly, saying,
"My sworn kin, Khmelnytskyi, oh, military scribe,
Why should we read the king's letters together, the two of us,
Why should we issue the proper orders to the Kozaks?
Would it not be better for us to work with the Poles,
To get along with the powerful lords,
So that we could forever partake of our bread and salt in peace?"
At that point Khmelnytskyi became greatly enraged,
Very angry with his sworn kin, Barabash,
And he treated him to even more expensive liquors.
Well then, Barabash, the young hetman,
When he drank the expensive liquors at Khmelnytskyi's, his sworn
   kinsman's, house,
Well then he fell down drunk and went to sleep.
Then Khmelnytskyi took great care,
He took the pure gold ring off his right little finger,
He pulled the key out of his left pocket,
He tugged the silk handkerchief out from under his belt,
And he called his trusted servant and summoned him,
"Oh, my servant, trusted servant of Khmelnytskyi,
I order you to take great care,
I order you to saddle a good horse,
And to ride to the city of Cherkasy, to the home of Barabash,
And to request that the king's letters be handed over to you."
Well then, Khmelnytskyi's trusted servant did as was commanded,

He mounted a fine horse,
He rode to the city of Cherkasy, to the home of Barabash,
He entered Barabash's courtyard,
He came into the entryway – he took off his hat,
He came into the drawing room – he bowed low,
He took the tokens and laid them out on a bench,
And then he spoke quietly, saying,
"Madame," he said, "wife of Barabash, young hetman's wife,
Your husband, Barabash, the young hetman,
He is in Ukraine at a great banquet with Khmelnytskyi,
And they ordered that I pass these tokens over into your hands,
So that you would give me the king's letters,
So that the two of them, he and his sworn kin Khmelnytskyi,
Could read the letters together,
So that they could give the Kozaks their proper orders."
Then Madame Barabash, the hetman's wife,
Beat her hands against the floor,
She shed copious tears,
And she spoke quietly, saying,
"Oh, will not woe and sorrow befall my master Barabash,
Since he decided to go to glorious Ukraine, to Khmelnytskyi, his sworn kin,
So that they could hold a great banquet,
And so that they could also read the king's letters together?
Would it not have been better to be with the Poles,
With the powerful lords,
And share bread and salt in peace forever?
And now Barabash, the young hetman, had better be prepared,
To suffer through fires and thorns in glorious Ukraine,
To feed the mosquitoes with his white body –
All because of Khmelnytskyi, his sworn kin."
Then young Madame Barabash,
She spoke quietly, saying,
"Oh servant, trusted servant of Khmelnytskyi,
I cannot hand over the king's letters to you,
Instead I order you to go over to the gates,
And to dig up the chest with the king's letters."
Then Khmelnytskyi's trusted servant,
When he heard her words,
He went quickly and in a timely fashion to the gates,
And he dug up the chest with the king's letters.

He himself mounted his fine steed,
And quickly and in a timely fashion he arrived in Chyhyryn,
He handed over the king's letters to his master Khmelnytskyi,
    as was proper.
Then Barabash, the young hetman, awoke from his sleep,
He saw the king's letters in the hands of his sworn kin Khmelnytskyi,
Then he drank no more costly liquor,
He just left the household quietly,
And he called his elder, Krachevskyi, and summoned him,
"Oh, elder, my elder Krachevskyi,
If you would do the right thing,
Then you would capture my sworn kin Khmelnytskyi,
And hand him over to the Poles, to the powerful lords,
So that the Poles, the powerful lords, would thank us for our foresight."
Well, when Khmelnytskyi heard these words,
He became greatly enraged with his sworn kin Barabash,
He himself mounted a fine steed,
He took his trusted servant with him.
And then he was joined, on his right hand,
By four colonels:
The first colonel was Maksym Olshanskyi, `
And the second colonel was Martyn Poltavskyi,
And the third colonel was Ivan Bohun,
And the fourth – Matvii Borukhovych.
Then they arrived in glorious Ukraine,
They read the king's letters,
And they gave the proper orders to the Kozaks.
Then, on the holy day, on blessed Tuesday,
Khmelnytskyi woke up the Kozaks before the break of dawn,
And he spoke quietly, saying,
"Hey, Kozaks, my children, my friends, brave men,
I ask you to heed my words,
Arise from your sleep,
Recite the Rusian Lord's prayer,
And attack the Polish encampment,
Break the encampment up into three parts,
And hack the Poles, the powerful lords, to pieces,
Mix their Polish blood in the field, mix it with the yellow sand,
Never allow anyone to slander your Christian faith!"
Then the Kozaks, the friends, the brave men, they heeded his words,

They awoke from their sleep,
The recited the Rusian Lord's Prayer,
They attacked the Polish encampment,
They separated the encampment into three parts,
And they hacked the Poles, the powerful lords, to pieces,
They mixed their Polish blood in the field, mixed it with yellow sand,
They let no one slander their Christian faith.
Then Barabash, the young hetman, rode up on his horse,
He wept and shed tears,
And he spoke quietly, saying,
"Oh, sir, Khmelnytskyi, my sworn kin, military scribe,
Why did you take the king's letters from Madame Barabash,
Why did you issue orders to the Kozaks?
Would it not have been better to eat bread and salt,
With us, with the Poles,
With the powerful lords,
Share bread and salt in peace?"
Then Khmelnytskyi,
He spoke quietly saying,
"Oh, sir, oh Barabash, my sworn kin, young hetman,
If you are going to accuse me and attack me with these words,
Then I won't forgo taking your head off of your shoulders as if it were a
    jackdaw,
I won't forgo taking your wife and your children captive,
And sending them off to the Turkish sultan as a present."
Well then, Khmelnytskyi, when he said these words,
Then he did exactly as he had said,
He attacked his sworn kin, Barabash, the young hetman,
And took his head off his shoulders as if it were a jackdaw,
He took his wife and his children alive,
And sent them off as a present to the Turkish sultan.
From that hour, it was Khmelnytskyi who took over as hetman.
Then the Kozaks, his children, his friends, the brave men,
Spoke quietly saying:
"Oh, Hetman Khmelnytskyi,
Our father, Zynovii Bohdan from Chyhyryn,
God grant us that we may drink to your health and celebrate,
Let us protect our Christian faith from slander forever!"
Dear Lord, grant the people of the tsar,
The Christian people,

And all who are listening,
All Orthodox Christians,
Grant, God, grant them many years.

The duma "Khmelnytskyi and Barabash" presents history in its own way. According to Antonovych and Drahomanov, there was a historical Barabash, a lower-echelon figure rather than a hetman, who did indeed keep Kozak registers and may have been responsible for concealing the true number of registered men permitted by royal decree.[17] Beyond that, the relationship between the song and fact is more tenuous and the song's goal is to present Khmelnytskyi as the champion of his men. As will be discussed later in this chapter, the registration issue and the question of possible peaceful relations with Poland continued to plague the Kozaks. This song restates the problem of registers and reaffirms that the Poles are indeed the enemy. The term "Rusian Lord's Prayer" appears in this and in other songs from the Khmelnytskyi cycle. It is not to be found in dumy from other cycles. The addition of Rusian (not Russian) in front of Lord's Prayer is probably meant to underscore the distinction between the Catholic Poles and the Orthodox Ukrainians. This difference was of paramount importance during the Khmelnytskyi Uprising and would also have been important to Orthodox seminarians in later periods.

The historical Khmelnytskyi, once he became hetman, quickly demonstrated his abilities as a leader. The man was a tactical genius. He soon realized that Kozak forces needed more cavalry to ensure military success and made a deal with the Crimean Tatars. In 1648 he engaged a Polish force at Zhovti Vody. The issue of registered Kozaks came into play during this conflict. Those Kozaks who were registered by the Polish state were obliged to fight with the Poles. However, as Khmelnytskyi's effectiveness as a leader of a force opposed to Polish rule became evident, several thousand Ukraine men in the service of Poland deserted over to him, preferring ethnic solidarity to the obligation placed on them by their registered status.[18] What happened at Zhovti Vody, a name that means "yellow water," is reflected in an upbeat historical song which features wordplay on the name of the location and also on Khmelnytskyi's name, the first part of which does indeed mean "hops." At this point in the history of the Uprising, optimism was justified and wordplay was appropriate to the joyful, playful atmosphere. The text here was published by Antonovych and Drahomanov.[19]

Oh, is that hops growing along the fence?
Hey, it is Khmelnytskyi, battling the Poles.
Hey, Khmelnytskyi rode to Zhovti Vody,
And more than one Pole now lies with his head in the water.
Don't drink too much of that yellow water, Khmelnytskyi,
Because forty thousand Poles are coming on horseback,
"I'm not afraid of Poles and I have no concern,
I know that I have a great force behind me,
And you, Poles, it will mean your destruction."
The Poles fled; they lost their fur coats,
Hey, more than one Pole is lying there with a dead man's grin.
The Poles built houses of oak,
And now their little children will need to flee to Poland!
The Poles fled, they fled as they could,
And dogs and wolves were eating [their corpses].
Hey, there's a meadow over there and flowers in the meadow,
And more than one Polish child is crying for his father.
Hey, there a river over there and its opposite bank is muddy,
And more than one Pole has left a widow behind.

The Poles retreated from Zhovti Vody only to be ambushed near Korsun and suffer a decisive defeat.[20] This event is commemorated in the duma which is named after the Korsun battle. The text translated below was first published by Panteleimon Kulish. It was recorded by Nihovskyi from a kobzar named Ivan Ryhorenko.[21]

Khmelnytskyi made his presence known,
The father-hetman from Chyhyryn called out:
"Hey, my friends, brave young men,
My brothers, Zaporozhian Kozaks,
Heed my words and guess my proper meaning,
Start to brew beer with the Poles.
We'll use Polish malt and Kozak water,
We'll use Polish wood and Kozak labour."
Well, using that beer,
The Kozaks performed a great feat with the Poles,
They encamped near the city of Korsun,
Near Stebliv they soaked the malt,
And they hadn't even gotten around to brewing the beer,
When Khmelnytskyi's Kozaks had already quarrelled with the Poles,

And because of that brew,
The Kozaks started a great scuffle with the Poles,
And because of that grain,
The Poles started a great fracas with the Kozaks,
And because of some bread-beer,
More than one Pole was treated like a bastard
And had his forelock pulled by a Kozak.
At that point, the Poles figured out that something was afoot,
And for some reason they started to flee from the Kozaks,
And the Kozaks reproached the Poles:
"Oh, you Poles, you sons of bitches,
Why don't you wait
And why don't you finish drinking our beer?"
Then the Kozaks caught up with the Poles,
And they caught Pan Pototskyi,
And the trussed him up like a ram,
And they quickly delivered him before Khmelnytskyi:
"Oh, Mister Pototskyi,
For some reason you act like you have the brains of a woman!
You didn't know how to stay in Kamianets-Podilskyi,
To eat roast pig, and chicken with peppers, and mushrooms,
And now you don't know how to fight us Kozaks,
And you don't know how to eat hardtack.
Perhaps I should turn you over to the Crimean Khan,
So that the Crimeans and the Nogais could teach you how to eat raw
    horse meat."
Then the Poles caught on,
And they started to blame the Jews:
"Hey, you Jews,
You pagan bastards,
Why did you start a great uprising, a great commotion?
Why did you place three check points every mile,
And collect enormous tolls?
From the rich man,
You took two gold coins,
And from the cart driver,
You took half a gold piece,
And from the traveller on foot – two pennies,
And you didn't even let the honest beggar pass,
You took his millet and his eggs!

Now you should gather all that you collected,
And hand it over to Khmelnytskyi,
And if you don't hand it over to Khmelnytskyi,
Then be prepared to flee beyond the River Vistula to Podillia."
Then the Jews figured things out,
And they fled beyond the Sluch River,
He who fled to the River Sluch lost his boots and his leg wraps,
And he who fled to the River Prut
Was forced by Khmelnytskyi's Kozaks to take a steep path,
And on the River Sluch,
They destroyed the bridge that crossed over,
And they sank all the skiffs,
And all the Polish drums.
Those who fled to the River Ros,
Were left naked and barefoot.
Then one Jew named Hychyk called out,
As he grabbed his side,
And then a Jew called Shleima called out,
"Oh, it looks like I won't make it home for the Sabbath,"
Then a Jew called Avram called out, saying,
"I have some wares,
I have pins and needles,
I have flints and pipes,
And I have put my wares
Into a box,
And fled from the Kozaks so that all they saw was my heels."
And then a fourth Jew called Davydko spoke,
"Oh, brother Lebko, you can see the Kozak banners over the mountains."
And a filthy Jew, Yudko, said,
"Hey, best to flee to Poland quickly."
Then a Jew called Leiba was running,
So fast that his tummy was bouncing up and down,
And he gets to a school and he looks,
And his Jewish heart wilts,
"Oh, my school, my school built of brickwork
I can't do anything with you,
I cannot stick you inside my shirt,
And I cannot hide you in my pocket,
I'll have to abandon you and let Khmelnytskyi's Kozaks shit all over you."
Well, gentlemen, it was not a black cloud descending over Poland,

It was many a Polish woman who became a widow.
And one Polish woman called out,
"My husband, my Pan Ian is no more,
The Kozaks trussed him up somewhere like a ram
And took him before their hetman."
And a second Polish woman called out,
"My Pan Kardash is no more,
Khmelnytskyi's Kozaks took him to their lair."
And a third Polish woman called out,
"My Pan Yakob is no more,
It seems that Khmelnytskyi's Kozaks hung him from an oak tree somewhere."

As with other texts, matching the events recounted in the dumy with events as they are presented in scholarly histories is difficult; it can be done only in the most general terms. A conflict with the Poles did indeed take place at Korsun and the Polish forces were indeed routed. The Jews did indeed flee and the Polish dead were surely mourned by their wives. The details which describe how the Jews fled and the indignities that Kozaks inflicted upon Polish soldiers are more a matter of artistic licence.

Another account of this period comes from a historical song that contrasts the fears of a young Kozak to the unjustified bravado of the Poles. The Kozak, a common soldier, is shown saying goodbye to his beloved and worrying about his stumbling horse, a bad omen. The Poles, by contrast, boast and claim that they will massacre the Kozaks. As in most folk poetry, arrogance is punished and the Poles flee. The song ends with Pototskyi's wife admonishing him and warning him of the dangers of fighting Kozaks. The translation provided below is based on a text published by Antonovych and Drahomanov.[22]

The Kozaks set out on an expedition at midnight,
And little Marusia cried her dark eyes shut.
"Don't cry, don't cry, Marusia, we will take you with us
When we set off for foreign lands."
"Go, go, my beloved, just don't have a good time there,
And do come back to me on your raven-coloured horse."
"Only God knows, only God can tell, if I will return,
For some reason, my raven-coloured horse stumbled at the gate."
Oh, the Poles walked along three roads and they asked as they went,
"Did the Kozaks pass this way, did you see them?"

All the Poles, as they went, each had three horses with him,
And they, the Poles, bragged as they went, saying they would win.
"We will go, dear brothers, to massacre the Kozaks,
But if misfortune falls upon us, then we will flee"
Pototskyi's wife will cry and she will lament:
"How long has it been, Pototskyi, sir, since I spoke to you,
It's been a long time since you, Pototskyi, have been fighting the Kozaks,
You will not be able to conquer the Kozaks; you will only waste your
    strength."

The switch from the description of Polish bravado to the picture of
Pototskyi's wife admonishing him for trying to defeat the Kozaks is
abrupt. The Poles' statement of their willingness to flee plus the par-
allelism between the Kozak's crying beloved at the beginning and
Pototskyi's lamenting wife at the end allows for this shift and underscores the contrast which is the core of this song.

In real life, the victory at Korsun led to bloody attacks on individual Jews and Poles. Ordinary citizens took it upon themselves to exact
revenge from their oppressors. Khmelnytskyi's success electrified the
ordinary people of the Ukrainian lands. They joined his army in droves.
As often as not, however, they acted on their own and not as part of a
disciplined and organized Kozak army. On their own initiative, they
attacked the Polish nobles who had exploited them and the Jews who
acted as their agents. Their rage against the masters who had oppressed
them was so great that their violence knew no bounds and was directed
against women, children, and clergy along with the hated magnates
who were the real source of oppression. The Poles responded in kind
with the most notorious practitioner of terror against the population
being Jeremi Wiśniowiecki.[23]

From the point of view of the ordinary people living on the territory of Ukraine, formal military actions were something distant, something outside their experience. For them, the most important issue was
exploitation and the oppressors with whom they dealt most directly
were Jewish leaseholders. Polish colonization of Ukraine meant that
Polish magnates were granted enormous tracts of land that they had
to administer and defend on their own. Many nobles responded by
turning to the practice of leasing out their rights so that they could
draw income from their landholdings without having to live there and
expose themselves to the hardships of the newly colonized territories.
Jews, while not allowed to own land, were allowed to lease it, and the

administration of the large Polish estates, or rather portions of them, was under their control. Hunting and fishing rights that belonged to the nobility could also be leased, and so circumstances combined to place Jews in the position of acting as intermediaries between the Poles and the Ukrainians; they were the people in immediate contact with the peasantry. Jews were under pressure to capitalize on their investment as quickly as possible; the consequences of this pressure are easy to imagine. In addition to leasing land, Jews leased the right to run taverns. A liquor monopoly prohibited home brewing and made the ownership of taverns most lucrative.[24] The local population's resentment of all this and more is expressed in the duma "The Leaseholders." The text below was recorded by Panteleimon Kulish from Andrii Shut in Oleksandrivka in 1853.[25]

Oh, from the time of the Kumeiky battle to the Khmelnytskyi period,
And from the Khmelnytskyi period to the time of Briansk,
And from the time of Briansk up until the present day,
Things were not good in the king's lands,
Because the Jews, the leaseholders,
Had leased all the Kozaks' paths and byways,
So that for every mile there were three toll posts,
And there were toll posts in the valleys,
And they were also on the high burial mounds.
And even this was not enough for the Jews,
The Jews assumed the right to tax all Kozak transactions,
And they took tolls that were very high,
From a cart-driver,
They took half a gold piece,
And from a man on foot they took three coins,
And even from the miserable beggar,
They took his chickens and his eggs,
And they even pressed him,
"Don't you have anything else, pussycat?"
And the Jews did not even stop there,
In glorious Ukraine they took control of all the churches,
So that if God gave a Kozak or a peasant a child,
Instead of going to the priest to have his child blessed,
He had to go to the leaseholder-Jew and give him a sixpence,
So that he would open up the church,
So that the man could have his child baptized.

And should God grant a Kozak or a peasant the joy of marrying off a child,
Instead of going to the priest for his blessing,
He had to go the leaseholder-Jew and produce a whole thaler,
So that he would open up the church,
So that the child could be married.
And the Jews, the leaseholders,
Did not stop even there.
They took leases on all the Kozak rivers in glorious Ukraine,
One (toll station) was on the Samara,
And the second was on the Saksanka [Savranka]
And the third was on the Hnyla [Hnylyi Tikych],
And the fourth was on the Probiina,
And the fifth was on the Desna River.
This meant that if a Kozak or a peasant wanted to catch some fish,
To feed his wife and children,
He didn't go to the landlord to ask for his blessing,
He had to go to the leaseholder-Jew and promise him a portion of the catch,
So that he would let him fish in the river,
And feed this wife and children.
At one point a Kozak was walking by an inn,
And carrying a musket over his shoulder,
He wanted to go down to the river to shoot a duck,
To feed his wife and children.
A leaseholder-Jew was looking out of the window,
And he spoke to his wife quietly, saying,
"Hey, wife, my wife Rasia,
What is this Kozak thinking? Why isn't he stopping by the inn,
And paying money for some horilka?
Why isn't he asking me, the leaseholder-Jew,
To allow him to go to the river to hunt for ducks,
So that he can feed his wife and children?"
Then the leaseholder-Jew approached the Kozak stealthily,
And grabbed him by the hair.
And the Kozak looked at the leaseholder-Jew askance, as a bear would,
And he called the leaseholder-Jew a mighty lord:
"Oh Jew," he said, "leaseholder-Jew,
Powerful lord,
Allow me to hunt ducks by the river,
So that I can feed my wife and children."
Then the leaseholder-Jew entered the inn,

And he spoke to his wife quietly, saying,
"Hey, wife, my wife Rasia,
I should become the rabbi in Bila Tserkva,
Because the Kozak is calling me a powerful lord."
Then on the holy day, on Thursday,
When the leaseholder-Jews were gathering in Bila Tserkva for prayers,
They spoke to each other quietly saying,
"Oh, Jews, oh you leaseholder-Jews,
What's the news in glorious Ukraine?"
"I heard," said one, "that Khmelnytskyi is now our hetman,
And that from Bila Tserkva to Zaporozhia,
Our life will not be the same."
Then a Jew named Ovram responded,
(He had a small cash of wares –
Just pins and needles,
With which he used to cheat Kozak wives),
"Hey, Jews, hey you leaseholder-Jews,
As a soft wind blows from the south,
So our entire Jewish structure will collapse."
Then on that holy day, on God's Tuesday,
Hetman Khmelnytskyi woke the Kozaks up before the break of day,
And he spoke to them quietly, saying,
"Hey, Kozaks, my children, my friends,
I ask you to take great care,
Arise from your slumber,
Recite the Rusian Lord's Prayer,
Go to glorious Ukraine,
And chop the leaseholder-Jews to pieces,
Mix their blood with the yellow sand in the field,
Don't let the Christian faith be slandered,
Don't honour the Jewish Sabbath."
Then the leaseholder-Jews figured out what was happening,
They all fled to the city of Polonne.
Then Khmelnytskyi arrived in glorious Ukraine
And he didn't find a single leaseholder-Jew there.
Then Khmelnytskyi was not proud,
He went to the city of Polonne,
He wrote letters with his own hand,
And he had them delivered to Polonne,
And in the letters he wrote:

"Oh, Polonnians, oh, citizens of Polonne,
If you would heed my words,
You would then turn the leaseholder-Jews over to me."
Then the Polonnians wrote back to him,
"Sir, Hetman Khmelnytskyi,
Even if we should fall dead one upon the other,
We cannot turn the leaseholder-Jews over to you."
Then Khmelnytskyi wrote letters again,
And had them delivered to the city of Polonne,
"Oh, Polonnians, of citizen of Polonne,
Your counsel is unwise,
I have a cannon Syrota [literally, orphan],
It will destroy your wide, iron gates."
Then on that holy day, on God's Thursday,
Khmelnytskyi arose before the break of day,
And he approached the city of Polonne more closely,
And he set up the cannon Syrota in front of his troops,
And he sent a greeting to the city of Polonne.
Then the leaseholder-Jews
Yelled in a loud voice,
"Hey, Polonnians, citizens of Polonne,
If you would do the right thing,
You would open the gates on the Polish side,
And let us cross the Vistula River, if even in just our shirts,
Then we would live beyond the Vistula River,
And wait for children to be born to us,
And we would teach them to do good deeds,
So that they wouldn't look toward Ukraine at all, not even sideways."
Then the Kozaks were given full run of the city of Polonne for three and
    one-half hours,
"Drink and be merry,
Take rich booty from the leaseholder-Jews."
Then the Kozaks drank and made merry in the city of Polonne,
They took rich booty from the leaseholder-Jews;
Then they returned to glorious Ukraine,
And they seated themselves by rank,
And they divided the silver and the gold into three parts,
The first part they donated to the church of the Protection of the Mother of
    God in the Sich,
And the church of Christ the Saviour in Mezhyhirria,

And the second part they spent on mead and on distilled horilka,
And the third part they divided amongst themselves, amongst the Kozaks.
Then more than one Kozak prayed to God for Hetman Khmelnytskyi,
Because he, that Kozak, had gotten a fine Jewish overcoat to wear.

The historical background behind this text is hard to uncover. It is certain that Jewish leaseholders did indeed oppress the local population, although the amount of tax they collected is exaggerated for effect in the above text. The accusation that Jews held the keys to churches and demanded the payment of a fee for church use is doubtful. Kohut states that no primary sources support this claim and then traces the appearance and development of this statement in historical writing. He hypothesizes that the image originated in Polish literature as an attempt to explain the success of the Khmelnytskyi Uprising and to divert blame away from the Poles.[26] What is especially noteworthy is the similarity between the accusations as they are stated in the variants of this duma and historical writing. The similarities are so extensive that assuming a literary source for the imagery found in oral texts seems justified.

After the list of accusations against the Jews, the text above focuses on interactions between the Jews and the Kozaks. At first, the Jews are thrilled by the deference shown by the Ukrainians. Soon, however, one of the Jews foretells that Khmelnytskyi's ascension to the position of hetman means that they will suffer. The Jews take action and flee to Polonne. This is a real city in the Khmelnytskyi region of Western Ukraine, located on the Khomora River rather than the Vistula. It is an ancient city and one that did have a Jewish community. Did Khmelnytskyi attack Polonne and massacre the Jews? Hrushevska, says that there is no evidence of a Khmelnytskyi attack on Polonne.[27] Antonovych and Drahomanov state that Jews did indeed flee Ukraine when they heard of Khmelnytskyi's assuming the position of hetman and that Polonne was a gathering point for those travelling westward. They do not, however, mention any Kozak attack and say that any Jewish deaths were the result of locals seeking revenge.[28] Jewish popular sources such as the website "The History of Jewish Communities in Ukraine" disagree and state that a massacre led by Kozaks did indeed occur and that ten thousand people lost their lives.[29]

After his victory at Korsun, Khmelnytskyi regrouped at Bila Tserkva, organizing his many new recruits.[30] The Poles used the lull in fighting to try and gain time by engaging in protracted negotiations with the hetman, a situation that may have given rise to the "Bila Tserkva Duma," although Antonovych and Drahomanov claim that this duma is based on later events.[31] In both cases Bila Tserkva marks a lull in the fighting that the ordinary population found unacceptable. The Poles and Khmelnytskyi's forces engaged each other that fall at Pyliavtsi, and the victory of the Kozaks was decisive. At that point, with nothing standing in Khmelnytskyi's way, he and his troops advanced westward. They besieged Lviv, but did not destroy it, and were about to attack the fortress at Zamostia when news arrived that Jan Casimir, a man who Khmelnytskyi thought would support the Kozak cause, had been elected to the Polish throne and was offering the hetman an armistice. Khmelnytskyi accepted and returned to Kyiv in January 1649.[32]

Casimir was not the friend that Khmelnytskyi thought he would be. He himself led an attack against the Kozaks in the spring of 1649. He was joined by the notorious Wiśniowiecki with a force of Polish magnates from the Ukrainian territories. Khmelnytskyi and his Tatar allies managed to trap Wiśniowiecki in the fortress at Zbarazh. The siege at Zbarazh was meant to starve Wiśniowiecki and the Poles into submission and it was horrific, with the population reduced to eating horses, dogs, and cats.[33] In a peculiar twist of fate, this event is commemorated in a song that, in the nineteenth century, accompanied a spring circle dance. Groups of young women and men would dance and sing the following:[34]

There at the house
There at the edge,
    [Refrain of 5 lines]
    Oh, go forth
    Vyshnevetskii, sir,
    You who are a Greek warrior,
    You should dance
    A dance in the German style.
By that house,
There the gentlemen sat,
[Refrain] Oh, go forth …
The gentlemen sat
And they skinned dogs,
[Refrain] Oh, go forth …
They broke their knives,
They tore with their teeth,
[Refrain] Oh, go forth …
Oh, there on the edge,

I will build a house,
[Refrain] Oh, go forth …
I will go forth quietly
As the water flows over a rock
As it flows over a white stone
Even more quietly still.

Casimir and the Polish army moved to the aid of Wiśniowiecki and his troops, but Khmelnytskyi again took the upper hand and surrounded the Polish army at Zboriv. All would have gone well for the Kozaks had not their Tatar allies taken a buy-out from the Poles and withdrawn. This forced Khmelnytskyi to accept a negotiated settlement instead of a victory, losing much of the momentum that he and his forces had enjoyed after Korsun. What was perhaps worse was that the Tatars, on their way homeward, took captives to sell on the slave market following the custom described in the chapter on slavery and, when they did so, they did not distinguish Ukrainian from Pole, taking many of the people whom the Kozaks were supposed to protect.[35]

One of the reasons that the Tatars deserted Khmelnytskyi was that they did not want any of the Christian powers in the region to get too strong; the bribe was not their main motivation. Thus, having used the Kozaks to weaken the Poles and the Poles to keep the Kozaks in check, the Tatars now approached Khmelnytskyi with a proposal to raid Russian territory. Fearing that an attack on a fellow Orthodox power, especially one conducted in coordination with a Muslim force, would anger his people, Khmelnytskyi succeeded in redirecting the Tatars' energies to the much more accessible and less powerful Moldova. The Kozaks participated in this venture, which also is reflected in a Khmelnytskyi duma. The Moldovan campaign was tragic for Khmelnytskyi because he lost his son Tymish. The text that follows was recorded by Panteleimon Kulish from Andrii Shut.[36]

As the soft wind blows from the south, from the Dniester,
Only Holy God knows, only Holy God can comprehend,
What Khmelnytskyi is thinking and planning.
That means neither the centurions nor the colonels could know,
Nor the Kozak pages,
Nor the ordinary citizens,
That our leader Hetman Khmelnytskyi,
Our father Zynovii Bohdan of Chyhyryn,

Had sent twenty pairs of cannons ahead of his troops,
And he himself had departed from Chyhyryn.
The Kozaks walk behind him,
It is like a swarm of bees buzzing.
If a Kozak did not have a steel sword,
Or a long-barrelled rifle,
Then that Kozak threw a cudgel over his shoulder,
And he set off after Hetman Khmelnytskyi as a member of
    the volunteer army.
When they arrived at the River Dniester,
Khmelnytskyi divided the Kozaks into three units,
And when he arrived at the city of Soroky,
He dug trenches around the city of Soroky,
And he camped in the trenches,
And he wrote letters with his own hands,
And sent them to Vasyl Moldavskyi,
In the letters he wrote:
"Oh, Vasyl Moldavskyi,
What will you do now and what do you plan,
Will you fight me,
Or will you make peace?
Will you yield your Wallachian cities to me,
Or will you fill bowls with gold coins,
Or will you beg Hetman Khmelnytskyi for mercy?"
Then Vasyl Moldavskyi,
The ruler of Wallachia,
He read the letters,
And he sent them back,
And to the letters he added:
"Hetman Khmelnytskyi, sir,
Father Zynovii Bohdan of Chyhyryn,
I will not fight with you,
Neither will I make peace,
I will not yield my Wallachian cities to you,
Neither will I fill bowls with gold coins;
Would it not be better for you to yield as my junior
Rather than having me, your senior, yield to you?"
Well, when Khmelnytskyi heard these words,
Then he himself mounted his good horse,
He rode past the city of Soroky,

And he gazed at the city of Soroky,
And he spoke quietly, saying,
"Oh, city, city of Soroky,
You have not yet become a source of amusement for my Kozaks,
I will capture you,
And I will get great riches from you,
I will take care of the poor amongst my ranks,
I will pay them wages of a thaler a month."
Well, just as Khmelnytskyi had boasted,
Then he did just as he had said,
He captured the city of Soroky on Sunday, before the hour of noon,
He ate his noon meal in the marketplace,
Then he attacked the city of Suchava in the afternoon,
He burned the city of Suchava with fire,
And he plundered it with the sword.
Well then, before the Suchavans had even seen Hetman Khmelnytskyi,
They fled to the city of Yassy (Iashi),
And they spoke quietly to Vasyl Moldavskyi, saying,
"Oh, Vasyl Moldavskyi,
Our Wallachian leader,
Are you going to stand up for us?
If you do, we will support you.
If you will not properly defend us,
Then we will shed our blood for a different lord."
Well then Vasyl Moldavskyi,
The Wallachian leader,
He hitched a pair of horses to a wagon,
And he drove to the city of Khotyn,
He set up camp with Captain Khvyletskyi,
And then he wrote letters with his own hand,
He sent them to Ivan Pototskyi, the Polish king,
"Oh, Ivan Pototskyi,
King of Poland,
You are drinking and making merry in Ukraine,
And you know nothing about my misfortunes,
It seems that Hetman Khmelnytskyi, the Rusyn,
Has ruined my entire Wallachian land,
He has dug up all my fields with the sword,
He has taken the heads of all my Wallachians,
He has taken them off their shoulders as if they were jackdaws.

Where there were paths and roads in the fields,
He has paved them with Wallachian heads,
Where there were deep valleys in the fields,
He has filled them with Wallachian blood."
Well then Ivan Pototskyi,
The king of Poland,
He read the letters,
And he sent letters back,
And he wrote in the letters,
"Oh, Vasyl Moldavskyi,
Leader of Wallachia,
If you wanted to live in your Ukraine,
Then you should not have touched Khmelnytskyi at all,
For I have come to know Hetman Khmelnytskyi very well,
In the first war,
At Zhovti Vody,
He met fifteen of my knights,
And he answered them summarily,
He took their heads off the shoulders of all of them as if they were jackdaws,
He captured three of my sons alive,
And sent them off as a present to the Turkish sultan;
And he held me, Ivan Pototskyi,
The Polish king,
Tethered to a cannon for three days,
And he gave me nothing to eat or drink.
Thus, I came to know Hetman Khmelnytskyi well.
I will remember him now and forever."
Well, Khmelnytskyi eventually died,
But his Kozak fame will not die and will not perish.
As for now Lord God confirm and support,
All the tsar's people,
And all the audience,
And all Orthodox Christians,
And the master of this house,
The master and mistress of the house,
May God grant them many years.

Again, the correspondence between history and the duma is tenuous. There were, in fact, two campaigns into Moldova, one in 1650 and one in 1652. They were led by Bohdan Khmelnytskyi and his son Tymofii/

Tymish. The latter married Rozanda Lupul in an effort to create a union between the two polities, but was killed in 1653 at the battle of Suchava/ Suceava. There was indeed a Pototskyi, although he was not the king of Poland but a military hetman. Furthermore, the Pototskyi who was the head of the Polish army and who was defeated at Korsun was Mykolai, not Ivan. But historical accuracy is not what matters from the folk point of view. What matters is Khmelnytskyi's promise to take care of his men, especially the poorest among them, to let them profit from his campaigns, and to guarantee them a regular salary. The other message of importance is the one that Pototskyi delivers to Vasyl Moldavskyi, the besieged ruler, and that message is that opposition to Khmelnytskyi is futile. The idea that the champion of the people cannot be opposed was surely a welcome one to the Ukrainian audience.

In terms of historical events, what followed was not good for Khmelnytskyi and his men. The Poles attacked again in 1651 and the battle of Berestechko was disastrous for the Kozaks.[37] While there are no dumy about this conflict, there are several historical songs about individuals who fought with Khmelnytskyi. Ivan Bohun and Danylo Nechai were especially popular in song. A song about Nechai published by Antonovych and Drahomanov is translated below:[38]

> Oh, from beyond the high mountain, from beneath the dark grove,
> The Kozaks yelled: "Flee Nechai!"
> "Don't worry, don't worry, Hetman, sir,
> I've posted a guard on all the roads,
> How can I, the Kozak Nechai, flee from here,
> How can I lose my Kozak fame and honour?"
> "Oh, my Nechai, I am not disparaging you,
> But keep your horse saddled, as is our custom!"
> "I have with me Shpak, Shpak and he is a good lad,
> He'll let me know when I have to flee."
> "Oh, my Nechai, I am not disparaging you,
> But keep your sword [ready] beneath your cloak.
> When the Poles come, my Nechai, when they come to attack you,
> You should have, my Nechai, a way of defending yourself."
> "My boy, my page, saddle my raven-coloured horse,
> Ride into the open field and see if there are many Poles."
> The boy returns, he returns from Polonne:
> "Forty thousand Poles are coming, forty thousand minus one."
> And the young Kozak Nechai does not pay attention to this,

He drinks mead and wine with Khmelnytskyi, his sworn kin;
Because he, Kozak Nechai, has posted three guards in the city,
And he himself went to his sworn kin to eat sturgeon and fish.
Oh, Kozak Nechai looks out on the still waters,
A company of forty thousand Poles comes riding along the good paths.
The Kozak Nechai glanced through the top window,
There are as many Poles as chickens walking in the marketplace.
"Oh, I am a young Kozak and I'm not afraid of the Poles,
I have my Kozaks with me and I will defend myself."
And Kozak Nechai yells to his small servant,
"Boy, saddle my horse, saddle the raven one,
Saddle the raven one for me and the dappled one for you,
We will defeat the enemy Poles down to the last man!"
Oh, Nechai did not have time to jump on his horse,
Before he began to mow down Poles like sheaves of hay.
Oh, Kozak Nechai darted from house to house,
And he knocked some one thousand Poles from their horses as if they
    were hay,
Nechai looked over his left shoulder,
And what he saw was rivers of blood running from the Poles, the bastards,
Nechai looked to the right,
And his horse got stuck in the corpse of a Pole.
And Nechai addressed his horse with words:
"My horse, don't touch the ground with your hooves."
Well, then Nechai spurred on his horse,
And forty thousand Poles pursued him with their sabres drawn.
The horse strained and struggled under Nechai
While he [Nechai] caught Poles, the sons of bitches, by the hair.
Oh, Kozak Nechai struck his side with his hand
"Looks like I will need to part from my wife and my children!"
"Well, Nechai, where are you raven-coloured horses?"
"They are in the hetman's stables in Polonne."
"And where, Nechai, are your wagons armed with metal?"
"They are by the town of Berestechko, sunk into the swamp."
"Oh where, Nechai, are you wife and children?"
"In the town of Berestechko, sitting at home."
"Oh, whichever one of you Kozaks goes to that town,
Bow before my wife and tell her the bad news,
Let her gather together gold and silver in abundance,
Let her buy me out, let her buy my freedom."

The bastard Poles did not want to take gold or silver,
They ordered that Nechai be hacked into little bits.
"Oh, young Kozaks, whichever one of you goes to the city,
Bow before my mother and tell her the sad news.
Let her weep and let her cry, let her cry without end,
Above her son, above Nechai, a black raven is screaming."
In time, in an hour, in just a minute,
Nechai's head is rolling around the marketplace.
Oh, the bastard Poles did not respect Kozak customs,
They tore apart his body and floated it down the river.

There were two Nechai brothers, Danylo and Ivan. Danylo was the brother who was killed in the conflicts of 1651 and so this is his song. In tone, it is much closer to the dumy of the fourteenth to sixteenth century period because it deals with the emotions of an individual, a lower-echelon figure whose feelings can be explored in greater depth. Like the dumy that reflect events of the earlier period, this historical song warns against excessive confidence. Although Nechai cannot be accused of hubris, he does put more trust in his men, his horse, and himself than is warranted. Like the heroes of the dumy related to earlier periods, he does kill huge numbers of the enemy before he himself succumbs. In the end, his body is desecrated by the Poles. Considering the beliefs about body integrity discussed in the previous chapter, this makes the Poles seem even more vile.

Another historical song about Berestechko presents Khmelnytskyi as being surprised by the defeat. Perhaps because the idea of a champion as promising as Khmelnytskyi suffering such a rout was almost impossible to accept, the song focuses on his incredulity and his expectation of a positive outcome.[39]

I will toss my feathers, I will soar like an eagle, I will spin on my horse,
And I will get back to my Otaman.
"Sir, our hetman, sir, I bow before you [literally, touch my forehead
   to the floor]
[You must know] that a big part of our company is gone."
"Oh, my boys, my young men, how did this happen to you
How could you lose your companions, lose them forever?"
"We stood, Hetman, sir, stood shoulder to shoulder,
And the Poles yelled, "We will cut them down to nothing.""
"Oh, perhaps you, you young men, perhaps you captured booty."

"We had horses in fine array, but the Poles took them."
Winter has come. There is no bread. This is not good for us,
Spring has come and the forest has thawed and we have all been defeated.

Yet a third song is about Khmelnytskyi himself, and uses some of the imagery found in the Nechai song to chastise the hetman.[40]

The Kozaks came charging out from the high mountains,
And in front of them there was Khmelnytskyi on his raven horse,
"Step, my horse, prance along the wide path with your hooves,
Berestechko is not far and the Horde supports us.
Beware, Sir Yan, and remember Zhovty Vody,
A fine force of forty thousand is coming toward you!"
When a page, a young lad, started to saddle his [Khmelnytskyi's] horse,
That horse's knees began to tremble.
Then Khmelnytskyi spoke to the horse; he spoke, saying,
You, you bad horse, do not let your hooves touch the ground!"
"Oh, are these those hops (khmil),[41] those hops which grow up the stake,
Oh, are you not the Kozak Khmelnytskyi who fights the Poles?"
"Oh, I am not the green hops and I do not twist up a stake,
I am not that Kozak Khmelnytskyi who battles the Poles."
"Where, Khmelnytskyi, where is your raven horse?"
"He is tied up in Pototskyi's stable."
"Where, Khmelnytskyi, are your wagons armed with metal?"
"In the town of Berestechko, they have sunk into the swamp."
"How is it, you Poles, my enemies, that I did not really fight you:
I spurred on my horse and the bridge broke beneath me."

This song captures the combination of bravado and unexpected defeat – and the resulting confusion – that befell the Kozaks. What made the defeat at Berestechko especially painful psychologically was the fact that so many men died, not because they were killed in combat, but because they drowned in the swamp. This is not glorious defeat in heroic combat, and there is something ignoble about dying in a muddy quagmire, a fact that affected the spirit of both leaders and the rank-and-file.

For Khmelnytskyi and the Kozaks, the Bila Tserkva treaty that followed the defeat at Berestechko meant accepting numerous concessions. It is this treaty that Antonovych and Drahomanov claim is the source of the duma that is named after this city.[42] It was the humiliation suffered

by the population of Ukraine following this treaty, they explain, that
led Khmelnytskyi to break it and to attack the Poles. The text translated here was recorded by Panteleimon Kulish from the kobzar Andrii
Shut.[43]

Oh, did our Hetman Khmelnytskyi do the right thing, the good thing,
When he made peace with the Poles, the powerful lords, at Bila Tserkva?
And he ordered the Poles,
The powerful lords,
To hold power over the Kozaks and the peasants,
At the same time, he told them not to consider excessive control.
Well, then the Poles,
The powerful lords,
Took control over the Kozaks and the peasants,
And they plotted to seize much power,
They took away the keys from everyone,
And they started to exercise control over their homes.
One [of them] would send the master of the house to the stable,
While he himself would rest on pillows with the other man's wife.
Well, when the Kozak or the peasant would return from the stable,
And look into the home,
Then he would see the Pole, the powerful lord, resting on pillows
   with his wife.
And he has but one coin in his pocket,
But from grief and from sorrow he goes to the inn and spends even that.
Then the Pole, the powerful lord, would wake up,
And walk down the street,
I would say that it's like an unwashed pig pricking up its ears,
And he listens, and he listens closely,
To see if he is being judged by the Kozak or the peasant.
Then he enters the tavern,
And it seems to him,
That the Kozak is greeting him with a cup of mead and a shot glass of
   horilka,
Instead, the Kozak takes aim to hit him between the eyes with the cup,
And the Kozak speaks quietly, saying,
"Oh, you Poles, you Poles,
You powerful lords,
You have taken away our keys,
And you have become the masters of our houses,

You should at least stay away from our company!"
Then the Kozaks gathered in rows, like little children,
And they wrote letters with their own hands,
And they sent them to Hetman Khmelnytskyi,
And in the letters they wrote:
"Hetman Khmelnytskyi, sir!
Our father Zynovii from Chyhyryn,
Why are you so angry with us
That you have placed such a great burden upon us,
We have no freedom of any sort,
The Poles, the powerful lords, have taken away our keys,
They have become masters in our houses."
Then Khmelnytskyi read the letters,
And he spoke quietly, saying,
"Hey, Kozaks, my children, my friends, my nephews,
Wait just a bit, wait just a little while,
Wait from the blessed day of the Protection of the Mother of God, until the
    thrice-ninth Sunday,
When God allows the coming of beautiful springtime,
Then even the poor among you will be well clothed."
Then lord Khmelnytskyi took great care,
He dispatched the Kozaks on their campaign before sunrise,
And he spoke to them quietly, saying,
"I beg you to take heed,
Go to glorious Ukraine,
Chop the Poles, the powerful lords, to pieces,
Mix their Polish blood with yellow sand in the field,
Don't let your Christian faith be slandered."
Well, the Poles, the powerful lords, showed foresight,
And they fled through the wastelands and the forests.
Well, a Kozak runs through the forest,
And there is a Pole lying under a bush and trembling,
Then the Kozak finds the Pole under the bush,
And hits him between the eyes with a cudgel,
And he adds softly, saying,
"Oh Poles, oh you Poles,
You powerful lords!
Enough of this lying around under the bushes,
It is time to go sleep with our wives,
Our wives have already fluffed up the pillows,

And are waiting for you Poles, you powerful lords."
Well, then the Poles called the Kozaks their brothers,
"Oh, Kozaks,
Oh, our dear brothers,
If you would do the right thing,
You would let us flee across the Vistula River at least in our shirts!"
At that point God helped the Poles out,
And the ice on the River Vistula cracked,
And the Kozaks rescued the Poles,
They grabbed them by the hair,
And they pushed them further beneath the ice,
And they spoke quietly, saying,
"Oh, Poles, oh you Poles,
You powerful lords,
At one point our grandfathers were Kozaks along this river,
And they hid treasures beneath the waters,
If you can find those treasures,
Then we will live with you as brothers!
Go then – there is only one road open to you,
To the very bottom [of the river]."
Well, Khmelnytskyi did die,
But his glory will not perish.

This duma starts by questioning Khmelnytskyi and his decisions, but then quickly goes on to say that the problems created by the treaty were not his fault. In the text, Khmelnytskyi makes sure that the terms of the Bila Tserkva agreement protect his people. It is the Poles who violate these terms and do so by quite literally violating the homes and the wives of their Ukrainian subjects. Of course, when Khmelnytskyi learns the truth, he takes action and, as in other texts, promises that the poor will be rewarded.

The attack on the Poles with which the Bila Tserkva duma ends refers to the counteroffensive which Khmelnytskyi began in 1652. During this campaign, the Kozaks defeated the Poles at Batih, and again inspired the local population to launch their own small-scale attacks on Polish magnates. This time, however, Khmelnytskyi did not take advantage of the popular desire to get rid of the Poles. Weakened by years of conflict, he decided that the Kozaks needed a larger polity to serve as an ally and sponsor. He considered becoming an Ottoman vassal, but was opposed by his compatriots and eventually chose the Orthodox option – Moscow. The treaty signed at Pereiaslav affected the future course of what was to become Ukraine. It recognized the Hetmanate, a Ukrainian state under the protection of Moscow. Yet the process of signing was an indication of how Muscovy would behave towards its new ally: Khmelnytskyi swore an oath of loyalty to the Russian tsar and expected the representative from Moscow to do the same. Buturlin, the tsar's envoy, stated that the tsar was an absolute ruler who could not be made to take an oath to his subjects. Khmelnytskyi baulked at first, but eventually accepted the treaty as offered. Unfortunately, just as the Russian side had refused to swear its loyalty to the Kozaks, so it failed to keep the terms of the treaty.[44] Ukrainian lands were besieged by Tatar raids and Polish attacks, forcing Khmelnytskyi, who could not get support from Moscow, to look for support from the Swedes. When the Swedes decided to move against Moscow, Khmelnytskyi was caught in an awkward position. Tensions mounted as newly conquered Belarus preferred Kozak hegemony over their lands to rule by Moscow and as Ukrainians were alarmed at Russian garrisons stationed in Kyiv and elsewhere on Ukrainian soil. At this point, the Russian tsar formed an alliance with Poland, the enemy from whom he was supposed to protect Ukraine. At the war's conclusion, he did not include Ukrainian representatives in the peace negotiations, leading Khmelnytskyi and others to fear that Ukrainian interests were about to be sacrificed. These fears were indeed realized, only in a gradual manner. The incursion of Muscovy was slow, but relentless. Russian intrusion into Ukrainian politics and progressive domination of Ukrainian lands continued until all traces of Ukrainian independence vanished. Khmelnytskyi would not live see this outcome. Disheartened, he died in 1657.[45]

The Khmelnytskyi duma cycle concludes with the account of its namesake's death. Khmelnytskyi had hoped to have one of his sons succeed him, but Tymish was dead, killed in the defence of Suceava, and Yurii (called Yevras or Yuras in most dumy texts), the son who was elected hetman, was only sixteen years old and clearly not up to the task. In the duma that describes the death of Khmelnytskyi, the selection of the young Yurii is presented as the choice of the Kozaks and not the young man's father, even though it takes place while Khmelnytskyi is still alive. The song then describes an episode that shows the young man's irresponsibility and lack of judgment. The mistake that Yurii makes is putting his own pleasure before family duty as he entertains himself instead of keeping vigil over his father's dying moments. The death vigil is considered as important for the soul as integrity of the body of the deceased is for its proper resurrection. Thus, what Yurii commits is a personal error rather than a military one and one that would have resonated with seminarians and the folk audiences of minstrels. In the duma Yurii is described as only twelve years old, not the age of the historical Yurii at the time of his father's death, to underscore his immaturity. The text below is also a recording from Andrii Shut made by Panteleimon Kulish.[46]

> Khmelnytskyi's grey head grew sad; it grew troubled,
> Because he had with him neither a captain nor a colonel,
> All he had with him was Ivan Luhovskyi,
> He was the military scribe,
> And he was a registered Kozak.
> Then they held counsel,
> Like small children,
> And they wrote letters with their own hands,
> And they sent them to cities where regiments and military columns
>   were stationed.
> In the letters they wrote to the Kozaks:
> "Hey, Kozaks, our children, our friends,
> We beg you to take heed,
> Take your flour and stockpile it,
> Travel to the Zahrebelnyi burial mound,
> And wait for me, for Khmelnytskyi, to hold counsel with you."
> Well, the Kozaks did as they were told,
> They gathered their flour together,
> And they travelled to the Zahrebelnyi burial mound.
> They waited until Easter,
> But they did not lay eyes on Khmelnytskyi;
> And they waited until Ascension Day,
> But they did not see Khmelnytskyi;
> They waited until Trinity Sunday [Pentecost]
> But they did not lay eyes on Khmelnytskyi;
> They waited until the Feast of Peter and Paul,
> But they did not lay eyes on Khmelnytskyi;
> They waited until the Day of the Protection of the Mother of God,
> But they did not lay eyes on Khmelnytskyi.
> Then the Kozaks gathered and held a council,
> Like little children.
> "Hetman Khmelnytskyi boasted before us,
> Father Zynovii, Bohdan of Chyhyryn, promised,

That he would host a fair at the Spas Preobrazhennia [Christ of
  the Transfiguration] Church."
Then the Kozaks did the right thing,
They travelled to the city of Subotiv,
And they met Khmelnytskyi there.
They stuck their spears into the earth,
They took off their hats,
They bowed low before Khmelnytskyi:
"Hetman Khmelnytskyi, sir,
Father Zynovii, our man from Chyhyryn,
Why do you need us and why did you summon us?"
Well, then Khmelnytskyi spoke quietly, saying:
"Oh, Kozaks, my children, my friends,
I ask you to heed my words,
To select a hetman from amongst you,
See if you have among you a man of great maturity,
A man who is an administrative hetman.
Because now I get sick from time to time,
And I don't have the strength to be your hetman.
Thus, I order you to select a Kozak from amongst you to be hetman,
Let him be your hetman,
And he will keep order amongst the troops."
Then the Kozaks spoke quietly, saying:
"Hetman Khmelnytskyi, sir,
Our father, Zynovii of Chyhyryn,
We cannot select a Kozak from amongst ourselves to be hetman
We cannot do this on our own,
We want to hear your advice."
Well, then Khmelnytskyi spoke quietly, saying,
"Oh Kozaks, my children, my friends,
I ask you to heed my words,
I have with me Ivan Luhovskyi,
He has served as my page for twelve years,
He knows all my Kozak ways,
He can be your hetman,
He can keep order amongst you."
Then the Kozaks spoke quietly, saying,
"Hetman Khmelnytskyi, sir,
Our Father Zynovii of Chyhyryn!
We do not want Ivan Luhovskyi,

Ivan Luhovskyi is too closely tied to the Poles;
He will join the Poles, the powerful lords, in oppressing us,
He will treat us as if we were nothing."
Then Khmelnytskyi spoke quietly, saying,
"Hey, Kozaks, my children, my friends,
If you do not want Ivan Luhovskyi,
Then I have with me Pavel Teterenko."
"We do not want Pavel Teterenko."
"Then tell me, who do you want?"
"We," they said, "want Yevras Khmelnytskyi."
"My Yevras is still very young;
It is only twelve years since he was born,
He is still young of age and immature of mind."
"Well, we will seat him on the shoulders of twelve people [we will
    have twelve people take care of him],
And they will teach him how to do good deeds,
And he will be hetman amongst us Kozaks,
He will keep order amongst us."
Then the Kozaks behaved properly,
They lay down the mace and the staff,
They elevated Yevras to the position of hetman;
Then they fired their rifles,
And they congratulated the young Khmelnytskyi on ascending to
    the position of hetman.
Then the elder Khmelnytskyi blessed his son,
And he returned to his house,
And he said to his son:
"Son," he said, "heed my words,
If you spend but a short time by the River Tashlyk,
Playing trumpets and drums,
Then you will find your father alive when you return.
But if you spend a long time by the River Tashlyk,
Playing trumpets and drums,
Then you will not find your father alive."
Well, then Yevras, the young hetman,
Spent a long time by the River Tashlyk [Chornyi Tashlyk]
Playing trumpets and drums,
And when he returned home,
He did not find his father alive.
Then he commanded that in Shtomyn,

On a high mountain,
A grave be dug.
Then the Kozaks dug the soil with their swords,
And they carried the dirt with their caps,
And they buried Khmelnytskyi,
And they fired their rifles in his honour,
They celebrated Khmelnytskyi's funeral.
Well, while the Kozaks felt the presence of the elder Khmelnytskyi,
Then they honoured Yevras as their hetman,
But when they no longer felt the presence of the elder Khmelnytskyi,
Then they no longer recognized Yevras, the younger Khmelnytskyi, as
   their hetman.
"Hey, Yevras, son of Khmelnytskyi, young hetman,
It is not fitting that you lead us as our hetman,
It is fitting that you sweep out our Kozak quarters."

The song is somewhat confusing. At first it is the Kozaks who want Khmelnytskyi's young son to take over as hetman and refuse the more experienced leaders suggested by Khmelnytskyi himself. Then, once Yurii does become their leader, they support him only as long as the elder Khmelnytskyi is alive. The contradictory statements are the folk text's way of presenting the confusion that followed the loss of a leader of the stature and genius of Khmelnytskyi. Yurii Khmelnytskyi was indeed deposed and Ivan Vyhovskyi became hetman. What happened under his leadership was typical of what was to follow. Vyhovskyi favoured reviving a relationship with Poland, but other men did not. A particularly adamant opponent was Yakiv Barabash, who led a revolt against Vyhovskyi. Yurii again became hetman and favoured a union with Russia over cooperation with Poland. He was deposed again and entered a monastery only to re-assume various leadership posts in which he was more of a pawn than a leader. The complexities of the political relations both within Kozak ranks and between the Kozaks and Russia and Poland are great.[47] They are extensively treated in historical literature. Suffice it to say that the territory split into Right Bank Ukraine and Left Bank Ukraine and that this period is widely referred to as The Ruin. The effects of The Ruin on the lives of ordinary people are the subject of the cycle of songs called "The Dumy about Everyday Life." They are treated in the next chapter.

Khmelnytskyi continues to excite the popular imagination. Ukrainians see him as both a symbol of struggle against oppression and as a failed leader who surrendered Ukraine to Russia, thus replacing the Polish yoke with the even more onerous Russian one. Russian, Polish, and Jewish views are equally complex, if not contradictory. The recent tendency in historical scholarship to examine literary treatments of historical figures has produced an excellent compilation of articles, similar to the study of literary treatments of Roksolana cited in the chapter on slavery.[48] Khmelnytskyi is written about in historical treatises and literature, and is also the subject of films. The various media which treat this figure offer a variety of images of the hetman. In 1941, the film *Bohdan Khmelnytskyi* was one of a series of Stalin-era biographical features which championed class struggle and Russian imperialism. It portrays the hetman as a strong and valiant leader with a tragic flaw: an irrational love for Helen, his second wife. In the film, she is presented as a woman with Polish sympathies so strong that she is willing to poison her husband. The unflattering picture of Helen was likely meant as an anti-Polish statement.[49] Jerzy Hoffman's 1999 filmic adaptation of Henryk Sienkiewicz's novel *With Fire and Sword* uses Ukrainian actor Bohdan Stupka to portray Khmelnytsky.[50] Khmelnytskyi is not a major character in this narrative, yet the film gives him more dignity than the novel and presents a more positive image of the Ukrainian leader. Ukraine's contribution to the films about Khmelnytskyi is Mykola Mashchenko's 2007 *Bohdan-Zynovii Khmelnytskyi,* cited at the beginning of this book for its scene of Poles destroying Ukrainian minstrels.[51] This is the least successful of all the films where Khmelnytskyi appears as a character. Mashchenko's vision of the hetman was overly ambitious and the film was over budget and had to be cut. The result is a narrative with a confusing plot which presents the hetman as a conflicted character. Several films based on the Khmelnytskyi era, though not featuring the hetman himself as a character, have also been made. The most controversial was the 2009 filmic adaptation of Mykola Hohol's (Nikolai Gogol) *Taras Bulba.* Directed by Vladimir Bortko and financed by the Russian Ministry of Culture, it starred the powerful actor Bohdan Stupka, who, in this case, played not Khmelnytskyi, but the title character, Taras Bulba.[52] The film was widely criticized for its blatant attempts to assimilate Ukrainians into the Russian fold, a charge based on the fact that numerous characters, as they fall in battle, declare their love for the Russian land. Ukrainians responded to this filmic appropriation by producing their own Taras Bulba film, a low-budget drama that was soon relegated to television and received little attention.

The image of Bohdan Zynovii Khmelnytskyi retains its power, especially at the boundary between elite artistic expression, much of which has political overtones, and popular imagination. It is a multifaceted image, capable of articulating Ukrainian nationalist sentiments and of promoting Russian hegemony. The recent popular interest in Khmelnytskyi, manifested in films about him and his era, makes examination of earlier artistic portrayals of the hetman, namely, the dumy of the Khmelnytskyi cycle, most timely.

6 Dumy about Everyday Life – Songs Reflecting the Post-Khmelnytskyi Period

Kateryna Hrushevska assigns the dumy that are categorized as belonging to the everyday life cycle to the period that followed the Khmelnytskyi Uprising. This period is known as The Ruin, and it was not a happy time. Russian domination of Ukrainian lands increased. The Kozaks quarrelled among themselves, some preferring to cooperate with Moscow and others siding with Poland. Yurii Khmelnytskyi led a checkered career. He was deposed as hetman but, when Ivan Vyhovskyi's pro-Polish policies began to displease a number of the Kozak Host, he was reinstated and signed a new Pereiaslav Treaty in 1659. The treaty yielded more control to Moscow and allowed Russians to demand more from the Kozak Host. Thus, the Kozaks were obliged to fight alongside Moscow against the Poles and lost, at which point Yurii annulled the Pereiaslav treaties and signed a new agreement with the Poles. This did not prove popular and Yurii abdicated and joined a monastery. He was captured by the Crimean Tatars and taken to Istanbul, where the Turks first gave him a high ecclesiastical position and then used him in their attempts to consolidate their hold over Right Bank Ukraine. In 1677 he was proclaimed hetman by the Turkish sultan and established a capital of sorts in Nemyriv, whence he conducted military attempts to annex the Left Bank. He failed, and Moscow, Turkey, and the Crimean Khanate established a truce. Yurii was finally executed by strangulation in 1685 for disobeying Turkish orders.[1]

Yurii Khmelnytskyi's sad career is indicative of the tumult that upset the course of people's lives all over Ukraine and at all levels of society. Because of the unsettled situation, this was a time of extreme poverty. Some people did profit. In fact, one of the problems was that certain factions of the Kozak Host wanted to assume the positions once held by the Polish nobility, or szlachta, and become hereditary nobles themselves. Their willingness to sacrifice the interests of rank-and-file Kozaks contributed to the divisions in the Kozak Host.[2] Thus, while a few people did manage to do well in the chaotic situation that characterized The Ruin, the average person struggled, surviving as best as he or she could.

A precarious state on the edge of survival is the situation depicted in the everyday life cycle of dumy. There are no scenes of battle. Most of the action takes place in the home, although many of the actors in the songs are forced to leave their birthplace and venture into foreign territory because that is the only way to make some sort of living. The men who go to seek their fortune in a place far away leave of necessity; they do not see their travels as a grand adventure that they willingly undertake. Rather, it is a burden forced upon them by poverty. Along the same lines, while in the dumy connected to life in the fourteenth to sixteenth centuries mothers try to keep their sons at home, in the everyday life dumy mothers urge their sons to leave, feeling that this is what will offer them the best chance for success and prosperity.

Everyday life dumy, like Khmelnytskyi songs, are different from the dumy about captivity and the songs about Kozaks fighting on land and on the sea. Unlike Khmelnytskyi dumy, this cycle bears no trace of literary influence. These are songs about the life of simple people and the genres that influenced them are folk genres, namely, ballad and lament. Ballads and laments have their own distinctive features and some of these, especially content elements, were transferred to dumy. Laments are sung when a person dies. They are not really songs, but a rhythmic and melodic chant that lets those who have experienced the loss of someone near and dear, like a family member, express grief and, through that expression, achieve some comfort and mitigation of sorrow. Laments are performed in Ukraine, especially the rural parts of this country, to this day. I heard lamentation at every funeral I attended.[3] When working in the field, I did not record what I heard out of consideration for the mourners, but other folklorists did. The work of Svientsitskyi will be cited below.[4] Laments express sad emotions, and so the fact that they share images with the dumy that reflect The Ruin is not surprising. Entire duma passages seem to be taken from laments and are used to express longing for a family member who is so far away that he might as well be dead. The duma passages summon that family member, just as laments do, with images that describe travel over vast distances, often in the form of a bird or a series of several different kinds of birds. In the end, they state that the reunion will never come to pass, again using lament imagery and describing things that are impossible, such as trees blooming in winter, lakes and rivers freezing in summer, and flowers growing on rocks from sand sprinkled as if it were seed.

The material that everyday life dumy share with ballads concerns family conflict. Ballads are story songs, like dumy, but they are shorter, more melodramatic, and have a very clear structure of either rhymed couplets or four-line stanzas. Ballads typically describe problems such as courtship and the seduction and abandonment of a gullible young woman. They talk of infidelity, murder, and spousal abuse. Conflicts between siblings and between parents and their children are also typical subject matter. The severe economic hardship that people suffered during the time of The Ruin led to tensions within families and thus encouraged the presence, or perhaps introduction, of ballad subject matter into dumy. The dumy of this cycle emphasize the importance of kin and also describe the sad situation of family tension and conflict. Like ballads, everyday life dumy depict struggles between blood kin and kin by marriage. They describe misunderstandings that sometimes produce tragic results. At the same time, the everyday life dumy are in dialogue with ballads and provide a different point of view. Many ballads are about the struggles of the young and quite a few texts sing about the young wife whom her mother-in-law dislikes so intensely that she plots her destruction, if not her death. In everyday life dumy we see the mother's point of view. It is the mother who is mistreated when the son brings a new bride into the household. Epic songs sing of the mother's plight and arouse sympathy for the indignities she must suffer.

What connects everyday life dumy most closely to the historical circumstances of The Ruin is the idea of injustice. This is a lawless time. There is no stable governmental authority. Everyone must look out for him- or herself. The only people who can be counted on are relatives, and even some of those are not trustworthy. Only parents genuinely have the interests of their offspring at heart. This idea is best expressed in a song entitled "Justice and Injustice," recorded by Lysenko from the kobzar Ostap Veresai. It is not a duma, but it was a very popular minstrel song. Since ill treatment of the poor and

A Kozak saying goodbye to his beloved. Unknown artist, mid-twentieth century. Courtesy of Rodovid Press.

downtrodden continued into the nineteenth century, this song lived
on in all its power.[5]

There is no Justice in this world, Justice cannot be found!
These days Justice has gone to live with Injustice.
Now Justice is held captive in the nobleman's prison,
And Injustice visits in the nobleman's drawing room?
These days Justice must wait at the doorstep,
And Injustice dines with the noblemen at the head of the table!
Justice is trampled underfoot by the nobles,
And Injustice sits among them and keeps them company.
Now Justice is stepped upon and crushed,
And Injustice is treated to wine and liquor!
Now Justice is in deep trouble with the nobles,
And Injustice is granted free rein!
Well now, Justice – Justice is dying,
And Injustice is devouring the whole world!
Well now, Justice – Justice is dead,
And Injustice has smothered the whole world!
There is no Justice in this world, Justice cannot be found …
The only Justice in this world is your father and your mother!
And where can Justice be found? It cannot be bought and it cannot be
     earned,
You can travel the whole world and not find Justice.
Once there were children; now they have become orphans;
They have nowhere to turn for help,
They cry and they cry; they cannot hang on,
They cannot forget their own dear mother:
"Oh, mother, oh falcon, where can we find you?
We cannot buy you and we cannot earn you,
You can travel the whole world and not find Justice."
If only we had the wings of angels,
Then we would fly and we would gaze upon you,
Because the end of the age is approaching,
And you have to be wary of even your own brother!
Because even when you stand with him in court – you will not find Justice,
All you will find is the need to placate the nobles with gold and silver.
Whichever man can still carry out Justice,
Him God will reward with Heavenly grace.
Because God Himself – He is divine Justice,

He will conquer Injustice; He will vanquish pride,
He will raise up the blessed,
From now and forever!

The dumy of the everyday life cycle do not share military subject matter with the songs about Turkish and Tatar captivity or with the dumy about battles on the steppe and on the Black Sea. What they do share with the folk epic poetry that reflects the fourteenth through sixteenth centuries is their ability to convey the heroism of the main character. In the dumy about battles, the hero displays his valour through his determination to act despite intense pain and suffering. He is on the verge of death and yet, like Fedir, the man without kin, he makes sure that his page can take his place in the Kozak ranks and aid them in their struggle. He is about to succumb after days without food or water, like the youngest of the three brothers escaping from Azov, and yet he expresses concern for his older brothers and their safety. He is quite willing to sacrifice his life and accept the painful ordeal of drowning in the stormy seas to save his fellow Kozaks, like Oleksii Popovych. Throughout his ordeals, despite the intense pain that he experiences, he maintains his dignity, like the Kozak in the Kodyma Valley who holds off predators even as he is dying. The hero of the dumy connected to the fourteenth through sixteenth centuries does not need fancy clothing to know what he is worth. Character, not external trappings, are the true indication of the value of a man, and even a leader, a hetman like Khvesko Handzha Andyber, is willing to dress like a rank-and-file Kozak. Dignity in the face of suffering also characterizes the dumy about Turkish and Tatar captivity and life as a slave. The captives in both the captives' laments dumy endure unspeakable cruelty. Their masters make a special effort to inflict pain on their bodies, and yet the men endure and even express resistance through the words they speak or sing. Dignity and respect are important to Ivan Bohuslavets. He is happy with his Turkish wife until she insults his religion. This is an affront that he cannot tolerate and he kills his wife and embarks on a perilous journey out of the Ottoman Empire. Marusia Bohuslavka may be the ultimate example of courage, self-sacrifice, and maintaining face. She frees the Kozaks being held in prison by her Turkish master but, unlike Samiilo Kishka, she does not herself escape. Furthermore, she hides from the men whom she has just freed the horrific fate that likely awaits her. She does not say that she will probably be killed, if not also tortured, when her master finds out what she has done. Rather, she presents a picture that will let the men escape with a clear conscience.

The heroes of the everyday life dumy similarly maintain their dignity despite the great hardships that they suffer. Sometimes the pain is mental rather physical. In many cases it is both, with mental cruelty compounding what the body must endure. In all cases, the sufferer maintains his or her dignity, sometimes even, like Marusia Bohuslavka, covering up horrid reality for the sake of others. It is this ability to retain one's dignity, one's essential humanity, in the face of forces that seek to destroy all that is right and true that makes the women and men of everyday life dumy admirable. As the song "Justice and Injustice" states, "There is no justice in this world." And yet the people of these songs and the people of Ukraine did endure. From the point of view of the grand march of history, enduring hardship may not seem like a great act of courage. From the folk point of view, however, this was indeed something to express, if not celebrate, in song.

Of the everyday life cycle of dumy, the song that contains the most battle-related subject matter is "Kozak Life." The similarities between this duma and dumy that talk about the fourteenth to sixteenth centuries, as well as the differences between these two cycles, are indicative. In this text, a man sets out on a campaign against his wife's wishes. There are no place names that would indicate which campaign the song refers to, and it is not clear if the man is a registered Kozak and therefore obliged to go when summoned to service, or if he sets out of his own accord: the opening lines could be interpreted either way. Angry with her husband, the wife curses him much as Ivas Konovchenko's mother curses her son. In this case, however, the curse proves ineffectual. The horse plays an important role in both texts, and just as Ivas's mother sends him a horse to try to make up for cursing him, so the nameless man in "Kozak Life" does his best to take extra care of his horse, trying to make sure his wife's angry words do not come to pass. From this point on, the texts diverge dramatically. The duma about Ivas Konovchenko describes the hero's life at the front in great detail. In the song that belongs to the later period, most of the attention is focused on what happens back in the village. Left alone, the wife turns to drink and neglects her household. Her motives are not explained, though one could surmise they are some combination of resentment and feeling overwhelmed by the task of singlehandedly caring for a house and children and farm animals. In some versions of this song the Kozak lists what the wife must do in his absence and the list is long indeed. The Kozak is successful while serving in the military, and even ridicules his wife's efforts to curse him. Eventually he returns and his wife tries to make do with what she has, heating up old borshch for her husband's homecoming meal. He, however, will have none of this and beats her severely: the blows across her back are so intense that the woman ends up with black eyes. The man is a brute. He has no sympathy for what his wife suffered in his absence. He offers her no love, no comfort; all he does is inflict physical pain on top of the emotional pain the woman has already endured. And this produces the result that the man desires. The poor wife makes fresh borshch and she sells her best fabric, probably linen that she wove herself, to buy him the best liquor. When neighbourhood women question her about her appearance, she maintains her dignity and even covers up for her husband, claiming that the bruises were her own fault and the result of an accident. What is more, the Kozak, instead of fixing the gate that he had broken, does exactly what his wife had done and what presumably had made him angry with her: he wastes his money drinking in a tavern. The duma ends decrying the sad state into which Kozaks have fallen. During the time of the Khmelnytskyi Uprising the Kozaks were the hope of Ukraine, the men who would restore justice and equality and bring prosperity. Now, the song tells us, they are the epitome of poverty and decrepitude. It is telling that the last line mentions children, implying that even the future of the country is affected by this sad state of affairs. The text that follows was recorded by Nihovskyi from Ryhorenko and was first published by Panteleimon Kulish.[6]

More than one Kozak did himself a disservice
By leaving his young wife and joining the army.
His wife cursed him and she reviled him:
"May you, wretched Kozak, be plagued with three misfortunes –
Three misfortunes while in the open field.
May the first misfortune be that your horse collapses beneath you,
And may the second misfortune be that you fail to catch up to the Kozaks,
And may the third misfortune be that the Kozaks dislike you,
That they do not allow you to join their company."
Then the Kozak took great care,
He did not heed his wife,
He did not believe what she said.
He took his horse and fed him regularly with fresh hay,
And he gave him yellow oats
And he gave him fresh, cold well water to drink.

He set out on his campaign,
And God helped him,
He made sure that his horse did not collapse beneath him,
He caught up with the Kozaks
And they took a liking to him
And admitted him into their company;
They even asked him to be their hetman.
As the Kozak spends his time in the army,
He informs his fellow Kozaks:
"Listen, fellow Kozaks,
A woman's curse is for naught.
It is like the wind blowing past a dried-up tree,
A woman's tears are useless, like flowing water."
The wife was in the tavern, drinking and partying,
And she neglected her house;
It was as if her house had gone to hell and started to reek of emptiness.
Soon she began to expect that her Kozak would return home from the
    campaign,
And she went back to the house,
She started to fire up the stove,
She took out the sour borshch,
The one that was like vinegar, God knows how old,
She started to take it out from under the bench,
She started to put it on the stove,
She wanted to use it to greet her Kozak.
Soon the Kozak came home from his campaign,
He rode up to the new gate, which was now broken;
He did not get off his horse,
He opened the gates by hitting them with his cudgel,
And he called out with his Kozak voice.
Soon the Kozak's wife heard his Kozak voice,
And she did not come to the door to greet him.
Instead, she tried to flee out the window like a grey dove.
Then the Kozak took heed,
He greeted her by striking her between the shoulders with his cudgel,
He slashed her across her back with his whip.
Then the Kozak's wife ran into the house,
She knocked over the borshch, as if accidentally, with a piece of firewood,
She spilled it to hell, spilled it all over the stove,
And she started to cook new borshch, cook it afresh.
She went into her trunk,

She took out thirty measures of cloth, not plain, but special linen cloth,
And she dragged them down to the tavern,
She bought three quarts of horilka, not plain but double-distilled,
She heated it with honey and with hot peppers,
And she used it to greet and treat her Kozak.
Well, on the next day the Kozak's wife walked outside her gate,
And there was a group of women sitting there.
As they say, women are like magpies,
They gazed one upon the other,
And they passed judgment on the Kozak's wife,
But they did not say anything to her.
Finally, one of the old women could no longer contain herself,
And she said to the Kozak's wife:
"Hey, Kozak's wife, oh Kozak's wife!
It seems that your Kozak came back from his campaign rather late,
Since he has left you black circles under your eyes as presents."
Well then, the Kozak's wife did the right thing,
She covered up everything for her Kozak's sake:
"Ladies, dear ladies, don't you know,
That my Kozak came back from his campaign quite late.
And he made me fire up the stove in the middle of the night,
And prepare his supper for him.
I went to fetch the firewood,
And instead of finding the firewood,
I stumbled across the frame saw,
And I injured my eyes on a grappling hook.
And then I was also mixing bluing for the wash,
And it didn't turn out quite right,
As I was mixing it, it got into my eyes."
The Kozak was sitting in the tavern drinking mead and wine,
And he praised the tavern:
"Oh, tavern, tavern, queen of taverns,
Why does a great deal of Kozak wealth disappear within your walls?
And meanwhile you yourself are not well dressed.
And you lead us, poor Kozaks, about without coats, dressed in practically
    nothing."
Oh, it is easy, it is easy to recognize a Kozak's house,
Even amidst ten houses,
For it is not covered with straw,
And it does not have a stoop around it.
The yard is dirty and it has not a single fence post,

In the shed there is not a single stick of firewood.
In the house there sits a woman and she is numb,
And it is easy to recognize a Kozak's wife,
Because she walks around barefoot, even in winter,
She carries water in a pot,
And she feeds it to the children with a ladle.

Some versions of this song, such as the one published by Horlenko and the one collected by Sudovshchykov, end with lines that sing Kozak glory. What is more, they credit the wife for maintaining the Kozak's dignity as well as her own:[7]

The Kozak's wife rescued him from shame,
"Women, ladies, don't believe this [meaning, that the husband beat her]
I went out late at night looking for a light
And I bruised my eyes [stumbling] over a log!"
Grant, oh Lord, that Kozaks may drink and enjoy themselves,
That they may never lose their Kozak glory!
Although a Kozak may die, although he may be buried,
His fame will not disappear for all ages,
Not for many years,
Not until the end of time.

Modern sensibilities would not praise a woman for covering up an abusive situation. In the seventeenth century, however, and even through the eighteenth century and into the nineteenth, a woman with a brutish husband would have no recourse but to stay with him. In fact, a group of ballads tell of a woman whose brothers take pity on her and kill her abusive spouse. This song category ends by saying that getting rid of the wife-beater leaves the woman worse off than she was before. One example of this ballad is translated below:[8]

A widow had nine sons [each odd line is sung twice]
Nine sons and one daughter.
She had one daughter,
And she gave her in marriage to Roman.
Roman says that he does not love her,
And he boasts that he will destroy her.
He gave her three tasks:
He told her to get up early,

And to use her hands to spin,
And to use her feet to pasture the flocks.
She pastures the flocks
And she takes them along the Danube River.
Along come three merchants –
Her three young brothers:
"Good day, Romanivna [Roman's wife]
You, who are our own sister.
Where is Roman [your husband]?"
"My Roman is in the marketplace somewhere,
He's drinking horilka with the other gentlemen."
"Why are you pasturing the flocks by yourself?
Why don't you hire servants to do this?"
"Oh, I have many servants,
But I have no access to them."
"We're going to go on a visit,
We will go and talk to Roman;
We will go and talk to Roman,
And hack him with our swords."
"Please punish him with your words,
But don't hack him with your swords."
They chopped of his right hand,
"This, Roman, is a lesson for you."
They chopped off his right leg
"This, Roman, is to pay off a debt."
They chopped off a piece of his flesh,
"This, Roman, is because she is our sister."
She came home and started to weep,
Because she did not find Roman [alive].
"What have you done, my brothers,
Why have you killed Roman,
Why have you made orphans out of my children?
Even though I had to pasture the flock myself,
Yesterday I was at least Roman's wife,
And now I am a poor widow."

Dei and Yasenchuk published six ballads on this topic, which would indicate that it was a common theme and that the belief that an abusive husband was better than none at all was widely held. Thus, if the wife of the duma "Kozak Life" has no options and risks ending up in the

Village scene with a large rural monastery. Oleksandra Shabatura, "By the Wall of the monastery," 1930s. Courtesy of Rodovid Press.

same bad situation as the woman in the ballad, then her ability to maintain her dignity in a very difficult situation is indeed heroic.

Whether the Kozak who forces his wife to tend the house alone while he goes out on a campaign profits from this military foray is not clear. Presumably going on a campaign in the seventeenth century, as in the past, could produce booty, goods taken from enemy combatants or from captured populations. Presumably there would also be a salary for participating in a campaign, though most sources say that such salaries were more often promised than paid. What is clear is that Kozaks are the poorest of the poor, much like the steppe riff-raff from which they had developed several centuries earlier. But Kozaks were not the only people in the village who were poor, and going on a campaign was not an option for most men. As a result, young men were forced to seek other employment. Right Bank Ukraine, especially in the period when Yurii Khmelnytskyi was hetman, became progressively depopulated. Bad administrative policies forced people to leave and search elsewhere for work. In most texts, just as in the one that follows, they are pictured as going to a foreign land. "Foreign" had a different meaning in the past, especially at a time when political borders were fluid and administrative systems, particularly on Ukrainian territory, were unstable. Still, going away was so bad that it was akin to death. In the text translated below and first published by Hrushevska, the young man who is leaving against his will lives in a house at the edge of town, which means that his home, like the Kozak house in the first duma of this chapter, is among the poorest dwellings. His family is relatively large, for he has three sisters, all of whom need to be fed and cared for until they are married off and become the responsibility of other families. The poverty of the household may mean that the parents simply cannot support all their children, thus forcing the son to leave so that the rest of the family can survive. The text can also be interpreted to mean that the parents want the best for their son and see his departure as his only chance at a better life. The older two sisters are not saddened by their brother's departure and bring him what he will need for his journey. Only the youngest is concerned about her sibling's return and asks him when she will see him again. He answers in images taken from laments listing the impossible situations mentioned earlier.[9] The text was recorded from Ivan Zoria and first published by Hrushevska.

On Sunday, early in the morning,
It was not church bells that were pealing,

It was people talking in the household on the edge [of town]:
A father and mother were sending their son off into foreign lands,
They were sending him off and they were saying:
"Go, son, go amongst the people,
Maybe things will be better for you there."
"I don't want to go, Mother,
I don't want to live in a foreign land,
People there, my mother,
They will call me a stranger."
The oldest sister leads the horse out,
The middle sister brings the armour,
And the youngest sister also sends him off,
She bids her brother farewell and speaks, saying:
"In which direction shall I look to see your return,
[Shall I look] towards the stormy sea or towards the open field
Or [shall I expect you to come] from the good people in Zaporozhia?"
"Don't look for me, sister, either in the direction of the stormy sea
Or the open field; do not expect me to come from the good people in
    Zaporizhzhia.
Take, my sister, take a handful of yellow sand,
Sow it, my sister, sow it upon a white stone,
Arise, sister, early in the morning,
Water the sand often, my sister,
At the twilight of dawn and at the twilight of dusk,
Water it with your copious tears.
Oh, sister, when do the rivers freeze on the day of Saints Peter and Paul
    [June 30 Old Style/July 12 New Style],
Oh, when does the rowan tree in the field become covered with white
    flowers at Christmas,
Oh, when does it bear fruit on the day of St Basil [January 1 Old Style/
    January 14 New Style],
When does the yellow sand sprout forth on the white rock,
When does it bloom with lavender flowers,
When does cross-shaped periwinkle cover it four times over?"
"I don't know what's become of me, brother,
But I never heard from our elders,
That the rivers might freeze on the day of Saints Peter and Paul,
That the rowan might bloom with white flowers at Christmas time,
Or bear fruit on the day of St Basil,
That yellow sand might sprout upon a white rock,
And bloom with lavender flowers,

That cross-shaped periwinkle might cover it four times over."
"Have you not guessed, sister,
That rivers will not freeze on the day of Saints Peter and Paul,
That the rowan tree will not produce white blossoms on Christmas,
That it will not have berries on St Basil's Day,
That yellow sand will never sprout upon a white rock,
That it will never bloom with lavender flowers,
That cross-shaped periwinkle will not cover it four times over."
Then the sister spoke, saying,
She shed bitter tears:
"Things will be good for you in the foreign land, brother,
It will be good being in a foreign land, visiting stores,
People will take you as their sworn kin, as their blood brother,
But, brother, when misfortune strikes you, when evil befalls you,
Then all your sworn kin will forsake you!"
On the Day of the Holy Spirit people go to church,
They go to church and it sounds like a swarm of bees,
The hem of one garment flashes past the hem of another,
One shoulder brushes the next,
One sworn brother enquires about the health of the other,
They invite each other over for dinner.
As for the poor man, it's as if no one knows him,
It's as if they never visited his house,
As if they never partook of his bread and salt!
Oh, as hard as it is for a beast or a bird to live without a forest,
As hard as it is for a fish or a pike to be on dry land,
As hard as it is to pull a heavy boulder out of the damp earth,
It is equally hard to live in a foreign land without one's father and
    mother,
To live without having one's beloved family at one's side.

After the sister figures out that her brother will not come back, she
foretells his good fortune, assuring him that prosperity is possible. But
she also warns him that, should he fall on hard times, his situation will
be bad indeed because sworn kin treat you well only when you have
money. Sworn kin, also called social kin, are a widespread institution in
Ukraine. For example, my son was "adopted" by a family of my close
friends who had no male grandchildren. People who are not biologically
related can verbally accept others as kin, assuming the mutual obligations that normally go with family relations. In other words, they can
swear to honour a relationship and to treat it as analogous to biological

kinship. Sworn kinship is taken very seriously and indicates special closeness, as in the case of Khmelnytskyi and Barabash in the duma about the two men translated in the preceding chapter. In the song from the Khmelnytskyi cycle, the hero reluctantly breaks the bonds of sworn kinship for the sake of his men. In the everyday life dumy, economic hardship is so extreme that it can prove more powerful than any social kinship obligations; only biological kin can truly be relied upon and trusted regardless of circumstances. Unfortunately, hard times are also the cause of people moving far away from biological kin and thus losing the comfort and support that they provide.

Because of the hardships that he will endure when separated from his family, it is possible to argue that the young man who is forced to depart for a foreign land exhibits heroism. Although he initially expresses his desire not to leave, he accepts his fate. Like men dying on the field of battle and maintaining their composure and dignity even as they succumb to mortal wounds, the young man of this duma also exhibits stoicism. He does not tell his parents to hurry up and marry off his sisters so that they can afford to keep him at home. He departs and has the strength to describe his fate to his youngest sister in the most beautiful of images. This is a courageous act that may not be immediately recognized as such. It is easy to see the courage of a dying combatant. The situation is dramatic and of short duration. The duma translated above and entitled "A Kozak Bids Farewell to His Family" reminds the audience that to accept a life of hardship, a life where pain and suffering might last for a long time, may require far more courage than accepting imminent death.

Ukraine in the fourteenth century was routinely described by travellers as the most fertile and bountiful of lands. It is ironic that, in the period of The Ruin, it was seen as a desolate land, one that could barely sustain a nuclear family. If that family was disturbed in some way, if the father was killed in battle, for example, survival became even more difficult. Women would remarry if they could, but new household heads were not always sympathetic to children who were not their own. Stepsons were perhaps in the most precarious position because, as potential male household heads, they posed a threat to new husbands. In the duma variously titled either "Stepfather" or "A Son Returns from a Foreign Land," a man married to a widow deeply resents his stepson. He lets the young man know how he feels by saying all sorts of hurtful things, including expressing his anger over the cost of the young man's food. As in other dumy, words are powerful and the young man's mother urges him to leave so that the stepfather's expressions of resentment will not have the adverse effect of a curse. The young man does depart and, in this text, he prospers in his new home. Furthermore, he finds himself a good wife who, when he asks permission to go home and see his mother, grants him leave. As he departs, his horse stumbles, a bad omen. The man does arrive at his place of birth and his stepfather again launches a verbal assault, this time accusing the young man of staying away far too long and not being mindful of his mother and her needs. This is, of course, untrue. In the final lines of the song, we learn that the mother's words, uttered in prayer, have brought her son back home and allowed her to see him one more time before her death.[10] This text was first published by Pavlo Chubynskyi.

On Sunday, at morning twilight, the church bells were ringing,
And still earlier, people were talking on a new farmstead,
It was a stepfather, a second father, swearing and cursing the son,
He was belittling his Kozak fate, the good fortune of the youth,
He was chastising him for the bread and salt that he ate,
He was chasing him out of the house.
The elderly mother felt pity and she spoke, saying,
"Oh, my son, widow's son, man without fate or good fortune,
I do not want you to live and dwell with your second father,
Let the old man not swear at you and curse you,
Let him not besmirch your Kozak fate,
Or blame you for your bread and salt and the roof over your head,
I want you to ride away to a foreign land."
Well, he said farewell to his elderly mother,
And he rode off to a foreign land.
He lived and he dwelled in the foreign land,
Not laying eyes on anyone whom he knew,
Neither his father nor his mother nor his beloved blood relatives,
All he had was his beloved, his faithful wife and spouse.
And he spoke to his wife, saying:
"My wife, my true beloved,
In a different land, in my native land, I have an elderly mother,
Should I go, should I travel and visit her?"
The wife heard this,
And she spoke, saying,
"You know and you comprehend [what is best]."
So, the widow's son quickly mounted his horse,

And soon the widow's son rode out of the gate,
And then the horse beneath him stumbled,
At which point the widow's son spoke, he shed copious tears,
"I don't know if I will be able to catch my mother alive."
Soon, in the fourth week of travel, the widow's son,
He started to arrive at the home of his stepfather,
And the second father, the stepfather, came out on the doorstep,
"Well, gentlemen, God has led this man here,
A man who spent his time in a foreign land, far away,
And who has come to his mother as she is about to die."
Soon his mother, who was on her deathbed, saw him,
She crossed her face with the sign of the cross,
"That which I wanted, that I have received,
I have seen my son with my own eyes before I die."

In addition to the emphasis on words, this duma again talks about the importance of blood kin and says that, in times of turmoil, they are the only people who can be relied upon. Step-parents, just like sworn kin, place their own interests first and, when money is tight, they resent sharing limited resources.

Fear of step-parents appears even in laments. Iliarion Svientsitskyi published a collection of laments in 1912. A text addressed by a woman to her deceased father specifically admonishes him for abandoning his children and making them vulnerable to mistreatment by a step-parent. The lament also contains much of the imagery of the impossible return found in dumy such as "A Kozak Bids Farewell to His Family" and "A Sister and a Brother." The lament text goes as follows:[11]

My father, my dear one!
My father, my old one!
Why are you abandoning us?
To whom are you entrusting us?
Is it to the dried-up oak,
Or to a father who is not ours,
Or to a cold wall?
A dried-up oak, my father, will never start to grow,
And a father who is not ours will not respond,
And a cold wall will not keep us warm.
Oh, it would be easier, my father, for me to move a heavy stone,
Than it would be to please a father who is not mine.

With such a man, if you do something, it will [need to] be redone,
And if you say something, it will be ignored.
My work, my father, will not be considered right,
And my words will be wrong as well.
In which direction should I, father, look for your return?
In which direction should I gaze?
Will you come from the field,
Or will you come by sea,
Or will you come from a high mountain,
Or will you come from a strange, foreign land?
Oh, don't come through the fields, father, for you will scrape your feet,
And don't come along the shores, for you might drown.
But walk, father, walk those paths which we walk,
Where we have watered the paths with tears shed for you.
Father, on which holiday will you come to visit,
When should we set the festive tables for you?
Will it be for the Christmas holidays,
Or for the Easter holidays,
Or will it be on holy Sunday?
At Christmas time snow will cover the paths and the byways,
And at Easter time rains will flood the paths,
And on Sunday the paths will be overgrown with thorns.
We will cut the thorns,
And we will await our father as our guest.
Oh, the gardens are blooming and the cuckoos are calling,
And I will go out to fetch water,
And I will ask the nightingales,
Oh, you grey cuckoos,
And oh, you little nightingales,
You fly high in the air,
You see a great deal of the earth,
Have you heard of my own dear father,
Have you heard of my own old father?
And the cuckoos fly and they call,
And they stir up pity in the hearts of orphans.

Perhaps the most horrific step-parent account is found in a song that many minstrels performed and that was very popular in the nineteenth century. It is sometimes classified as a ballad. Several versions of it were published by Dei and Yasenchuk in their collection of family life ballads.[12] The text translated below is the version most often recorded from minstrels. In it the step-parent is the mother who mistreats her stepdaughter so horribly that the girl wants to die. The orphan seeks her mother's grave and pleads with her mother, asking her for permission to join her beneath the earth. The mother describes the horrors that are suffered by a corpse and instructs the daughter to go to her new mother, meaning her stepmother, and to ask her for the care that would be due a child. As it turns out, the stepmother not only does not provide the care requested, she makes a special effort to abuse the girl. The girl does die and her reward is being granted a place in Heaven, whereas the stepmother is punished by being sent to Hell. The text below was recorded from the lirnyk Rydka and first published by Demutskyi.[13]

A strange time has come [been ordained] by God's will,
And more than one orphan has been left by his mother.
The mountains rustle and the rivers murmur,
Oh, a mother has died and the children are left behind …
Children, you are now orphans forever!
Your father will find himself a new wife; they will live as a couple;
And the poor orphans will have to go and become servants.
The ones who are older will go and work;
The one who are younger will go and perish.
When the son of a father works, his work prospers;
When an orphan works, he is always considered lazy.
No matter how hard an orphan works, his work is for nothing:
The stepmother will always say that the orphan is a sluggard.
The orphan girl went wandering out into the world –
She went in search of her own dear mother.
The Lord meets her and begins to question her:
"Where are you going, orphan?" "To find my mother."
"Go back, orphan, you will wander far across the world,
And you will not find your mother, not ever or never,
Because your mother is on top of a high mountain,
Because your mother rests in a house which is a coffin."
The little orphan girl went to the coffin to cry,
And her mother answered her tears:
"Oh, why are you crying atop my coffin?"
"It is me, Mommy, take me in there with you!"
"Oh, as hard as it is to take the sun down from the heavens,

So it is even harder to take you in here with me.
Here, my little orphan girl, there is nothing to eat or drink,
Because God has willed that I rot in the grave.
Why don't you go, little orphan, go ask your stepmother,
[Ask her] if she would be merciful, if she would wash your hair."
But the evil stepmother did not wash her hair,
She destroyed the health of the unfortunate orphan ...
"Why don't you go, little orphan, go ask your stepmother,
[Ask her] if she would not be merciful, if she would sew you a new shirt."
But the evil stepmother did not sew a shirt,
She dressed the unfortunate orphan for her funeral ...
God sends an angel from the heavens:
"Come, little orphan, come to the bright heavens;
As long as you obey God's will,
You will rule with the saints in Heaven.
As for you, evil stepmother, you have prepared yourself for Hell,
You had orphaned children and you did not take care of them.
Open up, Hell, and in it will burn
The one who would not take care of orphaned children."

Being an orphan is understood differently in Ukraine than in the West. While speakers of English expect the term "orphan" to refer to a child with no parents, in Slavic countries, Ukraine included, a person becomes an orphan when he or she loses a single parent. Parents are considered so important that the loss of even one of them renders the child an orphan or *syrota*. The importance of parents is underscored by the fact that relations with dead biological parents continue. When issuing invitations for a wedding, a man or a woman who has lost a parent is expected to go to that parent's grave and invite him or her to the festivities. But a dead parent cannot provide for a child the way a living parent can and being an orphan is considered a pitiable state. Theoretically, the surviving parent should protect the child and keep the step-parent from taking out any animosity on him or her. Apparently, this was not always the case, and especially at the time of The Ruin, when parents did die, whether from accidents or disease – or even starvation – the number of blended families was great. In situations of limited good, as folk songs tell us, the level of resentment of people who were not biologically related was high.

An interesting duma from the everyday life cycle presents the orphaned girl as the most desirable of all possible brides. It is called

"The Dream," and in it a young man goes to his mother to ask for an interpretation of the strange things that he has seen. In the son's dream three colours appear and, according to the mother's explanation, each of these colours represents a type of woman. The first is a married woman looking for an affair. The second is a widow. The third is a poor orphan girl. All three are interested in the young man, the mother says, but he should not succumb to the charms of the first two. It is the orphan who will bring the young man happiness. The text which follows was recorded from a kobzar called Okhtyrets and was first published by Amvrosii Metlynskyi.[14]

On Holy Sunday a widow's son had a dream, he dreamt a dream,
It was a strange dream and a marvellous one.
Shortly thereafter he awoke from his dream,
And he could not figure out the meaning of his Kozak dream,
He speaks to his elderly mother and he says:
"My elderly mother, you interpret dreams for people and you help small
    children,
Please interpret my dream for me, mother.
In it I saw – in our family farmstead,
I saw three mounds of glowing rocks,
And the first mound it glowed red, it was wine-coloured."
"This means that a married woman wants to take you as a lover;
You will have no life of any sort with her;
If God lets you live until Christmas
Or even until Holy Sunday [Easter]
Then she will leave the house,
And she will look toward the market place,
To see if her first husband is coming to look for his wife."
"As for the second mound, it glowed green."
"A widow wants you, a rich and proud woman;
I don't want you to take her, my son,
You will have no luck or good fortune with her,
If God lets you live until Christmas,
Or even until Holy Sunday,
Then her friends and her sworn kin will come to visit her,
They will drink and make merry,
And you will be forced to wait on the doorstep,
They will call you a hired hand,
And they will make fun of you."

"The third mound – it glowed white."
"An unfortunate orphan girl, a young girl without kin wants to marry you,
Son, I want you to marry her.
With her you will find happiness and good fortune,
Where a man and his wife live together and live well,
There St Nicholas delivers joy and contentment."

What makes the orphan girl desirable as a spouse has much in common with the traits that Ottomans found in the slave girls they bought as children and then married to their sons. As Zilfi points out, women with no access to their birth family would be entirely dependent on the family into which they married.[15] If there was any abuse of the bride, she would have no recourse to brothers who, as in the ballad translated above, might appear and punish the husband for mistreatment of their sister. The woman would also feel grateful to the family that accepted her as a bride and daughter-in-law. As discussed in the chapter on captivity, slaves who were given high status, whether or not they were manumitted and given their freedom, often developed feelings of intense loyalty to their masters. The psychological experience of going from deprivation and desperation to a position of respect created positive feelings that were stronger than those that might exist in a situation where there had been no suffering. This was true even if the person who eventually granted the slave a good life had been the one who had previously exhibited cruelty and inflicted abuse. The mother in the duma above assumes a psychological situation like the one expressed in dumy about slavery. She is convinced that, if her son takes an orphan as his wife, she will feel gratitude so great that she will become a most devoted spouse. Also, as in the case of Ottoman slave girls, the orphan girl will have no ties to relatives, either biological or sworn kin, and will be entirely dependent on her family of marriage. Because of the parallels between the orphan bride and the slave spouse, it is tempting to see the duma "The Dream" as a text originally about slavery, but one that evolved to become a song about the times of The Ruin. This may indeed be the case, but without transitional texts such a process of evolution can only be conjectured; it cannot be proven.

In "The Dream," an orphan with no attachments whatsoever is contrasted to women who do have ties. Such ties, the mother explains to her son, are dangerous. Extramarital affairs get one into a great deal of trouble; the mother warns her son that a woman who would betray her husband could, just as easily, betray her lover, should the young man of this song be willing to accept such a role. Widows may have no legal ties to their deceased husbands, but the emotional ties are still there. And then there are also the sworn kin accumulated during the time of the first marriage. Furthermore, here, as in historical songs and ballads, the widow is presented as rich. Marrying a rich woman may make one physically comfortable, but it will simultaneously create an emotional burden. Men who marry for money, who achieve wealth through marriage rather than by their own hard work, are looked down upon and scorned, just as this song states. Accepting a union for the sake of financial gain is akin to hiring one's self out. This song says that the friends and relatives of a widow will indeed treat the man as a hireling and let him know that they see his position in precisely that light. While this topic does not appear in the song translated here, in ballads young widows are often suspected of poisoning or otherwise getting rid of their husbands. As the adulteress may betray the hero, just as she betrayed her husband, so the widow may be a woman who loses husbands on a regular basis and is complicit in their deaths. A particularly sad ballad tells of a poor woman tricked into poisoning her husband so that she can marry a rich person, a nobleman. Her potential lover makes her believe that she cannot simply leave; she must make sure that her spouse is dead. But once the husband is dead, the nobleman rejects her for fear that she might just as easily poison him.[16]

> In the green field,
> A woman was pasturing a flock of sheep.
> A nobleman approached her:
> "Will you be my wife?"
> "How can I be your wife,
> I have a husband at home."
> "And what if you could manage,
> To poison that husband of yours?
> Go to where the fence is,
> And dig up some white mint.
> Soak it in a wine glass,
> Set the glass [with wine] in the entryway
> And when your husband comes home from the field,
> Then give it to him to drink, my beloved."
> The husband came home from the field,

"Give me something to drink, wife!"
[Then later he speaks again:]
"Oh, my wife, oh, my wife, pity the children
Because I am about to rot in the earth."
The woman gathered the children together,
And she sent the nobleman a letter:
"My nobleman, my nobleman, my fine one
I can now be your wife."
"How can you be my wife,
When you poisoned your husband?
You poisoned your husband,
You might poison me as well,
You may become angry with me
And you may do the same thing to me."
"My nobleman, my nobleman, my fine one,
May you be punished by whipping with a flail!
For you turned me into a widow,
And my children into orphans."

During the time of The Ruin, young men were supposed to leave home and seek their fortune in foreign lands. Marrying rich widows, while tempting, was not advisable, precisely for reasons of maintaining one's dignity. The situation for women was different. They were expected to leave their household of birth when they married. When the economic situation was stable, women would marry someone in their own or a neighbouring village. In hard times, women could be forced to marry further afield. Even if there were no step-parents to resent the drain on the household finances that children represented, reasons to send children far away were plentiful. Marrying a daughter to someone in a distant village or even a foreign land, especially one that was more economically secure, could be financially advantageous for both the girl and her family. In the duma translated below and usually entitled "A Sister and a Brother," a woman calls upon her brother for help. She is far away from home and has fallen on hard times. Women did not have the option of leaving home to look for work, so the fact that the speaker here is far from her homeland needs to be explained by her parents giving her in marriage to a rich, and probably older, person to secure her future. Whether the husband has died or has simply lost his fortune is not stated. What is made abundantly clear is that the woman, now poor, is completely ignored in the place where she lives. Not only do people not come to her aid, they treat her as if she was not there – even on their way to church. Life had been good when she lived with her parents and own people, the girl states, because both relatives and sworn kin treated her with respect. Now that she is both far from home and poor, the girl is reduced to suffering. This leads her to plead with her brother and to ask him to come and to restore her dignity. Of course, the brother cannot come, and this is conveyed metaphorically by listing the usual funeral imagery of distant travel and phenomena occurring impossibly out of season. In the end, the woman must accept her fate and anticipate the additional burden of being laid to rest far from home and in a foreign land.[17] This text was first published by Speranskyi.

Oh, on Sunday, early in the morning
Just at daybreak,
It was not a grey cuckoo calling,
And it wasn't a small bird chirping,
It was a sister praying to her brother,
She opened a small window,
And she spoke with words, and she said,
"My dear brother,
Fair as a turtledove,
Come to me
Come visit me
In a strange and foreign land,
During times of misfortune,
In times of ill fate."
"Oh, my sister," he said, "my dear one,
My beloved kin,
I cannot come and be with you,
For I live beyond the dark meadows,
Beyond the wide fields,
And beyond fast-flowing rivers."
"My beloved brother,
Fair as the turtledove,
Come, [please] do, to see me,
Fly to see me,
Fly across the dark meadows as a bright hawk,
And swim across the swift rivers as a white swan,
And run across the wide fields as a small and agile quail.

Alight and rest as a grey dove in my courtyard,
Lean your head to one side,
And call mournfully,
So that people may come outside [to our yard]
And recognize your voice,
And call you dear and beloved kin,
So that they may inquire about your health."
"Sister," he said, "dear one,
My own beloved kin,
You can expect me to come visit you,
When on the feast of Saints Peter and Paul the rivers and lakes freeze over,
When a rowan tree blooms in the field at Christmas.
Go, my sister, go to the swift-flowing Danube River,
Take, sister, take sand in your white hands,
And sow that sand upon a white rock.
When that sand starts to sprout on that white rock,
When it blooms with blue flowers,
When it covers the white stone with cross-shaped periwinkle,
That is when, sister, that is when I will come and be your guest,
That is when I will care for you in your poverty."
"My brother," she said, "my dear one,
Fair as the turtledove,
I am not an infant [literally: I have not just begun to stand on my own
    two feet].
Yet I have never heard old people talk of such a possibility,
That swift rivers and lakes might freeze on the Feast of Saints Peter and
    Paul,
Or that the rowan tree might bloom in the field at Christmas time,
Or that yellow sand might sprout upon a white stone,
And bloom with blue flowers,
That it might cover the white stone with cross-shaped periwinkle,
Does it mean that I will not lay my eyes on you, my brother, not see you for
    all eternity?
As people go to the church for a service on a holiday,
They make a sound like the buzzing of bees,
Men who are brothers come together,
And brother walks with brother,
And matchmaker walks with matchmaker,
And godparent walks with godparent,
And sister walks with sister,

As for me, [people's] shoulders touch mine and so do the hems of their
 skirts,
But they do not look me in the eye.
When we lived with our father and our mother and celebrated feast days,
When we ate and drank,
Then our godparents and our sworn kin honoured us;
But when misfortune befell us,
Then all kin forsook us, both close relatives and relatives in name [meaning,
 godparents]."
"Oh, it is very hard," she said, "my brother,
As it is hard for a winged bird to spend the night in an open field without
 a tree,
Oh, as it is hard, as it is difficult, my brother, for a live fish to be without
 water,
As it is hard and difficult to pull a white stone out of the damp earth,
So also it is hard and difficult to die in a foreign land without one's own
 blood relatives."

The fate of a woman given in marriage to a husband living far from
the household of birth is articulated even more clearly in a ballad
published by Dei and Yasenchuk.[18] As in dumy and other Ukrainian
songs, the human actor is compared to a bird and, in this case, actually flies like a bird to her parents' household. The flight in the form
of a bird is part of a system of bird imagery found in all Ukrainian
folk songs.

My mother gave me away in marriage into a land beyond the distant
 mountains,
And she told me never to come back to visit.
I did not come back for a year, and for two, and in the third year I began to
 pine,
If I had wings made of gold, I would fly and pay a visit.
As I flew over the forest, I charred it with my wings,
And as I flew over the meadow I flooded it with my tears.
Oh, I will alight and I will come down in the grove of cherries; I will sit on a
 cherry tree,
I will coo and I will murmur and perhaps my mother will hear me.
My mother sits by the window and she hears all of this,
And my brother walks in the new entryway, getting his arrows ready.
Oh, my son, my dear one, don't shoot the cuckoo,

For she suffers, as our daughter does, in a faraway land.
Oh, if you are a grey cuckoo, then I ask you to coo,
And if you are my sister, my dear one, I ask you to come inside.
Oh, mother, I will not come into your house,
Oh, you should not have bound me to a man I did not love.

Financial considerations are not present in this song. There is nothing to indicate that the mother married her daughter to a man she did not love to better either her own situation or that of her child. Yet such motives could easily be attributed to the actors of this song and the mother's injunction to her daughter telling her not to come home to visit may be a way of ensuring that she would be incorporated into her new household and her new life. Certainly, ties to kin, whether by blood or by marriage, play an important role and there are clear implications that such ties may be in conflict. Financial considerations leading to a most unhappy marriage are the subject of another ballad.[19]

Oh, there beyond the mountain, beyond the rocks,
A husband and his wife live unhappily.
She makes for him a white bed,
And he prepares for her a whip studded with spikes.
The white bed has become covered with dust,
The studded whip has ripped the white flesh.
The dust has calcified on the white bed,
And the studded whip has become coated with blood.
"Oh, husband, my husband, don't beat me too severely,
My flesh is white and this is very painful for me.
Let me, husband, let me go into the cherry orchard,
And let me pick a red flower there."
She took the red flower and she tossed it in the water,
"Float away, float away, red flower, float to my homeland,
Float away, red flower, float down the Danube,
And when you see my mother, float toward the bank."
The old mother walked out to the Danube to fetch water,
And she saw the red flower and she started to cry.
"Where have you come from, red flower, that you have floated here,
Could it be that my daughter set this red flower afloat?"
"You thought, mother, that you would not be able to feed me,
And so you married me to a man I did not love – and now you are sad,

You thought, mother, that no one would take me in marriage,
Well, the hour will come when you will have to lament."

The sufferings of young women married to men whom they do not love cover a broad spectrum, ranging from loneliness and longing for the family of birth to having to endure extreme brutality and abuse. The last line of the text above is particularly poignant because it implies that the brutal husband will eventually kill the speaker. In ballads, however, problems with husbands are not as prominent as conflicts between the young bride and her mother-in-law. There are more ballads on this topic than any other subject, and the conflict takes many forms. The mother-in-law turns out to be much like the stepmother described in the song about the plight of an orphan. In ballads, the mother-in-law resents the new addition to her household. In real life in the time of The Ruin and beyond, young brides were considered very desirable because they contributed additional labour and gave birth to children who would expand the household workforce further still. But both young brides and the children they produced needed to be fed and cared for. Furthermore, there are hints that mothers-in-law resented not only the food that these additional family members consumed, but also the emotional ties between their sons and the son's wives. In most ballads, mothers-in-law exploit the labour potential of the young women married into their households, sometimes with disastrous results. The saddest song of this type is the one where that bride is given so many tasks, such great demands on her ability to work, that she makes a most dreadful mistake – she forgets her infant.[20]

Halia had a mother who was not her own [meaning, a mother-in-law]
And she sent her out to reap wheat,
"Reap, Halia, and don't unbend your back,
Don't even look up at your child."
Halia reaped the crop and she worked hard,
And she gathered seven sheaves plus four.
And she managed to meet the cows coming home,
And she milked four cows.
And when she sat down to milk the fifth,
Her stepmother [mother-in-law] came and asked her:
"Halia, where is your little baby?"
"Oh, my God, I forgot him in the field!"
Halia walks along the field as it grows dark,

And in the field three ravens are calling,
Lying between them a little child is crying.
One raven is clawing at the head,
And the second is pecking out the eyes,
And the third one is pulling out the intestines.
"Oh, mother [addressed to the mother-in-law], give me a sharp knife,
I need to cut off a length of fabric,
So that I can cover my child's ribs."
Halia did not cut any fabric,
She plunged the knife into her heart.
"Well, mother [again addressed to the mother-in-law], now you have
    three sins,
The first sin is that you sent me out to reap on Sunday,
And the second sin is [the death of] my small child,
And the third sin is [the death of] me, young Halia."

Because the way that mothers-in-law treated young brides has much in common with the way that stepmothers treat stepdaughters, this song confuses the two at one point and the mother-in-law is called a stepmother. There are many variants of this ballad and, in almost all the others, the text states specifically that it is the mother-in-law who assigns the young woman an impossible workload. Other variants also contain lines that explain why the first sin is working on Sunday. In these texts the young woman, sometimes called Halia and sometimes given other names like Handzha, is indeed told that she must work on Sunday, even though this is a sin.[21]

Tensions between young brides and their mothers-in-law were great. The ballads on this topic in Dei and Yasenchuk's book take up sixty-seven pages. Because this is such a large category, the horrible things that the older women do to the newly arrived members of their households vary. In one group of texts, the mother-in-law turns her son's wife into a tree. Sometimes she does this by resorting to magic and sometimes she overworks the young woman to such an extent that she literally becomes stiff and wooden. Becoming wooden then leads to actual transformation into a tree. While all of this is happening, the son is away from home and unaware of the mistreatment of his beloved. When he returns, he spots a strange tree in an awkward, even inconvenient, place such as the middle of a field. His mother orders him to chop the tree down, which he does. Only when blood begins to run from the cuts in the wood or when the tree speaks with a human voice does the young man realize what is going on. By this point, however, it is too late because his beloved is mortally wounded.[22] In several ballads the mother-in-law tries to secretly poison her son's wife. But the son drinks from his beloved's glass and both die, leaving the old woman alone and despondent.[23]

Tense relations between mothers and daughters-in-law were not unidirectional. Young women could abuse their elders as well. The sufferings of the mother are most eloquently expressed in a duma called "The Widow and Her Sons." This was a very popular song, recorded in many variants; one such variant is given in the chapter on minstrelsy. The variants can be divided into two groups: in one, the sons mistreat their mother because they are concerned about their relations with their friends and, like Ivas Konovchenko, want to make the best possible impression on people whom they entertain as guests. The other group of variants emphasizes the potentially tense relations between mothers and the women whom their sons have married. All versions of this duma begin by describing the great sacrifices that the widow makes for her sons. As already noted, in the time of The Ruin, and among poor families even subsequently, the loss of a family member, especially an adult male, meant great hardship. The woman whose story this duma tells is precisely in this position: she is widowed and she has three young mouths to feed. Grown sons could be sent away to foreign lands where they might find good work and prosper. If the children were girls, foreign lands might be a place where they could find rich men to wed. Small children, however, could not be sent away. In hard times, and especially when an adult bread-earner was missing, small children were typically hired out to richer peasants or to nobles. In the chapter on minstrels and minstrelsy, we saw that the children of poor families could be hired out as guides to blind minstrels. Children could do any number of light tasks, from helping with the harvest to cleaning, to minding infants or children smaller than themselves. Some, as in the case of Ivan Kravchenko-Kriukovskyi, were hired as companions to the children of the nobility. These were not desirable jobs. The pay was a pittance and the chances of the child suffering physical and sexual abuse were high. Certainly, this was the case with Kravchenko-Kriukovskyi, who was rendered blind in the course of his service to the pannych, or master's son. Being fully aware of the mistreatment that her sons would likely suffer if they became hirelings, the widow of this duma keeps them at home. Of course, to get enough food to feed them, she must herself work. The song does not state whether the woman offers herself for hire or whether she owns a farm and is forced to work it single-handedly, as the Kozak's wife in the duma "Kozak Life" failed to do. What it does make clear is that the woman is overworked and ruins her health for her sons' sake. She hopes that her kindness will be repaid by her sons and that they will care for her properly when she is old and feeble. Unfortunately, this is not what happens. Perhaps the sons do not understand the magnitude of their mother's sacrifice, never having experienced hardship themselves. Perhaps it is a question of forgetting what want is like when one finds oneself in a situation of plenty. In any case, the sons grow to maturity and prosper. In fact, they do so well that their mother becomes an embarrassment to them. In the version published in the earlier chapter, the sons want to entertain rich people, people of high social standing – and are embarrassed by their mother's sorry state. She is a stark reminder that everything was not always prosperous and cozy. To save themselves the embarrassment of a sickly mother, one who, in one version of this duma constantly "coughs and moans," they kick her out of the house. In the other large group of variants, the reason for getting rid of the mother is the sons' wives and children. Here, the widow's sons are concerned about keeping their spouses and children happy. The version that appears below is one where relations between mothers and daughters-in-law comes to the fore. This text was recorded from the lirnyk Mykola Dibrova and first published by Hrushevska.[24]

In Kyiv, on the Podil,
A green pine was rustling;
But it was not a green pine:
It was a poor widow
Talking to her children.
Bitter, bitter, it is, Christian people,
For us to swallow a white stone while living in this bright world,
So it is more bitter, more difficult, more burdensome,
For a poor, lonely widow,
To raise her little children.
And one poor widow earned her bread in bitterness and through tears,
But she did raise her children,
And she did not let them go and work as hired hands,
She always stood before God and begged for good fortune:
"Oh, God, create a good destiny for my children,

[Give] them a time of good fortune."
This one widow, she succeeded in marrying off her children,
And she managed to secure a good life for them.
But when the children got married,
They started to forget their mother,
They started to reproach her with bitter, hurtful, painful, repulsive, mean
    words,
They even drove her out of the house.
The lonely widow steps over the threshold,
She cries so hard that she cannot see God's world through her tears.
She went outside the gate and became deeply depressed,
Because of her children's bitter, hurtful, painful, repulsive, mean words,
She fell to the ground.
The oldest brother looks out the window,
And speaks to his younger brother with arrogance and with pride,
"Go, younger brother, and escort our mother,
She seems to have become drunk on wine,
And now she cannot stand up on her feet."
"Oh, my dear children,
It's been three days since my lips touched bread,
Since I could cool my lips with water,
What a blood-filled curse has befallen me,
That, after I suffered for you when you were little,
I now receive this from you,
That bitter, hurtful, painful, repulsive, mean words,
Are what you give me."
A complete stranger comes along, a young woman,
She looks at the widow and she speaks to that widow,
"Come, Widow, come live in my house,
I will be mindful of your prayers,
And I will respect you in your old age,
I will honour your prayers in the morning and in the evening."
"Oh, my daughter, I will try to please you,
I will sweep your house and your entryway.
And if you have little children,
I will look after them,
Because you did not let me perish by the roadside [literally, under the
    fence],
As a result of the sorts of children that I have."
The lonely widow walked away from the household of her children,

And immediately their good fortune left as well.
As she walked away from her children's household,
God started to punish them,
Their cattle started to perish,
And fire and flames burned their home,
And green weeds started to overwhelm their yard.
That is when they started to remember their mother,
And on Sunday, early in the morning,
When all the bells were ringing,
You will see, you will believe, oh Christians,
That the widow's sons went most humbly to ask her forgiveness.
The oldest brother enters the stranger's house,
He falls on his knees before his mother,
And he begs for forgiveness, shedding bitter tears,
"Oh, Mother, come and live with us in our house,
We will not disrespect your prayers,
We will honour you in old age,
We will heed your prayers in the morning and in the evening,
Because, when we were little, you did not let us perish by the roadside."
The lonely widow did not pay much heed to their requests,
And she did not believe [in the sincerity of] their tears,
But she did have one concern,
And that was pity for their small children.
The lonely widow started to return to her children's household,
And she fell to the earth and she begged God to forgive them,
And their cattle began to prosper,
While their fierce weeds began to wither,
And the ashes, the mould, the decay started to disappear.
At that point they began to honour their dear mother.
The younger brother sets out on a trip,
And he begs his elder brother, speaking,
"Older brother, take care,
Don't upset our dear mother,
Keep your spouse and my spouse in check, brother,
So that luck and good fortune will aid us in our travels."
But the older brother again feels anger in his heart,
And taking his mother by the hands, he again leads her outside the gates.
The younger brother had a dream,
Far away on his long and distant trip,
He had a most marvellous dream,

And when he got up he cried and shed bitter tears,
And he spoke to the oldest brother, saying,
"It seems that our mother no long lives in our house,
Because luck and good fortune
No longer aid us in our travels."
Whoever respects his father and his mother,
God rewards that person with luck and good fortune,
And whoever makes his father and mother angry,
He falls down into Hell,
Forever and for all ages, Amen.

Dibrova's text is representative of the group of variants where the sons kick their mother out of their home because of their wives and children. As this song emphasizes, there is great tension between biological kin and kin by marriage. When young men marry, their attention focuses on their young families and they can forget their responsibilities to their elders, even elders who made great sacrifices to get them to the position of prosperity that they now enjoy. In some of the texts from this variant group, the sons' actual "bitter, hurtful, painful, repulsive, mean words" are given and they tell their mother that she must leave because she frightens their wives and small children with her shabby appearance and her poor health. While the sons' words themselves are not given in the text above, the song makes clear that the power of what they say is great. As the song continues, we learn that words wound the poor mother who sacrificed for her children to the point that she is virtually incapacitated. In fact, the older son exhibits double cruelty by compounding his ejection of the mother from the home with more hurtful words in the form of false accusations: he says that his mother stumbles, not because she has been rejected by her own children, but because she is drunk. He will not admit the great psychological hurt that is knocking her off her feet and places the fault on his parent instead of acknowledging the damage that he himself has caused. Words in all forms are important in this text, just as they are in other dumy and minstrel songs. Words can hurt and words can bring salvation, especially when they are said in prayer by a righteous person like the suffering mother. The mother's prayers on behalf of her sons when they are young do indeed produce the prosperity that the woman had hoped for. Once the sons see the error of their ways and bring their mother back home, her prayers restore the young men's good fortune.

Words are not the only important subject matter of this song. Bad and hurtful words are spoken because of a problematic family situation. Relations between mothers and daughters-in-law can be tense, and the duma translated above can be said to be in dialogue with ballads. As ballads artistically portray problems from a young bride's point of view, so this duma speaks from the point of view of the mother. While it is the sons who expel their mother, they do so because of their wives. When the younger brother leaves on a journey, he instructs his older brother to keep the wives in check and to protect their mother from the younger women. This motif is much like the one found in ballads where abuse of a wife occurs when the son leaves home and instructs his mother to care for his young wife, a charge that she cruelly violates. The contrast between instructions given and actions taken that appears in both duma and ballad strengthens the cross-genre connection. In addition to using imagery found in ballads to highlight problems between mothers and daughters-in-law, the text given above changes the number of brothers from three to two. This sets up a stark contrast between the younger son, who behaves correctly, at least once he has learned his lesson, and the older brother, who does not. The importance of the relationship between kin by blood and kin by marriage is also underscored by the fact that the neighbour who gives shelter to the homeless mother is explicitly said to be a woman; in other versions of this duma the neighbour is male or the gender of the neighbour is ambiguous. Because the neighbour is a woman in the text given here, the song uses her to show how proper daughters-in-law should behave. What the neighbour offers the widow is respect, exactly what daughters-in-law should give to their husbands' mother, and it is telling that what the widow promises in return are the things that would be expected from a grandmother in a proper household, namely, minding the children and doing light housework. As the younger son's proper behaviour is contrasted to the bad behaviour of his elder brother, so the female neighbour's behaviour is juxtaposed with the presumed disrespectful actions of the daughters-in-law.

Songs cannot correct a problematic family situation. They cannot bring prosperity in times of want. They cannot deliver justice in a situation where injustice predominates. But songs can give artistic expression to all these problematic situations. They can make injustice known. They can convey what is bad and what is good behaviour in the most powerful, effective, and memorable of terms. Songs are words with music. And, as so many minstrel songs say, words are very powerful indeed. As Nadia Suprun, Pavlo Suprun's blind wife, explained, songs help a person "sing out" pain and sorrow.[25] They provide relief and even pleasure. It is little wonder that songs are seen as a threat by those who would suppress others, who would take away their dignity and even their humanity. Songs keep dignity and humanity alive. They are indeed a form of resistance. Songs ensure that, even though a person may die, "his fame will not die and will not perish, now and forever, and unto all ages."

Conclusion

The Ruin was the last historical period reflected in dumy. Songs and singing did not die, of course, but the creation of new dumy ceased. Attempts to create new dumy were made. During the Soviet period, scholars aided lirnyky and especially kobzari in the creation of dumy about Lenin and about Stalin. These were top-down creations, however, imposed by the government. They were not songs born among the common people. As such, they held no popular appeal and disappeared as soon as the Soviet Union collapsed. At present they are fossils preserved in books. When Ukraine became independent, Pavlo Suprun and a few other kobzari did attempt to create new dumy. As already noted, Suprun composed the music to the duma about the accident at Chernobyl and another duma about the murder of the journalist Gongadze.[1] While the Chernobyl duma was initially successful, both these songs have since faded into obscurity. By the time Suprun produced his post-independence compositions, the age of dumy was over.

Songs and singing, however, did not die. Musical expression is impossible to kill. Ballads continued to flourish. I recorded numerous ones during my fieldwork in Ukraine. Ballads came with Ukrainian settlers to Canada. Robert Klymasz collected quite a number of them when he did his fieldwork among Ukrainians living on the Canadian prairies.[2] Songs on historical topics continue to be composed. In Ukraine, the Second World War prompted the composition of songs of great beauty and power. There are songs about young recruits leaving for the front and compositions about courageous women and men defending their homeland. Laments continue to be sung; lamentation was still active when I did my fieldwork. The laments and the complementary genre of folk psalms retain their importance.[3] When the Euromaidan crisis occurred in 2014, traditional folk songs were modified to express the suffering of the Ukrainian population and to praise the courage of the people manning the barricades. Dumy continued to be sung, whether at rallies or at festivals promoting Ukrainian identity such as Kraina Mrii (Land of Dreams). These are traditional dumy like the ones translated here. New dumy are not being composed and old texts are not modified and made fresh and relevant the way other genres are reworked to suit modern times. The age of dumy is over.

The fact that new dumy are no longer composed gives them a special usefulness in today's situation, both in Ukraine itself and among the many people in the Ukrainian Diaspora. As a genre reflecting the past, dumy help us understand history, not from the perspective of the elite, the leaders of battles, the rulers of nations – but from that of the common man around whom the events unfolded. Because dumy are something from the past, they provide people today with the distance that allows us to better understand the present. If we can look back in time to situations that were both different from ours – and similar to what we are experiencing – we can have the objectivity to see our own situation better. We can have the clarity to sing the past, to find emotional release, and to face the future.

Epilogue

I have spent much of my life writing about the poetry of war. My own interest in epic poetry began with a nightmare. In my dream I am running … I am running. I am trying to get away from men who are chasing me. I am carrying a gun, but it is of no use. I do not know why. Is it out of bullets? Am I too scared and disoriented to fire a gun? I am trying to hide, but the buildings through which I run are shattered by the bombs that have been dropped on them and only their skeletons remain. Not only are there no windows, but most of the walls are missing. I see only girders with some bits of wall clinging to them here and there. I am running and stumbling and falling. There is nowhere to hide. I am shot. Everything is red. Red is what I see and the faint outline of the bombed-out buildings in which I had been trying to hide. I die.

This nightmare plagued me for years and years. I do not remember when it stopped, but it persisted through childhood and well into adulthood. Why did I have this nightmare? Am I a reincarnated German soldier who was killed in the Second World War? For some reason I am convinced that I am a German soldier even though I have no German ancestors. In the dream, I am not aware of the identity of the people chasing me; all I know is that they are the enemy and that they want me to die. Were my nightmares caused by the horrors I saw around me as a child? I was born in Germany right after the Second World War. I was born in a displaced persons camp and, if the camp was not bad enough, around me, in the city of Munich, I saw people missing arms and legs and even parts of faces. I was surrounded by the bombed-out buildings that I saw in my dreams. This could certainly cause nightmares in a child. Were my nightmares an attempt to understand the wounded men that I saw around me and the horrors that they must have experienced? These are questions I cannot answer.

What I do know is that I discovered epic poetry and found solace. When I was five we moved to the United States and, several years later, when I was in second grade, I was allowed to go to the library on my own, and there I found *The Iliad* and *The Odyssey*. These were stories of blood and gore, of conflict and heroism, of fantasy and adventure. They were just what I needed. I was hooked. Once I had identified the genre that fascinated me, I quickly found other epic stories. I read *The Song of Roland* and *Beowulf* and all the other classic epics of the Western world. There are certain commonalities to epic as a genre. Sad to say, the sorts of conflicts that generate epic poetries persist.

Ukrainian epic is not my only war-themed topic. When I was in graduate school, Ukraine was under Soviet rule and I could not go there to do research. Instinctively, I chose Turkish minstrel tales and the conflict between Turkey and Iran as the subject matter of my doctoral dissertation. War does not seem like an attractive topic. My husband has always been somewhat puzzled, if not repulsed, by my fascination with war and blood and gore. But it is not the blood and gore itself that I must explore again and again and again. It is the artistic transformation of war and carnage. Artistic transformation is precisely what I have found in epic songs, Ukrainian dumy included. To deal with the horrors of my nightmares and perhaps the horrors of post-war Germany that greeted my first investigation of the world as a child, I needed to see them transformed. Perhaps paradoxically, but I think not, I also have a strong attraction to the beautiful. I crave pretty things. Even when I cook, tasty food in and of itself will not do; the meal must be pretty and colour-coordinated. I like the beauty of my house and I work hard on the beauty of my person. I love crafts. I am constantly making pretty things, be it sweaters which I knit, or embroideries which I make, or my newest craft, jewellery. I want to somehow overcome the horrors of my nightmares by creating things of beauty.

This means that I approach dumy not as a Ukrainian nationalist; I approach them as a child of war. To me, it is imperative that dumy be recognized as artistic creations, not just talismans of Ukrainian national identity. Dumy do indeed reflect the birth of Ukrainian national consciousness. They are indeed unique and attest to the distinctiveness of Ukrainian culture. They are unlike Russian epic song, and they do not resemble the epic poems of Ukraine's other neighbours, both Slavic and Turkic. They do indeed feature brave Kozak heroes, men who fight to the very end, refusing to give up even as they lie mortally wounded, men who make sure to pass on horse and armour to another combatant so that the fight can continue. Recognizing the importance of dumy to Ukrainian identity, this book tries to show that, as artistic creations, dumy have a power beyond their connection to national consciousness. To underscore the artistic aspect of dumy I have made a special effort to discuss these songs as folk creations, exploring the images selected, the language used, the poetic devices employed. Such an analysis is unusual in a collection of epic poetry and it is motivated by my own fascination with artistic expression.

Understanding dumy as art also allows recognition of the fact that these songs can have a multitude of meanings and suit the needs of a variety of people. Right now, the ability of art to transform destruction and war into something that can be handled by a human soul is of paramount importance – and not just for me as a war baby or for the Ukrainians frightened by the Russian annexation of Crimea and the continuing war in Donbas. My students come from all over the world and my classes look like the United Nations. These students are fascinated by my presentation of epic songs in my beginning folklore classes. War films are what they want to talk about when I teach folklore and film. With conflicts not just between Ukraine and Russia, but also in the Middle East, with periodic clashes between China and its minority populations, with rising tensions in Southeast Asia, having art to transform war is vital and my students sense this. Furthermore, scholarly exploration of the transformative power of art is imperative to understanding the human condition. Dumy offer a case study of effective ways of dealing with the trauma of war and destruction.

Dumy have other meanings and functions as well. They can help people understand the emotional needs of others. I learned a great deal by working on this book and I found that these songs helped me achieve empathy for current situations that I had found difficult to comprehend. When I began this book, I did not know its subject matter would come to have such wide applicability. I originally set out to meet the needs of the Ukrainian Diaspora in a time of threats to Ukrainian nationhood. Working on the book, I came to better appreciate one aspect of the Diaspora which has always puzzled me. Many members of the Ukrainian community insist on calling attention to and memorializing Ukrainian suffering and this made no sense to me. The primary focus of attention has been the Holodomor, the famine of 1932–3. Efforts to get governments to recognize this event as genocide are numerous. They include protests by Ukrainian activists in Canada that accuse the Canadian Museum of Human Rights of not giving sufficient attention to the Holodomor, and thus not recognizing that Ukrainians have suffered human rights violations. The Shevchenko Society states that graduate student scholarship applicants who plan to research the Holodomor will be given priority over those researching other topics. My colleagues at the University of Alberta compiled the Holodomor reader, published by the Canadian Institute for Ukrainian Studies in 2012.[1] There are even Holodomor activities for children and online guides telling teachers how to incorporate the Holodomor into the elementary school curriculum. As someone who experienced actual starvation, I found efforts to inform the young about its horrors to be most ill advised.

The internment of Ukrainian Canadians has similarly prompted people to action and here too the goal is recognition of suffering. There are various internment monuments across Canada, but the biggest single effort was the one coordinated by the Shevchenko Scientific Foundation which helped sponsor the production of one hundred commemorative plaques. These were simultaneously unveiled at one hundred sites across Canada on 28 October 2015, and were meant to mark, and thus recognize, the suffering of Ukrainians and other East Europeans mistakenly labelled as enemy aliens.

My reaction to all these commemorations of suffering has long been one of puzzlement. Why commemorate something bad? Why not celebrate Ukrainian accomplishments? Why not ask for recognition of great writers and artists and composers? Why not praise the Kozaks, who insisted on struggling against impossible odds? The sufferings of the Holodomor and the Internment are so passive. What good can be found in memorializing passivity? Looking at dumy in the context of history, along with reading about Ernesto de Martino's theory of presence, has helped me understand why suffering is important and needs to be artistically expressed.[2] The key to my understanding the drive to validate suffering are the dumy about everyday life. These songs, though usually assigned to the post-Khmelnytskyi era, have no explicit references to a period, and are songs which are almost exclusively about suffering. A mother suffers because she works to excess to keep her children at home and to prevent them from assuming the burden of becoming hired labourers. She then suffers again in old age when her sons forget all that she has done and kick her out of their home. A wife suffers when her husband goes off to join a military battalion and leaves her to take care of the entire farmstead single-handedly. She suffers again when the husband returns and beats her for the disrepair of their home. Stepfathers abuse stepsons and sisters suffer as they long for brothers who will never come to their aid. Misery abounds. Suffering is everywhere. Joy is nowhere to be found. At first glance, this seems like wallowing in misery, but it is not. Artistic expression of suffering, I have come to understand, is a testament to endurance, even an assertion of power. Songs about the post-Khmelnytskyi period cannot be songs of struggle like the dumy connected to earlier epochs. After the fall of the Hetmanate, there was nothing to struggle against: no Turks and Tatars to battle, no Polish lords with their Jewish agents against whom to rebel. Life was miserable, and this period is often referred to as The Ruin. Nonetheless, Ukrainians continued to exist and, by continuing to "be," by enduring their lot, they demonstrated strength that must be admired. This is not agency in the sense in which this term is used in contemporary scholarship. It is a power of a different sort; it is the power to endure. Dumy about everyday life powerfully articulate fortitude. For me, looking at dumy provided the distance I needed to understand that efforts to commemorate the Holodomor are similar to dumy about everyday life: they too are artistic expressions of the power to endure. Like dumy, Holodomor monuments say that Ukrainians have suffered and persevered. They did not fight and they did not struggle – they could not. As in the post-Khmelnytskyi period, struggle during the time of the Holodomor or against Internment was just not possible. Ukrainians did endure, however, and their presence is a testament to their strength. Commemorating what they had to withstand to simply "be" honours their fortitude.

Working with dumy, I also learned a lesson about the causes of conflict. Studying dumy in historical context has led me to realize the importance of economic considerations in driving human behaviour. Looking at war through the prism of artistic transformation and examining songs about conflicts that took place at a time long before the one in which I live and in a homeland that I was not able to experience until I was an adult, has allowed me to see that wars often start for practical, rather than ideological, reasons. Artistic transformation leads to the glorification of duty and honour and the presentation of the struggle as a moral one, an effort to defend a people, a nation, a religion. Yet the cause of most struggles presented in epic is injustice in the allocation of resources; in other words, the cause is economic. People settled the area that was to become Ukraine because they saw opportunity for economic betterment. In the dumy from the fourteenth through sixteenth centuries, namely, those about captivity, those about the steppe, and those about the sea, Turkish desire for cheap labour led to raids on the population of Ukraine either by the Turks themselves or by the Crimean Tatars and the Nogais who profited from selling Ukrainian captives to the Ottomans. Polish exploitation of the Ukrainian lands led to the Khmelnytskyi Uprising. The Poles often used Jewish intermediaries, and thus the Jews bore the brunt of Ukrainian fury for pushing the land to the edge of its capacity and the people who worked it to the limits of their endurance. Dumy survived into the nineteenth century and beyond because the people who listened to them felt that they were as badly treated as Turkish slaves and as exploited as the men who rebelled against Polish nobles and fought with Khmelnytskyi. Dumy from the cycle about everyday life speak of economic hardship separating family members and causing emotional and physical suffering.

Wars are often presented as conflicts over ideology, battles between people of different faiths, clashes over abstract principles such as national identity and cultural integrity. Epics are interpreted as songs about honour and glory and that they are. But the conflict in which a brave hero sacrifices his life for his people, his culture, his faith, was, as often as not, precipitated by economic problems. Wars come from the desire to profit at the expense of others. Uprisings happen when the exploited are pushed too far. Military conflicts may be masked by ideology and, as the "Duma about the Widow and Her Sons" reminds us, it is easy to forget what desperate need is like once we are comfortable and well fed. Forget as we might, it is the desire to exploit and the resistance to being exploited that drive wars. May dumy teach us how powerful a motive the economy can be. May they lead to the elimination of the economic disparities that lead to wars. May there be no more children who need to make poetry out of the misery of war.

Notes

Introduction

1 Hrushevska, *Ukrainski narodni dumy* (Ukrainian Folk Dumy).
2 Baycroft and Hopkin, eds, *Folklore and Nationalism in Europe during the Long Nineteenth Century*.
3 *Bohdan-Zynovii Khmelnytskyi*, directed by Mykola Mashchenko.
4 Kononenko, *Ukrainian Minstrels: And the Blind Shall Sing*, 52, 53, 293–4.
5 Volkov, editor, *Testimony: The Memoirs of Dmitri Shostakovich*, 214–15. The writer argues that because minstrels were blind, they were harder to control than people to whom an edict could be issued. Because minstrels could not be controlled by edicts, they were shot.
6 Kuromiya, *The Voices of the Dead*. The section on Ukrainian minstrels is on pp. 108–24.
7 *Povodyr* (The Guide), directed by Oles Sanin, 2014.
8 Tarnawsky and Kilina, translators, *Ukrainian Dumy: Editio minor*.
9 See, for example, Zilfi, *Women and Slavery in the Late Ottoman Empire: The Design of Difference*.
10 Antonovych and Drahomanov, *Istoricheskie pesni malorusskogo naroda* (The Historical Songs of the People of Little Russia).
11 Ukrainian transliteration: Resolution no. 55 of the Cabinet of Ministers of Ukraine, 27 January 2010. http://zakon1.rada.gov.ua/laws/show/55-2010-п.

1. The Recording and Publication of Dumy

1 Anttonen, "Oral Traditions and the Making of the Finnish Nation," 345.
2 McDowell, *Poetry and Violence: The Ballad Tradition in Mexico's Costa Chica*.

3 Anttonen, "Oral Traditions and the Making of the Finnish Nation," 345.
4 Leerssen, "Oral Epic: The Nation Finds a Voice."
5 Webber, *Folklore Unbound: A Concise Introduction*, 13.
6 Danilov, *Drevnie rossiiskie stikhotvoreniia, sobrannye Kirsheiu Danilovym* (Ancient Russian poems collected by Kirsha Danilov) (1818).
7 Tsertelev, *Opyt sobraniia starinnykh malorossiiskikh pesnei* (An Experiment in Collecting Ancient Ukrainian Songs).
8 Hrushevska, *Ukrainski narodni dumy* (Ukrainian Folk Dumy), vol. 1, xviii–xxi.
9 Maksymovych, *Malorossiiskie pesni, izdannye M. Maksimovichem* (Songs of Little Russia Published by M. Maksimovich).
10 Maksymovych, *Ukrainskie narodnye pesni* (Ukrainian Folk Songs).
11 Maksymovych, *Sbornik ukrainskikh pesen* (A Collection of Ukrainian Songs).
12 S(reznevskii), *Zaporozhskaia starina* (Zaporozhian antiquities).
13 Kulish, *Ukraina: Od pochatku Vkrainy do batka Khmelnytskoho* (Ukraine: From the birth of Ukraine to Father Khmelnytskyi).
14 Tsertelev, "O starinnykh malorossiiskikh pesniakh" (About the Ancient Songs of Little Russia), 124.
15 Kononenko, *Ukrainian Minstrels*, 286.
16 Ibid.
17 Ibid.
18 Raynard, *The Teller's Tale*, 135–51.
19 Bazylevych, "Mestechko Aleksandrovka Chernigovskoi gubernii, Sosnitskogo uezda" (The Town of Oleksandrivka in the Sosnytskyi Region, Chernihiv Province).
20 Kononenko, *Ukrainian Minstrels*, 288. See also Kulish, "Pisma P. A. Kulisha k O. M. Bodianskomu."
21 Kononenko, *Ukrainian Minstrels*, 290. See also Zhemchuzhnikov, *Moi vospominanniia iz proshlogo* (My Recollections of the Past) and Rambaud, *La Russie épique: Étude sur les chansons héroiques de la Russie.*
22 Kononenko, *Ukrainian Minstrels*, 291. See also Martynovych, "Ukrainskie zapisi Porfiriia Martynovicha" (The Ukrainian Notes of Porfirii Martynovych).
23 Speranskii, *Yuzhno-russkaia pesnia i ee nositeli* (South Russian Song and Its Performers).
24 See bibliographic essay in Kononenko, *Ukrainian Minstrels*, 292.
25 Lysenko, "Kharakterystyka muzychnykh osoblyvostei ukrainskykh dum i pisen u vykonanni kobzaria Veresaia" (Characteristic Musical Features of Ukrainian Dumy and Songs as Performed by Kobzar Veresai).
26 Kononenko, *Ukrainian Minstrels*, 294.
27 Tylor, *Primitive Culture.*
28 S(reznevskii), *Zaporozhskaia starina* (Zaporozhian Antiquities).

29 Kulish, *Ukraina*. Kulish, *Istoriia vozsoedineniia Rusi* (The History of the Reunification of Rus).

30 Lukashevych, *Malorossiiskie i Chervonorusskie narodnye dumy i pesni*.

31 Kononenko, *Ukrainian Minstrels*, 114.

32 Antonovych and Drahomanov, *Istoricheskie pesni malorusskogo naroda*.

33 Lord, *Singer of Tales*. While Milman Parry died too young to be able to publish, his work was carried on by Albert Lord. Parry's contribution to the oral theory is discussed in the introduction to Lord's *Singer of Tales*, 3–12. Parry is also referenced throughout this book.

34 Bauman, "Verbal Art as Performance."

35 Matiash, *Kateryna Hrushevska: Zhyttia i diialnist* (Kateryna Hrushevska: Her Life and Works).

36 Kolessa, "Etnograficheskaia ekskursiia" (Ethnographic Excursion).

37 Hnatiuk, "Lirnyky: Lirnytski pisni, molytvy, slova, zvistky i t.i. pro lirnykiv povitu Buchatskoho" (Lirnyky. Lirnyk Songs, Prayers, Speech, Customs etc. concerning the Lirnyky of the Buchach Region). Hnatiuk, "Zhebratski blahalnytsi" (Mendicant Begging Songs).

38 For an account of the harassment of Yehor Movchan see Kononenko, *Ukrainian Minstrels*, 30.

39 Kvitka, "Profesionalny narodni spivtsi i muzykanty na Vkraini" (Professional Folk Singers and Musicians in Ukraine).

40 See bibliographic essay in Kononenko, *Ukrainian Minstrels*, 296.

41 Pavlii, Rodina, and Stelmakh, editors, *Ukrainski narodni dumy ta istorychni pisni* (Ukrainian Folk Dumy and Historical Songs).

42 Kononenko, *Ukrainian Minstrels*, 42. See also Lavrov, *Kobzari, Narys z istorii kobzarstva Ukrainy* (Kobzari: A Sketch of the History of Ukrainian Minstrelsy) and Kyrdan and Omelchenko, *Narodni spivtsi-muzykanty na Ukraini* (Folk Singer-Musicians in Ukraine).

43 Miller, *Folklore for Stalin*.

44 Kyrdan, "Varirovanie kobzarem M. Kravchenko dumy 'Bednaia Vdova i Tri Syna'" (M. Kravchenko's Variations of the Duma The Poor Widow and Her Three Sons).

45 Kyrdan, *Ukrainskie narodnye dumy* (Ukrainian Folk Dumy).

46 Kulish, *Zapiski o Yuzhnoi Rusi* (Notes on South Rus).

47 Tarnawsky and Kilina, *Ukrainian Dumy*.

48 Kushpet, *Startsivstvo: Mandrivni spivtsi-muzykanty v Ukraini (XIX–poch. XX st.)* (Mendicancy: Wandering Singer-Musicians in Ukraine, 19th–Beginning of the 20th Centuries).

49 *Ukrainski narodni dumy* (Ukrainian Folk Dumy), ed. Skrypnyk et al.

50 *Sotsialistychna kultura* (Socialist Culture), August 1990, 32–3.

51 Klymash (Klymasz), *Ukrainska narodna kultura v kanadskykh preriiakh* (Ukrainian Folk Culture on the Canadian Prairies).

52 Brooks, *Why We Left: Untold Stories and Songs of America's First Immigrants.*

53 Khanenko-Friesen, *Ukrainian Otherlands: Diaspora, Homeland, and Folk Imagination in the Twentieth Century*, 23–43.

54 Kononenko, *Ukrainian Minstrels.*

55 Kononenko, "Ukrainian Folklore Audio," *Oral Tradition*, vol. 28, no. 2, 2013, 243–52. See also http://journal.oraltradition.org/issues/28ii/kononenko; Kononenko, "Groupsourcing Folklore Sound Files: Involving the Community in Research."

2. Kobzari and Lirnyky – The Singers of Dumy

1 Bushak, Sakharuk, and Sakharuk, *Cossack Mamai.*

2 Kononenko, *Ukrainian Minstrels*, 140–2. See also Yastrebov, "Gaidamatskii bandurist" (The Bandura Player Who Was Also an Outlaw).

3 Not all the people who lived and worked at the Sich were Kozaks. The Kozaks were military men and, while they did a great deal of their own upkeep and maintenance, such as cooking, boat building, and housing and equipment repair, they also hired labourers for all these jobs. Bandurko was such a labourer.

4 Kononenko, *Ukrainian Minstrels*, 141–2. See also K.F.U.O., "Kodenskaia kniga i tri bandurista" (The Book of Koden and Three Bandura Players).

5 Kononenko, *Ukrainian Minstrels*, 142. See also G.V., "Pridvornyi bandurist v begakh" (An Escaped Court Bandura-Player), 21–3.

6 Kononenko, *Ukrainian Minstrels*, 134–7.

7 Ibid., 137–9. See also Efimenko, "Bratstva i soiuzy nishchikh" (The Brotherhoods and Unions of the Poor) and Efimenko, "Shpitali v Malorossii" (Hospices in Little Russia).

8 Mishalow, *Kharkivska bandura* (Kharkiv-style Bandura).

9 Bezsonov, *Kaleki perekhozhie: Sbornik stikhov i izsledovanie* (Wandering Mendicants: Collected Poems and Scholarly Works).

10 Kononenko, *Ukrainian Minstrels*, 50–6.

11 *Marusia Bohuslavka*, directed by Nina Vasylenko.

12 Hrushevsky, *A History of Ukraine by Michael Hrushevsky*, 249.

13 Kononenko, *Ukrainian Minstrels*, 142–7. See also Zhytetskyi, *Mysli o narodnykh malorusskikh dumakh* (Thoughts about the Folk Dumy of Little Russia), 39–56.

14 See table of married minstrels in Kononenko, *Ukrainian Minstrels*, 299.

15 Ibid., 14–15.

16 Ibid., 48. See also Hrinchenko and Lavrov, *Kobzar Fedir Kushneryk* (The Kobzar Fedir Kushneryk), 21–4.

17 Kononenko, *Ukrainian Minstrels*, 48.

18 Ibid., 50.
19 Ibid., 49–50. See also Martynovych, "Ukrainskie zapisi Porfiriia Martinovicha" (The Notes of Porfyrii Martynovych), *Kievskaia starina*, vol. 84, 1904, 272–6 and separately, 1906, 52–3. At http://www.runivers.ru/lib/book8963/. Subsequent articles are also available at this site.
20 Kononenko, *Ukrainian Minstrels*, 97, translated from an archival source.
21 Ibid., 99–100.
22 Translated from an archival source and first published in ibid., 218–19.
23 Ibid., 214–15. See also Borzhkivskyi, "Lirniki," 655–7.
24 Kononenko, *Ukrainian Minstrels*, 95–6, 99.
25 See apprenticeship charts in Kononenko, *Ukrainian Minstrels*, 300–1.
26 First published in Ukrainian in Demutskyi, *Lira i ii motivy: zibrav v Kyivshchyni P. Demutskyi* (The Lira and Its Melodies: Collected in the Kyiv Region by P. Demutskyi), 52–4. First published in English translation in Kononenko, 220–3.
27 Demutskyi, *Lira i ii motivy*, 27–8. Translated in Kononenko, *Ukrainian Minstrels*, 223–5.
28 Published by Lysenko, "Kharakterystyka muzychnykh osoblyvostei ukrainskykh dum" (Characteristic Musical Features of Ukrainian Dumy), 339–66. First published in English translation in Kononenko, *Ukrainian Minstrels*, 227–9.
29 Kononenko, *Ukrainian Minstrels*, 101–2.
30 Ibid., 98.
31 Ibid., 101–2.
32 Ibid., 232–4 gives a translation of the Orphan Girl song recorded from the lirnyk Rydka and published by Demutskyi, *Lira i ii motivy*, 54–6.
33 Recorded by Lysenko from Veresai and first published in English in Kononenko, *Ukrainian Minstrels*, 230–1.
34 Ibid., 15, 98.
35 Ibid., 72–4. See also Hornjatkevyč, "The Secret Speech of Lirnyky and Kobzari Encoding a Life Style."
36 Kononenko, *Ukrainian Minstrels*, 27–9, as quoted in Efimenko, "Bratstva i soiuzy nishchikh" (The Brotherhoods and Unions of the Poor), 312–17.
37 Kononenko, *Ukrainian Minstrels*, 102–6. Descriptions of the initiation rite can be found in Martynovych, *Ukrainskie zapisi*, 272–6, and Hnatiuk, "Lirnyky." See also Speranskii, *Yuzhno-russkaia pesnia i ee nositeli* (South Russian Song and Its Performers).
38 Kononenko, *Ukrainian Minstrels*, 79–80. See also Borzhkivskyi, *Lirniki*, 674.
39 Kononenko, *Ukrainian Minstrels*, 79.
40 Ibid., 114–17, 120.
41 Ibid., 84–5.
42 Ibid., 68–72.

43 Ibid., 74–8.

44 Ibid., 10–11.

45 Ibid., 41. See also Borzhkivskyi, *Lirniki*, 666.

46 Kononenko, *Ukrainian Minstrels*, 13–14.

47 Ibid., 11–13.

48 Ibid., 91–2. See also Kharkiv, Volodymyr, in the archives at M.T. Rylsky Institute.

49 Hrushevska, *Ukrainski narodni dumy* (Ukrainian Folk Dumy), vol. 2, 24–8. First published by Zhytetskyi, *Mysli o dumakh*, 212–20.

50 Hrushevska, *Ukrainski narodni dumy*, vol. 2, 239–40. First published by Chubynskyi, *Trudy etnografichesko-statisticheskoi ekspeditsii v Zapadno-Russkii krai* (Studies of the Ethnographic and Statistical Expedition into the Region of Western Russia), vol. 5, 847–9.

51 Kononenko, *Ukrainian Minstrels*, 292–4. See also Ivanov, "Arteli slepykh: ikh organizatsiia i sovremennoe polozhenie" (The Guilds of the Blind: Their Organization and Current Condition) and Khotkevych, "Neskolko slov o banduristakh i lirnikakh" (Several Words about Bandura Players and Lirnyky).

52 Kononenko, *Ukrainian Minstrels*, 296–8. See also Pravdiuk, *Romenskyi kobzar Yevhen Adamtsevych* (Kobzar Yevhen Adamtsevych from the Romny Region) and Rylskyi and Lavrov, *Kobzar Yehor Movchan*. See also Hrinchenko and Lavrov, *Kobzar Fedir Kushneryk* (The Kobzar Fedir Kushneryk).

53 Kononenko, *Ukrainian Minstrels*, 41, from an interview with Pavlo Suprun, 31 March 1996.

54 At https://commons.wikimedia.org/wiki/File:Kucherenko_shoot.jpeg.

55 Kononenko, "Reviving Dumy: Epic Poetry at the Birth of a Nation" (Vozrozhdaia dumy: epicheskaia poeziia v zarozhdenii natsii), *Twenty Years Later: The Reshaping of Space and Identity*.

56 See the work of Taras Silenko, examples of which are readily available on YouTube.

3. Turko-Tatar Slavery

1 The term janissary comes from the Turkish *yeni cheri*. Janissaries were an elite military corps. Originally, they came from the one in every five captured slaves who were appropriated as a tax of sorts by the sultan. Later they were conscripts taken from the Balkans and from Christian families living in Anatolia through a system called *devshirme*. The janissaries received special training, making them into a military force that inspired fear in the enemies of the Porte. As a special social category, they were placed under severe restrictions, such as a prohibition against marriage, but also granted special privileges, such as a salary and high status.

2 Subtelny, *Ukraine: A History*, 78.

3 Lewis, *Race and Slavery in the Middle East*, 57.
4 Erdem, *Slavery in the Ottoman Empire and Its Demise 1800–1909*, 44.
5 Clarence-Smith, *Islam and the Abolition of Slavery*, 13; Hrushevsky, *History of Ukraine-Rus*, vol. 7, 21.
6 Zilfi, *Women and Slavery in the Late Ottoman Empire: The Design of Difference*, 192.
7 Clarence-Smith, *Islam and the Abolition of Slavery*, 67.
8 Erdem, *Slavery in the Ottoman Empire*, 152. See also Seng, "Fugitives and Factotums: Slaves in Early Sixteenth-Century Istanbul," 142.
9 Seng, "Fugitives and Factotums," 140.
10 Erdem, *Slavery in the Ottoman Empire*, 16, 19.
11 Ibid., 8.
12 Inalcik, "Servile Labor in the Ottoman Empire," 35.
13 Zilfi, *Women and Slavery*, 187–8.
14 Hrushevska, *Ukrainski narodni dumy*, vol. 1, 44–9. First published by Lukashevych, *Malorossiiskie i Chervonorusskie narodnye dumy i pesni* (The Folk Dumy and Songs of Little Russia and Red Russia). Recorded from the bandura player Strichka in the Poltava region, near Romny, on 20 July 1832.
15 Buturlak pretended that Alkan Pasha and his bride were abroad the ship so the ship would be granted safe passage.
16 Zilfi, *Women and Slavery*, 144.
17 Hrushevska, *Ukrainski narodni dumy*, vol. 1, 20.
18 Peirce, *The Imperial Harem: Women and Sovereignty in the Ottoman Empire*, 72.
19 Ibid., 65.
20 Abbott, *A History of Mistresses*, 57–8.
21 Seng, "Fugitives and Factotums," 147.
22 Suprun had turned the historical song about Baida into a duma by adding recited sections to the ones which he sang.
23 Antonovych and Drahomanov, *Istoricheskie pesni malorusskogo naroda* (The Historical Songs of the People of Little Russia), vol. 1, text 145–6; discussion 144–59. For historical information on Dmytro Vyshnevetskyi, also known as Baida, see Hrushevsky, *History of Ukraine-Rus*, vol. 7, 88–98.
24 Antonovych and Drahomanov, *Istoricheskie pesni*, vol. 1, 270–1.
25 Zelenin, *Ocherki po russkoi mifologii: Umershie neestestvennoiu smertiu i rusalki* (Essays on Russian Mythology: Those Who Died Unnatural Deaths and Rusalki).
26 Field observations made in Ukraine by the author. See also Kligman, *Wedding of the Dead: Poetics and Popular Culture in Transylvania*.
27 Erdem, *Slavery in the Ottoman Empire*, 16.
28 *Mamai*, dir. Oles Sanin.
29 Hrushevska, *Ukrainski narodni dumy*, vol. 1, 104–7. First published by Kulish, *Zapiski o Yuzhnoi Rusi* (Notes about Southern Rus), vol. 1, 32–42.

30 Bohoslovets is a variant of Bohuslavets, which is the more common spelling and is derived from the city of Bohuslav. Bohoslov (Bohoslovets) means a theologian, a person who speaks God's word. The alternate spelling might be motivated by the close relationship between minstrels and the church.

31 Hrushevska, *Ukrainski narodni dumy*, vol. 1, 31–2. First published by Kostomarov: "Istoricheskoe znachenie iuzhno-russkogo pesennogo tvorchestva" (The Historical Meaning of South-Russian Song).

32 Zilfi, *Women and Slavery*, 167.

33 Ibid., 205.

34 Ibid., 198.

35 Ibid., 109.

36 Ibid., 109–15.

37 Ibid., 193.

38 Ibid., 204.

39 Hrushevska, *Ukrainski narodni dumy*, vol. 1, 24. First published by Kulish, *Zapiski o Yuzhnoi Rusi*, 210–14. The text was recorded by Nihovskyi from kobzar Ryhorenko in Krasnyi Kut, near Bohodukhiv, Kharkiv region.

40 Haase-Dubosc, "Lady Mary Wortley Montagu (1689–1762): Her Turkish Performances," 211–12.

41 Yermolenko, ed., *Roxolana in European Literature, History and Culture*. The biography of Roksolana is on pp. 2–16.

42 Halenko, "How a Turkish Empress Became a Champion of Ukraine."

43 Antonovych and Drahomanov, *Istoricheskie pesni*, vol. 1: discussion on pp. 286–96, text on pp. 287–9.

44 Ibid., 275–7.

45 Davis, *Christian Slaves, Muslim Masters: White Slavery in the Barbary Coast and Italy, 1500–1800*, 74–5.

46 Zilfi, *Women and Slavery*, 195.

47 Inalcik, "Servile Labor," 27.

48 Erdem, *Slavery in the Ottoman Empire*, 30.

49 Davis, *Christian Slaves*, 75, 79.

50 Ibid., 74.

51 Antonovych and Drahomanov, *Istoricheskie pesni*, vol. 1: text of this duma is on pp. 220–30.

52 Davis, *Christian Slaves*, 76–9.

53 Ibid., 98–9.

54 Erdem, *Slavery in the Ottoman Empire*, 29–30.

55 Davis, *Christian Slaves*, 70–1.

56 Hrushevska, *Ukrainski narodni dumy*, vol. 1, 7–8. First published in Kolessa, "Variianty melodii ukrainskikh narodnikh dum; yikh kharakterystyka i

grupovanie: Studiia" (The Variants of Ukrainian Duma Melodies, Their Characteristics and Their Categorization: A Study).

57 Ibid., 11–12. See also Antonovych and Drahomanov, *Istoricheskie pesni*, vol. 1, 95–6.
58 Erdem, *Slavery in the Ottoman Empire*, 21.
59 Ostapchuk, "Crimean Tatar Long-Range Campaigns."
60 Seng, "Fugitives and Factotums," 157.
61 Davis, *Christian Slaves*, 43.
62 Ibid., 44.
63 Antonovych and Drahomanov, *Istoricheskie pesni*, vol. 1, 83–4.
64 Ibid., 1–61.
65 Zilfi, *Women and Slavery*, 117.
66 Davis, *Christian Slaves*, 57.
67 Zilfi, *Women and Slavery*, 144.
68 Davis, *Christian Slaves*, 62–3.
69 Antonovych and Drahomanov, *Istoricheskie pesni*, vol 1: discussion on pp. 100–6, text on 102–3.
70 Zilfi, *Women and Slavery*, 150.
71 Peirce, *Imperial Harem*, 65–6.
72 Ibid., 63–5.
73 Hrushevsky, *History of Ukraine-Rus*, vol. 7, 72, quoting Karamzin, *Istoriia gosudarstva Rossiiskogo* (The History of the Russian State).
74 See http://oca.org/saints/lives/2013/05/27/101545-st-john-the-russian -and-confessor-whose-relics-are-on-the-island. The print source for St John the Russian is *Pravoslavnaia entsyklopediia* (The Encyclopedia of Orthodoxy), vol. 24, 598–600. Moscow, 2010. John the Russian is given as Ioann Russkii.
75 Seng, "Fugitives and Factotums," 154–5.
76 Ibid., 160.
77 Hrushevska, *Ukrainski narodni dumy*, vol. 1, 102–3.
78 Durak, "Performance and Ideology in the Exchange of Prisoners between the Byzantines and the Islamic Near Easterners in the Early Middle Ages."
79 Hrushevsky, *History of Ukraine-Rus*, vol. 7, 1–30.
80 Seng, "Fugitives and Factotums," 145.

4. The Rise of the Kozaks – Battles on Land and on Sea

1 Hrushevsky, *History of Ukraine-Rus*, 1.
2 Ibid., 3–4.
3 Ibid., 6.

4 Antonovych and Drahomanov, *Istoricheskie pesni malorusskogo naroda* (The Historical Songs of the People of Little Russia), vol. 1. See pp. 79–83 for the song, its variants, and a discussion. The text was taken from Novytskyi's manuscript.

5 Hrushevsky, *History of Ukraine-Rus*, vol. 7, 8–16.

6 Ibid., 27–37.

7 Antonovych and Drahomanov, *Istoricheskie pesni*, vol. 1, 75–6.

8 Hrushevsky, *History of Ukraine-Rus*, vol. 7, 43.

9 Ibid., 44–5.

10 Hrushevska, *Ukrainski narodni dumy* (Ukrainian Folk Dumy), vol. 1, 147. Based on a manuscript found in the collection of Bilozerskyi. Hrushevska postulates that it was written down by I.F. Trush.

11 Kononenko, "Folk Orthodoxy: Popular Religion in Contemporary Ukraine," 46–75.

12 Kononenko, *Ukrainian Minstrels: And the Blind Shall Sing*, 171–95.

13 Hrushevska, *Ukrainski narodni dumy*, vol. 1, 149, version A2.

14 Hrushevsky, *History of Ukraine-Rus*, vol. 7, 45.

15 Hrushevska, *Ukrainski narodni dumy*, vol. 2, 127–8. Originally published by Zhytetskyi in *Mysli o narodnykh malorusskikh dumakh* (Thoughts about the Folk Dumy of Little Russia), 238–40.

16 Ibid., vol. 2, 124–5. Originally published in Zhytetskyi, *Mysli o dumakh*, 240–3. Recorded from Kobzar Ivan, date circa 1810, location somewhere in the Myrhorod region.

17 Hrushevska, *Ukrainski narodni dumy*, vol. 1, 143–4. Originally published in Kolessa, *Melodii ukrainskykh narodnykh dum* (Ukrainian Folk Duma Melodies). The text is on pp. 98–100, the music on ii–iii. Recorded by Kolessa from Mykhailo Kravchenko, Sorochyntsi, Poltava region.

18 Hrushevska, *Ukrainski narodni dumy*, vol. 2, p. 9. Originally published in Kulish, *Zapiski o yuzhnoi Rusi* (Notes about Southern Rus), vol. 1, 14–19. Recorded by Kulish from Arkhyp Nykonenko, Orzhytsia, circa 1852.

19 Hrushevsky, *History of Ukraine-Rus*, vol. 7, 47.

20 Ibid., 64–8.

21 Ibid., 61.

22 Ibid., 68–9.

23 Ibid., 217–21.

24 Antonovych and Drahomanov, *Istoricheskie pesni*, vol. 1, 271–2.

25 Hrushevska, *Ukrainski narodni dumy*, vol. 2, 118–20. First published by Martynovych, "Ukrainskie zapisi Porfiriia Martinovicha" (The Ukrainian Notes of Porfirii Martynovych); recorded from Ivan Kravchenko-Kriukovskyi in Lokhvytsia, 1876.

26 Krvavych and Stelmashchuk, *Ukrainskyi narodnyi odiah XVII–pochatku XIX st. v akvareliakh Yu. Flohovskoho* (Ukrainian Folk Costume of the

XVII–Beginning of the XIX Centuries, as Presented in the Flohovskyi Watercolours).

27 Seng, "Fugitives and Factotums," 164.

28 Hrushevska, *Ukrainski narodni dumy*, vol. 2, 13–137. First published by Metlynskyi, *Narodnye yuzhnorusskie pesni* (South Russian Folk Songs), 377–82.

29 Ibid., vol. 2, 135.

30 Ibid., vol. 7, 232–3.

31 Ibid., vol. 1, 74–6. First published by Kolessa, *Melodii ukrainskykh dum*, 490–4. Wax cylinder recording by Kolessa from Hnat Honcharenko at the Hubaiv khutir near Kharkiv. The text was also recorded in writing by Lesia Ukrainka.

32 Hrushevska, *Ukrainski narodni dumy*, vol. 1, 64. First published by Tsertelev, *Opyt sobraniia starinnykh malorossiiskikh pesnei* (An Experiment in Collecting the Ancient Songs of Little Russia), 26–9.

33 Hrushevska, *Ukrainski narodni dumy*, vol. 1, 83. Recorded from kobzar Ostap Veresai and first published by Kulish in *Zapiski o Yuzhnoi Rusi*, 28–31.

34 Antonovych and Drahomanov, *Istoricheskie pesni*, vol. 1, 245–7.

35 Hrushevska, *Ukrainski narodni dumy*, vol. 1, 87. First published by Zhytetskyi, *Mysli o dumakh*, 244–5.

5. The Khmelnytskyi Period

1 Kohut, "The Khmelnytsky Uprising," 262–8.

2 Kononenko, *Ukrainian Minstrels*, 288.

3 Hrushevsky, *A History of Ukraine by Michael Hrushevsky*, 182–3. Cf. Subtelny, *Ukraine: A History*, 113–14.

4 Hrushevsky, *A History of Ukraine*, 188–93; Subtelny, *Ukraine: A History*, 114.

5 Subtelny, *Ukraine: A History*, 78–9; Hrushevsky, *A History of Ukraine*, 168–70.

6 Subtelny, *Ukraine: A History*, 123.

7 Hrushevsky, *A History of Ukraine*, 232–7.

8 Ibid., 177–80.

9 Ibid., 247–9.

10 Ibid., 257.

11 Antonovych and Drahomanov, *Istoricheskie pesni malorusskogo naroda* (*The Historical Songs of the People of Little Russia*), vol. 1, 262–3.

12 Hrushevsky, *A History of Ukraine*, 255–6.

13 Ibid., 268–70.

14 Subtelny, *Ukraine: A History*, 125–6.

15 Hrushevsky, *A History of Ukraine*, 278, does mention the report that Khmelnytskyi stole letters written by the king from the pocket of a Kozak officer and used these to add weight to his cause when he called upon Kozaks in the Sich, both registered and unregistered, to rebel.

16 Hrushevska, *Ukrainski narodni dumy* (Ukrainian Folk Dumy), vol. 2, 157–9. First published in Metlynskyi, *Narodnye yuzhnorusskie pesni* (South Russian Folk Songs), 385–91. Text recorded by Kulish from Andrii Shut in Oleksandrivka, Sosnytskyi region. The text was probably conflated with a recording from Andrii Beshka, village of Mena. Probable recording date: 1852.

17 Antonovych and Drahomanov, *Istoricheskie pesni*, vol. 2, 15–17.

18 Hrushevsky, *A History of Ukraine*, 279–80; Subtelny, *Ukraine: A History*, 127.

19 Antonovych and Drahomanov, *Istoricheskie pesni*, vol. 2, 18–19.

20 Subtelny, *Ukraine: A History*, 127; Hrushevsky, *A History of Ukraine*, 280.

21 Hrushevska, *Ukrainski narodni dumy*, vol. 2, 167–8. The text was first published by Kulish in *Zapiski o Yuzhnoi Rusi* (Notes about Southern Rus), vol. 1, 223–8 and recorded by Nihovskyi, probably from Ivan Ryhorenko in Krasnyi Kut in the 1840s or early 1850s.

22 Antonovych and Drahomanov, *Istoricheskie pesni*, vol. 2, 38–9.

23 Hrushevsky, *A History of Ukraine*, 280–1; Subtelny, *Ukraine: A History*, 127–8.

24 Subtelny, *Ukraine: A History*, 124, Kohut, *The Khmelnytsky Uprising*, 260–1; see also Teller, "A Portrait in Ambivalence," in *Stories of Khmelnytsky*, ed. Glaser.

25 Hrushevska, *Ukrainski narodni dumy*, vol. 2, 174–6.

26 Kohut, *Khmelnytsky Uprising*, 250–9.

27 Hrushevska, *Ukrainski narodni dumy*, vol. 2, 170–2.

28 Antonovych and Drahomanov, *Istoricheskie pesni*, vol. 2, 30–2.

29 For a history of Jewish communities in Ukraine see http://www
    .jewishencyclopedia.com/articles/4685-cossacks-uprising.

30 Subtelny, *Ukraine: A History*, 128; Hrushevsky, *A History of Ukraine*, 280–2.

31 Antonovych and Drahomanov, *Istoricheskie pesni*, vol. 2, 115–16.

32 Hrushevsky, *A History of Ukraine*, 282–3; Subtelny, *Ukraine: A History*, 129.

33 Antonovych and Drahomanov, *Istoricheskie pesni*, vol. 2, 55. See also Hrushevsky, *A History of Ukraine*, 285–6; Subtelny, *Ukraine: A History*, 129.

34 Antonovych and Drahomanov, *Istoricheskie pesni*, vol. 2, 54.

35 Hrushevsky, *A History of Ukraine*, 285–8; Subtelny, *Ukraine: A History*, 129–31.

36 Hrushevsky, *A History of Ukraine*, 292–4; Subtelny, *Ukraine: A History*, 131; Hrushevska, *Ukrainski narodni dumy*, vol. 2, 189–90. The text was first published by Metlynskyi, *Narodnye yuzhnoruskie pesni*, 391–5.

37 Subtelny, *Ukraine: A History*, 132; Hrushevsky, *A History of Ukraine*, 291–2.

38 Antonovych and Drahomanov, *Istoricheskie pesni*, vol. 2, 55–7.

39 Ibid., 108–9.

40 Ibid., 107–8.

41 The word *khmil* has the same root as Khmelnytskyi's name. The connection between hops and Khmelnytskyi may be part of the reason behind the beer-brewing song that comes up early in the Khmelnytskyi cycle.

42 Ibid., 115–16.

43 Hrushevska, *Ukrainski narodni dumy*, vol. 2, 197–8.
44 Hrushevsky, *A History of Ukraine*, 293–7; Subtelny, *Ukraine: A History*, 132–6.
45 Hrushevsky, *A History of Ukraine*, 297–301; Subtelny, *Ukraine: A History*, 136–7.
46 Hrushevska, *Ukrainski narodni dumy*, vol. 2, 205–6.
47 Subtelny, *Ukraine: A History*, 143–8. See also *Encyclopedia of Ukraine*, http://www.encyclopediaofukraine.com/display.asp?linkpath=pages\ K\H\KhmelnytskyYurii.htm. The print source for this is *Encyclopedia of Ukraine*, Canadian Institute of Ukrainian Studies, vol. 2, 473–4.
48 Glaser, ed., *Stories of Khmelnytsky*.
49 Kalinowska and Kondratyuk, "Khmelnytsky in Motion."
50 *With Fire and Sword*, dir. Jerzy Hoffman.
51 *Bohdan-Zynovii Khmelnytskyi*, dir. Mykola Mashchenko.
52 *Taras Bulba*, dir. Vladimir Bortko.

6. Dumy about Everyday Life – Songs Reflecting the Post-Khmelnytskyi Period

1 Encyclopedia of Ukraine, http://www.encyclopediaofukraine.com/display.asp?linkpath=pages\K\H\KhmelnytskyYurii.htm. See also Subtelny, *Ukraine: A History*, 143–8 and Hrushevsky, *A History of Ukraine by Michael Hrushevsky*, 307–11.
2 Subtelny, *Ukraine: A History*, 141–3.
3 Kononenko, "When Traditional Improvisation Is Prohibited," 52–71.
4 Svientsitskyi, "Pokhoronni holosinnia i tserkovno-relegiina poeziia" (Funeral Laments and Church and Religious Poetry) and Svientsitskyi, and Hnatiuk, "Pokhoronni holosinnia, pokhoronni zvychaii i obriady" (Funeral Laments, Funeral Customs and Rituals).
5 Lysenko, "Kharakterystyka muzychnykh osoblyvostei ukrainskykh dum i pisen u vykonanni kobzaria Veresaia" (Characteristic Musical Features of Ukrainian Dumy and Songs as Performed by Kobzar Veresai). Text on pp. 22–3. First published in English translation in Kononenko, *Ukrainian Minstrels*, 230–1, translation by the author.
6 Hrushevska, *Ukrainski narodni dumy* (Ukrainian Folk Dumy), vol. 2, 212–13. First published by Kulish, *Zapiski o Yuzhnoi Rusi* (Notes about Southern Rus), vol. 1, 215–20.
7 Hrushevska, *Ukrainski narodni dumy*, vol. 2, 214–15.
8 Dei and Yasenchuk, texts, and Ivanytskyi, music, *Balady: Rodynno-pobutovi stosunky* (Ballads about Family Relations and Daily Life), 391–2.
9 Hrushevska, *Ukrainski narodni dumy*, vol. 2, 222–3. This is an archival text first published by Hrushevska, 1931. Recorded from Ivan Zoria in the village of Bilotserkovets, Poltava region. Date of recording not known.

10 Ibid., vol. 2, 229. First published by Chubynskyi, *Trudy etnograficheskostatisticheskoi ekspeditsii v Zapadno-Russkii krai* (Studies of the Ethnographic and Statistical Expedition into the Region of Western Russia*)*, vol. 5: 849–50. Recorded by M. Kostomarov, circa 1840, in the Kharkiv region.

11 Svientsitskyi and Hnatiuk, *Pokhoronni holosinnia; pokhoronni zvychai*, 108–9.

12 Dei, Yasenchuk, and Ivanytskyi, *Balady: Rodynno-pobutovi stosunky*; see 405–27 and especially 414–19.

13 First published in Ukrainian in Demutskyi, *Lira i ii motivy: zibrav v Kyiivshchyni Demutskyi* (The Lira and Its Melodies: Collected in the Kyiv Region by Demutskyi), 54–6. First published in English translation in Kononenko, *Ukrainian Minstrels*, 232–4.

14 Hrushevska, *Ukrainski narodni dumy*, vol. 2, 230–1. First published by Metlynskyi, *Narodnye yuzhnorusskie pesni* (South Russian Folk Songs), 354–5.

15 Zilfi, *Women and Slavery in the Late Ottoman Empire*, 167.

16 Dei and Yasenchuk, texts, and Ivanytskyi, music, *Balady: Kokhannia ta doshliubni vzaemyny* (Ballads about Love and Premarital Relations), 92.

17 Hrushevska, *Ukrainski narodni dumy*, vol. 2, 286–7. First published in Speranskii, *Yuzhno-russkaia pesnia i ee nositeli* (South Russian Song and Its Performers), vol. 5, 197. Recorded from T. Parkhomenko, village of Voloskivsti, Sosnytskyi region.

18 Dei, Yasenchuk, and Ivanytskyi, *Balady: Rodynno-pobutovi stosunky* (Ballads about Family Relations and Daily Life), 302.

19 Ibid., 331.

20 Ibid., 238–9.

21 The full set of ballads is found ibid., 237–47.

22 Ibid., 216–36.

23 Ibid., 255–62.

24 Hrushevska, *Ukrainski narodni dumy*, vol. 2, 256–8. First published by Hrushevska from a manuscript in the S.I. Maslov collection. Text recorded from the lirnyk Mykola Dibrova, village of Hrymanky, near Pryluky, 1902.

25 Kononenko, *Ukrainian Minstrels*, 56.

Conclusion

1 Kononenko, "Duma pro Chornobyl: Old Genres, New Topics."

2 Kononenko, "Ukrainian Ballads in Canada: Adjusting to New Life in a New Land."

3 Kononenko, "When Traditional Improvisation Is Prohibited: Ukrainian Funeral Laments and Burial Practices."

Epilogue

1 Klid and Motyl, *The Holodomor Reader: A Source Book on the Famine of 1932–33*.

2 Ferrari, *Ernesto de Martino on Religion: The Crisis and the Presence*.

Bibliography

Note: For publications that are not readily available at major libraries, I have added an electronic source where one exists. The URL follows the publication information. I have included URLs for several major Ukrainian resources, such as the Encyclopedia of Ukraine, which, even in my university library, is not available in print. Only the index is accessible as a book; the remainder of the hard copy is stored in our book repository. Some of the electronic sources that come out of the former Soviet Union do not work reliably, but I have included them regardless.

Abbott, Elizabeth. *A History of Mistresses*. Harper Flamingo Canada, 2003.

Antonovych, Volodymyr, and Mykhailo Drahomanov (Vladimir Antonovich and Mikhail Dragomanov). *Istoricheskie pesni malorusskogo naroda* (The Historical Songs of the People of Little Russia). 2 vols. Izdatelstvo Imperatorskogo Russkogo geograficheskogo obshchestva, 1874–5.

Anttonen, Pertti. "Oral Traditions and the Making of the Finnish Nation." In *Folklore and Nationalism in Europe during the Long Nineteenth Century*, edited by Timothy Baycroft and David Hopkin, Brill, 2012, pp. 325–50.

Bauman, Richard. "Verbal Art as Performance." *American Anthropologist*, new series, vol. 77, no. 2, 1975, pp. 290–311.

Baycroft, Timothy, and David Hopkin, editors. *Folklore and Nationalism in Europe during the Long Nineteenth Century*. Brill, 2012.

Bazylevych, Hryhorii. (Grigorii Bazilevich, sviashchennik). "Mestechko Aleksandrovka Chernigovskoi guberni, Sosnitskogo uezda" (The Town of Oleksandrivka in the Sosnytskyi Region, Chernihiv Province). *Etnograficheskii sbornik* (Ethnographic Journal), vol. 1, 1853, pp. 313–36. Reprinted in *Chernigovskie gubernskie vedomosti* (Chernihiv Provincial News), 1854, nos. 12–14.

Bezsonov, P.A. *Kaleki perekhozhie: Sbornik stikhov i izsledovanie* (Wandering Mendicants: Collected Poems and Scholarly Works). 6 vols. Moscow: Tipografiia

A. Semena, 1861–4. Reprinted in 2 vols. with a new intro. by Very Rev. Sergei Hackel, Gregg International Publishers, Ltd., 1970.

Borzhkivskyi, Valerian. (Valeriian Borzhkovskii). "Lirniki" (Lirnyky). *Kievskaia starina*, vol. 26, 1889, pp. 653–708.

Brooks, Joanna. *Why We Left: Untold Stories and Songs of America's First Immigrants*. University of Minnesota Press, 2013.

Bushak, Stanislav, Valeriy Sakharuk, and Irine Sakharuk. *Cossack Mamai*. 2nd ed., Rodovid Press, 2008.

Chubynskyi, P(avlo). *Trudy etnografichesko-statisticheskoi ekspeditsii v Zapadno-Russkii krai* (Studies of the Ethnographic and Statistical Expedition into the Region of Western Russia). 1874, vol. 5: *Pesni liubovnyia, semeinyia, bytovyia i shutochnyia* (Songs about Love, Family Life, Everyday Life, and Humorous Songs). http://www.ex.ua/2942282.

Clarence-Smith, William Gervase. *Islam and the Abolition of Slavery*. Oxford University Press, 2006.

Danilov, Kirsha. *Drevnie rossiiskie stikhotvoreniia, sobrannye Kirsheiu Danilovym*. Vtoroe dopolnennoe izdanie podgotovili A.P. Evgeneva i B.N. Putilov (*Ancient Russian Poems Collected by Kirsha Danilov*, 1818. 2nd expanded ed., prepared by A.P. Evgeneva and B.N. Putilov). Izdatelstvo Nauka, 1977. https://archive.org/details/drevniiarossiis00danigoog.

Davis, Robert C. *Christian Slaves, Muslim Masters: White Slavery in the Barbary Coast and Italy, 1500–1800*. Palgrave/MacMillan, 2003.

Dei, O.I., and A.Yu. Yasenchuk, texts, and A.I. Ivanytskyi, music. *Balady: Kokhannia ta doshliubni vzaiemyny* (Ballads about Love and Premarital Relations). Naukova dumka, 1987.

Dei, O.I., and A.Yu. Yasenchuk, texts, and A.I. Ivanytskyi, music. *Balady: Rodynno-pobutovi stosunky* (Ballads about Family Relations and Daily Life). Naukova Dumka, 1988. http://chtyvo.org.ua/authors/Ivanytskyi _Anatolii/Balady_Rodynno-pobutovi_stosunky/.

Demutskyi, P. *Lira i yii motivy: Zibrav v Kyiivshchyni P. Demutskyi* (The Lira and Its Melodies: Collected in the Kyiv Region by P. Demutskyi). Kyiv: Notopechatnaia i drukarnia I.I. Chokolova, 1903. http://etnoua.info/ novyny/zbirnyk-lira-i-jiji-motyvy-porfyrij-demuckyj/.

Durak, Koray. "Performance and Ideology in the Exchange of Prisoners between the Byzantines and the Islamic Near Easterners in the Early Middle Ages." In *Medieval and Early Modern Performance in the Eastern Mediterranean*, edited by Arzu Ozturkmen and Evelyn Birge Vitz, Brepols Publishers, 2014, pp. 167–80.

Efimenko, P. "Bratstva i soiuzy nishchikh" (The Brotherhoods and Unions of the Poor). *Kievskaia starina*, vol. 7, 1883, pp. 312–17.

Efimenko, P. "Shpitali v Malorossii" (Hospices in Little Russia). *Kievskaia starina*, vol. 5, 1883, pp. 709–27.

Encyclopedia of Orthodoxy (Pravoslavnaia entsyklopediia): "St John the Russian." Vol. 24 (Moscow: 2010). http://oca.org/saints/lives/2013/05/27/101545-st-john-the-russian-and-confessor-whose-relics-are-on-the-island.

Encyclopedia of Ukraine (published by the Canadian Institute of Ukrainian Studies, 1984–).

Erdem, Y. Hakan. *Slavery in the Ottoman Empire and Its Demise. 1800–1909.* MacMillan Press, 1996.

Ferrari, Fabrizio M. *Ernesto de Martino on Religion: The Crisis and the Presence.* Equinox Publishers, 2012.

Glaser, Amelia M., editor. *Stories of Khmelnytsky: Competing Literary Legacies of the 1648 Ukrainian Cossack Uprising.* Stanford University Press, 2015.

G.V. "Pridvornyi bandurist v begakh" (An Escaped Court Bandura-Player). *Kievskaia starina*, vol. 23, 1888, pp. 21–3.

Haase-Dubosc, Danielle. "Lady Mary Wortley Montagu (1689–1762): Her Turkish Performances." In *Medieval and Early Modern Performance in the Eastern Mediterranean*, edited by Arzu Ozturkmen and Evelyn Birge Vitz, Brepols Publishers, 2014, pp. 203–13.

Halenko, Oleksander. "How a Turkish Empress Became a Champion of Ukraine." In *Roxolana in European Literature, History and Culture*, edited by Galina I. Yermolenko, Ashgate Publishing Limited, 2010, pp. 109–23.

Hnatiuk, Volodymyr. "Lirnyky: Lirnytski pisni, molytvy, slova, zvistky; pro lirnykiv povitu Buchatskoho" (Lirnyky. Lirnyk Songs, Prayers, Speech, Customs etc. Concerning Lirnyky of the Buchach Region). *Etnohrafichnyi zbirnyk* (Ethnographic Journal), vol. 2, 1896, pp. 1–76, and separately, Lviv 1896.

Hnatiuk, Volodymyr. "Zhebratski blahalnytsi" (Mendicant Begging Songs). *Zapysky Naukovoho tovarystva imeni Shevchenka* (Notes of the Shevchenko Scientific Society), vol. 110, 1912, pp. 158–63.

Hornjatkevyč, Andrij. "The Secret Speech of Lirnyky and Kobzari Encoding a Life Style." *Folklorica*, vol. 9, no. 2, 2004, pp. 32–54. https://journals.ku.edu/index.php/folklorica/article/view/3751/3590.

Hrinchenko, M.O., and F. Lavrov. *Kobzar Fedir Kushneryk* (The Kobzar Fedir Kushneryk). Tsentralna drukarnia naukovoho tovarystva URSR, 1940.

Hrushevska, Kateryna. *Ukrainski narodni dumy* (Ukrainian Folk Dumy). 2 vols. Derzhavne Vydavnytstvo Ukrainy, 1927–31.

Hrushevsky, Mykhailo (Mykhailo Hrushevskyi). *A History of Ukraine by Michael Hrushevsky*, edited by O.J. Frederiksen, Archon Books, 1970 (first published Yale University Press, 1941).

Hrushevsky, Mykhailo. *History of Ukraine-Rus*. Vol. 7. Translated by Bohdan Struminski, edited by Serhii Plokhy and Frank Sysyn, Canadian Institute of Ukrainian Studies, 1999.

Inalcik, Halil. "Servile Labor in the Ottoman Empire." *Studies in Ottoman Social and Economic History*, part 7, pp. 25–52, Variorum Reprints, 1985.

Ivanov, V. "Arteli slepykh, ikh organizatsiia i sovremennoe polozhenie" (The Guilds of the Blind: Their Organization and Current Condition). *Trudy XII arkheologicheskogo sezda v Kharkove* (*Studies of the 12th Archeological Congress in Kharkiv*), vol. 3, 1905, pp. 303–11.

Kalinowska, Izabela, and Marta Kondratyuk. "Khmelnytsky in Motion: The Case of Soviet, Polish, and Ukrainian Film." In *Stories of Khmelnytsky: Competing Literary Legacies of the 1648 Ukrainian Cossack Uprising*, edited by Amelia M. Glaser, Stanford University Press, 2015, pp. 197–217.

Karamzin, N. *Istoriia gosudarstva Rossiiskogo* (The History of the Russian State). Vol. 7, 5th ed., St Petersburg, 1842–3.

K.F.U.O. "Kodenskaia kniga i tri bandurista" (The Book of Koden and Three Bandura Players). *Kievskaia starina*, vol. 2, 1882, pp. 161–6.

Khanenko-Friesen, Natalia. *Ukrainian Otherlands: Diaspora, Homeland, and Folk Imagination in the Twentieth Century*. University of Wisconsin Press, 2015.

Kharkiv, Volodymyr, in the archives at M.T. Rylskyi Institute of Art, Folklore Studies and Ethnology of the National Academy of Sciences of Ukraine, fond 6–2/23(1), ark. 53.

Khotkevych, Hnat (I. Khotkevich). "Neskolko slov o banduristakh i lirnikakh" (Several Words about Bandura Players and Lirnyky). *Izvestiia XII Arkheologicheskogo sezda* (Bulletin of the 12th Archeological Congress in Kharkiv), no. 6, 1902, pp. 81–3.

Klid, Bohdan, and Alexander J. Motyl. *The Holodomor Reader: A Source Book on the Famine of 1932–33*. Canadian Institute of Ukrainian Studies Press, 2012.

Kligman, Gail. *Wedding of the Dead: Poetics and Popular Culture in Transylvania*. University of California Press, 1988.

Klymash, Robert Bohdan. *Ukrainska narodna kultura v kanadskykh preriiakh* (Ukrainian Folk Culture on the Canadian Prairies). Kyiv: Duliby, 2013.

Kohut, Zenon. "The Khmelnytsky Uprising, the Image of Jews, and the Shaping of Ukrainian Historical Memory." In *Making Ukraine: Studies on Political Culture, Historical Narrative, and Identity*, Canadian Institute of Ukrainian Studies Press, 2011, pp. 242–70.

Kolessa, Filaret. "Etnograficheskaia ekskursiia" (Ethnographic Excursion).
Etnograficheskoe obozrenie (Ethnographic Observations), vol. 78, no. 3, 1908,
pp. 198–9.

Kolessa, Filaret. Melodii ukrainskykh narodnykh dum (Ukrainian Folk Duma
Melodies). 1913, reprinted 1969, Naukova dumka.

Kolessa, Filaret. "Varianty melodii ukrainskykh narodnykh dum: yikh
kharakterystyka i grupovanne: Studiia" (The Variants of Ukrainian Duma
Melodies; Their Characteristics and Their Categorization: A Study). Zapysky
Naukovoho tovarystva imeni Shevchenka (Publications of the Shevchenko Scientific
Society), vol. 116, 1913, pp. 126–65.

Kolessa, Filaret. Ukrainski narodni dumy (Ukrainian Folk Dumy). Lviv: Prosvita, 1920.

Kolessa, Filaret. Ukrainski narodni dumy u vidnoshenii do pisen, virshiv, i
pokhodzhennia holosin (Ukrainian Dumy in Relations to Songs, Verses and
the Origin of Laments). 1920–1.

Kononenko, Natalie. "Duma pro Chornobyl: Old Genres, New Topics." Journal
of Folklore Research, vol. 29, no. 2, 1992, pp. 133–54.

Kononenko, Natalie. "Folk Orthodoxy: Popular Religion in Contemporary
Ukraine." In Letters from Heaven: Popular Religion in Russia and Ukraine,
edited by John-Paul Himka and Andriy Zayarnyuk, University of Toronto
Press, 2006, pp. 46–75.

Kononenko, Natalie. "Groupsourcing Folklore Sound Files: Involving the
Community in Research." Canadian Slavonic Papers / Revue canadienne des slavists,
vol. 55, nos. 1–2, 2013, pp. 131–50. (See "Ukrainian Folklore Audio" below.)

Kononenko, Natalie. "Reviving Dumy: Epic Poetry at the Birth of a Nation"
(Vozrozhdaia dumy: Epicheskaia poeziia v zarozhdenii natsii). In Twenty
Years Later: The Reshaping of Space and Identity, Russian State University for
the Humanities, 2012, pp. 326–41.

Kononenko, Natalie. "Ukrainian Ballads in Canada: Adjusting to New Life in
a New Land." Canadian Slavonic Papers / Revue canadienne des slavists, vol. 50,
nos. 1–2, 2008, pp. 18–36.

Kononenko, Natalie. Ukrainian Minstrels: And the Blind Shall Sing. M.E. Sharpe, 1998.

Kononenko, Natalie. "When Traditional Improvisation Is Prohibited:
Ukrainian Funeral Laments and Burial Practices." In Musical Improvisation:
Art, Education and Society, edited by Gabriel Solis and Bruno Nettl,
University of Illinois Press, 2009, pp. 52–71.

Kononenko, Natalie. "Ukrainian Folklore Audio." Oral Tradition, vol. 28, no. 2,
2013, pp. 243–52. See also http://journal.oraltradition.org/issues/28ii/
kononenko.

Kostomarov, Mykola. Sobranie Sochinenii N.I. Kostomarova: istoricheskiia
monografii i izsledovaniia (The Collected Works of N.I. Kostomarov)
https://archive.org/details/sobraniesochinen00kost.

Kostomarov, Mykola. "Istoricheskoe znachenie yuzhno-russkogo pesennogo
tvorchestva" (The Historical Meaning of South-Russian Song), *Beseda*
(Conversation), 1872. Republished in his *Sobranie sochinenii* (Collected
Works), 1906.

Krvavych, D.P., and H.H. Stelmashchuk. *Ukrainskyi narodnyi odiah XVII–
pochatku XIX st. v akvareliakh Yu. Flohovskoho* (Ukrainian Folk Costume of
the XVII–Beginning of the XIX Centuries, as Presented in the Flohovskyi
Watercolours). Naukova dumka, 1988.

Kulish, Panteleimon. *Istoria vozsoedineniia Rusi* (The History of the Reunification
of Rus). St Petersburg, 1874.

Kulish, Panteleimon. "Pisma P.A. Kulisha k O.M. Bodianskomu (1846–1877)"
(P.A. Kulish's letters to O.M. Bodianskii [1846–1877]). *Kievskaia starina*,
vol. 60, 1898, pp. 283–313.

Kulish, Panteleimon. *Ukraina: Od pochatku Vkrainy do batka Khmelnytskoho*
(Ukraine: From the Birth of Ukraine to Father Khmelnytskyi). 1843.

Kulish, Panteleimon. *Zapiski o Yuzhnoi Rusi* (Notes about Southern Rus). 2 vols.
St Petersburg, 1856–7.

Kuromiya, Hiroaki. *The Voices of the Dead: Stalin's Great Terror in the 1930s.*
Yale University Press, 2007.

Kushpet, Volodymyr. *Startsivstvo: Mandrivni spivtsi-muzykanty v Ukraiini
(XIX–poch. XX st.)* (Mendicancy: Wandering Singer-Musicians in Ukraine,
19th–beginning of the 20th Century). Kyiv: Tempora, 2007.

Kvitka, Klement. "Profesionalni narodni spivtsi i muzykanty na Ukraini.
Prohrama dlia doslidu yikh dialnosti i pobutu" (Professional Folk Singers
and Musicians in Ukraine: A Program for Studying Their Activities and
Their Daily Life). *Zbirnyk Istorichno-Filolohichnoho Viddilu Ukrainskoi
Akademii Nauk* (Journal of the Historico-Philological Division of the Ukrainian
Academy of Sciences), no. 13, Pratsi etnohrafichnoi komisii, vol. 2, Kyiv,
1924; reprinted in *Izbrannye trudy* (Collected Works), vol. 2, Moscow 1973,
pp. 251–76.

Kyrdan, Borys P. (B.P. Kirdan). *Ukrainskie narodnye dumy* (Ukrainian Folk
Dumy). Nauka, 1972.

Kyrdan, Borys P. "Varirovanie kobzarem M. Kravchenko dumy 'Bednaia
Vdova i Tri Syna'" (M. Kravchenko's Variations of the Duma "The Poor
Widow and Her Three Sons"). *Tekstologicheskoe izuchenie eposa* (Studies in
the Textual Criticism of Epic), edited by V.M. Gatsak and A.A. Petrosian,
Nauka, 1971, pp. 47–63.

Kyrdan, Borys P. and Andrii Omelchenko. *Narodni spivtsi-muzykanty na Ukraini*
(Folk Singers-Musicians in Ukraine). Muzychna Ukraina, 1980.

Lavrov, Fedir. *Kobzari: Narys z istorii kobzarstva Ukrainy* (Kobzari: A Sketch of the History of Ukrainian Minstrelsy). Mystetstvo, 1980.

Leerssen, Joep. "Oral Epic: The Nation Finds a Voice." In *Folklore and Nationalism in Europe during the Long Nineteenth Century*, edited by Timothy Baycroft and David Hopkin. Brill, 2012, pp. 11–26.

Lewis, Bernard. *Race and Slavery in the Middle East*. Oxford University Press, 1990.

Lord, Albert B. *Singer of Tales*. Harvard University Press, 1960.

Lukashevych, Platon (P. Lukashevich). *Malorossiiskie i Chervonorusskie narodnye dumy i pesni* (Folk Dumy and Songs of Little Russia and Red Russia). St Petersburg: Tipografiia Eduarda Pratsa, 1836.

Lysenko, Mykola (N.V. Lysenko). "Kharakteristika muzykalnykh osobennostei malorusskikh dum i pesen, ispolniaemykh kobzarem Veresaem" (Characteristic Musical Features of Ukrainian Dumy and Songs as Performed by Kobzar Veresai). *Zapiski Yugo-zapadnogo Otdela Imperatorskogo Russkogo Geograficheskogo Obshchestva* (Publications of the Southwestern Division of the Russian Geographical Society), vol. 1, 1874, pp. 339–66. Reprinted 1978, new edition prepared by M. Hordiichuk, Kyiv: Muzychna Ukraina. http://lib.rgo.ru/dsweb/View/ResourceCollection-139.

Maksymovych, Mykhailo (Mikhail Maksimovich). *Malorossiiskie pesni, izdannye M. Maksimovichem* (Songs of Little Russia, Published by M. Maksimovich). Moscow: Tipografiia Avgusta Semena, 1827.

Maksymovych, Mykhailo. *Sbornik ukrainskikh pesen* (A Collection of Ukrainian Songs). Kyiv: Tipografiia Feofila Gliksberga, 1849.

Maksymovych, Mykhailo. *Ukrainskie narodnye pesni* (Ukrainian Folk Songs). Moscow, 1834.

Martynovych, Porfyrii (Porfirii Martynovych). "Ukrainskie zapisi Porfiriia Martinovicha" (The Ukrainian Notes of Porfirii Martynovych). *Kievskaia starina*, vol. 84, 1904, pp. 272–6.

Matiash, I.B. *Kateryna Hrushevska: Zhyttia i diialnist* (Kateryna Hrushevska: Her Life and Work). Ukraiina, 2004.

McDowell, John H. *Poetry and Violence: The Ballad Tradition in Mexico's Costa Chica*. University of Illinois Press, 2000.

Metlynskyi, Amvrosii. *Narodnye yuzhnorusskie pesni* (South Russian Folk Songs). Universitetskaia tipografiia, 1854. http://www.ex.ua.

Miller, Frank J. *Folklore for Stalin: Russian Folklore and Pseudofolklore of the Stalin Era*. M.E. Sharpe, 1990.

Mishalow, Victor. *Kharkivska bandura: Kulturolohichno-mystetski aspekty genezy i rozvytky vykonavstva na ukrainskomu narodnomu instrumenti* (The Kharkiv

Bandura: Its Culturo-artistic Origin and the Development of Ukrainian Folk Instrument Performance Styles). Kharkiv: Savchuk, 2013.

Ostapchuk, Victor. "Crimean Tatar Long-Range Campaigns: The View from Remal Khodja's *History Sahib Gerey Khan.*" In *Warfare in Eastern Europe, 1500–1800*, edited by Brian J. Davies, Brill, 2012, pp. 147–72.

Pavlii, P.D., M.S. Rodina, and M.P. Stelmakh, editors. *Ukrainski narodni dumy ta istorychni pisni* (Ukrainian Folk Dumy and Historical Songs). Vydavnytstvo Akademii nauk Ukrainskoi RSR, 1955.

Peirce, Leslie P. *The Imperial Harem: Women and Sovereignty in the Ottoman Empire*. Oxford University Press, 1993.

Pravdiuk, O. *Romenskyi kobzar Yevhen Adamtsevych* (Kobzar Yevhen Adamtsevych from the Romny Region). Muzychna Ukraina, 1971.

Rambaud, Alfred. *La Russie épique: Étude sur les chansons héroiques de la Russie; trad. ou analysées pour la première fois.* "Les derniers Kobzars," 1876. Reprinted De Gruyer Mouton, 1967, pp. 435–55.

Raynard, Sophie. *The Teller's Tale.* State University of New York Press, 2012.

Rylskyi, M.T. (M.T. Rylskii), and F.I. Lavrov. *Kobzar Yehor Movchan.* Akademiia nauk URSR, 1958.

Seng, Yvonne J. "Fugitives and Factotums: Slaves in Early Sixteenth-Century Istanbul." *Journal of the Economic and Social History of the Orient*, vol. 39, no. 2, 1996, pp. 136–69.

Shevchenko Scientific Society: http://chtyvo.org.ua/authors/Naukove _tovarystvo_imeni_Shevchenka/.

Sotsialistychna kultura (*Socialist Culture*), August 1990, pp. 32–3.

Speranskii, M.N. *Yuzhno-russkaia pesnia i ee nositeli (po povodu bandurista T.M. Parkhomenka)* (South Russian Song and Its Performers – Concerning Bandura-Player T.M. Parkhomenko). In *Sbornik Istoriko-filologicheskago obshchestva pri Institute kniazia Bezborodko v Nezhyne* (Publications of the Historico-Philological Society of the Prince Bezborodko Institute in Nezhyn), vol. 5, Kyiv, 1904, pp. 97–230. http://lib.ndu.edu.ua/dspace/handle/123456789/149.

S(reznevskii), I(zmail). *Zaporozhskaia starina* (Zaporozhian Antiquities). Parts I–III, Universitetskaia tipografiia, 1833–8.

Subtelny, Orest. *Ukraine: A History.* University of Toronto Press, 2009.

Svientsitskyi, Ilarion. "Pokhoronni holosinnia i tserkovno-relegiina poeziia" (Funeral Laments in the Context of Religious Poetry). *Zapysky Naukovoho tovarystva im. Shevchenka* (Publications of the Shevchenko Scientific Society), vol. 93, 1910, pp. 32–53. http://chtyvo.org.ua/authors/Naukove_tovarystvo _imeni_Shevchenka/Zapysky_Tom_093/.

Svientsitskyi, Ilarion. *Pokhoronni holosinnia* (Funeral Laments) and V. Hnatiuk *Pokhoronni zvychaii i obriady* (Funeral Customs and Rituals). *Etnografichnyi zbirnyk* (Ethnographic Journal), vol. 31–2, 1912. http://www.bookva.org/books/369.

Tarnawsky, George, and Patricia Kilina, translators. *Ukrainian Dumy: Editio minor.* Canadian Institute of Ukrainian Studies and Harvard Ukrainian Research Institute, 1979.

Teller, Adam. "A Portrait in Ambivalence: The Case of Natan Hanover and His Chronicle *Yeven metsulah.*" In *Stories of Khmelnytsky: Competing Literary Legacies of the 1648 Ukrainian Cossack Uprising,* edited by Amelia M. Glaser, Stanford University Press, 2015, pp. 23–35.

Tsertelev, Nikolai (Tsertelev, Mykola). *Opyt sobraniia starinnykh malorossiiskikh pesnei (An Experiment in Collecting the Ancient Songs of Little Russia).* St Petersburg, 1819.

Tsertelev, Nikolai (Tsertelev, Mykola). "O starinnykh malorossiiskikh pesniakh" (About the Ancient Songs of Little Russia). *Syn otechestva (Son of the Fatherland),* no. 45, book 16, 1818, pp. 124–36.

Tylor, Edward Burnett. *Primitive Culture: Researches into the Development of Mythology, Philosophy, Religion, Art, and Custom.* H. Holt, 1874.

Ukrainski narodni dumy (Ukrainian Folk Dumy). Edited by H. Skrypnyk, S. Hrytsa, A. Ivanytskyi, M. Dmytrenko, H. Dovzhenok, L. Yefremova, and O. Shevchuk. Ukrainian Academy of Sciences, Rylskyi Folklore Institute, 2007. Foreword by S. Hrytsa.

Ukrainian Cabinet of Ministers. Ukrainian transliteration: Resolution no. 55 of the Cabinet of Ministers of Ukraine, 27 January 2010. http://zakon1.rada .gov.ua/laws/show/55-2010- .

Volkov, Solomon, editor. *Testimony: The Memoirs of Dmitri Shostakovich.* Limelight Editions, 2004 (Harper and Row, 1979).

Webber, Sabra J. *Folklore Unbound: A Concise Introduction.* Waveland Press, Inc., 2014.

Yastrebov, V. "Gaidamatskii bandurist" (The Bandura Player Who Was Also an Outlaw). *Kievskaia starina,* vol. 16, 1886, pp. 379–88.

Yermolenko, Galina I., editor. *Roxolana in European Literature, History and Culture.* Ashgate Publishing Limited, 2010.

"Yurii Khmelnytskyi." Encyclopedia of Ukraine. Vol. 2, pp. 473–4. http://www.encyclopediaofukraine.com/display.asp?linkpath=pages\K\H\KhmelnytskyYurii.htm.

Zelenin, D.K. *Ocherki po russkoi mifologii: Umershie neestestvennoiu smertiu i rusalki* (Essays on Russian Mythology: Those Who Died Unnatural Deaths and Rusalki). Moscow: Indrik, 1995 [1916].

Zhemchuzhnikov, Lev Mikhailovich. *Moi vospominanniia iz proshlogo* (My Recollections of the Past), edited by M. Dmitrenko, Leningrad: Isskustvo, 1970.

Zhytetskyi, P. (P. Zhitetskii). *Mysli o narodnykh malorusskikh dumakh* (Thoughts about the Folk Dumy of Little Russia). *Kievskaia starina*, 1893. https://archive .org/details/myslionarodnykh00zhitgoog.

Zilfi, Madeline C. *Women and Slavery in the Late Ottoman Empire: The Design of Difference*. Cambridge University Press, 2010.

Filmography

Bohdan-Zynovii Khmelnytskyi. Directed by Mykola Mashchenko, Dovzhenko Studios, Ukraine, 2007.

Mamai. Directed by Oles Sanin, Dovzhenko Studios, Ukraine, 2003.

Marusia Bohuslavka. Directed by Nina Vasylenko, Kievnauchfilm, Ukraine, 1966.

Povodyr (The Guide). Directed by Oles Sanin, Pronto Film, Ukraine, 2014.

Taras Bulba. Directed by Vladimir Bortko, adapted from the novel by Nikolai Gogol (Mykola Hohol), Central Partnership Studios, Russia, 2009.

With Fire and Sword. Directed by Jerzy Hoffman, adapted from Henryk Sienkiewicz's novel *With Fire and Sword*. Studio not given, Poland, 1999.

Electronic Resources

http://www.runivers.ru/lib/book8963/ – "Киевская старина" from 1882 to 1906.

List of Songs

Dumy

Historical Songs

Ballads

Begging Songs, Religious Songs, and Other Minstrel Songs

Index

Ryhorenko (kobzar), 125, 221, 257, 304n39, 308n21
Rylskyi, M.T., and F.I. Lavrov, 302n52
Rylskyi Institute of Folk Art, Folklore, and Ethnology, 36, 38

Sahaidachnyi, Petro, 49, 53, 211–12, 214
Sahib Gerey, 142
St John the Russian, 149–50, 305n74
St Petersburg, Russia, 21, 32
Saltanka/Soltanka, 170
Samara, 119, 150, 164, 169, 227
Sanin, Oles, 6, 115
Saracens, 27
Savur-mohyla, 118, 120
Second World War, 35–6, 289, 291
Seng, Yvonne, 110, 186, 303n8
Shevchenko Scientific Society, 294
Shostakovich, Dmitri, 6, 91, 297n5
Shpytal, pl. shpytali. *See* hospice
Shut, Andrii (kobzar), 31–2, 215, 226, 232, 240, 244, 308n16
Sich, 41, 46, 109, 166, 175, 203, 205, 212, 214–15, 229, 300n3, 307n15
Siegfried, 27
Sigismund III, 211
Sigismund Augustus, 211
Sirko, Ivan, 166–9
Skalozub, Semen, 103–4
Slastion, Opanas, 32, 137
Socialist Culture (magazine), 39
Sorochyntsi, 306n17
Soroky, 233–4
Soviet socialist art, 35
Soviet Union, 3–4, 6, 34, 37, 90–1, 289
sovietization. *See* russification
Speranskyi (Speranskii), Mykhailo, 32, 73, 301n37, 310n17
Sreznevskyi (Sreznevskii), Izmail, 30, 34

Stalin, Josef, 5, 6, 35–7, 91–2, 248, 289
starosta (elder, head of an organization), 15–18, 172, 177, 209
Straparola, Giovan Francesco, 29
Strichka (kobzar), 96, 303n14
Studynskyi, Kyryl, 35
Subotiv, 214, 245
Subtelny, Orest, 17, 211, 307n3
Suchava/Sucaeva, 234, 236, 243
Sudovshchykov, Nikolai Radionovich, 260
Suleyman, Sultan, 93, 110, 124, 129–30, 147
Sumtsov, Mykola, 32
Suprun, Nadia, 288
Suprun, Pavlo (kobzar), 39, 90–2, 288–9, 302n53, 303n22
Sviatogor, 25–6, 28
Svientsitskyi, Ilarion, 251, 268
szlachta, 210, 251

Tarnawsky, George, 38
Tatar raids, 27, 41, 43, 94, 129, 132, 143–4, 157, 159, 179, 210, 243, 296
Tatars, Crimean, 8, 11, 14, 28, 51, 80–1, 94, 112, 114–15, 124, 132–3, 137, 142–3, 154–5, 159, 162, 164–6, 172–6, 180–1, 203, 206, 211, 220, 222, 231–2, 250
taxation, 12, 52, 158, 225–30
taxes, 52, 94, 158, 210–11, 226, 230, 302n1
Teller, Adam, 308n24
textualization of oral tradition, 23
Tiahynia, 77, 80, 177
Tiamat, 24
Tkachenko, Hryhorii (kobzar), 91